AF575988

The Art of Print

Elizabeth Jacklin

The Art of Print

Three Hundred Years of Printmaking

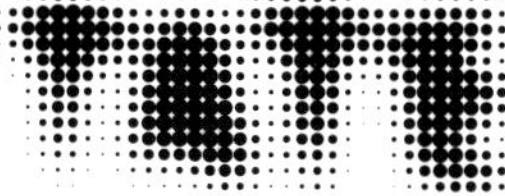

The Author

Elizabeth Jacklin is an art curator. She was previously assistant curator at Tate Britain and is currently Keeper of Art at Tyne & Wear Archives & Museums.

Contents

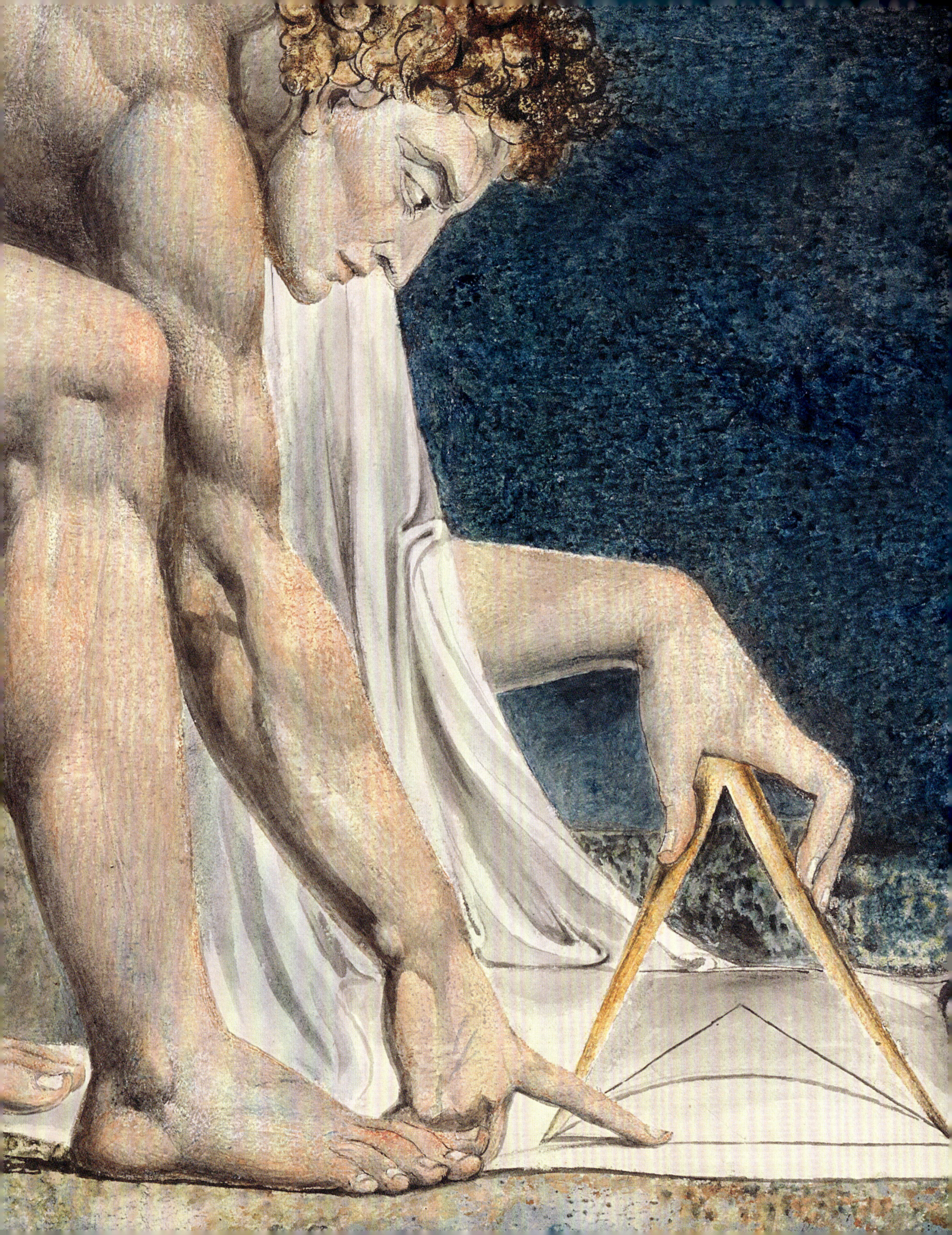

1 Introduction

William Blake *Newton* 1795–c.1805 (detail)

1 Introduction

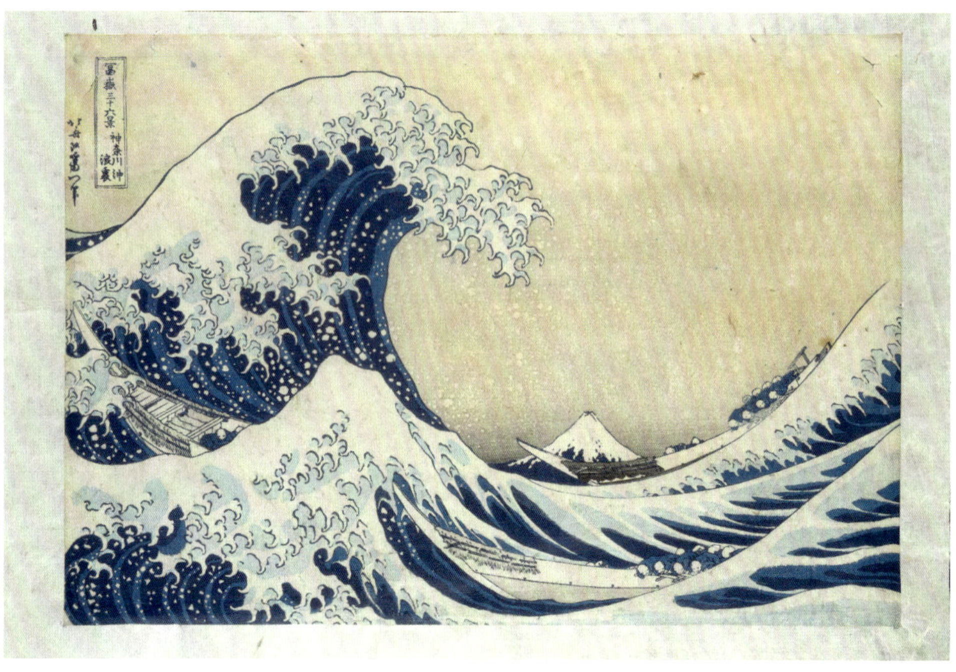

Katsushika Hokusai, *The Great Wave* c.1831 from *Thirty-six Views of Mount Fuji*, woodblock print on paper. Victoria and Albert Museum, London

> WARHOL p.10

Printmaking is the art of creating images by printing from a specially prepared block or plate, usually onto paper. Artists have been making prints for centuries, and some of the most celebrated images in the history of art, from Rembrandt's *The Three Trees* to Hokusai's *The Great Wave* and Warhol's *Marilyn* series, are prints. Importantly, each of these iconic works exists in more than one copy, and a key feature of most printmaking is the ability to create an image in multiples. And prints made by an artist's own hand – or under their supervision – are considered original works of art, despite potentially existing in many copies. For printmaking is a creative pursuit, about much more than multiplication. Some of the world's most famous artists have favoured its many methods, and prints have played a unique and important role in the history of art and image. Printmaking's enduring popularity is reflected both by the myriad artists who continue to experiment with its traditional methods, and by those using the new technologies of the digital age to pursue a different kind of print practice.

This book explores the multitude of ways artists have engaged with printmaking over the course of three centuries. The selection of artworks reflects a broad spectrum of techniques and purposes, from prints made by specialist metal engravers in collaboration with painters in the pre-photography era to recent mixed-method prints. The examples shown here – which range from works by William Hogarth in eighteenth-century London to William Kentridge in twenty-first century Johannesburg – are drawn from Tate's remarkable print collection.

> HOGARTH p.98
> KENTRIDGE pp.49, 218

Printmaking Techniques

'Printmaking' is an umbrella term covering numerous techniques. This book is structured around the key ones used to make artists' prints between 1700 and the present day. A joy of surveying the history of printmaking is the chance to explore lesser-known work by some of the best-loved artists: many famous painters, including Pablo Picasso, have also been printmakers. And, equally as important, works by less familiar names are also

> PICASSO pp.43, 71

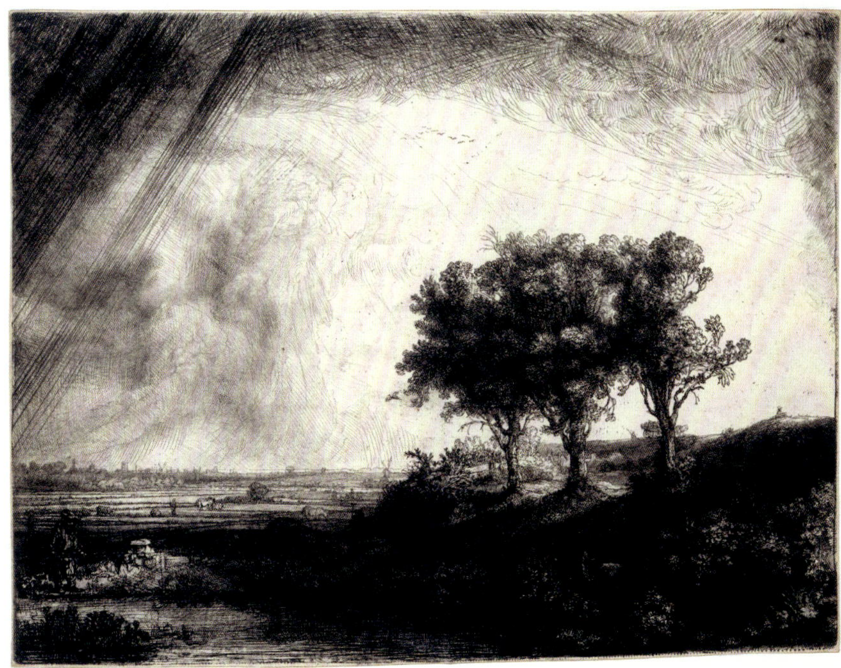

Rembrandt van Rijn, *The Three Trees* 1643, etching and drypoint with burin on paper. Victoria and Albert Museum, London

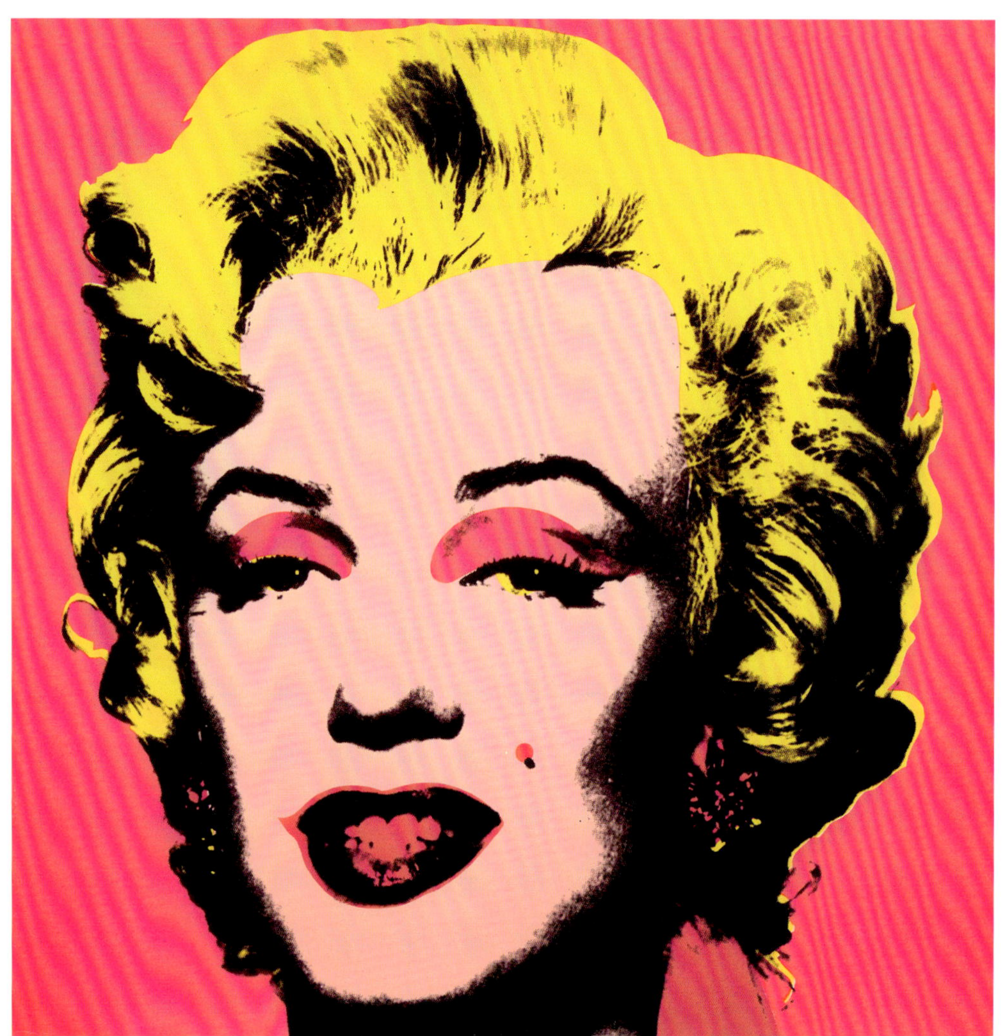

Andy Warhol, [No title] from *Marilyn* 1967, screenprint on paper

brought to the fore: Gertrude Hermes and Stanley William Hayter are among the many practitioners who deserve to be far better known.

> HERMES p.35
> HAYTER pp.85, 105

Hayter is an example of an artist who is chiefly celebrated as a printmaker, but most of the artists included in these pages have pursued printmaking alongside their work in other media. The history of 'painter-printmakers' is centuries-long and includes, for example, James Abbott McNeill Whistler, Lucian Freud, David Hockney and Paula Rego. There are also a significant number of sculptors with an important print practice, such as Germaine Richier, Kim Lim and Henry Moore. The proliferation of artists working across sculpture and printmaking is less discussed by comparison but is, perhaps, unsurprising

> WHISTLER p.68
> FREUD p.75
> HOCKNEY p.81
> REGO p.88
> RICHIER p.76
> LIM p.84
> MOORE p.139

given that sculptors are often used to both hands-on technical processes and to working with multiples, key features of most types of printmaking. Some of the artists featured have worked across an even wider range of disciplines, with practices encompassing areas such as installation and animation in addition to print.

While most of the prints illustrated here demonstrate mastery of one or more of the printmaking processes described below and imply a satisfaction in working directly with the medium, this is not an essential requisite of an artist's print. Artists have been working with engravers and 'master printers' to realise their ideas in print for centuries. More recently, some conceptual artists have consciously considered the medium itself as of secondary importance to the idea; this lessened emphasis on the artistic processes involved in printmaking has proven no barrier to print being used creatively as part of a wider ideas-driven practice, for example in the work of Sol LeWitt.

> LEWITT p.45

The book begins with 'In Relief', a section dedicated to relief printmaking – from woodcut, the oldest printmaking technique, to modern methods such as linocut – and includes works by artists ranging from William Blake to contemporary Latvian-American practitioner Vija Celmins. 'The Art of Etching' then explores the etching technique and how it has been used in a remarkable range of works, from eighteenth-century prints by Thomas Gainsborough to more recent works by artists such as Shirazeh Houshiary. Next, 'Metal on Metal' considers how artists ranging from William Hogarth to Louise Bourgeois have used metal tools to create metal engravings, drypoints and mezzotints.

> BLAKE p.26
> CELMINS p.112
> GAINSBOROUGH p.63
> HOUSHIARY p.87
> HOGARTH p.98
> BOURGEOIS p.114

The methods mentioned above have usually been considered most suited to monochrome images: it was in the twentieth century that new techniques allowed artists to fully embrace colour printmaking for the first time. 'Drawing on Stone' centres on artists' lithographs from this period, which are overwhelmingly colour prints, made by artists including Paul Cézanne and Barbara Hepworth. 'Through the Screen', meanwhile, explores screenprinting – a truly modern method practised by Andy Warhol, Roy Lichtenstein and Bridget Riley among others.

> CÉZANNE p.123
> HEPWORTH p.146
> WARHOL p.167
> LICHTENSTEIN p.204
> RILEY p.173

A final section, 'Print and Process', brings together some of the most technically innovative prints in Tate's collection. It covers mixed method approaches to printmaking and the rise of inkjet printing in relation to the predominantly handmade methods discussed. It also considers the use of print to create unique works which do not exist as multiples.

This publication makes no claims to be exhaustive when it comes to telling a broader history of printmaking. The examples included do, however, highlight some of the most interesting prints to be found among the more hidden of Tate's holdings, while also providing a sense of the various different printmaking techniques. I hope that this selection of artworks, from the iconic to the unfamiliar, will help others to discover the joys and wonders of the remarkable, diverse and occasionally mysterious art of print.

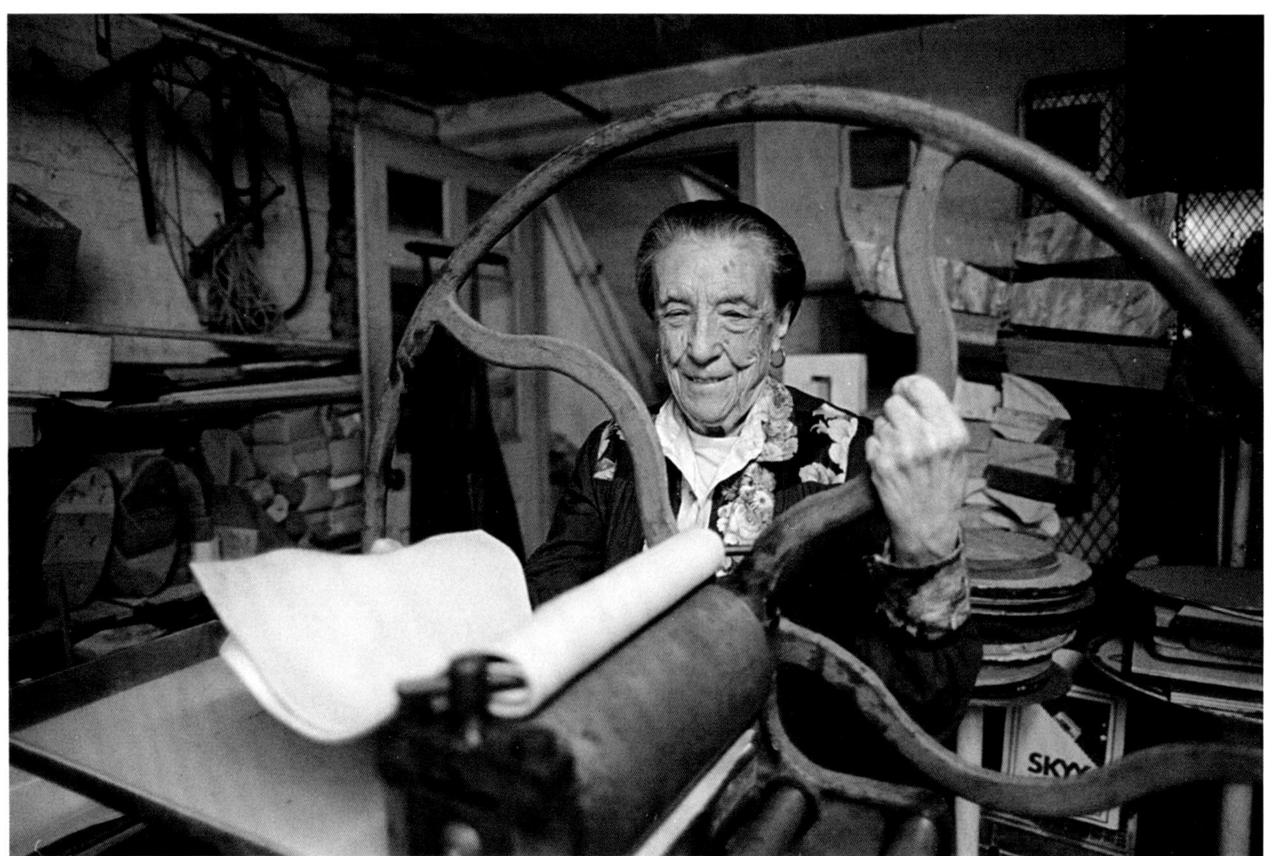

Louise Bourgeois with her printing press in the studio of her home on 20th Street, New York, 1995. Photo: Mathias Johannson

The Tate Print Collection

Tate's extensive print collection is surprisingly little known relative both to wider areas of its own collection and to the print holdings of other major institutions. In fact, with some notable exceptions, it has maintained a fairly low profile throughout the institution's history.

Tate's print collection reflects the gallery's broader collecting remit as the home of the national collection of British art from 1500 to the present day, and of modern and contemporary international art. Some of its strengths lie in the field of historic British art – William Blake, for example, is well represented in print, as are his followers; and the collection of prints made by, or in collaboration with, Joseph Mallord William Turner is outstanding. There are also prints by some of the other artists most strongly associated with Tate Britain, such as Thomas Gainsborough and George Stubbs. But holdings are patchy in other areas: there is very little pre-1700 material, and some significant printmakers from the following centuries – such as Thomas Bewick, who established wood engraving in late eighteenth-century Britain – are not represented at all. James Abbott McNeill Whistler, whose 'Nocturne' paintings are so well loved within Tate's collection, is currently represented only by a single print, despite his being one of western art history's best-known masters of the etching medium.

> BLAKE pp.26, 192
> TURNER pp.99, 101
> GAINSBOROUGH p.63
> STUBBS p.65
> WHISTLER p.68

When it comes to artists working from the late nineteenth century onwards, the print collection embodies Tate's commitment to collecting not only British, but also international, modern art. Key examples include a colour lithograph by Paul Cézanne and a portfolio of woodcuts by Käthe Kollwitz. Many of the twentieth-century's leading names are represented. Thanks to major gifts received around the time of the print collection's formal establishment in the 1970s, it is exceptionally strong in colour prints produced in London and New York during the same period; indeed the collection's particular strengths in its geographic range generally lie with British and North American examples. While it is true that the collections of the British Museum and the Victoria and Albert Museum are more comprehensive in

> CÉZANNE p.123
> KOLLWITZ p.33

their international and historical coverage, as both have a wider collecting remit, Tate's holdings also contain important prints not represented in either of these major collections.

The collection's somewhat eclectic nature is in part due to Tate's historically inconsistent approach to collecting prints. Although the gallery did acquire prints during the earlier years of its establishment, the selection was based more on opportune gifts than strategic purchases. An apparent reluctance to develop the print collection finally came to a head in 1951, when the gallery offered to relinquish its right to collect prints altogether: with concerns surrounding lack of space, it was thought the 'specialist' field of print collecting was better left to other institutions.[1] But when the Tate Gallery's offer to transfer all of its existing prints to the British Museum was rejected, this plan fell by the wayside and the print collection remained.

> STUBBS p.65

The institution truly began to embrace the art of print during the 1970s, by which time there was wider acceptance that printmaking formed a key part of the practice of many of the artists represented in the Tate collection. From eighteenth-century artists such as Stubbs through to then-contemporary practitioners, a great many of the artists represented within the gallery had pursued printmaking without seeing it as particularly 'specialist' or separable from their work in other mediums – but this aspect of their work had remained almost invisible at Tate.[2] Most notably among the changes that occurred at this time was a scheme in which artists and print studios donated prints to the collection via a trust called the Institute of Contemporary Prints. This initiative saw three thousand prints acquired on Tate's behalf by 1975, an extraordinary addition to the gallery's holdings that brought into the collection works produced by key print publishers including the Kelpra Studio, the Curwen Press and Waddington Graphics. Together, the artworks gifted via this scheme saw the print collection increase to ten times its previous size almost overnight, with a wealth of then-contemporary examples. A specific print department was also established, and Pat Gilmour was appointed the gallery's first curator of prints. Her transformative tenure oversaw new purpose-built storage for the growing modern print collection, establishing it as a key resource.[3]

Further important gifts followed, as well a series of exhibitions either focused on, or making use of, the print collection. While the emphasis was firmly on modern and contemporary prints, various historic prints were moved from the reference collection to the print room holdings, giving them status as art objects within the institution for the first time. This included a group of Hogarth prints with unknown origins. Although not pristine examples, their transfer into the realm of gallery objects reflected the new attitude towards printed material at Tate and helped to bridge a significant gap in the gallery's representation of an artist whose graphic work was central to his practice. From the 1970s onwards, prints were also actively acquired in the form of strategic purchases used to bolster the gallery's holdings, and to attempt to rectify some of the most obvious omissions. At the same time, the institution also became more selective in what it accepted as gifts, demonstrating a serious commitment to the art of print by prioritising the best examples. Once considered a specialist field, prints, like other art forms, were now being exhibited for all to see.

> HOGARTH p.98

In 1985 the original print study room closed and the print department was merged with the modern collection amid budgetary pressures.[4] But prints continued to be actively acquired and considered in the same terms as other art forms. Today, the print collection is still mostly housed at Tate Britain, where two study rooms cater for public visitors wanting to view prints not currently on display. The most significant development in the twenty-first century so far remains a 2004 gift from Tyler Graphics, one of the leading print publishers of the twentieth century. This sizable gift transformed the gallery's print holdings once again, making the institution a key European centre for modern – and often very experimental – North American prints by the likes of Frank Stella and Helen Frankenthaler.

> STELLA p.201

> FRANKENTHALER p.208

Acquisitions of the last two decades have included contemporary limited edition print portfolios, usually comprising either a series of prints by a single artist or a group of works by different artists responding to a particular subject or theme. For example, twelve British artists, including Anthea Hamilton, contributed to a portfolio commemorating the London Olympic and Paralympic Games in 2012. While printmaking and print collecting, like art and art collecting as a whole, have a long history of being male dominated, more recent acquisitions have also purposefully embraced the work of non-male artists. The examples included in this book reflect this as fully as possible, with women artists much more visible in the subject's more recent history. Naturally, given Tate's collecting remit, the historic examples included here are mostly British. However, in terms of modern and contemporary prints, recent acquisitions have increasingly embraced not only European and North American printmakers, but also artists from areas outside of the western art-historical canon. While there is undoubtedly much more to do in this area, developing these areas of the collection is another ongoing priority for Tate, and the selection of prints included here reflects the gradually increasing diversity of the collection in geographical terms as it endeavours to achieve a more global reach. It is also worth noting that the focus of Tate's print collection is primarily artists' prints made for display on the wall, though some examples of book illustrations and posters are included. Tate's Archive does, however, collect items reflecting a broader history of print culture, such as printed ephemera.

> HAMILTON p.184

Tate's print collection contains many treasures, from some of the most remarkable colour prints William Blake ever produced to great etchings by artistic giants such as Picasso and Giorgio Morandi and prints by the Guerrilla Girls that recapture one of the most important moments in feminist art history. This makes it all the more surprising that the gallery's print holdings remain relatively little known, and to note that this is the first book to delve into the institution's print holdings, historic and modern alike, and to consider the collection in its entirety.

> BLAKE p.192
> PICASSO p.71
> MORANDI p.70
> GUERRILLA GIRLS p.178

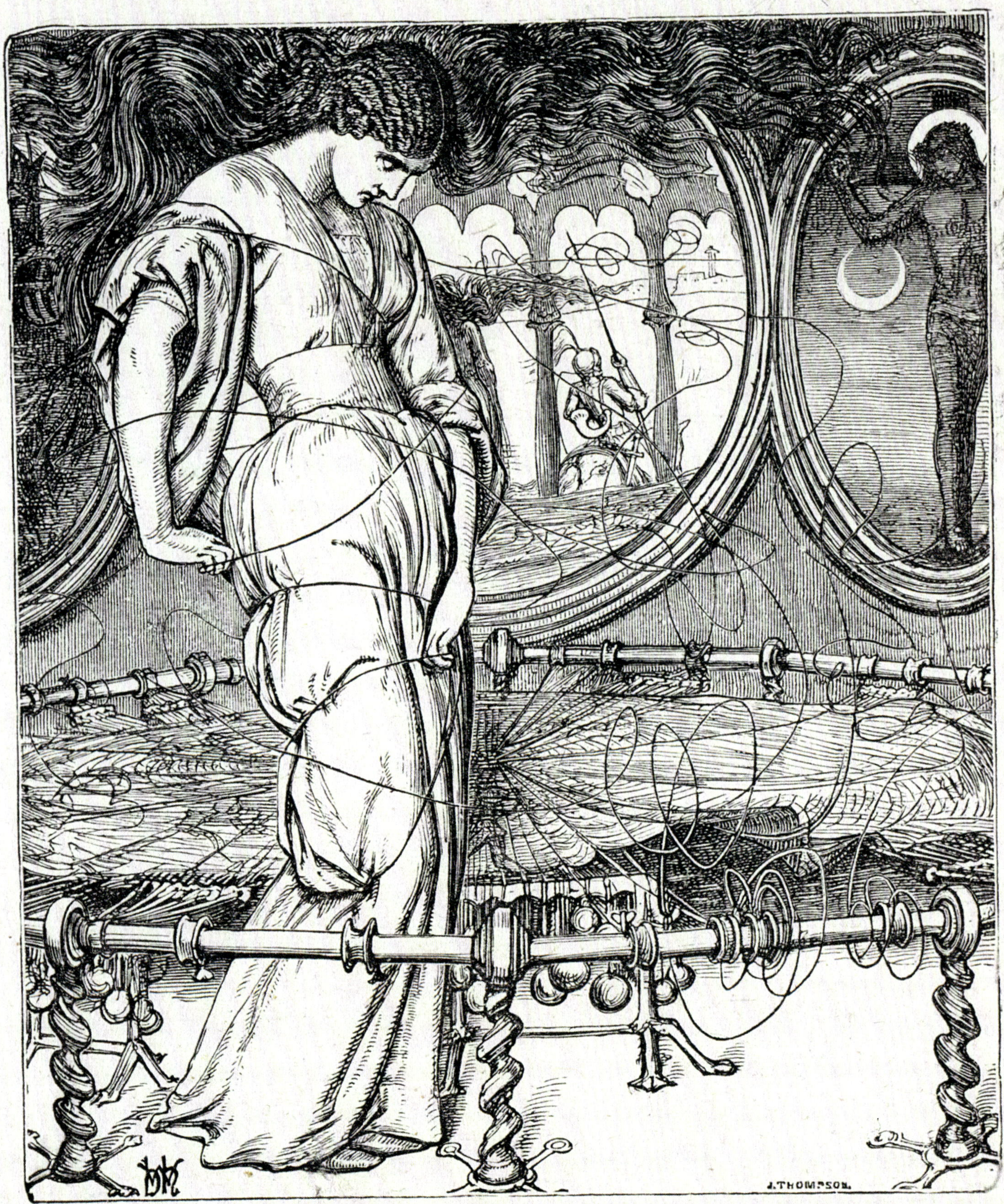
J.THOMPSON.

2 In Relief

John Thompson after William Holman Hunt *The Lady of Shalott* published 1857

2 In Relief

> WALLINGER p.48

In relief printmaking, ink is applied to the surface of a block or plate. When preparing a block, the printmaker generally uses tools to cut away the areas to be recessed, leaving the remaining areas to be inked and printed standing 'in relief' on the surface. The block or plate can be made from different materials depending on the particular technique being used: wood and linoleum are both common choices. One artist represented in this section, Mark Wallinger, has even employed potato printing, one of the most accessible printmaking methods of all. The other works illustrated here draw upon methods more commonly employed for artists' prints. The key techniques are described below.

Woodcut involves cutting into a block of wood using metal tools, such as knives and gauges. The areas of wood left behind by the cutter on the surface of the block are inked and printed onto paper, either using a relief printing press or by exerting pressure by hand.

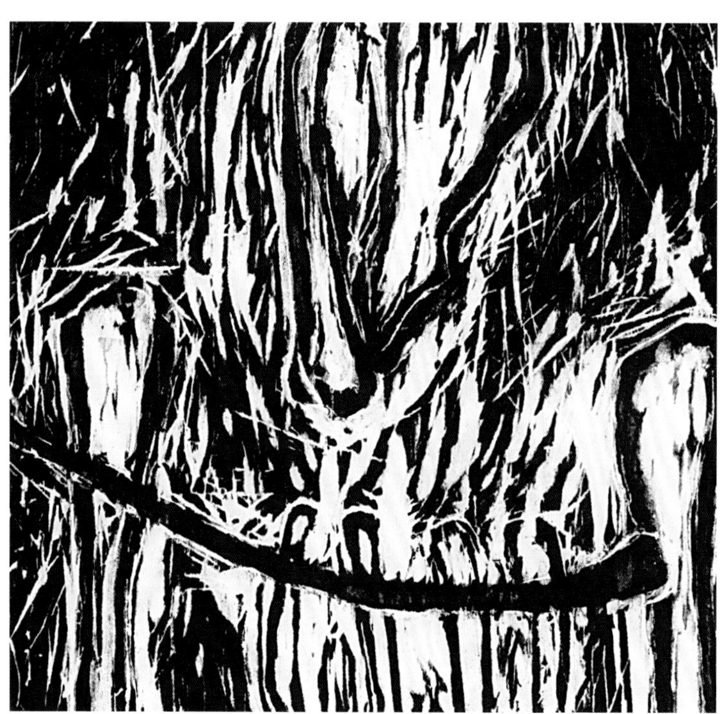

Detail from Susan Rothenberg, *Head and Bones* 1980

Linocut is similar in method and effect to woodcut, but linoleum provides a softer relief printing 'block', which is much easier for the printmaker to cut into.

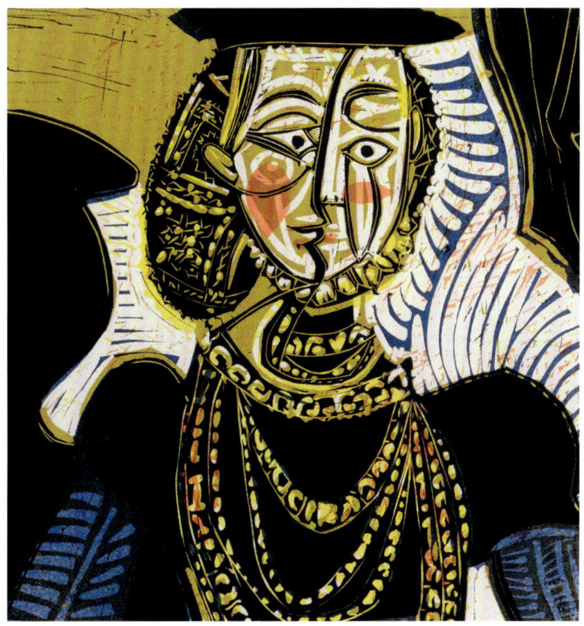

Detail from Pablo Picasso, *Portrait of a Woman after Cranach the Younger* 1958

Wood Engraving involves engraving into the end grain of a block of wood to create effects that are more intricate than those achieved with woodcut. The engraver

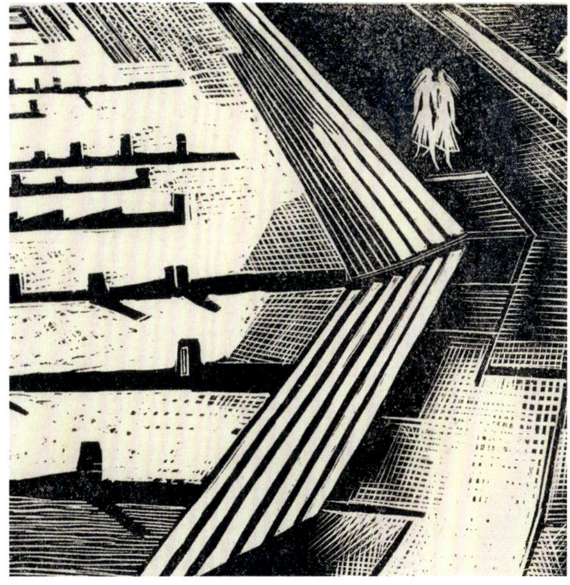

Detail from Paul Nash, *Promenade II* 1920

effectively 'draws' with a white line, as the lines incised into the wood will remain the white of the paper in the finished print. The surrounding areas 'left behind' on the wood by the engraver are the ones which stand in relief and take on the colour of the ink.

Relief Printmaking in Brief

Woodcut is the oldest printmaking technique described in these pages. The history of the method, which has its origins in fifth-century Chinese textile printing, has filled many books and recounting a comprehensive history is not possible here, but these brief notes aim to set the scene for the works of art highlighted in the pages that follow.

In Europe woodcut has been used for printing textiles since at least the Middle Ages. It developed as a process for making prints on paper in the late fourteenth century, when paper began to be manufactured in the west. The German artist Albrecht Dürer perfected the woodcut technique in the early sixteenth century, setting a near-impossible standard for other Northern European artists looking to follow his example. The technique was taken up in Italy around the same time, where sixteenth-century Italian practitioners began making multi-block 'chiaroscuro' woodcuts. These distinctive images, which used multiple blocks printed in different colours to echo the appearance of old master drawings, later inspired Georg Baselitz.

> BASELITZ p.46

As printed literature flourished in centres across Europe, woodcut's reach followed. Some artists worked – either alone or with professional cutters – to make expensive, collectible prints, but the technique was more commonly used for cheap popular illustrations. The medium's popularity waned during the seventeenth and eighteenth centuries, however, as etching became the preferred medium for artist's prints (see pp.59–61), and metal engraving, with its finer, more detailed effects, began to supersede woodcut as the preferred technique for reproducing images and illustrating books, despite being more costly (see pp.94–7).

In the late eighteenth century, the British illustrator and printmaker Thomas Bewick mastered the technique of wood engraving, which he famously used to illustrate his *History of British Birds*. This variation of the woodcut technique could – in the right hands – equal the intricacy of metal engraving. During the early nineteenth century, it was taken up by William Blake and his followers. Like Bewick, these artists used the technique to make original works with their own hands; but, as the century developed, wood engraving was increasingly used to reproduce images first made in other media, such as oil paint, and in the realm of book and periodical illustration. A highlight of this activity came during the 1850s, when highly skilled – and often anonymous – wood engravers translated Pre-Raphaelite illustrations into black and white. The best examples brought cutting-edge British art to the readers of lavishly illustrated books, such as the Moxon edition of Tennyson's *Poems*, which included John Thompson's engraving of William Holman Hunt's *The Lady of Shalott*. This intricate and often beautiful use of wood engraving was not restricted to Britain, and during the nineteenth century it similarly became the dominant medium for illustration in both France – where the illustrator and printmaker Gustave Doré was a key figure – and Germany.

> BLAKE p.26
> HOLMAN HUNT p.29

By the century's close, the growth of other print processes, most notably colour lithography, saw wood engraving overtaken as the leading reproductive illustration technique (pp.120–1). The method was revived during the twentieth century by artists including Paul Nash, Gertrude Hermes and Naum Gabo. Although it is now something of a niche skill compared with its nineteenth-century heyday, in Britain a Society of Wood Engravers exists to this day.

> NASH p.31
> HERMES p.35
> GABO p.40

Woodcut, meanwhile, enjoyed a more significant renaissance in the world of artists' prints during the early twentieth century. This was partly thanks to the examples set by Edvard Munch and Paul Gauguin, both of whom experimented with woodcut during the last years of the nineteenth century, embracing the wood's natural grain as part of their designs. It was then taken up by German expressionist artists including Käthe Kollwitz

> KOLLWITZ p.33

> PAPE p.41
> ROTHENBERG p.44
> BASELITZ p.46

and woodcut became increasingly associated with powerful, expressive images. More recent proponents of the method have hailed from all over the world, but the examples included here embrace artists from Europe and the Americas, such as Lygia Pape, Susan Rothenberg and Georg Baselitz.

> NICHOLSON p.36
> WALKER p.47
> PICASSO p.43

In the twentieth century linocut also emerged as a valid – and less technically arduous – alternative to working with wood. The Tate collection includes examples by artists ranging from Ben Nicholson to Kara Walker. The simplicity of form and clean lines possible with this medium are perfectly suited to Walker's historically informed monochrome imagery; other artists, meanwhile, have pushed the medium into the area of ambitious colour prints. Pablo Picasso, for example, used multiple linoleum blocks to create breathtakingly complex colour images.

William Blake (1757–1827)
The Blighted Corn c.1821
Wood engraving on paper 3.4 × 7.3

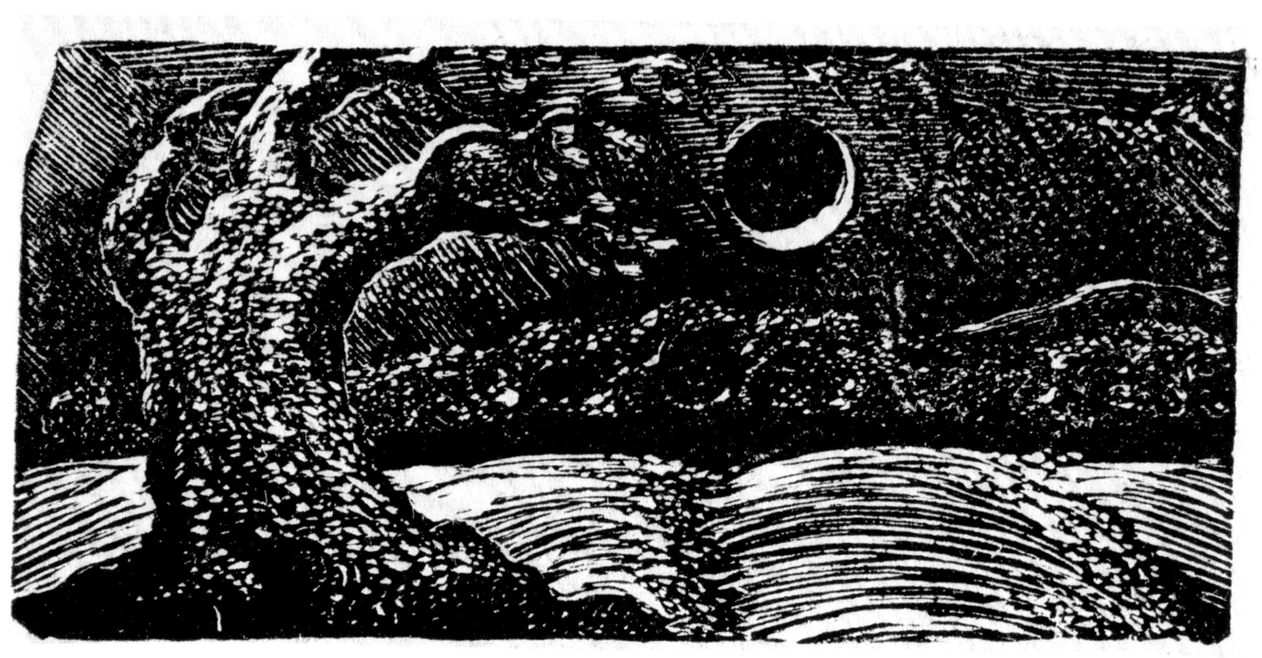

The artist and poet William Blake made this tiny print as part of a commission to illustrate a book, *The Pastorals of Virgil ... Adapted for Schools* (1821). To make the illustrations, the sixty-four year-old Blake attempted wood engraving for the first time. Although his patron, the book's author Dr Robert Thornton, doubted the quality of the resulting wood engravings, their appeal among Blake's fellow artists persuaded him to publish them. The breathtakingly intricate prints were particularly admired by two artists in Blake's circle: Edward Calvert and Samuel Palmer (see pp.27, 67). Palmer wrote that there was no way to describe the light and shade achieved in Blake's 'visions of little dells, and nooks, and corners of Paradise'.[1]

The Blighted Corn is a melancholic night-time scene, a moonlit sky and a swaying tree shown alongside the cornfield of the title. This 'impression' (or copy) of the print was probably printed from Blake's woodblock by Calvert shortly after his death.

Edward Calvert (1799–1883)

The Chamber Idyll 1831

Wood engraving on paper 4.1 × 7.6

Edward Calvert was one of the Ancients, a group of artists inspired by William Blake. Between 1826 and 1834 the group gathered in the Kent village of Shoreham, where their leading member, Samuel Palmer (see p.67), had a house. This wood engraving dates from this time, a particularly fruitful period for Calvert.

This print, often considered Calvert's masterpiece, reflects something of the intricacy and style of Blake's 'Virgil' illustrations from a decade earlier (see p.26), but also sees Calvert's style evolve into something unique. His vision is one of pastoral love, the setting of a rustic cottage and the landscape and shepherd's crook implying labour. But if the setting is rustic, the scene is still rich: apples fill the basket by the bed, well-kept animals wait outside and the human protagonists, undressed, are lovers. Like Calvert's other wood engravings, this one makes effective use of the technique to create a small, intimate scene that almost sparkles with light and shade.

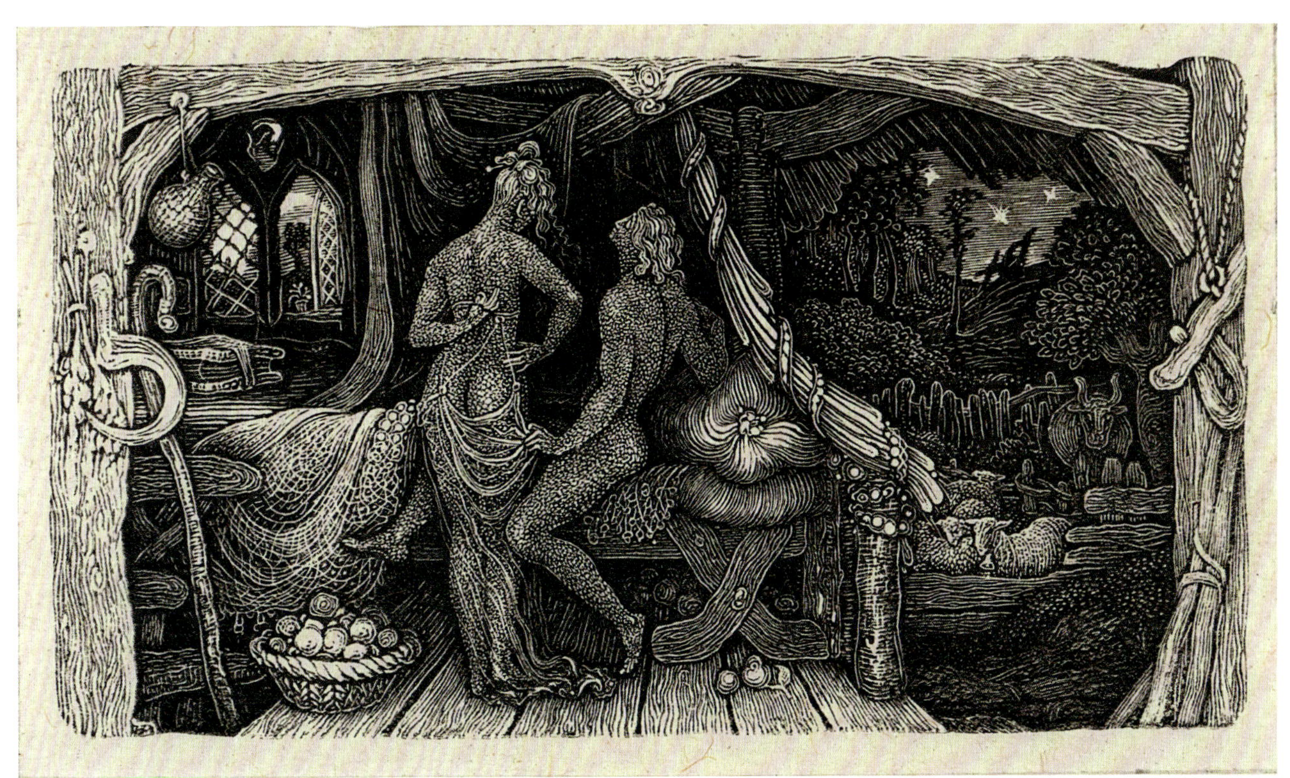

The Dalziel Brothers after
Dante Gabriel Rossetti (1828–1882)
Maids of Elfen-mere published 1855
Wood engraving on paper 12.7 × 7.6

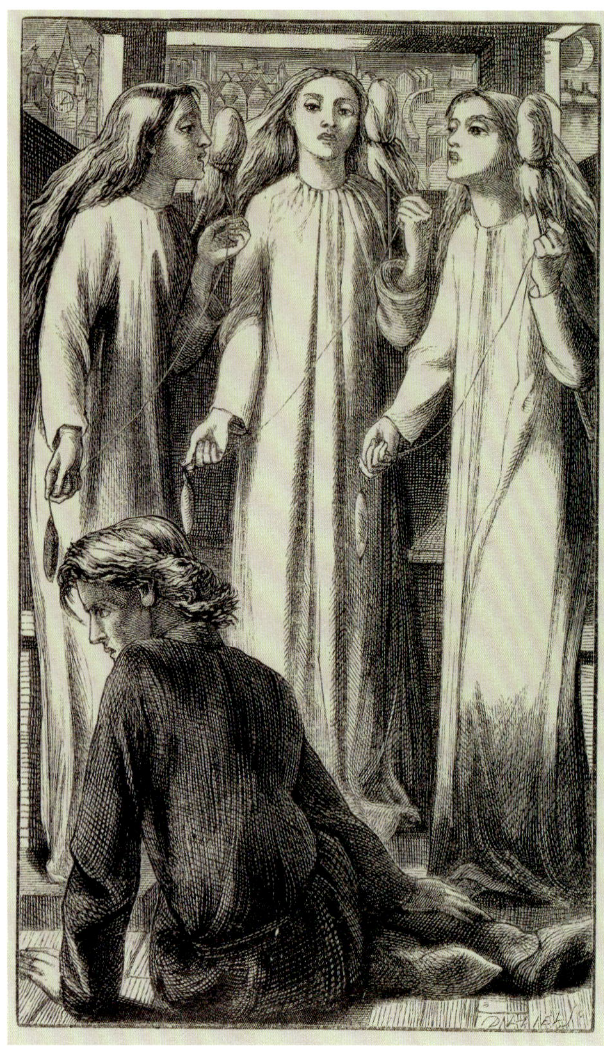

Dante Gabriel Rossetti was a founding member of the Pre-Raphaelite Brotherhood, which also included his artistic contemporaries William Holman Hunt (see p.29) and John Everett Millais. This illustration for William Allingham's *The Music Master* was considered by the younger artist Edward Burne-Jones to be the most beautiful illustration he had ever seen. He noted: 'the weirdness of the Maids of Elfen-mere, the musical timed movement of their arms together as they sing, the face of the man above all, are such as only a great artist could conceive.'[2]

Despite designing only ten significant illustrations, Rossetti has been credited with helping to raise the quality of British illustration as a whole during the 1850s by bringing his incredibly original designs to the pages of Victorian illustrated books.[3] Like Millais and Hunt, Rossetti benefited from the skill of the engravers who rendered his brilliant designs into the black-and-white language of wood engraving so successfully. This print was made after his design by the Dalziel Brothers, the largest and most influential wood-engraving firm in Victorian London.

John Thompson (1785–1866)
after William Holman Hunt (1827–1910)
The Lady of Shalott published 1857

Wood engraving on paper 9.5 × 7.9

William Holman Hunt designed this illustration for an edition of Tennyson's poems published by Moxon in 1857. This compilation of verses by Alfred, Lord Tennyson was accompanied by fifty-four wood-engraved illustrations by Victorian artists, thirty of which were by Pre-Raphaelite artists. In this image, Hunt shows the protagonist of Tennyson's *Lady of Shalott* struck by the curse described in the poem: the broken 'magic web' she has been weaving is imagined in amazing detail. Hunt's design was translated into the black-and-white idiom of wood engraving by John Thompson, one of Britain's leading wood engravers.

Reception of the Pre-Raphaelite Tennyson illustrations was mixed at the time, with Tennyson himself unimpressed. But it is now clear that the translation of these innovative designs into print represents a high point in the history of book illustration and, in turn, the history of printmaking in Britain.

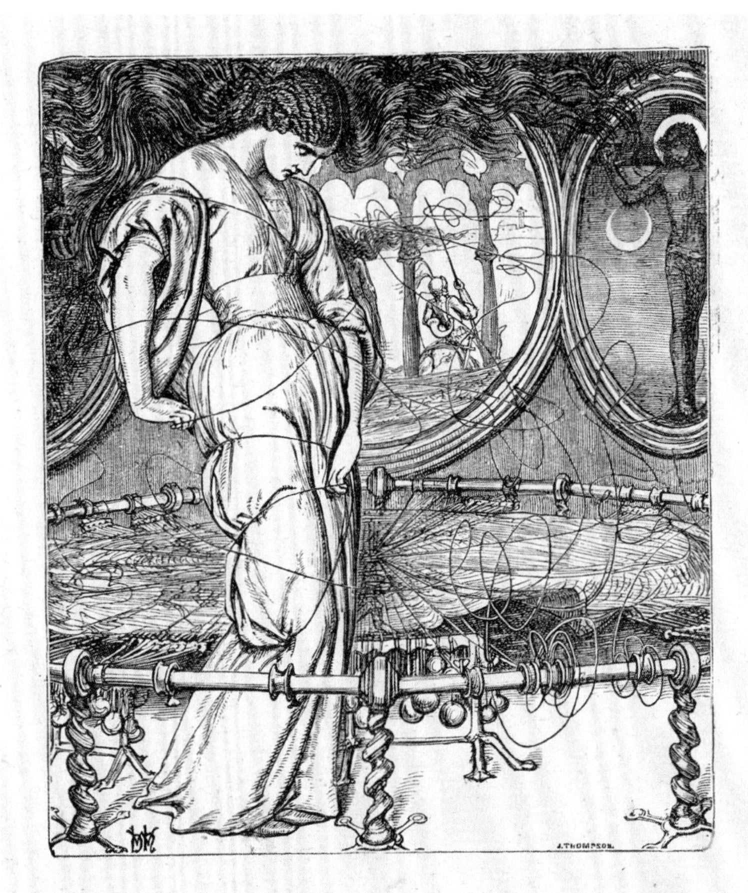

Edward Wadsworth (1889–1949)
The Port c.1915
Woodcut on paper 18.7 × 12.7

The Port is associated with Edward Wadsworth's 'vorticist' period. Vorticism was a short-lived movement that saw a group of British artists reject conventional approaches to landscape and figures in favour of a geometric style of working. None of Wadsworth's paintings from this period survive but his woodcuts reveal the ways he engaged with these modern ideas in terms of form, colour and abstraction.

Wadsworth burnt the woodblocks for his woodcuts before a house move in 1927, 'because they are finished and done with'.[4] As a result, the prints are rare: only the few unnumbered impressions Wadsworth himself took from each of his blocks, such as this one, survive. This woodcut is printed in two colours. Four different colour variations are known, revealing that Wadsworth experimented with printing it in different inks.[5]

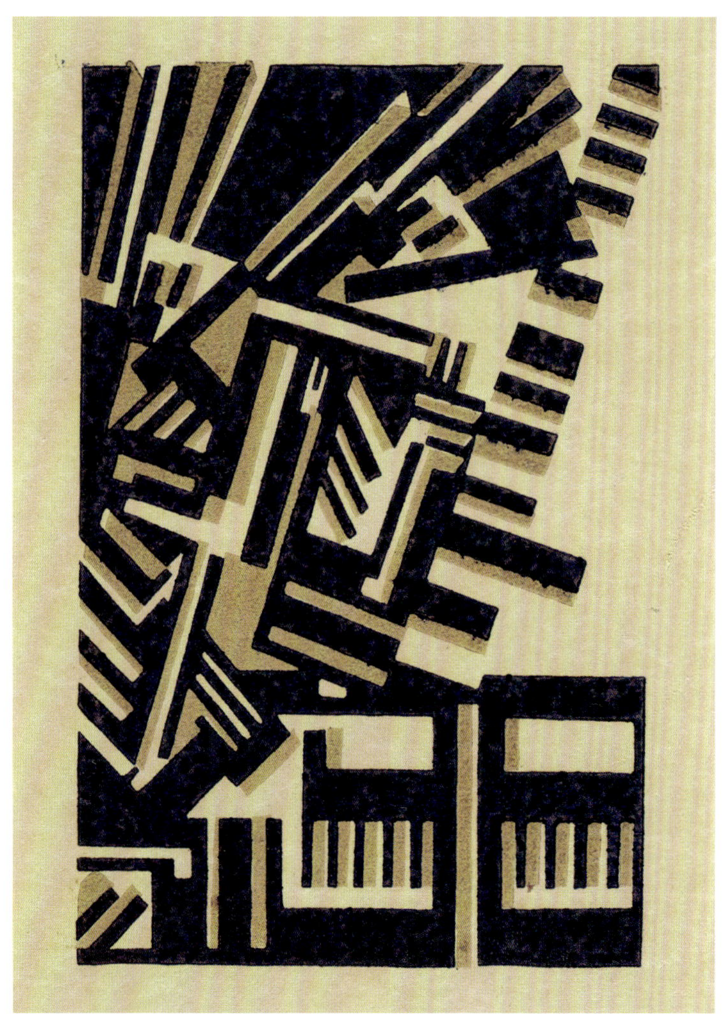

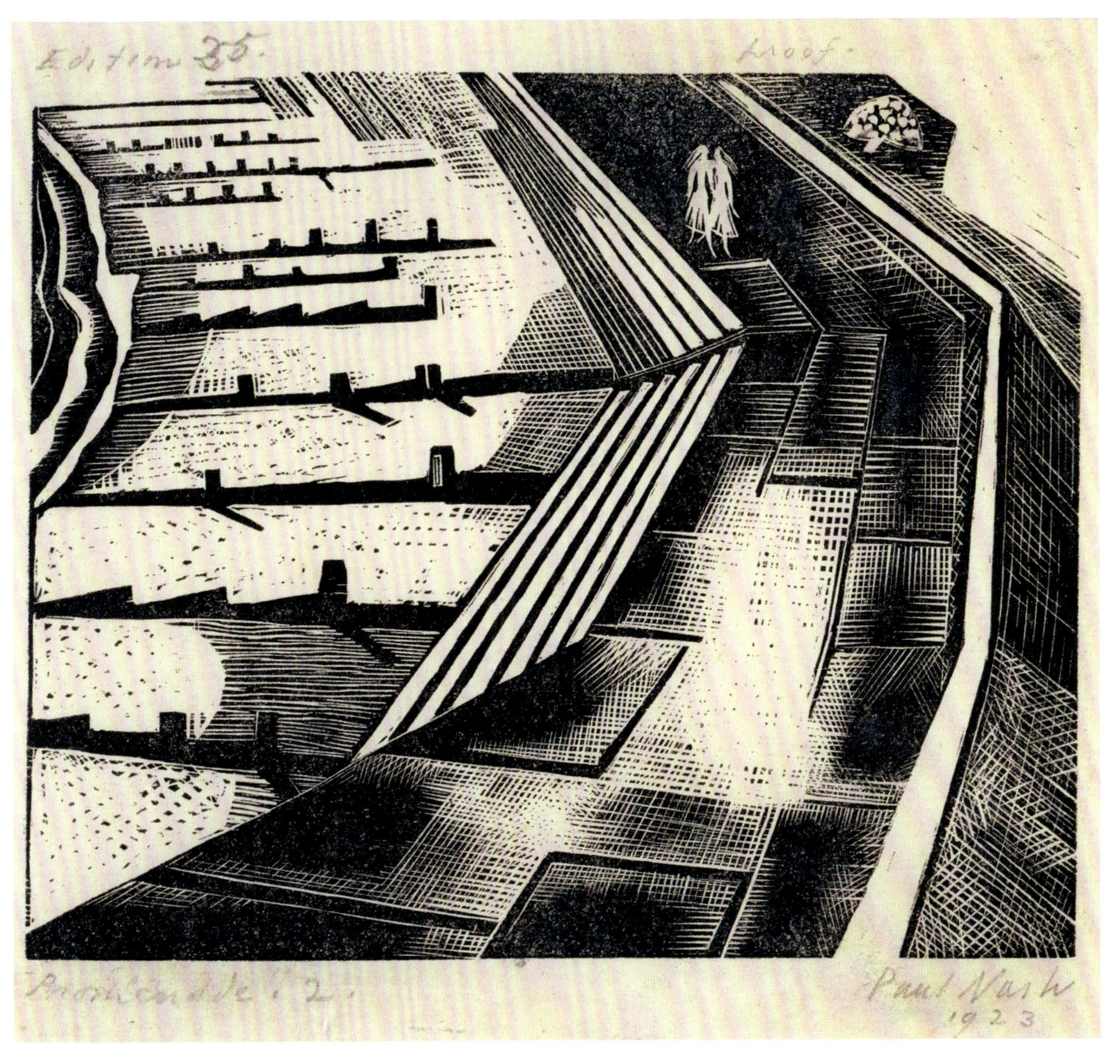

Paul Nash (1889–1946)
Promenade II 1920
Wood engraving on paper 13.7 × 15.6

Paul Nash, a British painter, printmaker, illustrator and photographer, is best known for his war landscapes. This wood engraving, though, was made between the two world wars that Nash famously documented. It shows the bay and seawall at Dymchurch in Kent, one of the artist's favourite subjects. It has been suggested that the two female figures glimpsed in this print are the artist's wife Margaret and his sister Barbara.

Nash's pencil inscription in the upper right, 'Proof', indicates that this impression of the print was an artist's test-piece, made outside of a planned edition. Although Nash dated it 1923, this apparently refers to the time of printing rather than the artist's work in creating the woodblock itself, which is believed to date from 1920.

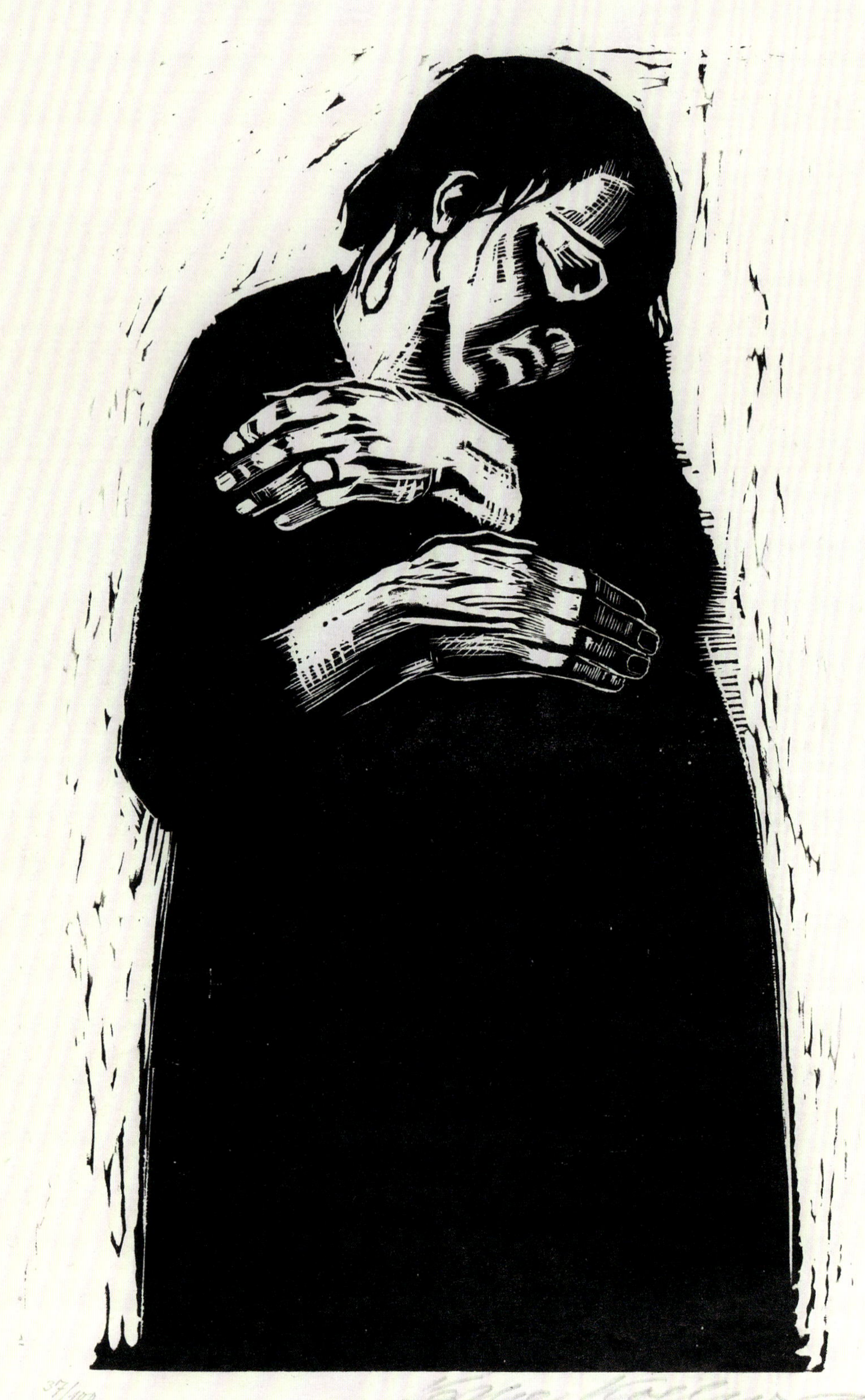

Käthe Kollwitz (1867–1945)
The Widow I from *War* 1921–2
Woodcut on paper 37 × 24

This striking woodcut is from Käthe Kollwitz's 'Krieg' (or 'War') portfolio, a series of prints she made in response to the First World War. Most of the prints explore the suffering of mothers, widows and children left behind during the war, and this piece is one of two to depict a grieving widow. Only one print in the series shows the soldiers themselves. In it, Kollwitz's son Peter takes his place next to Death. Peter was killed in 1914, at the age of eighteen.

Kollwitz favoured the woodcut technique due to its potential to create stark, arresting images: she revised each woodcut in the series until it was as refined as possible. The 'War' prints demonstrate her ability to evoke the horror of human suffering – and personal loss – in the face of events beyond an individual's control. In *The Widow I* a woman's grief is laid bare and presented in black and white, her sagging head and empty hands unforgettable.

Gertrude Hermes (1901–1983)
Waterlilies 1930
Wood engraving on paper 22.9 × 13.4

The sculptor and printmaker Gertrude Hermes played a key role in the revival of British wood engraving during the early twentieth century. In 1929 she made twenty wood engravings to illustrate Irene Gosse's botanical book *A Florilege: Chosen from the Old Herbals* (1931). The intricate, flowing images she produced are considered a turning point in her printmaking career, combining the abstract qualities of her earlier work with closer observation of the natural world. They have been credited with fusing the historical methods of wood-engraved illustration with the contemporary concerns of modern art.[6] It certainly seems possible to read this image's brilliant combination of naturalistic representation and crisp, bold marks in this way.

Waterlilies (or *Nonefar*) was the final illustration in the *Florilege*. The other subjects included clematis, deadly nightshade and various additional flowers and plants, such as *Mistletoe*, a print of which is also held in the Tate collection.

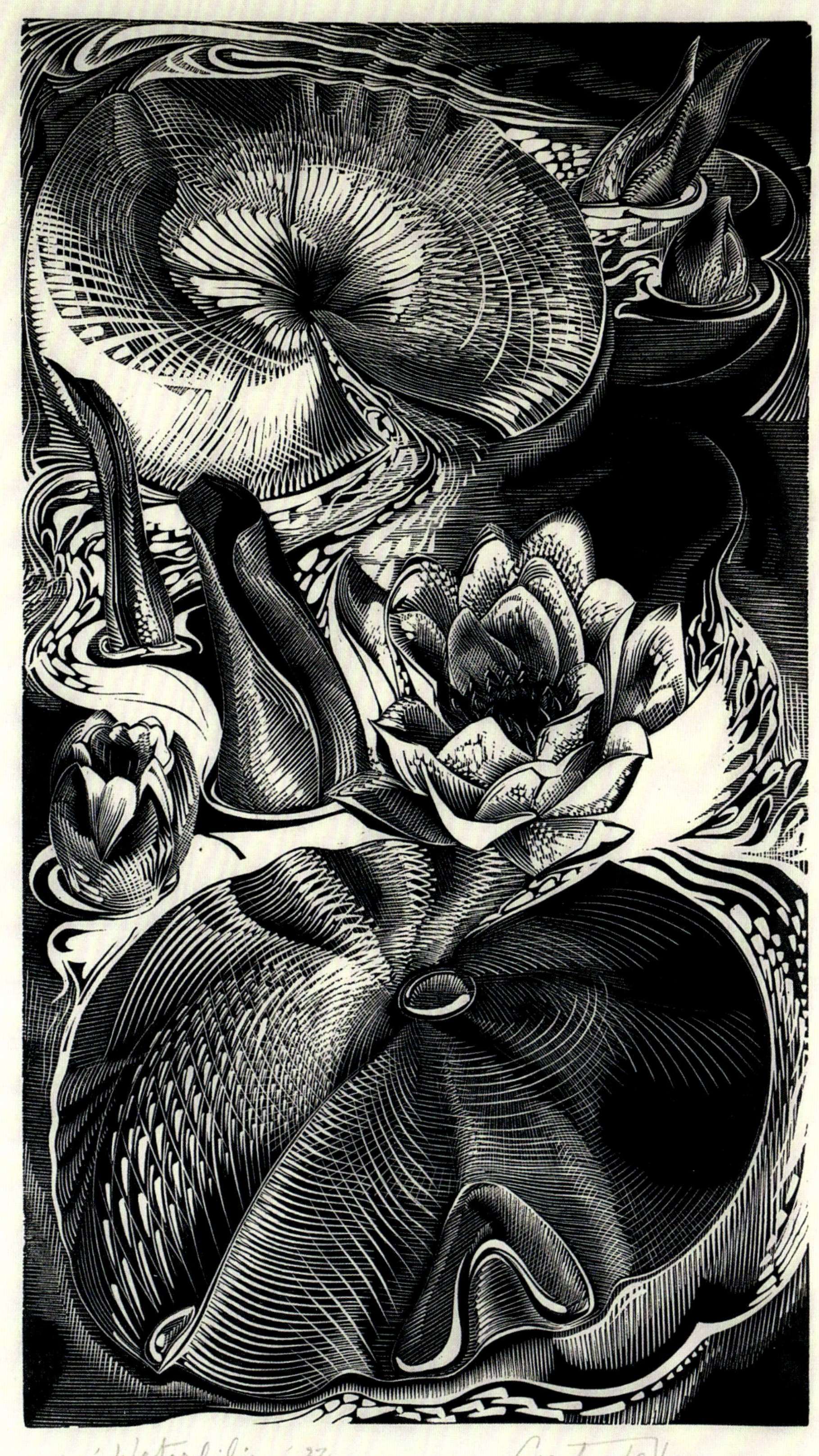
'Waterlilies' 27/30
Gertrude Hermes
1930.

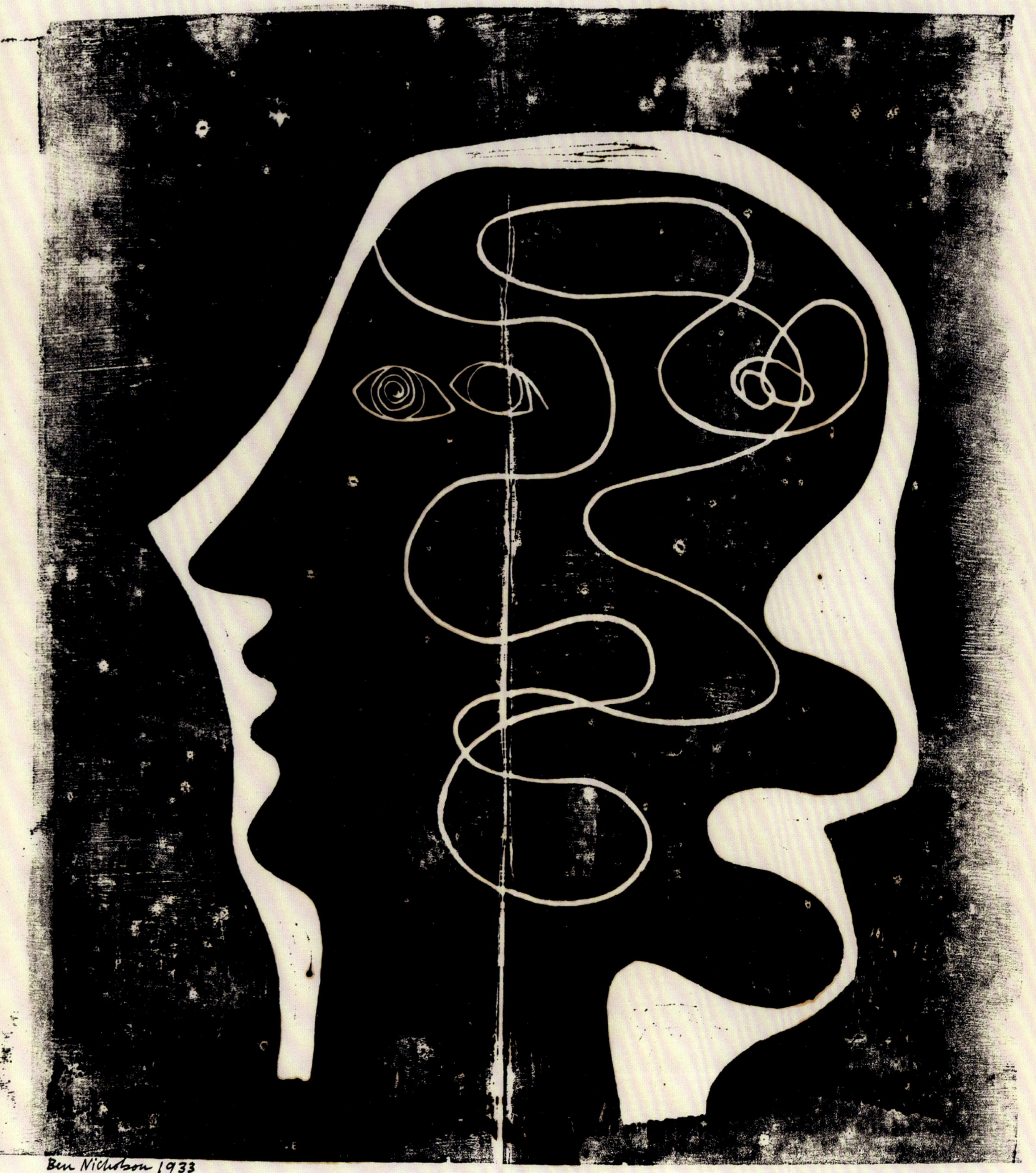
Ben Nicholson 1933

Ben Nicholson (1894–1982)
1933 (Profile) 1933
Linocut on paper 60 × 45

For this print, the British artist Ben Nicholson used linocut to create an image of a woman in profile. The head's graphic form and spiralling white lines perhaps suggest the influence of Picasso,[7] while the contrast between the neat blocks and lines at the centre of the image and the unfinished edges imply the work is an informal experiment. This is also suggested by the fact that the artist did not make a numbered edition, instead making various trial prints from the lino, using different inks in an ad hoc fashion.

The woman Nicholson depicts in this image is believed to be the artist Barbara Hepworth (see p.146), with whom he was romantically involved. It has been suggested the two artists were working collaboratively around this time, and that this print, with its sweeping linear depiction of Hepworth, is one result of their artistic exchange.[8]

Leonard Baskin (1922–2000)
The Anatomist 1952
Woodcut on paper 50.2 × 27.9

While many of the artists highlighted in this book are better known for their work in other media, the American artist Leonard Baskin came to prominence as a printmaker. His prints probably remain the best-known aspect of his oeuvre, although he also worked as a sculptor, painter, illustrator and book publisher.

The Anatomist is one of the early woodcuts which made Baskin's name. It was printed in red and black in an edition of fifteen. The image reflects the artist's interest in anatomy: the anatomist of the title holds a scaled-down skeletal model and stands next to a diagram of the human body, which is printed in red. The anatomist himself seems to become part of his own field of study in Baskin's image, the lines of the man's skin merging with the blood vessels that usually lie unseen beneath the surface.

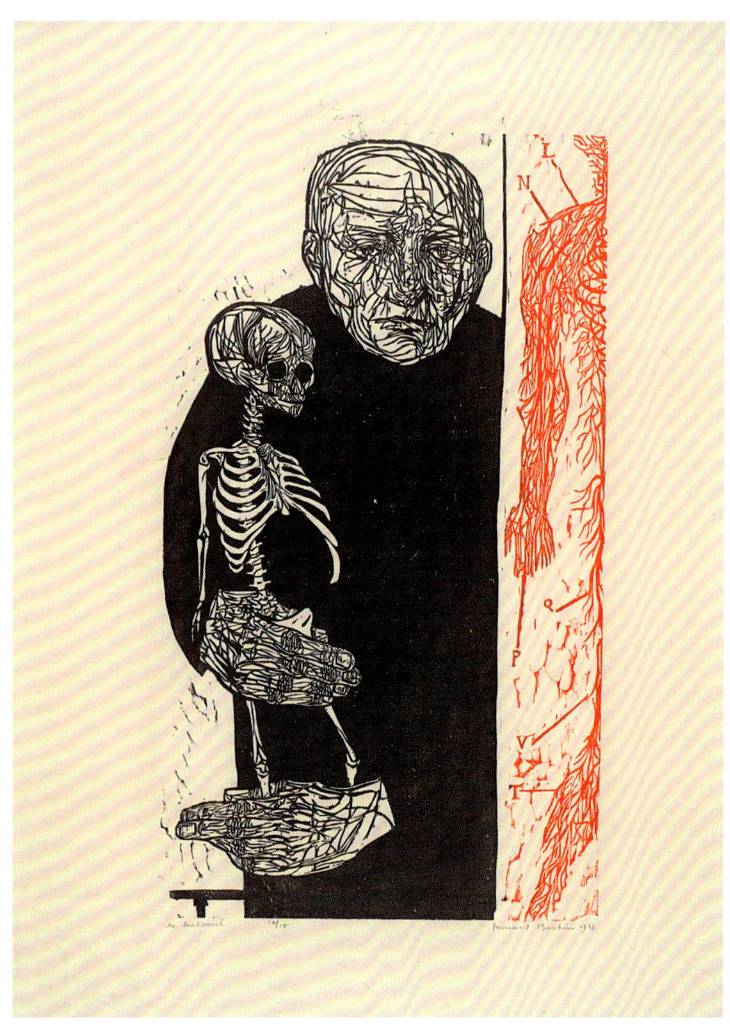

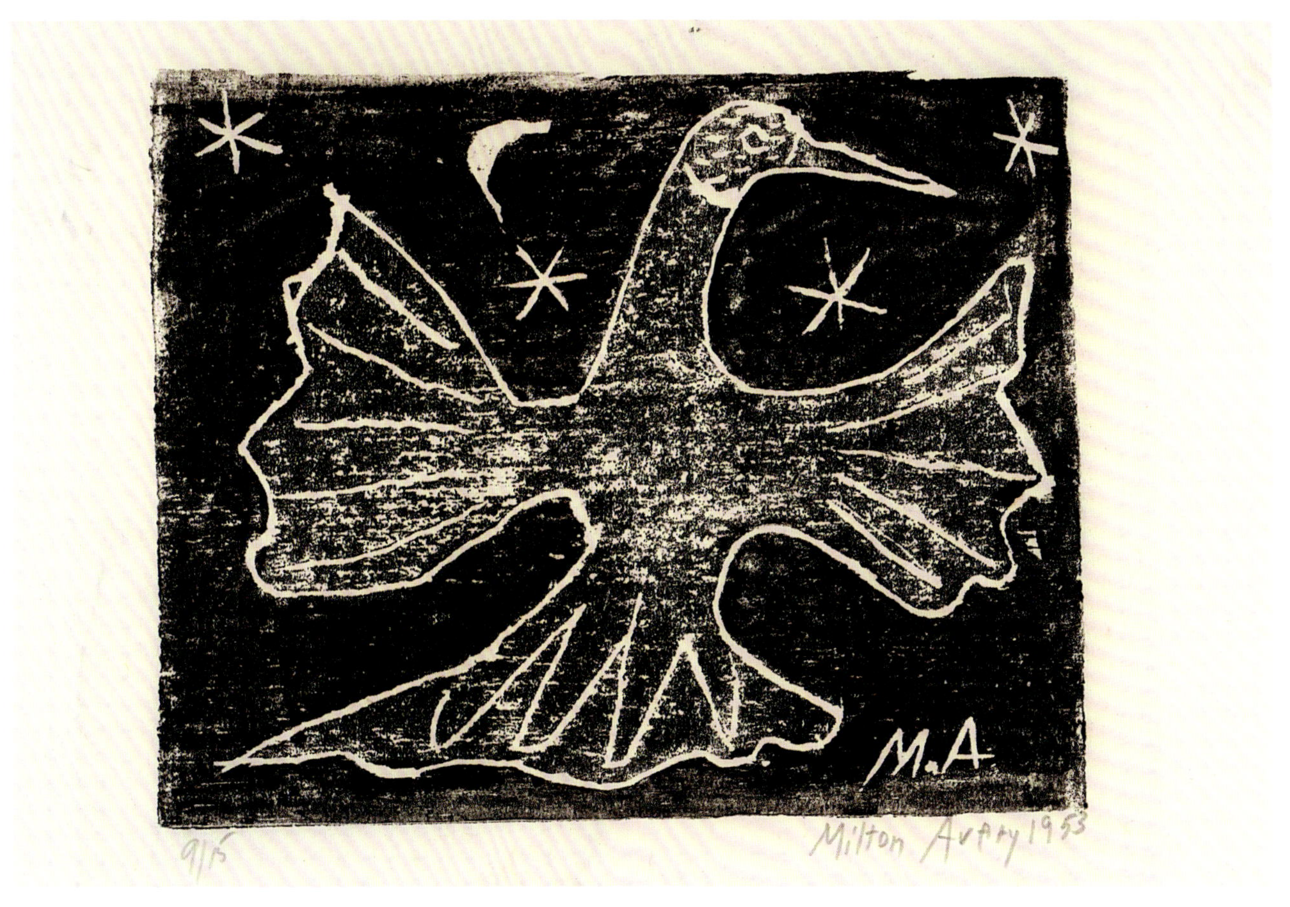

Milton Avery (1893–1965)
Dawn 1952
Woodcut on paper 18 × 23

The American artist Milton Avery made this woodcut in 1952, during an intense period of printmaking activity. This impression belongs to a small edition of fifteen printed in black.

Avery's incisions into the woodblock resulted in the central image of a flying bird, which was gouged out of the wood and appears in the final image as white lines. The stars and crescent moon suggest the night sky behind the bird. The subject reflects Avery's wider interest in flying seabird motifs around this time: he made numerous drawings and paintings of the subject, as well as prints. His widow, Sally Avery, noted: 'We spent many summers by the sea. The birds were there … Milton did hundreds of sketches of birds in flight.'[9]

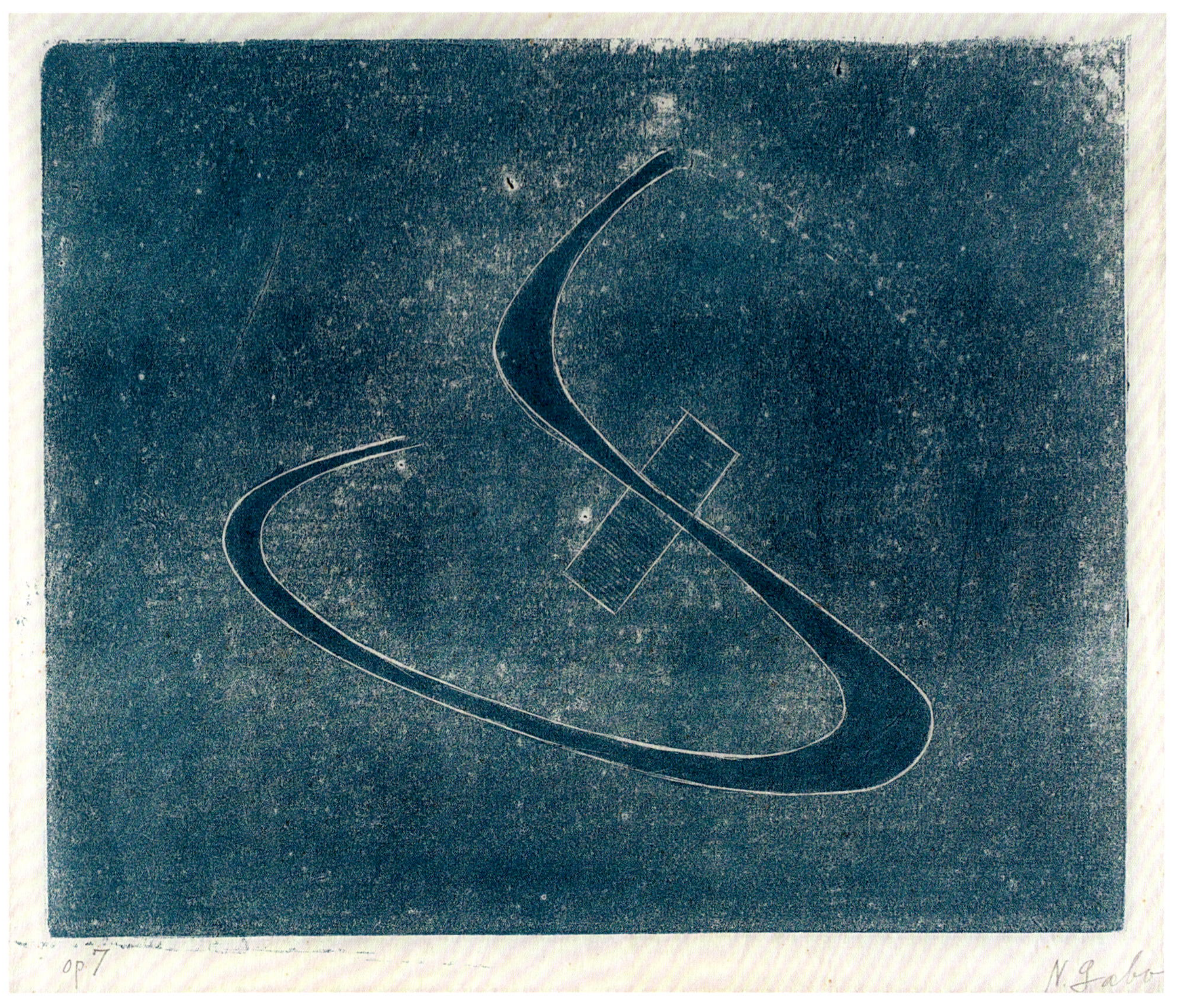

Naum Gabo (1890–1977)
Opus 7 1956–73
Wood engraving on paper 20.3 × 25.3

The Russian-born artist Naum Gabo arrived in England as a refugee in 1935. He went on to work in St Ives, Cornwall, where his artistic contemporaries included Ben Nicholson and Barbara Hepworth (pp.36, 146), before moving to the United States after the Second World War. He took up wood engraving in the mid 1950s and experimented with it during the next two decades.

This work is from Gabo's momentous 'Opus' series, which he printed himself. As he printed each impression slightly differently, each print is unique. The blue ink he used here imbues the abstract, sculptural form of the central shape with the suggestion of a twilight sky.

Lygia Pape (1927–2004)
Weaving 1957
Woodcut on paper 45 × 33

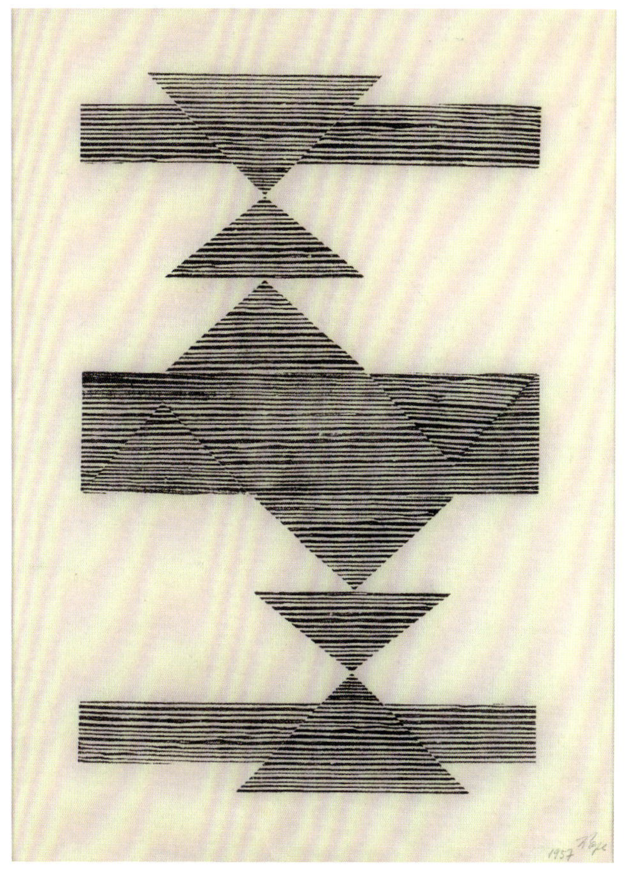

Lygia Pape made this print during the 1950s, when the government of her native Brazil encouraged use of the 'democratic' woodcut technique in a move inspired by the cultural policy of Stalin's Soviet Union.[10] But while the government celebrated woodcut's potential for mass production – something demonstrated by the medium's historic use for book illustration – Page actually did the opposite, printing her woodcuts as unique pieces in single editions.

Although the image might appear straightforward at first glance, this is deceptive: the arrangement of geometric shapes is actually quite complex. The triangles and rectangles that make up the image are also seen in visual dialogue with the wood grain used to make the woodcuts, which has a complex effect on the eye.[11] This and other *Weaving* prints by Pape seem to emphasise the natural texture of wood grain – and the texture of the ink – against the manmade texture or 'weave' of paper. The piece anticipates Pape's work of the following decade, when the 'neo-concretist' artistic group she belonged to emphasised natural and organic elements within geometric abstract art.[12] This concern is also seen in the uneven application of ink, which draws attention to the imperfect nature of human hand over the perfect mathematical qualities of geometry.

Pablo Picasso (1881–1973)
Portrait of a Woman after Cranach the Younger 1958
Linocut on paper 64.5 × 53.3

An exceptionally experimental printmaker, Pablo Picasso first tried linocut in 1939 before returning to it with seriousness in the mid 1950s. This print, his first colour linocut, was inspired by a postcard of a sixteenth-century painting, *Portrait of a Woman* by Lucas Cranach the Younger. To make the print, Picasso fashioned five different linoleum blocks, one for each of the colours seen in the print (sepia, yellow, red, blue and black). The blocks moved through different 'states' (or stages) as Picasso refined them before arriving at a final image. The completed work was printed in an edition of fifty signed and numbered copies, while this impression is one of around fifteen artist's proofs.

Picasso's image appears the reverse of Cranach's, as the printing process reversed the marks he drew and cut onto the lino. The other Picasso piece included in this book also sees the artist reinterpret the art of the past (p.71).

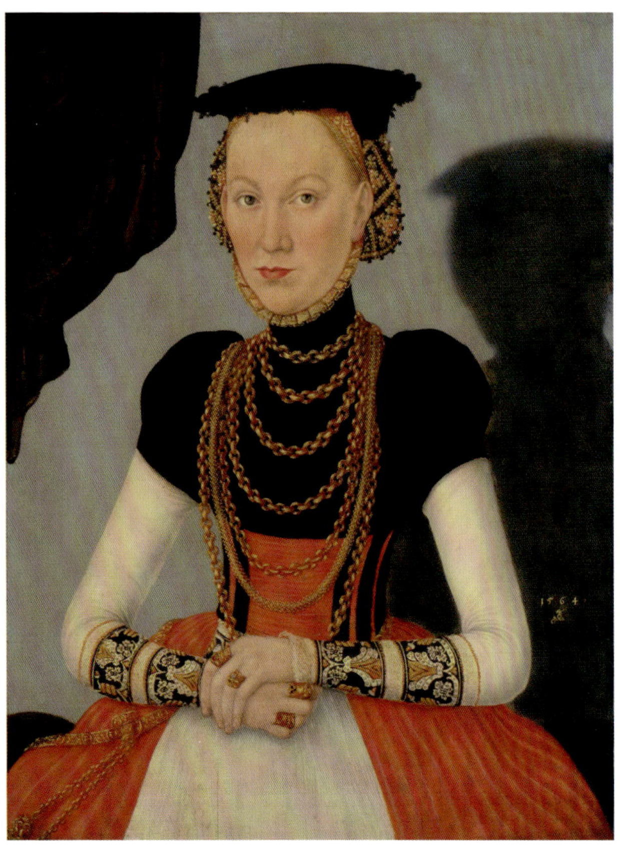

Lucas Cranach the Younger (1515–86), *Portrait of a Woman* after 1565. Kunsthistorisches Museum Wien, Vienna

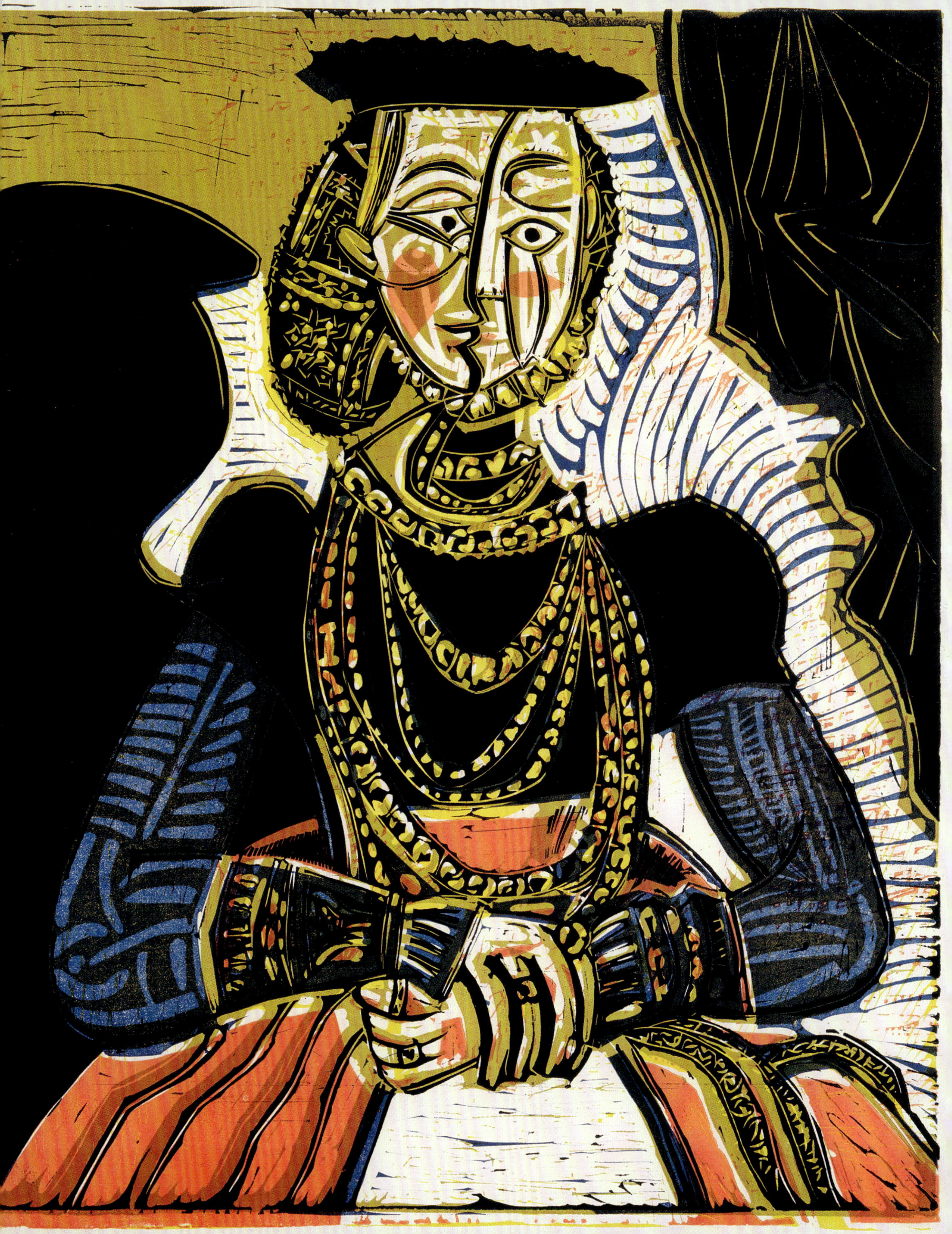

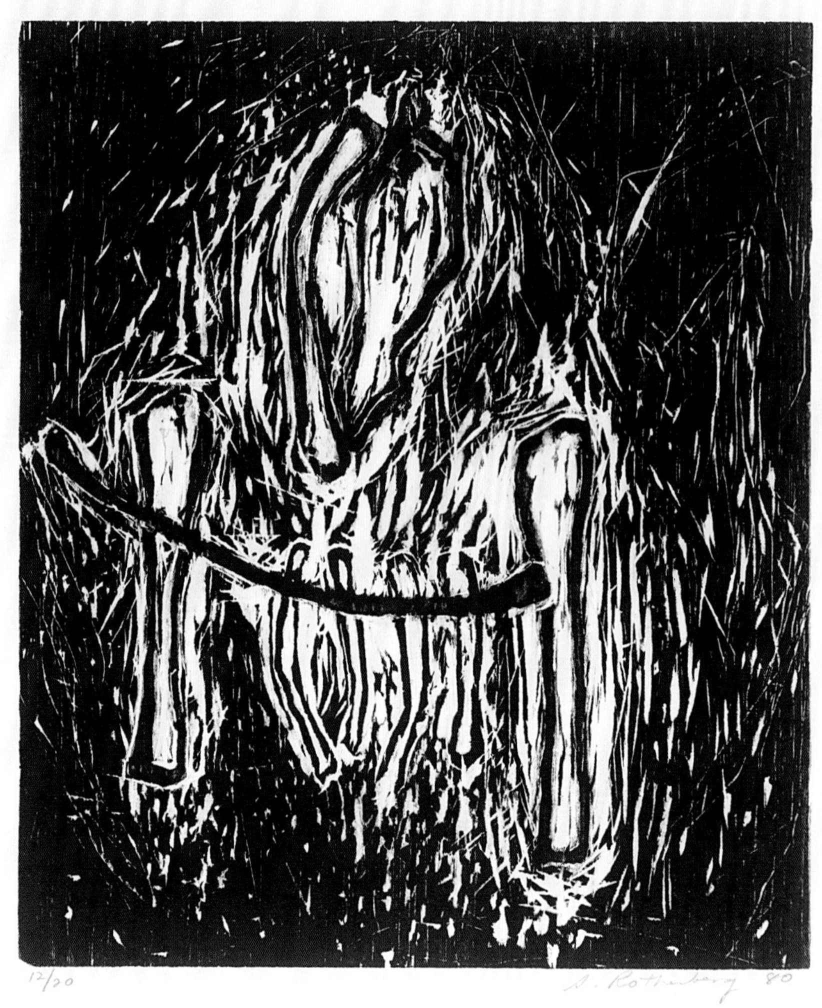

Susan Rothenberg (1945–2020)
Head and Bones 1980
Woodcut on paper 33 × 28.6

Susan Rothenberg's print practice embraced the techniques of woodcut, etching, lithography and mezzotint (see also p.113). Her prints echo the subject matter of her paintings, which focused first on horses and then the human figure.

In this, one of Rothenberg's first editioned woodcuts, she depicted a horse's head and leg bones. These are seen alongside other bone-like forms the artist gouged from the woodblock, and the animal features seem to emerge almost organically from the wood-printed background. Perhaps because of this, the image feels slightly mysterious. The woodcut was printed by Gretchen Gelb at Aeropress and published by Multiples Inc., New York, in an edition of twenty.

Sol LeWitt (1928–2007)

A Square Divided Horizontally and Vertically into Four Equal Parts, Each with a Different Direction of Alternating Parallel Bands of Lines 1982

Woodcut on paper, printed with watercolour 60.7 × 60.7

The American artist Sol LeWitt fully engaged with printmaking from 1970, working with lithography, screenprinting, etching and, later, woodcut. Unlike most of the artists featured in these pages, LeWitt did not make his own prints; instead he provided drawings and instructions to specialist printmakers. This reflects his emphasis on the importance of concept over making: he did not see working with his own hands as important to his art, or to his engagement with printmaking.

This print is one of a series of six woodcuts projecting forms drawn from a cube. It was printed in Boston and published by Multiples Inc., New York in an edition of forty.

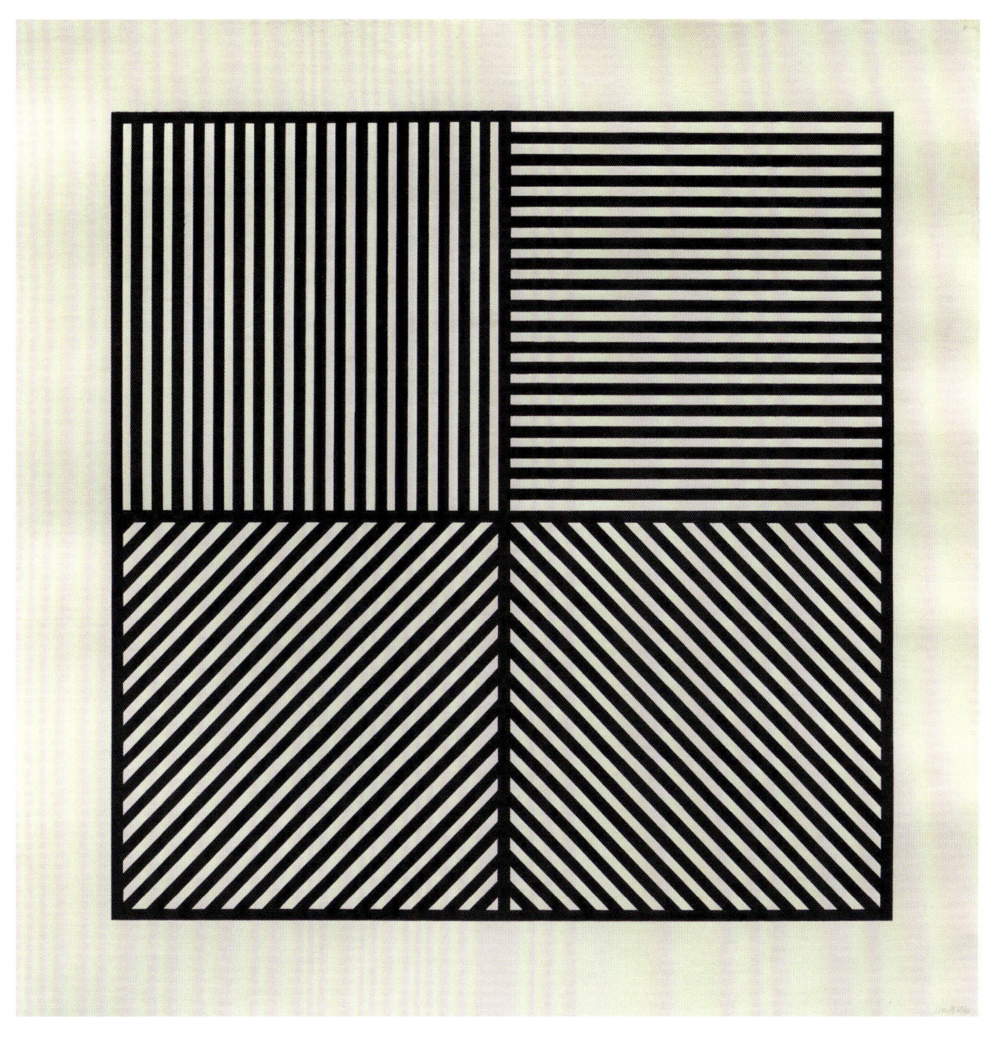

Georg Baselitz (born 1938)
Von vorne [From the Front] 1985
Woodcut on paper, printed in ink 65 × 49

Georg Baselitz discovered sixteenth-century 'chiaroscuro' woodcuts during his scholarship in Florence in 1965. In these distinctive prints, separate blocks were used to create line and tone; these were then printed in different tones or colours. Inspired to adopt this centuries-old technique within his own work, Baselitz sought to 'rediscover the woodcut' in an era he saw as dominated by conceptual art and screenprinting (pp.154–7).[13] In this print he, like the chiaroscuro woodcutters of old, introduced a second woodblock, making expressive use of red as a contrast colour against the black and white of the main image. As in many of Baselitz's images, the figure depicted here is purposefully shown upside down.

Baselitz's oeuvre includes almost two thousand prints. His wife Elke, who often assisted him with printing using a press in his studio, printed the present edition of fifteen prints, which was published by Maximilian Verlag/Sabine Kunst in Munich.

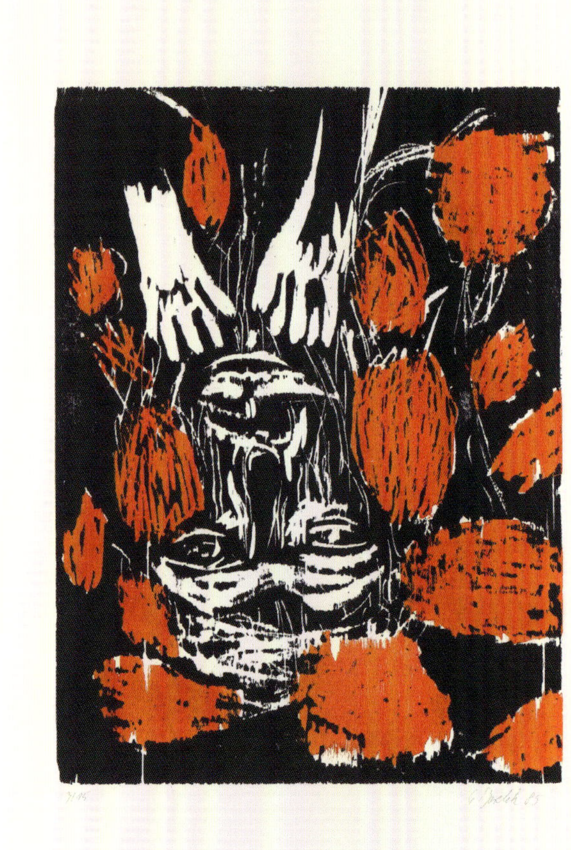

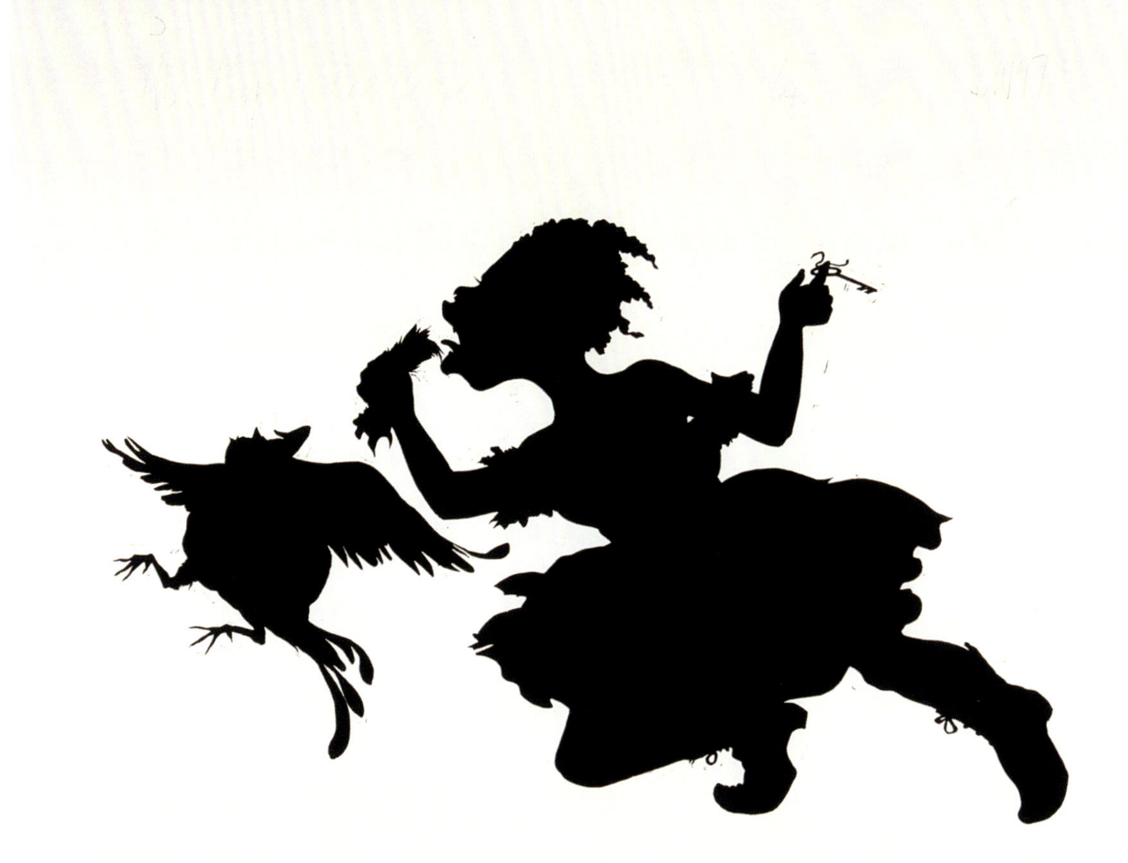

Kara Walker (born 1969)
The Keys to the Coop 1997
Linocut on paper 117.5 × 154

During her teenage years the American artist Kara Walker lived in Stone Mountain, Georgia, the birthplace of the Ku Klux Klan in its twentieth-century manifestation. Experiencing this setting was formative, and the history of Black people in the United States became the central theme of Walker's work.

Walker is best known for her room-size tableau of cut-paper silhouettes depicting the violence towards and abuse of Black slaves, with the profiled figures referencing the 'polite' silhouette format developed in the eighteenth century. Here, she used linocut to explore the silhouette form in print on a similarly large scale. The African American girl in the image is depicted twirling a set of keys in one hand and a chicken's head and neck, which she is about to eat, in the other. The keys and the 'coop' of the title may allude to ideas of imprisonment, while the girl's decision to eat a part of the chicken which is usually discarded could suggest her lack of choice, her rebelliousness, or both.[14]

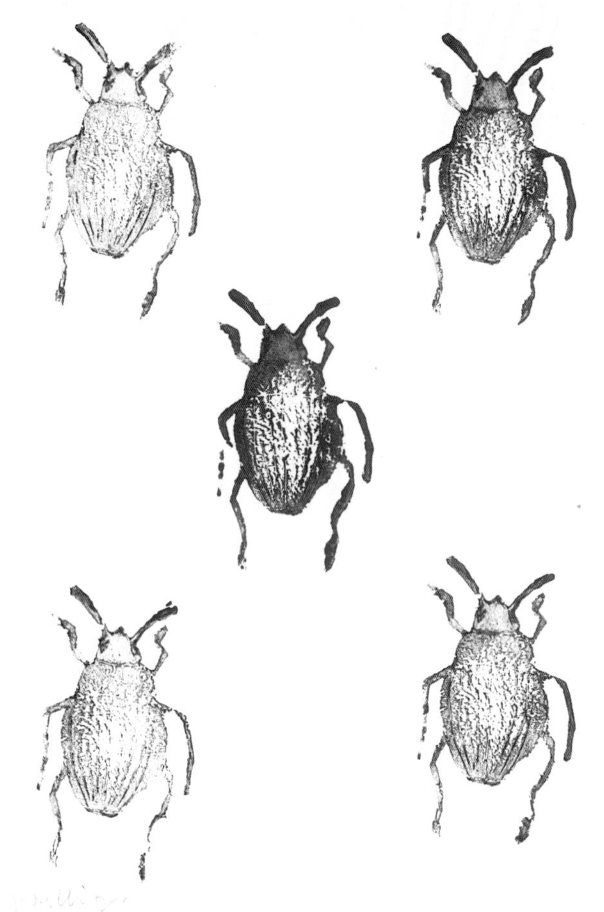

Mark Wallinger (born 1959)
King Edward and the Colorado Beetle, from *Bugs* 2000
Potato print on paper 37 × 25.5

Potato printing, perhaps the humblest print technique of all, is here employed by the British artist Mark Wallinger to create an image of a Colorado beetle. While the method is relatively simple, Wallinger's choice is conceptual. The Colorado beetle and its larvae feast on potato plants, with the species considered a major pest to potato growing. As such, the beetle's image is here created using its potential victim. The same beetle is printed five times on the sheet, with the amount of ink used within each print varying from darkest in the central image to almost fading away on the left.

Wallinger was one of ten artists to make a print for the portfolio *Bugs*, which was published to support bursaries for students at London's Byam Shaw School of Art. Each artist responded to the overall theme, but the prints were made in various different ways, using both handmade and photo-mechanical techniques. The portfolios were published in an edition of ninety.

William Kentridge (born 1955)
Untitled (Woman Turning into a Telephone) 2000

Linocut on paper Sheet size: 224.3 × 119.8

In this piece William Kentridge, one of South Africa's leading artists, used the linocut technique on such a grand scale that the prints were made using the largest printing press in South Africa. The image seems intended both to disturb and amuse: a woman's figure, which is life-sized, steps across a landscape, but her upper half has transformed into an old-fashioned telephone. This might suggest the changing nature of society and the way it communicates. Transformation is an important theme in Kentridge's work, and a related linocut shows a man turning into a tree.

Printmaking is central to Kentridge's practice; for an example of his work using the etching medium in combination with collage, see p.218.

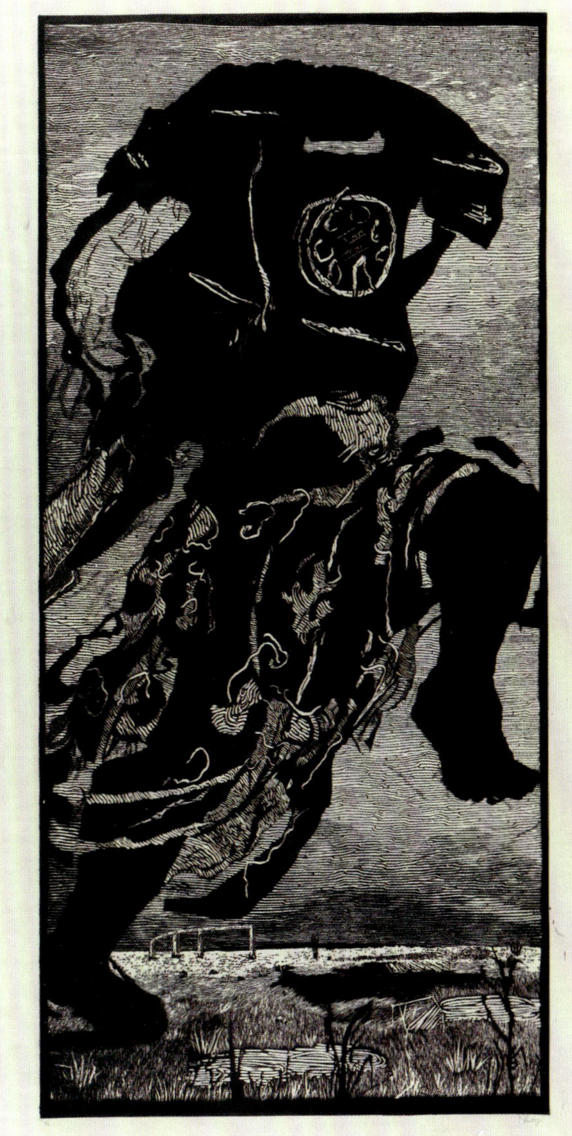

Zarina (1937–2020)

Letters from Home 2004

Portfolio of 8 woodcuts and metalcuts on paper   sheet: 56.5 × 38.1

The Indian-born artist Zarina (as Zarina Hashmi was known professionally) studied printmaking at Atelier 17 in Paris with Stanley William Hayter (see pp.85, 105) during the 1960s. This portfolio of eight prints (opposite; *Letter VII* is shown below), designed as a single work, reflects her knowledge of different printmaking techniques as well as her interests in layering and memory. Letters written in Urdu from the artist's sister, Rani, were recreated as metalcuts that Zarina printed herself in sepia ink. She then added woodcut to the prints by printing from wood-blocks representing different locations, eventually publishing *Letters from Home* in an edition of twenty.

Zarina left India in 1958. Shortly after her departure, the partition of India and Pakistan forced her family to relocate from Delhi in India to Karachi in Pakistan. It is from Karachi that Rani wrote to her, and as such Karachi might be seen as the 'home' the title refers to. But in this work – as in Zarina's mind – home is not a single place; other places she has lived, including her first home in pre-Partition India as well as places she travelled to later, also feature as routes and plans printed onto the letters. Text is also very important in Zarina's work, and she has spoken of the significance of including words in Urdu, her mother tongue, within her prints.[15]

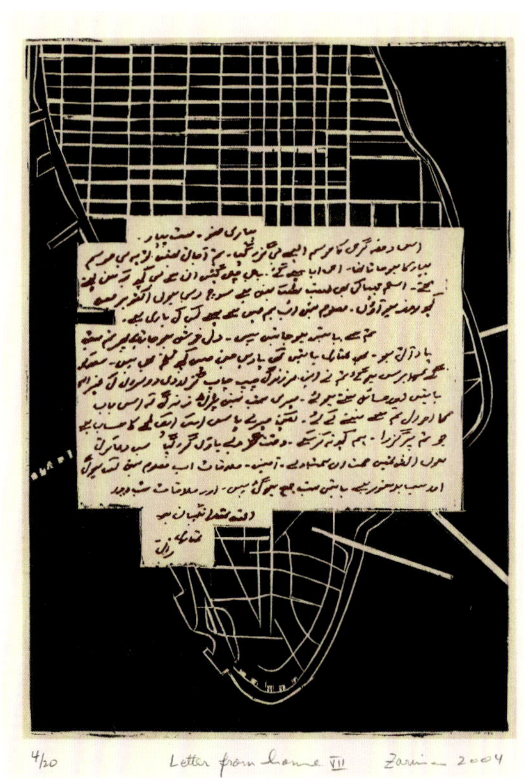

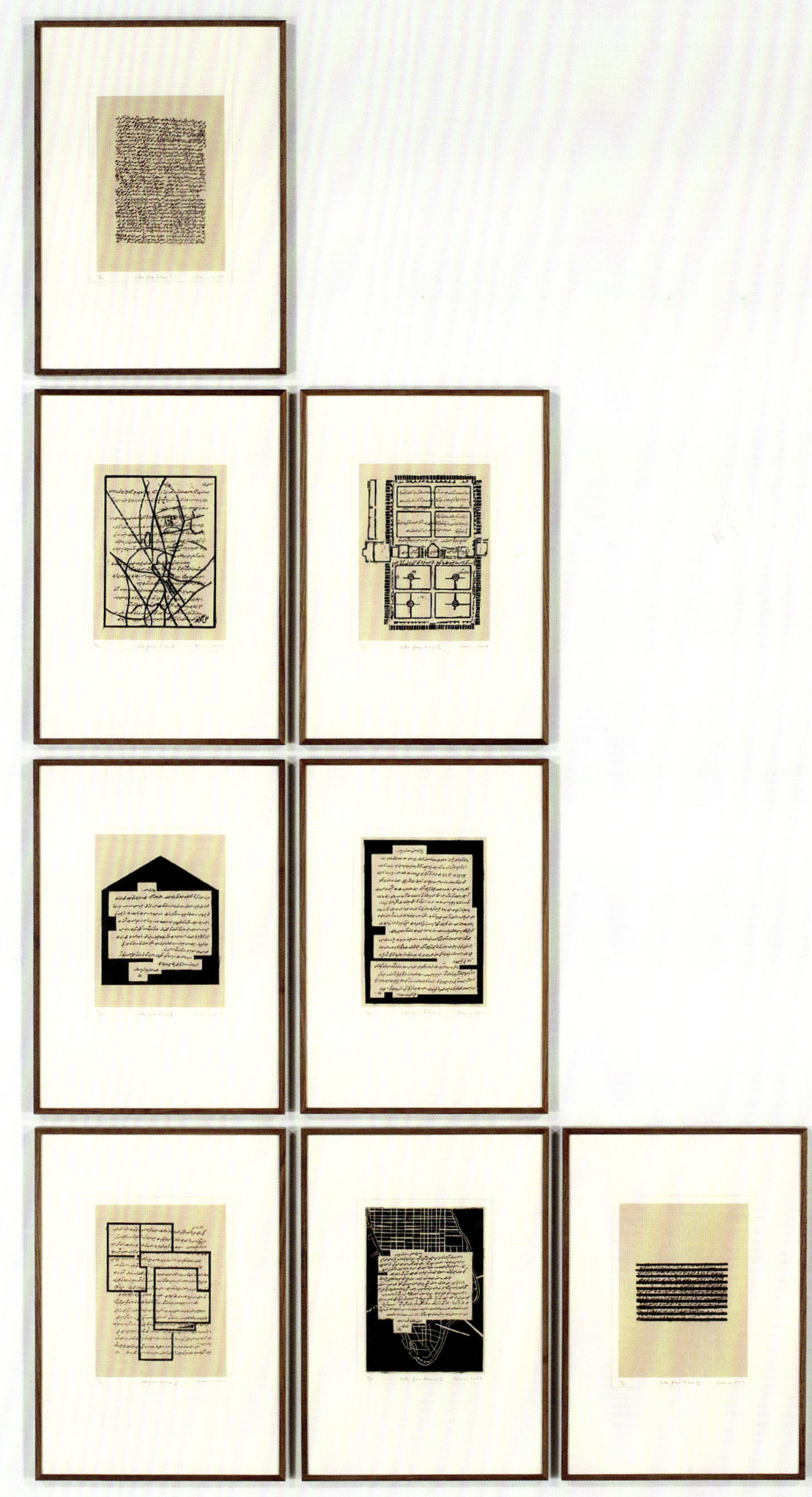

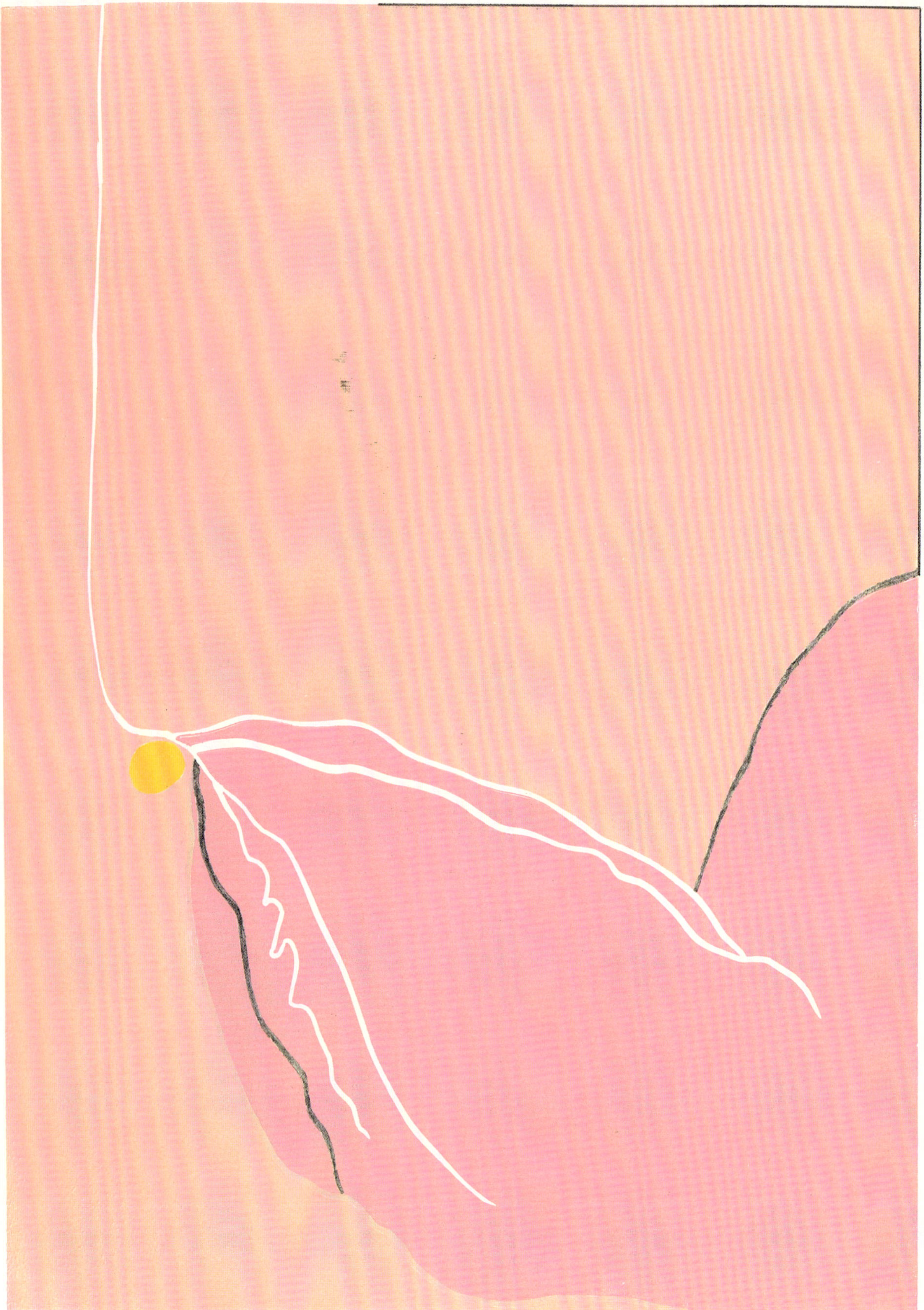

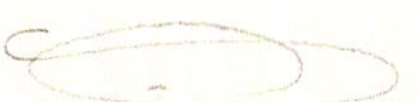

06.

Gary Hume (born 1962)
Untitled 02 2006
Linocut on paper 55.5 × 40

Gary Hume is associated with the Young British Artists, who came to prominence in the 1990s. *Untitled 02* is from a series of eight linocuts exploring floral imagery, a familiar motif in Hume's practice. In this print the details of the flower have become abstracted and the delicate colour combinations achieved come to the fore.

Hume created this linocut series, *Here's Flowers*, with Hugh Stoneman, a printer known for his many notable collaborations with leading artists. When Stoneman died in 2005, Hume completed the project alone and the prints were published by Charles Booth-Clibborn's Paragon Press. As a series they go some way to describing the planes of flat colour and the crisp lines achievable using the linocut method, while also displaying a subtlety of tonal and colour contrasts unusual for the medium.

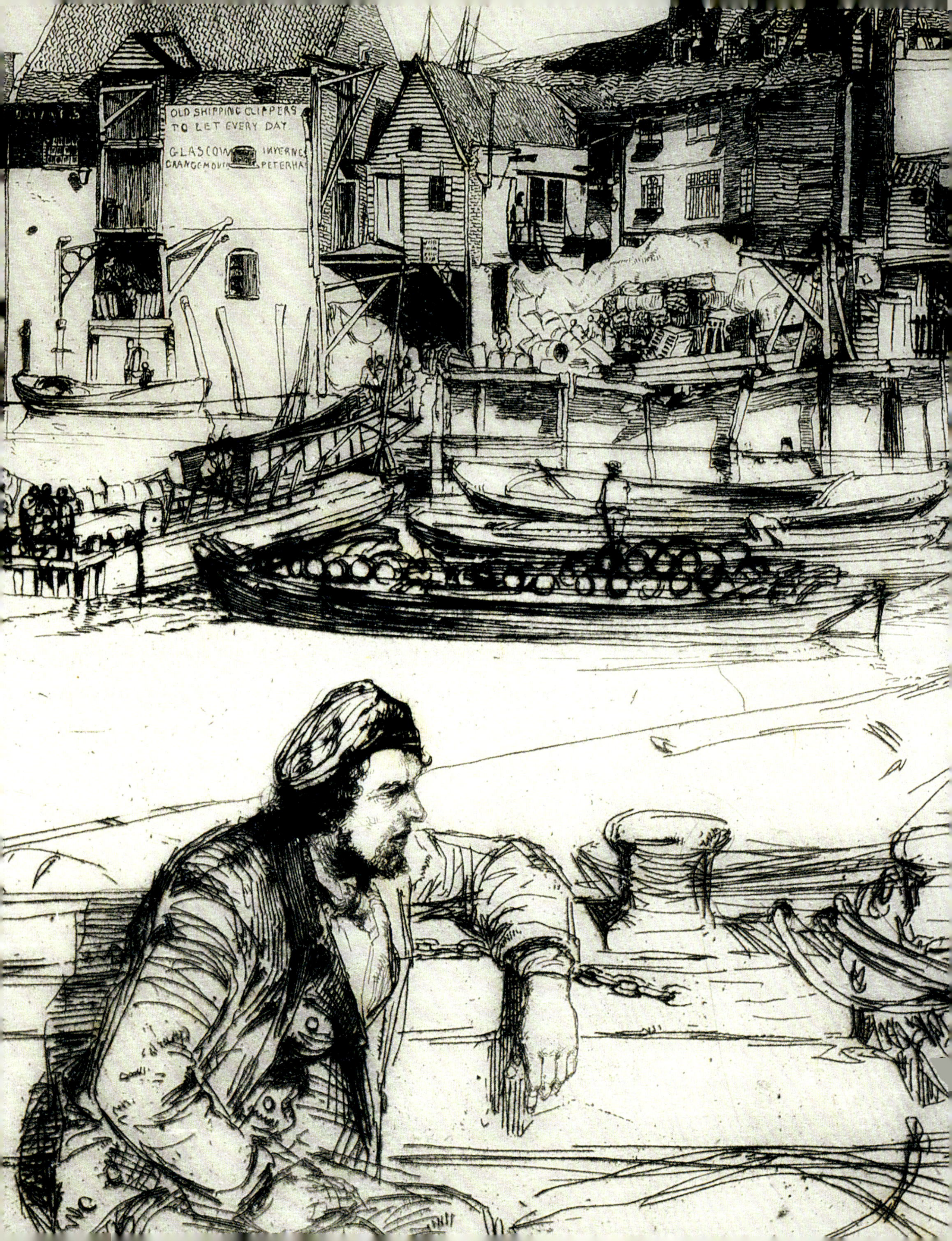
OLD SHIPPING CLIPPERS
TO LET EVERY DAY
GLASGOW
INVERNES
PETERHA

3 The Art of Etching

James Abbott McNeill Whistler *Black Lion Wharf, Wapping* 1859 (detail)

3 The Art of Etching

Etching, with its acid baths, metal plates and various 'grounds', can seem a mysterious art form, but it is one of the easiest print techniques to try. Anyone able to make an image on paper can usually also 'draw' on a prepared etching plate without too much trouble. This is one reason etching has appealed to many artists known primarily as painters, from Parmigianino (Girolamo Francesco Maria Mazzola) in sixteenth-century Italy, one of the earliest to experiment with the medium, to most of the artists featured in the following pages; David Hockney, for example, learnt the essentials 'in fifteen minutes' from a fellow student at London's Royal College of Art.[1] Another reason for its popularity is the medium's endless potential for experimentation, with any number of different visual effects possible.

> HOCKNEY p.81

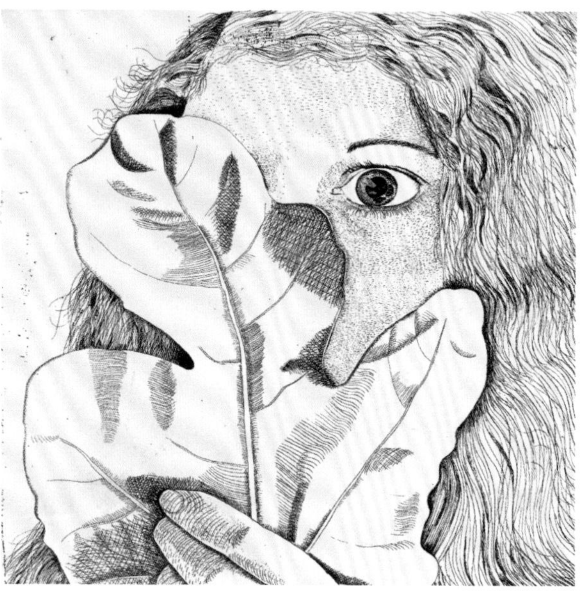

Detail from Lucian Freud, *Girl with a Fig Leaf* 1947

To make a line etching, an artist coats a metal plate with a waxy, acid-resistant ground, usually made up of beeswax, bitumen and resin. They can then 'draw' into the ground using a sharp tool. When the plate is placed in a bath of dilute acid, the acid eats away at (or 'bites') the artist's marks, while the ground protects the rest of the plate. It is possible to bite or etch different parts of the plate for different amounts of time by 'stopping out' areas with varnish and returning the plate to the acid bath. This creates depth and variance in the lines. When the artist is ready to see their creation, they wipe away the ground and clean the plate. The plate is then inked by hand, with the ink pushed into the artist's marks and the excess wiped away. Finally, the plate is run through a rolling printing press with a sheet of moistened paper placed over it. The artist's marks hold the ink and print black (or whatever colour ink has been used). A 'plate mark' is left around the image, caused by the plate's edges pushing into the paper as it passes through the printing press.

Once an artist has mastered the basic technique described, a plethora of additions and variations are possible.

Soft-Ground Etching is a variation of line etching in which the plate is prepared with a waxy ground softer than that used for traditional line etching. A thin sheet of paper is placed over this ground and the artist draws onto it with a pencil before removing the paper and placing the plate in the acid bath as usual. The resulting printed marks have the appearance of a drawing.

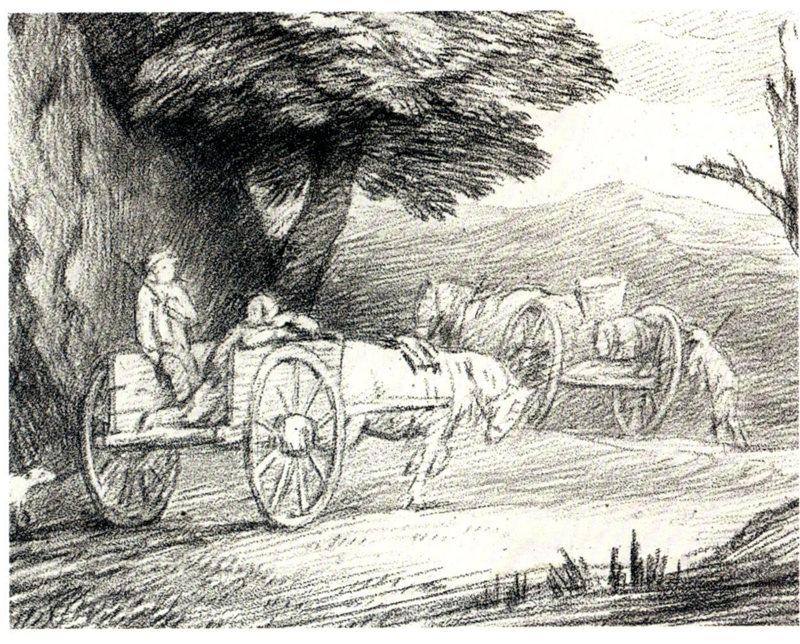

Detail from Thomas Gainsborough, *Wooded Landscape with Two Country Carts and Figures* 1779–80

Aquatint is used to create areas of tone. Traditionally, the technique involves heating a granular resin onto the metal plate; these days granular-effect spray paint is also used. When the plate is placed in the acid bath, only the areas in-between the grains 'bite', resulting in broad areas of tone. Different tones are achieved by varying the amount of time different areas of the plate are exposed to the acid.

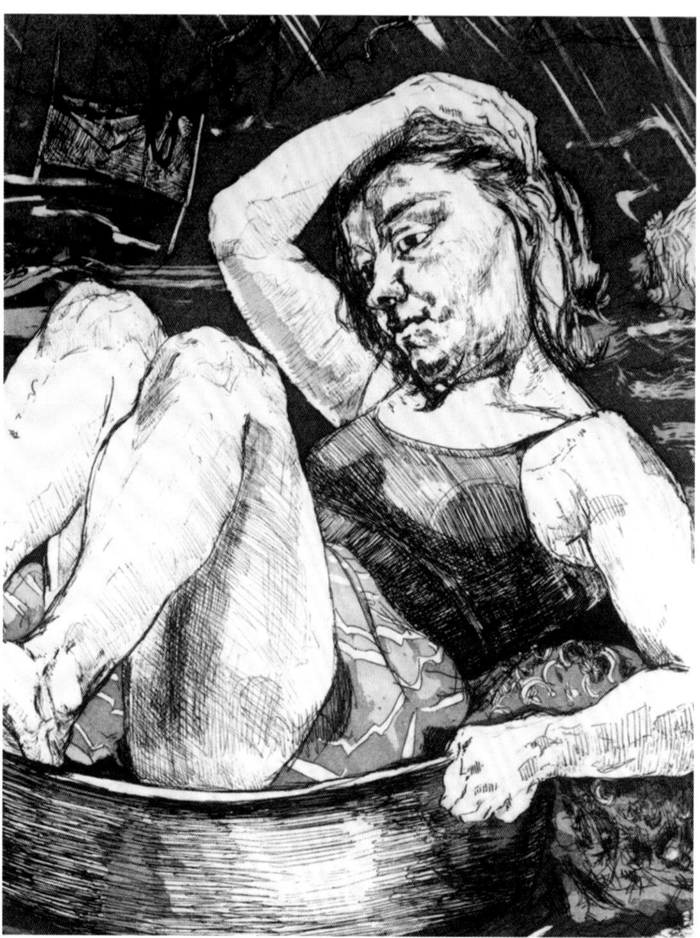

Detail from Paula Rego, *Flood*, from *Pendle Witches* 1996

Sugar Lift is used with aquatint to create more spontaneous-seeming and dramatic effects. The artist brushes marks onto an aquatinted plate using a sugar solution. The plate is then covered with a varnish and placed in hot water, which 'lifts' the varnish from the sugar solution. When the plate is exposed to acid, only the artist's marks etch as the rest of the plate is still protected by varnish.

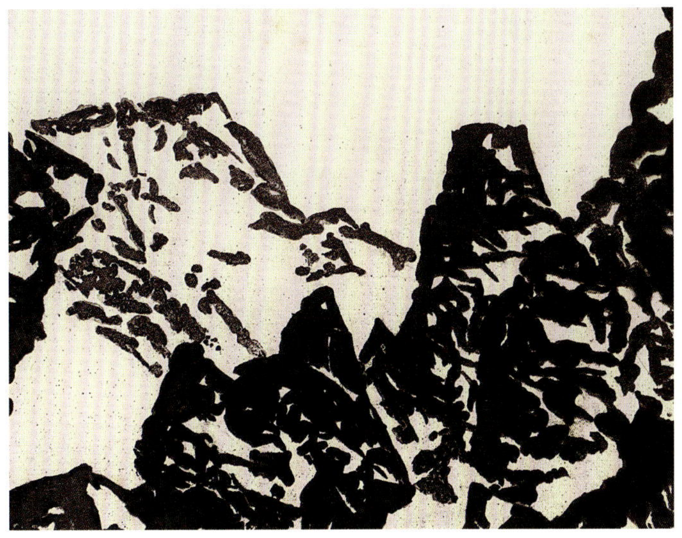

Detail from Alexander Cozens, Plate 2, *A New Method for Assisting the Invention in the Composition of Landscape* c.1785

Etching In Britain And Beyond

Etching has been used to make prints since the early sixteenth century, when the practice was first taken up by artists in Northern Europe and Italy. From the latter 1500s it was also increasingly used by professional printmakers working from centres across Europe. They often employed etching alongside metal engraving to create prints after designs first produced as paintings or drawings. As a standalone technique, though, etching was most notably used for artists' prints, and by the seventeenth century it was thriving in Italy and many other parts of Europe. Working in Amsterdam, Rembrandt van Rijn made some of the most admired etchings in the history of the medium. As portable multiples, his carefully inked prints travelled across national borders and seas more readily than his paintings. And the masterly use of aquatint by the Spanish artist Francisco de Goya around the first quarter of the nineteenth century has a continuing influence to this day, as is evident in the work of such artists as Paula Rego.

> GOYA p.88

> REGO p.88

Etching has also held a long appeal for British artists, including for two of the best-known painters of eighteenth-century England: Thomas Gainsborough and George Stubbs; each made some of the period's most experimental prints, embracing a variety of techniques including soft-ground etching.

> GAINSBOROUGH p.63

> STUBBS p.65

> PALMER p.67
> WHISTLER p.68

In the nineteenth century, British artists continued to make etchings. Samuel Palmer is one standout etcher of the period, but the century's leading proponent was James Abbott McNeill Whistler. Along with his brother-in-law, Francis Seymour Haden, Whistler absorbed the etching scene in both Paris and London. He both contributed to and capitalised on the medium's increasing popularity in the latter part of the century, varying the effects of the ink from print to print and developing the practice of printing etchings in small numbered 'limited editions'. This approach emphasised each etching's role as an original, valuable work of art. The practice of limited editioning has become standard today.

> SUTHERLAND p.72
> PICASSO p.71
> HAYTER p.85
> FREUD p.75
> HOCKNEY p.81
> REGO p.88

The twentieth century saw some of the most celebrated artists working in Britain and beyond experiment with etching in its various forms. During the first half of the century, Graham Sutherland made prints in the 'visionary' tradition of Palmer and others, before moving towards abstraction. In France, meanwhile, artists clustered around experimental centres in Paris, notably the studio of Roger Lacourière, who worked with artists including Pablo Picasso, and Atelier 17, the workshop of Stanley William Hayter, who made astonishing prints of his own. When Hayter relocated to New York for a decade after the start of the Second World War, the Atelier 17 workshop he established there became a centre for both European émigré and American artists. Etching's appeal for notable artists such as Lucian Freud, Hockney and Rego continued in the years that followed.

While existing histories of etching are mostly confined to the technique's use in Europe, reflecting its origins, a wider history remains ripe for fuller exploration; Tate's collection of modern international prints increasingly reflects these concerns, although there is much room for continued development. In its earlier days, the technique's spread tended to mirror that of European colonisation, with etching reaching Australia, New Zealand and the Americas via European settlers; in India, Western printmaking was taught in art schools from the mid-nineteenth century.[2] Etching has also been practised in Japan since the late eighteenth century. A truly international presence, though, came with the twentieth century, when significant centres were established in countries as far flung as Argentina and South Korea.[3] South Africa, too, has produced notable etchers, most famously William Kentridge.

> KENTRIDGE p.218

The practice of handmade etching continues to attract artists based in Europe and beyond, sometimes in combination with photo etching, in which photographic images can be etched onto metal plates and then worked into in the traditional, handmade manner – as in the work of Ellen Gallagher, for example. This is despite the plethora of printmaking techniques available to contemporary artists. Concerns about the environmental and health implications of using acid have led to the development of more eco-friendly variations of the technique, while the traditional approach is also still extensively practised.

> GALLAGHER p.216

Alexander Runciman (1736–1785)
Fingal Encounters Carbon Carglass c.1773
Etching on paper 14.9 × 24.5

Alexander Runciman was one of the first Scottish artists to take up etching. He drew freely with the etching needle to create small narrative scenes. He based some of his prints on his paintings, while others were independent compositions.

The subject of this print is taken from Ossian, a legendary Gaelic poet whose works had recently been 'translated' (and, in fact, expanded or even invented) for publication by Runciman's contemporary, James Macpherson. Runciman captured a moment described in the poem 'Fingal': in the moonlight, Fingal finds the captive Carbon Carglass, held prisoner by his enemy King Starno. Runciman's 'Ossian' etchings relate to a plan to paint twelve scenes on the ceiling of the Great Room in Sir James Clerk of Eldin's new Palladian house at Penicuik in Midlothian. These were destroyed in a fire of 1899, but Runciman's compositions survive in drawings and prints.

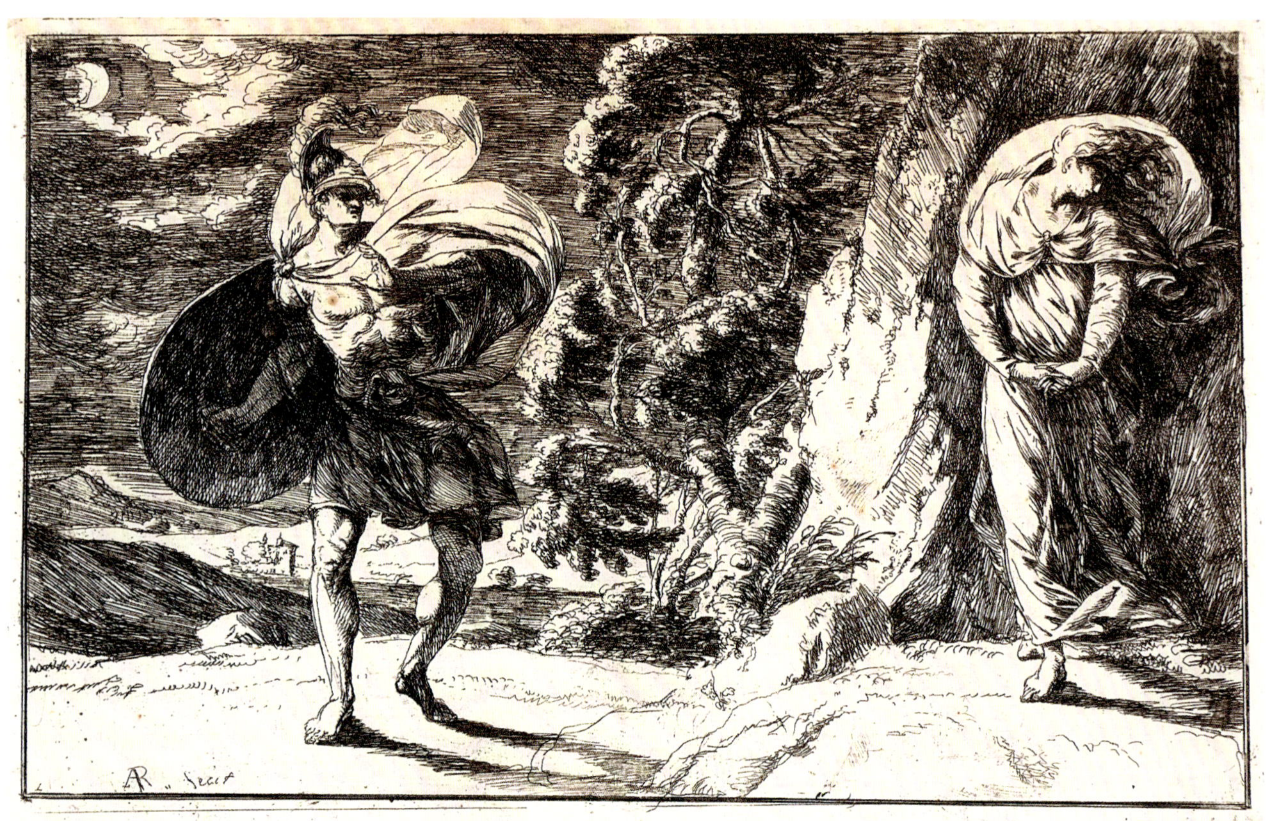

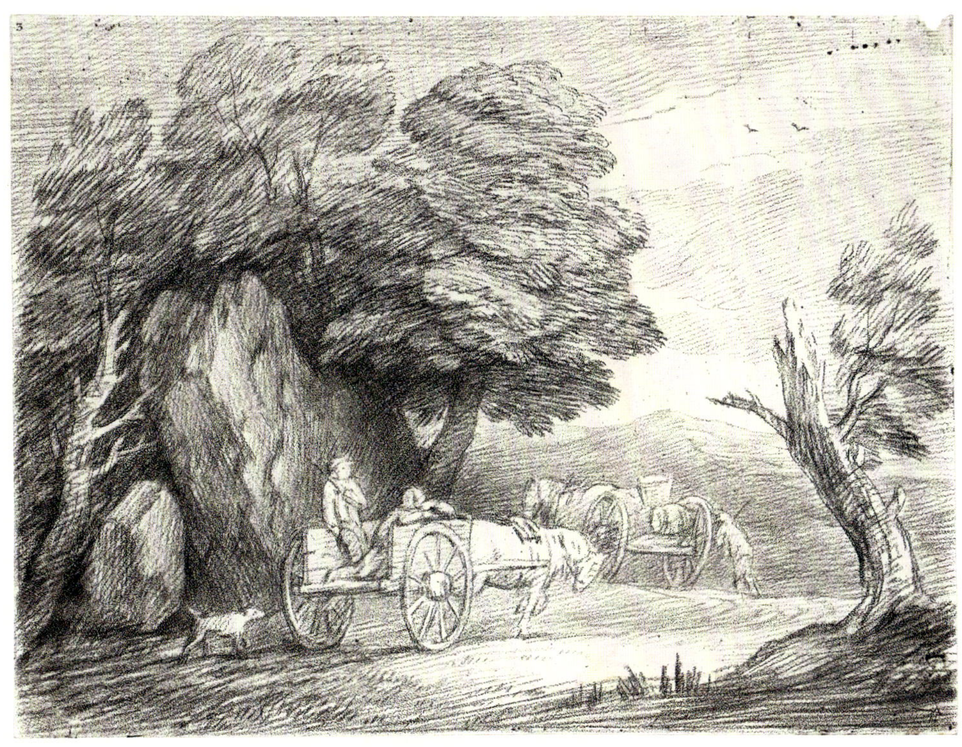

Thomas Gainsborough (1727–1788)
Wooded Landscape with Two Country Carts and Figures
1779–80
Soft-ground etching on paper, state ii/ii 29.8 × 39.4

Despite only making around twenty prints, Thomas Gainsborough has – along with George Stubbs – been called the most innovative English printmaker of the eighteenth century.[4] He tried out a few different printmaking techniques, but it was seemingly the recently rediscovered method of soft-ground etching that most appealed.

Although Gainsborough's soft-ground etchings are now celebrated for their immediacy and apparent spontaneity – which makes them incredibly akin to his chalk drawings – most remained unpublished in his lifetime. A very rare earlier 'state' (or version) of this etching was printed by Gainsborough himself, suggesting he did intend to publish it. The state illustrated here is also rare; although the publication details have been trimmed off, it is from the first published edition of the artist's etchings. This was published by J. & J. Boydell in 1797, nearly twenty years after Gainsborough's death. It was the third in a series of twelve prints: the number '3' can be seen in the upper left.

Tate holds a group of Gainsborough's copper printing plates, which can be studied alongside prints made from them.

Alexander Cozens (1717–1786)
Plate 2, *A New Method for Assisting the Invention in the Composition of Landscape* c.1785
Aquatint with sugar lift on paper 22.9 × 30.3

The British artist Alexander Cozens made some surprisingly experimental prints for his *New Method*, a manual instructing artists in how to work up random 'blot drawings' into landscape scenes. This print illustrates 'the tops of hills or mountains', the second of Cozens's 'types' of landscape composition.[5]

While Cozens employed a professional engraver to work up other prints in his publication, these aquatint 'blot' landscapes seem to be his own work. It has been suggested he used the then hardly known sugar lift technique, which certainly seems to be the case.[6] This method, which later found popularity in the hands of twentieth-century artists including Picasso, can be used to create strong and spontaneous-seeming marks.

Cozens's blot drawing system interested some important British artists of the day: Joseph Wright of Derby knew the *New Method*, and George Romney and Joseph Farington also apparently 'made blots ... as first preparatory sketches for compositions of history and landscape'.[7]

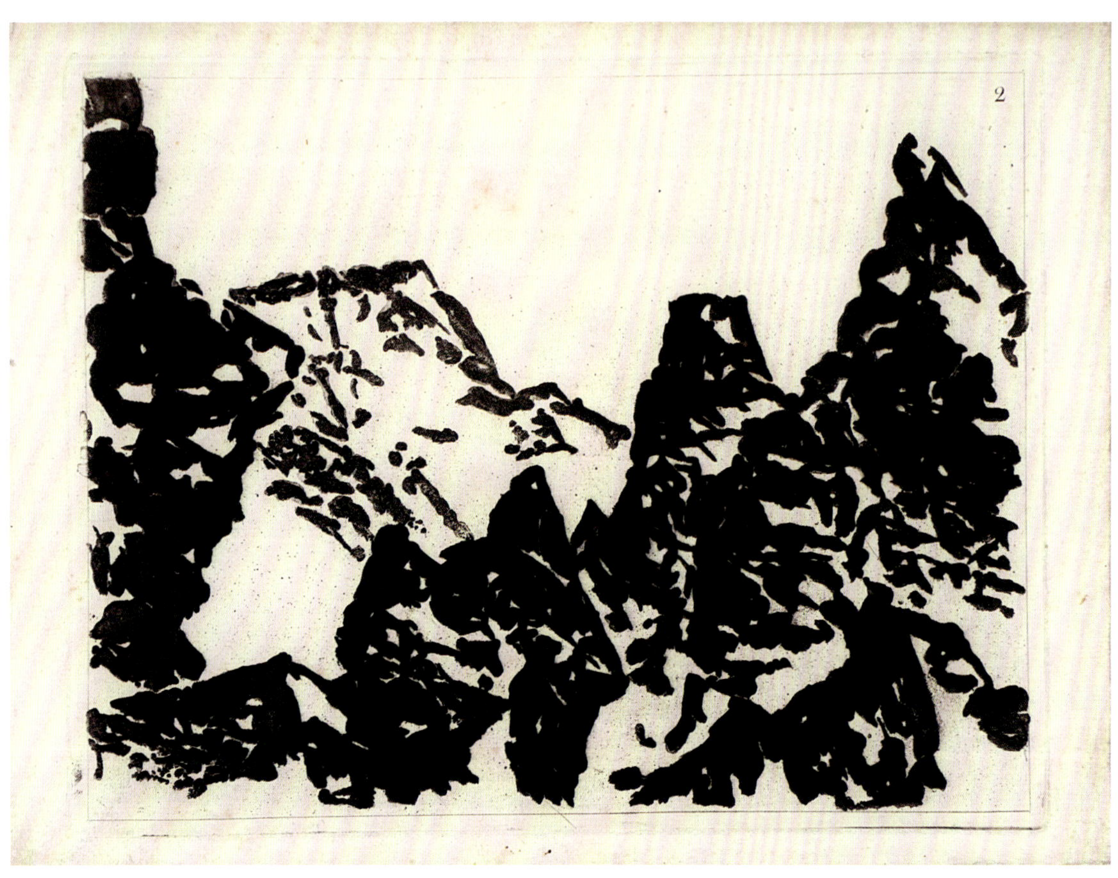

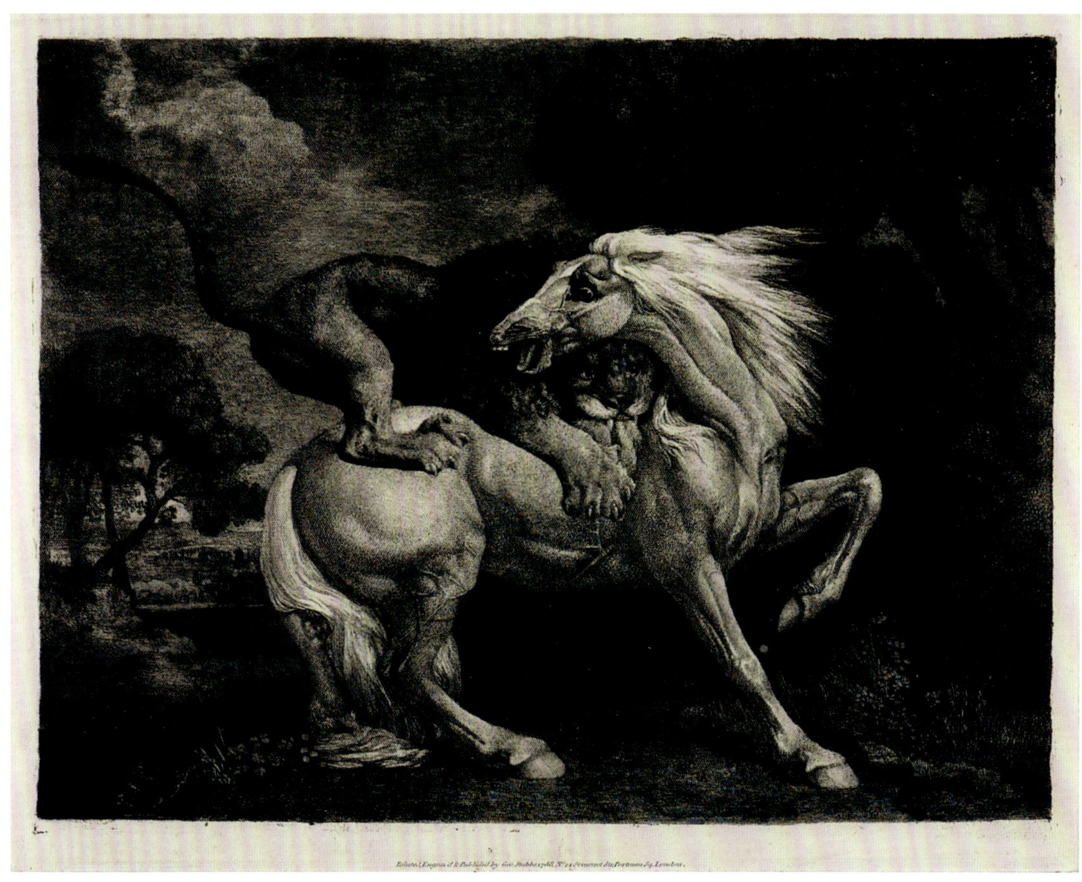

George Stubbs (1724–1806)
A Lion Devouring a Horse published 1788
Soft-ground etching with roulette work on paper, state iii/iii 25 × 33.5

In this dramatic etching by George Stubbs, a distressed horse is attacked by a lion, which has leapt onto the horse's back. Stubbs treated the 'lion and horse' theme multiple times, both in paint and in print.

Stubbs's status as an innovative and interesting printmaker remains surprisingly little known. The way he combined different techniques on a single plate to create rich effects, however, sets him apart from most of his contemporaries. On this plate he employed soft-ground etching for the first time, allowing him to effectively render the textures of the animals' coats and manes. Stubbs's extensive knowledge of anatomy is demonstrated by his detailed depiction of the animals, including the horse's veins, visible on the head and legs as it stretches. The dark and shadowy tones of the landscape background and the lion, meanwhile, emphasise the paler features of the doomed horse.

Stubbs published this etching alongside a further eleven of his most accomplished prints in 1788.

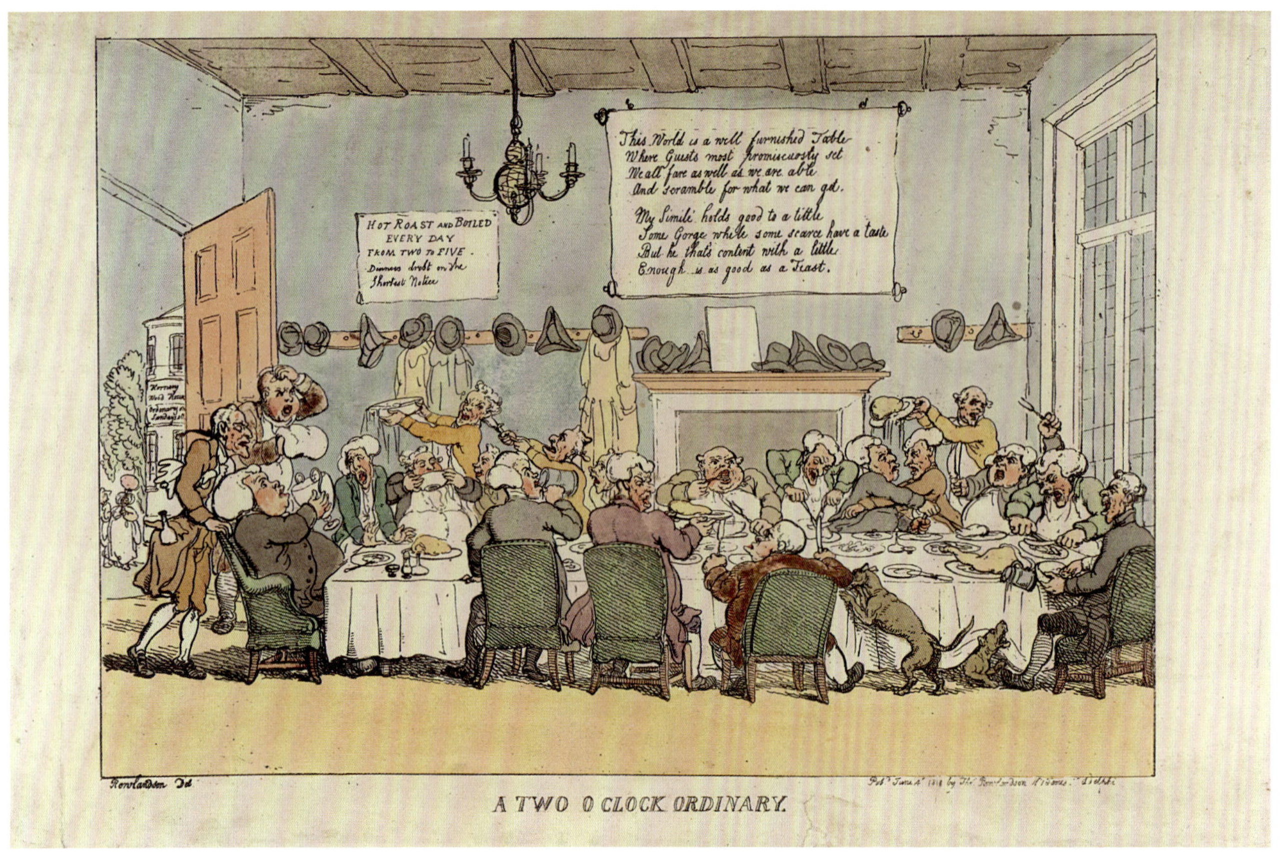

Thomas Rowlandson (1756–1827)
A Two O'Clock Ordinary 1811
Etching and watercolour on paper 23.8 × 35.2

This work by Thomas Rowlandson, one of the greatest satirists of late Georgian Britain, is a rare example of a satirical print in Tate's collection. The etching has been hand coloured with watercolour: this was a common, and usually cheap, means of adding colour to prints. The scene shows a contemporary eatery, Hornsey Wood House, which offered a 'Hot roast and boiled' set price meal (or 'ordinary') on Sunday afternoons. Rowlandson injects the scene with humour: diners jostle each other for food and latecomers look in vain for a slice of the pie. The writing seen on the wall behind them includes the phrase: 'We all fare as well as we are able / And scramble for what we can get.'

Rowlandson etched and published the print himself in 1811. Both the print and a related drawing came to Tate via the Oppé Collection, which was formed by the scholar Paul Oppé (1878–1957) and includes over three thousand works on paper.

Samuel Palmer (1805–1881)
The Weary Ploughman 1858–65
Etching on paper, state viii/viii 13.3 × 20.3

Although Samuel Palmer's output of etchings was small, these works reflect his true enthusiasm for the process. He took up etching in 1850, aged forty-five, and quickly mastered the technique. He completed most of his work on this plate during an intense period between late May and early July 1858, making notes about the 'biting' times used to etch different areas of the plate.[8] The print was eventually published in 1865, following further alterations; such extensive reworking seems to have been typical of Palmer's approach.

Like most of Palmer's etchings, this one depicts a landscape in dramatic light conditions; the scene is beautifully illuminated by the glow of the full moon, with foreground details sparkling in the low light.

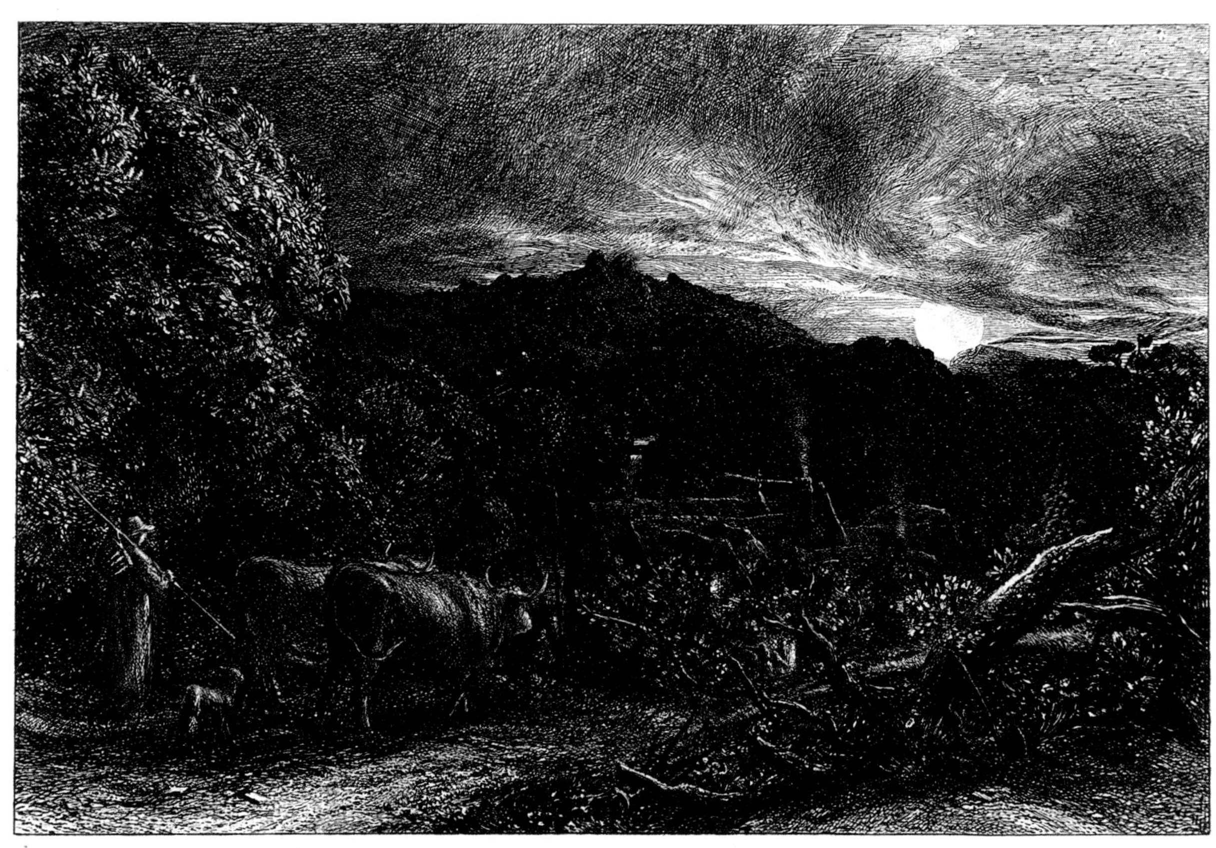

James Abbott McNeill Whistler (1834–1903)

Black Lion Wharf, Wapping 1859

Etching on paper, state iv/iv 14.3 × 22.5

American-born James Abbott McNeill Whistler was one of the leading printmakers of the nineteenth century. This etching is from his 'Thames Set', a series of views of the river's warehouses and wharves. Whistler began working on it shortly after returning to London from Paris in May 1859. He explored the stretch of the river running through Wapping in East London, an impoverished area which, Charles Dickens wrote, reflected the 'accumulated scum of humanity'.[9] Whistler found much to interest him, from the decaying riverside buildings to the local workers, such as the male figure who takes centre stage in this scene. He observed the river from the water, capturing long backgrounds like this one by moving back and forth along the river in a boat.

Black Lion Wharf was displayed at the Royal Academy in London in 1860, making it one of the first of the Thames etchings to be exhibited. It was eventually published as part of the 'Thames Set' in 1871.

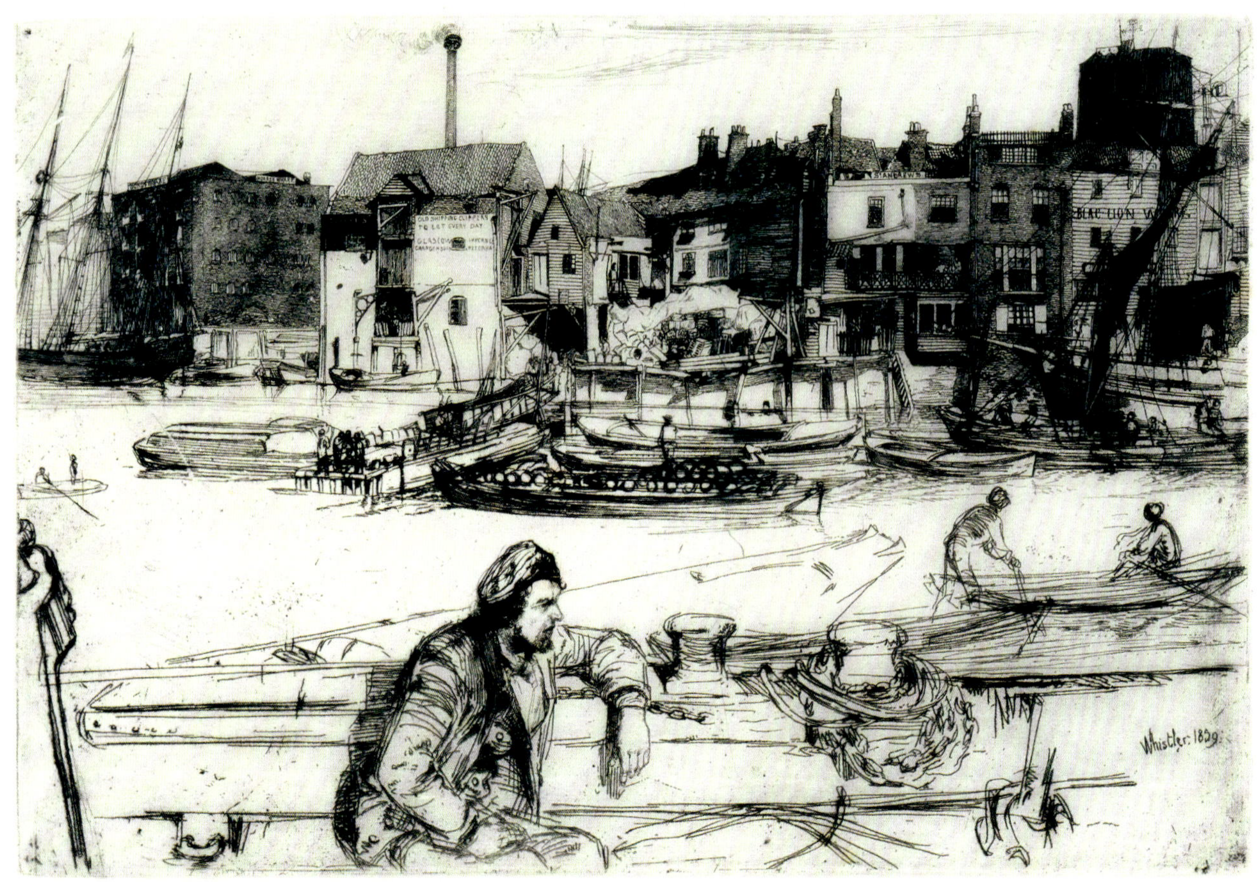

David Young Cameron (1865–1945)
The Admiralty 1889
Etching on paper, state i/i 19.4 × 13.7

The Scottish artist David Young Cameron was a prolific and successful printmaker, producing over five hundred etchings during his career. His crisp etched lines were particularly suited to architectural subjects, and this print shows the facade of the Ripley Building, the entrance to London's Admiralty House, the government headquarters of Britain's Royal Navy. It is part of Cameron's 'London Set', a series of twelve prints of central London. The set also included views of the Custom House, Horse Guards, Downing Street, Waterloo Bridge and St Paul's Cathedral.

Cameron built up a significant collection of Rembrandt etchings, and his own prints reflect the influence of the Dutch master. They were also admired on their own terms during his lifetime, and Cameron is still considered one of the leading British etchers of the late nineteenth and early twentieth centuries.

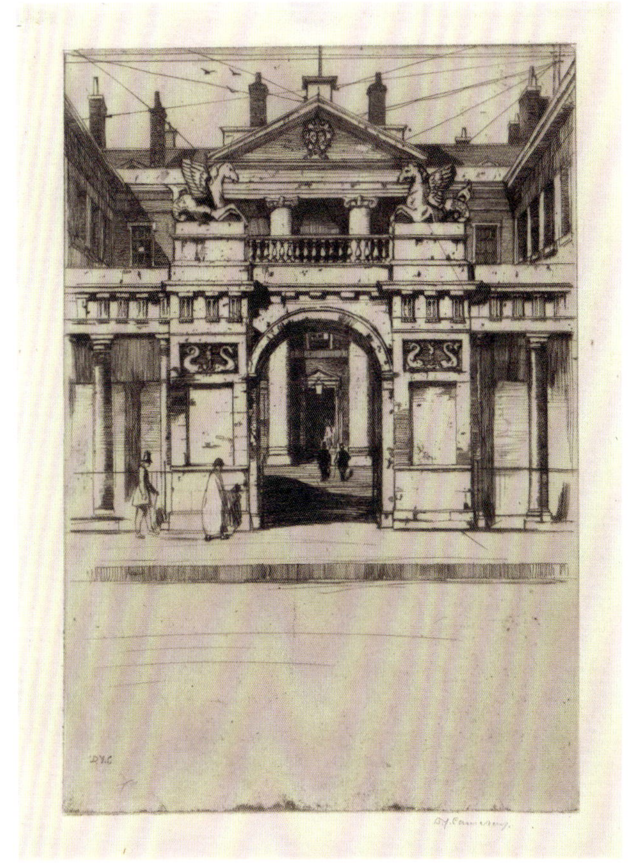

Giorgio Morandi (1890–1964)
Still Life with Very Fine Hatching
[Natura morta a tratti sottilissimi] 1933
Etching on paper 24.8 x 23.8

The Italian artist Giorgio Morandi made his first etching in 1912, having taught himself the method using a seventeenth-century treatise. Almost half of his 135 known prints were executed between 1927 and 1933, his most productive period as a printmaker.

Morandi is best known for still life subjects, which he observed from life, drawing directly onto his etching plates. He often returned to the same everyday objects, rearranging them to make new compositions. His etchings are characterised by intricate use of cross-hatching, which is even referred to in the title of this work. In this he probably followed the example of Rembrandt, yet Morandi employed the technique to quite different, very subtle effect. His restrained approach resulted in silvery prints awash with calm, tonal effects; his etchings are much admired for their technical brilliancy and a pervading sense of stillness.

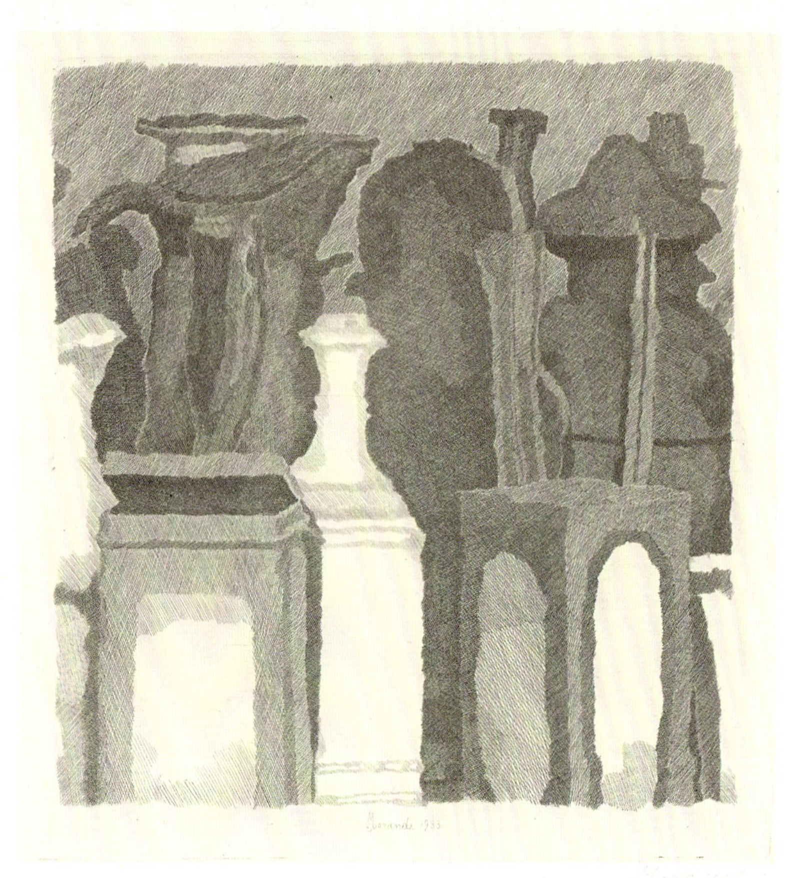

Pablo Picasso (1881–1973)
Faun Revealing a Sleeping Woman (Jupiter and Antiope, after Rembrandt) 1936
Etching, engraving and aquatint with sugar lift on paper, state vi/vi 31.6 × 41.7

Pablo Picasso approached the print medium with his characteristic enthusiasm for artistic processes. This print is from the 'Vollard Suite', a series of 100 prints commissioned by the art dealer Ambroise Vollard that have become Picasso's most celebrated etchings. This, the final scene in the series, is based on Rembrandt's 1659 etching of the same mythological subject, which shows Jupiter disguised as a satyr (a lustful, drunken woodland god), peering over the naked form of a sleeping young woman, Antiope, who, according to Greek myth, he raped and impregnated.

Picasso seamlessly combined strong, fluid, engraved lines (for more information about metal engraving, see pp.94–7) with etching and aquatint on this plate, creating a dramatic interplay between light and dark.

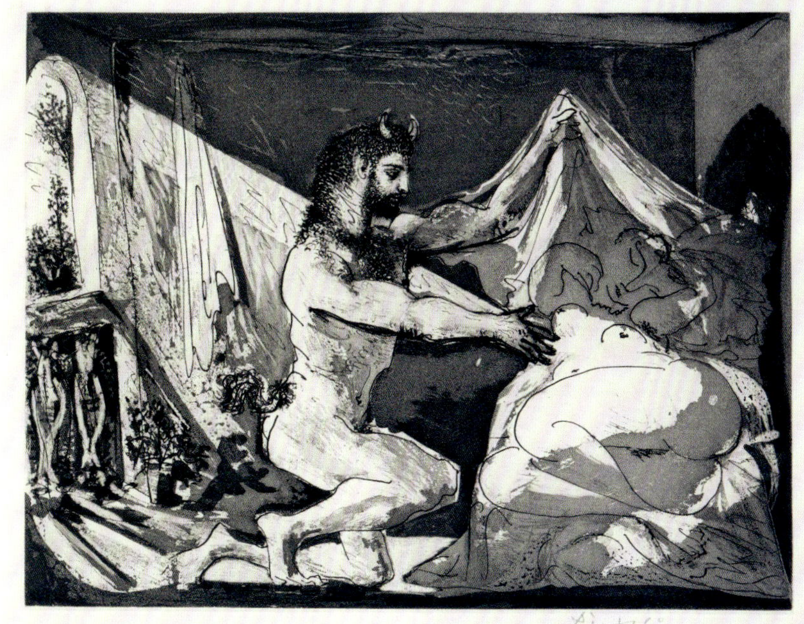

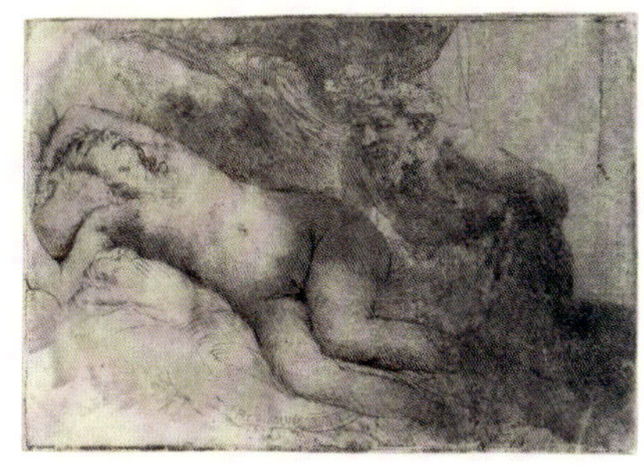

Rembrandt van Rijn (1606–1669), *Jupiter and Antiope: larger plate* 1659, etching and drypoint on paper, British Museum, London

Graham Sutherland (1903–1980)
Clegyr Boia, frontispiece for *Signature No.9*, July 1938
Etching and aquatint on paper 12.4 × 18.8

Clegyr Boia is a rocky outcrop near St David's in Pembrokeshire. Graham Sutherland visited this area every summer from 1934 to 1939, making brooding studies of the Welsh landscape in the mediums of painting, drawing and print.

Although distinctive in style, this, like other etchings by Sutherland, has been compared to prints by Samuel Palmer (p.67). Sutherland had been inspired by Palmer since the day his close friend William Larkins showed him one of Palmer's etchings, *The Herdsman's Cottage*.[10]

The word 'Herons', which can be glimpsed in the bottom centre of this plate, was intended to be the title, 'Herons Ghyl', which Sutherland later abandoned. This was the first of Sutherland's etchings to include aquatint to add tone. Although appreciated for its entwining of Palmer's visionary style and modern surrealist forms, this print was Sutherland's last etching until the 1970s. Deciding to concentrate on painting, Sutherland gave his etching tools to another British artist who would become an important etcher: Lucian Freud (pp.74–5).[11]

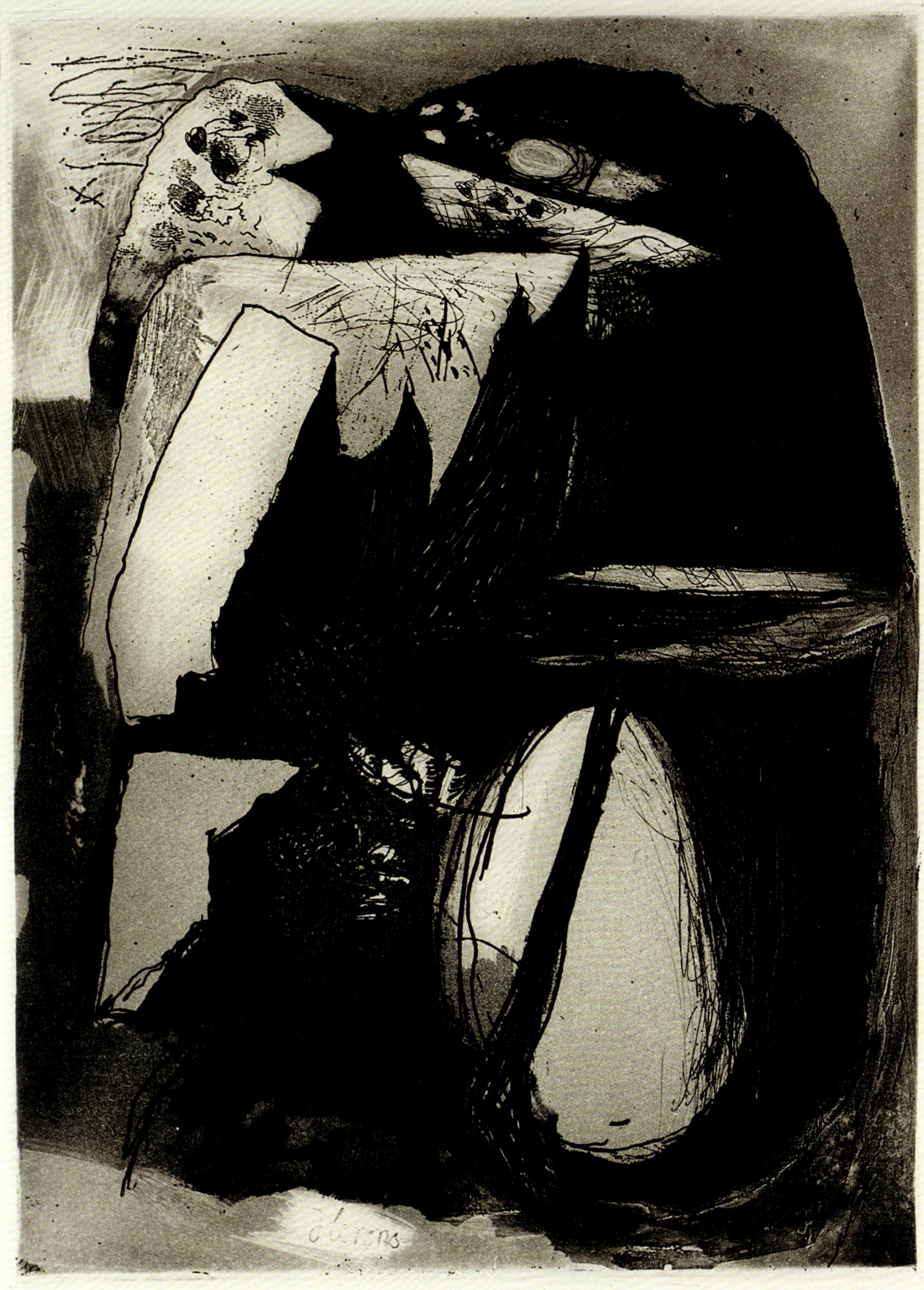

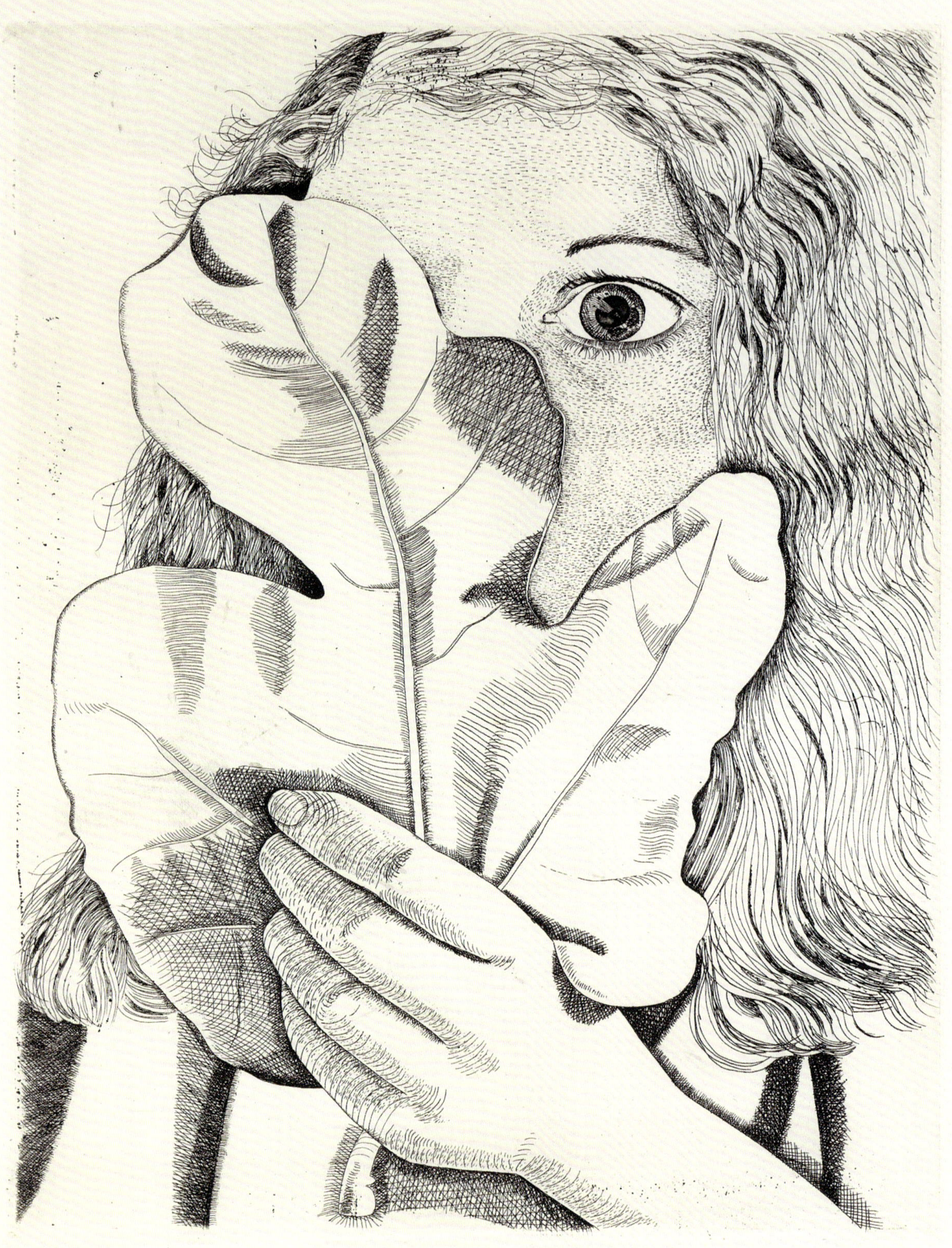

7/10 Lucian Freud

Lucian Freud (1922–2011)
Girl with a Fig Leaf 1947
Etching on paper 29.8 × 23.8

Girl with a Fig Leaf is one of Lucian Freud's earliest etchings. The artist captured his wife, Kitty, holding up a leaf, her one visible eye staring out intensely. Freud's crisp lines appear restrained and almost silvery. He used different types of mark for different parts of the plate, from the stipples that shade Kitty's face to the cross-hatching used to create the shadow beneath her hand.

Freud's etching practice developed alongside his other work, and his prints often relate in some way to a contemporaneous painting or its sitter. Some of his later etchings have a fluidity and boldness that feels very different to the more restrained and strangely unsettling atmosphere of *Girl with a Fig Leaf*. But other qualities, such as the careful and effective use of white space, are common to most of Freud's work in the etching medium.

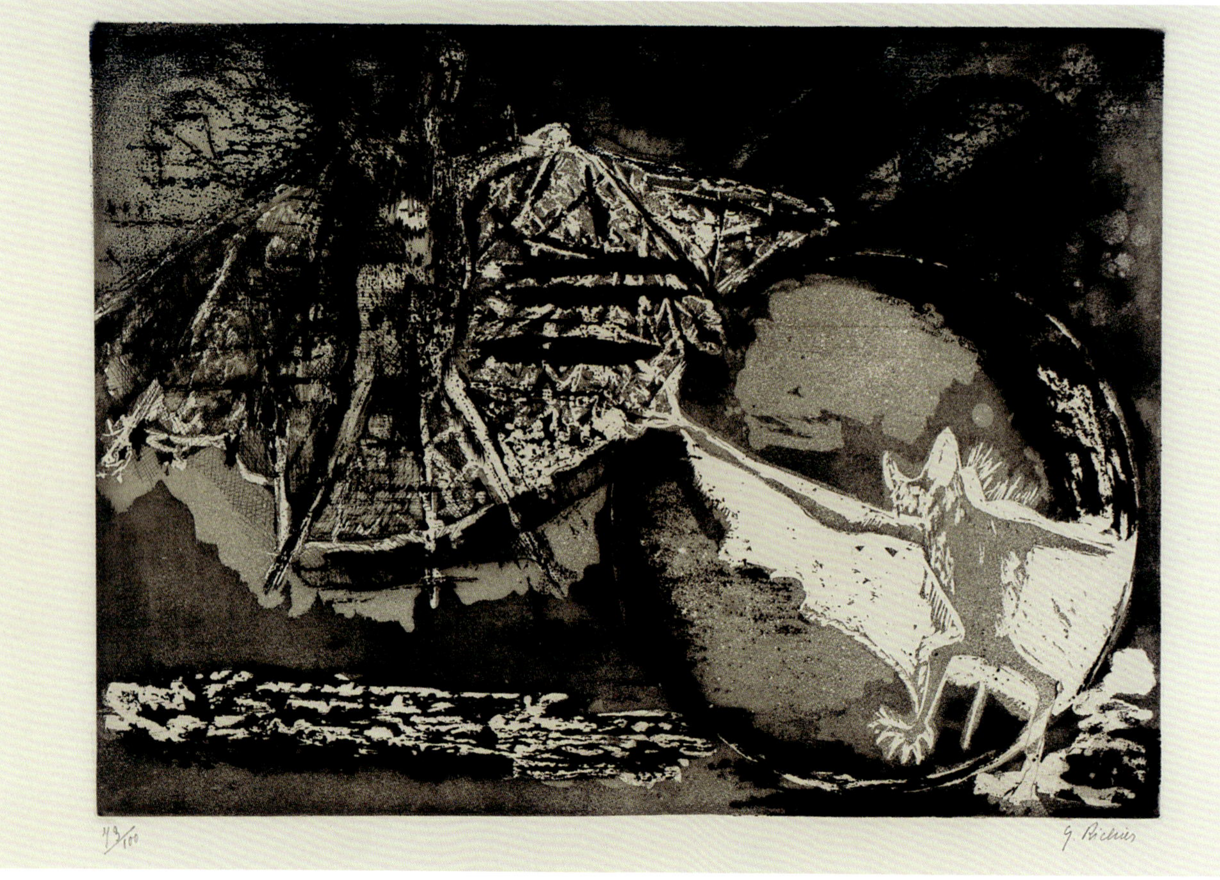

Germaine Richier (1902–1959)
Bat 1948–51
Etching and aquatint on paper 38.5 × 53.6

The French artist Germaine Richier lived and worked in Paris for much of her career, gaining considerable acclaim as a sculptor; she also experimented with ceramics, mosaic and printmaking. This etching relates to a sculpture of 1946, *The Bat*, a version of which is also held in the Tate collection; both pieces were made during a productive period following Richier's return to Paris from Zürich, where she had spent the war. A bat's skeleton with its wings spread out was found in Richier's studio after her death – the artist often worked from life and it is possible the skeleton served as a model for both the print and the sculpture.

Richier began making hybrid figures in 1944, combining human features with those of animals and insects in her sculptures. In this etching, too, the left-hand bat has a human-looking face. Although she was primarily a sculptor, the variety of textures and tones on this, one of her most accomplished plates, reveals the considerable time Richier dedicated to mastering etching techniques.

Joan Miró (1893–1983)
Untitled, from *Series II* 1952
Etching and aquatint on paper 37.7 × 45.5

Joan Miró's distinctive, otherworldly imagery evolved in 1920s Paris, where he moved in surrealist circles. His interest in etching developed in a new way in the 1940s, during an extended stay in New York. While there, he spent time at Atelier 17, the renowned studio of the experimental printmaker Stanley William Hayter (pp.60, 85).

This piece is from a series of five etchings, all printed from the same plate using different combinations of coloured inks. The plate was apparently made at Atelier 17 during Miró's stay in New York, but printed later at Atelier Lacourière in Paris, another highly regarded print studio, between 1952 and 1953.[12] Miró introduced mysterious, amoeba-type forms into his work during his New York period; in this print, the strange semi-abstract images floating in green space seem suggestive of the scientific imagery used to illustrate sex and reproduction.

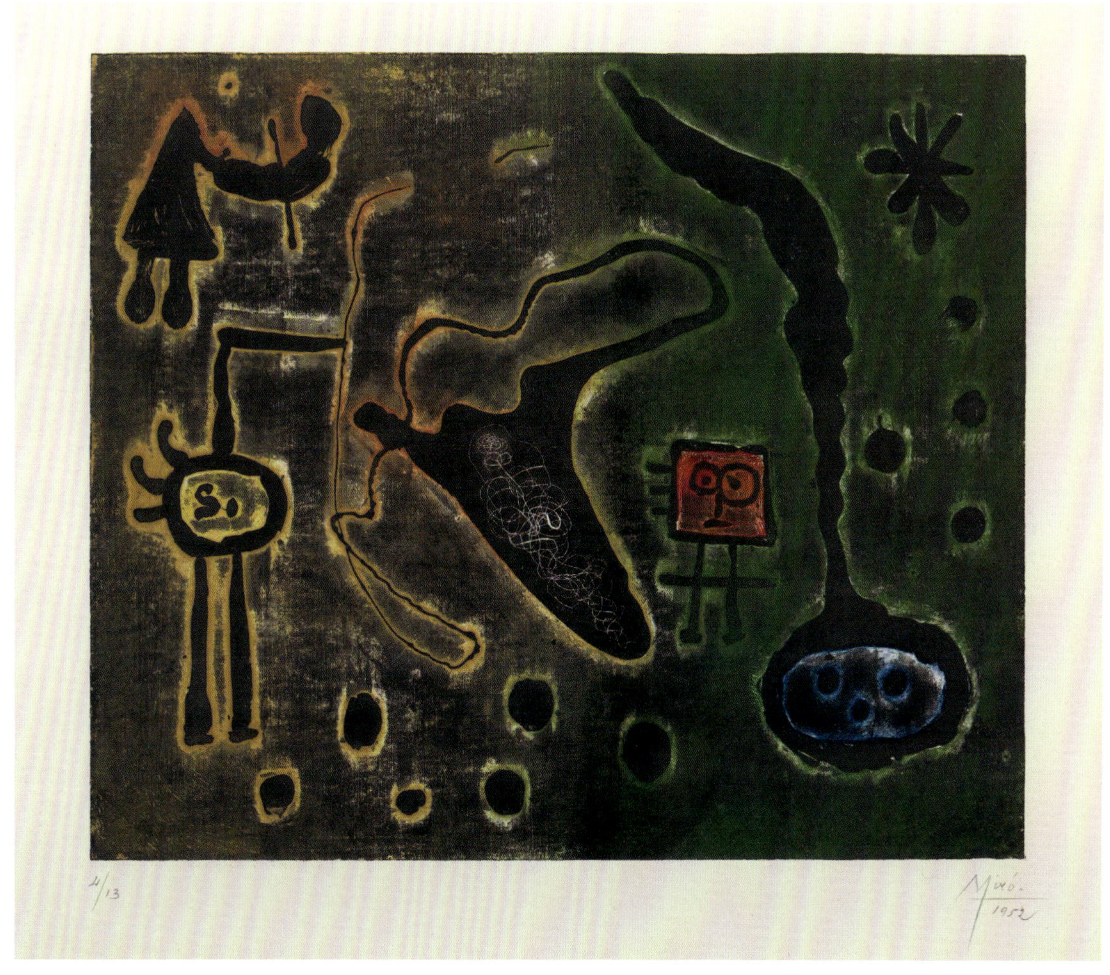

Pierre Soulages (born 1919)
Etching No.2 1952
Etching and aquatint on paper 30 × 55.3

In the second half of the twentieth century the small black-and-white etchings most associated with the history of the medium began to be superseded by large colour prints. Paris was central to this activity, and Pierre Soulages a leading proponent; he brought the characteristic abstract combination of black and colour seen in his paintings to printmaking.

Soulages first tried etching in 1952, following a visit to the studio of the master printer Roger Lacourière, whose wife had seen one of Soulages's paintings through the window of the Galerie Carré in Paris. This was only his second etching; he noted that later, as his confidence as an etcher grew, his use of the technique became more distinct.[13] Nonetheless, *Etching No.2* is a powerful work, translating the balance of colour, tone and line Soulages achieved on canvas to the etching plate in a way that is sensitive to the print medium; already Soulages was exploiting the unique textures that can be achieved using etching and aquatint.

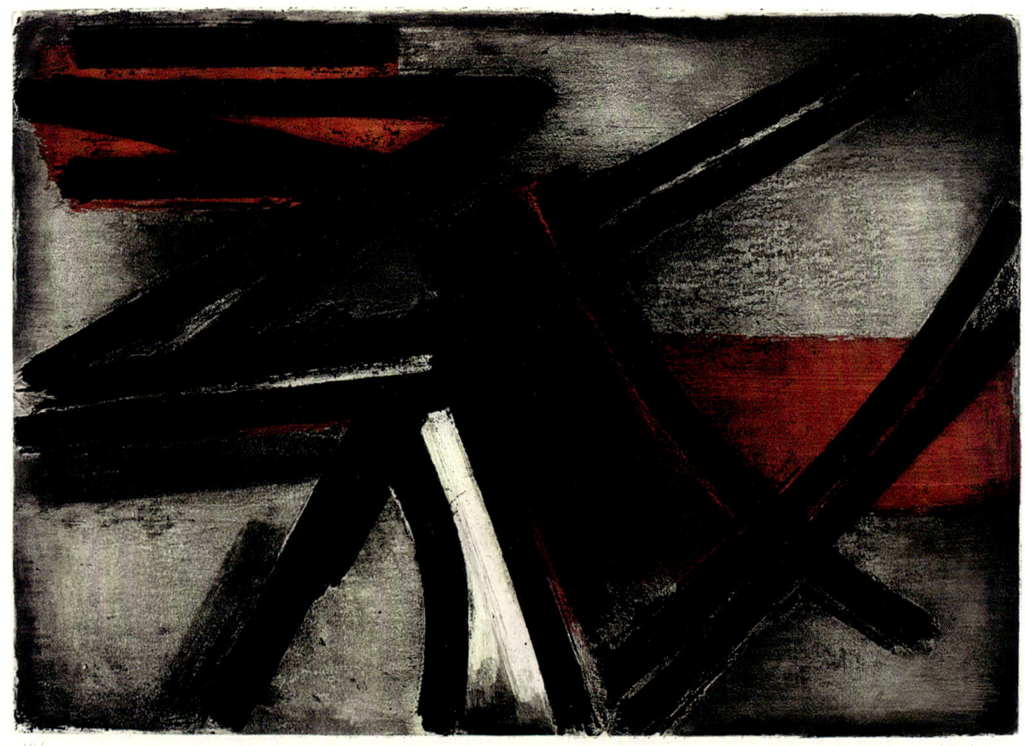

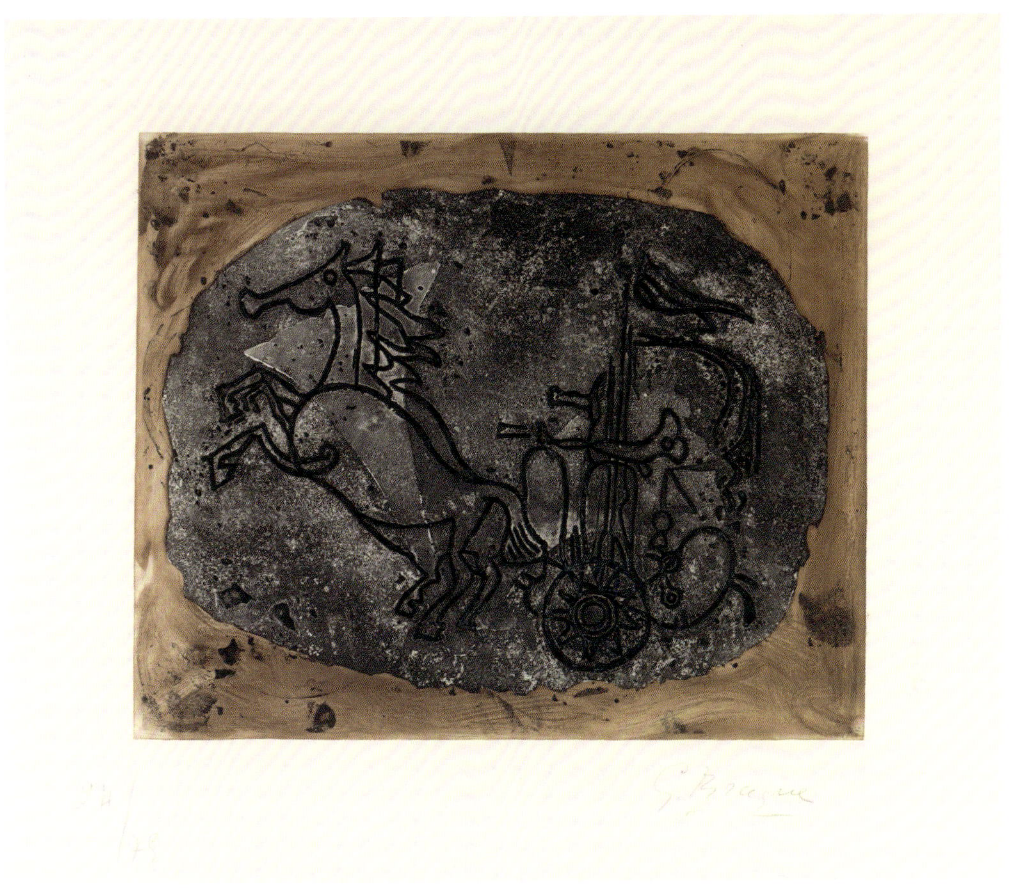

Georges Braque (1882–1963)
Black Chariot 1958
Etching and aquatint with sugar lift on paper, printed in two colours 23.6 × 29.5

Georges Braque, who made most of his prints during the latter part of his career, greatly enjoyed the printmaking process, writing in one of his notebooks: 'It is not the finished product that is interesting so much as the means of achieving it.'[14]

For this etching Braque collaborated with the printer Aldo Crommelynck, who called Braque a patient perfectionist.[15] Braque found working with a technical specialist – particularly an artistically gifted one such as Crommelynck – helped him to create increasingly ambitious prints. For *Black Chariot* two separate plates were used, one of which was printed black and the other brown. The brown brush-like marks framing the image were achieved using sugar lift, while the black image of the chariot was deeply etched using a combination of line and aquatint.

Many of Braque's prints, including this depiction of a figure in a horse-drawn chariot, were inspired by ancient Greece, and this is one of a group to include chariots.

Asger Jorn (1914–1973)
Untitled C [Ohne Titel C] 1958–9
Etching and aquatint on paper 24.4 × 20.8

Asger Jorn, a Danish artist, made paintings, sculptures and ceramics as well as prints. In *Untitled C*, a strange image of an open-mouthed face, Jorn's etched line has a sense of urgency and directness. The mottled edges reveal his experiments with aquatint and 'spit biting' (the direct application of acid to the metal plate) to create contrasting effects – he had been 'dripping' acid onto plates to distort images since as early as 1953.[16] The heavy curved lines bordering the face appear, by contrast, both tightly controlled and almost scrawled. The use of colour printing, too, creates power, the head red and raw against the blue-brown of the background.

Jorn travelled widely in Europe, forming different artistic networks. He founded and joined some significant artistic collectives, including CoBrA, an artistic movement which sought to break away from both naturalistic and abstract modes of artistic representation.

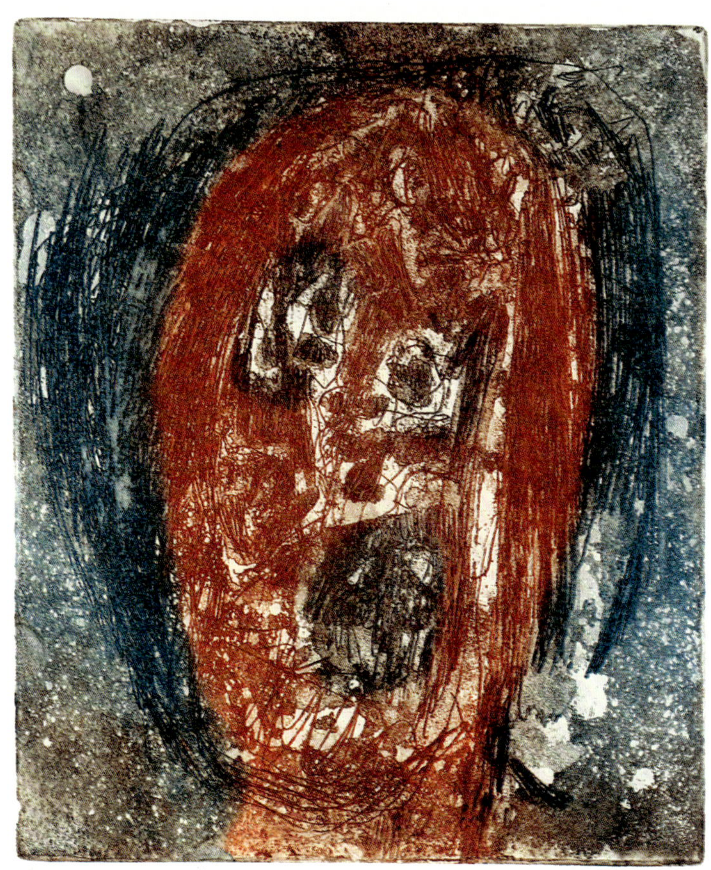

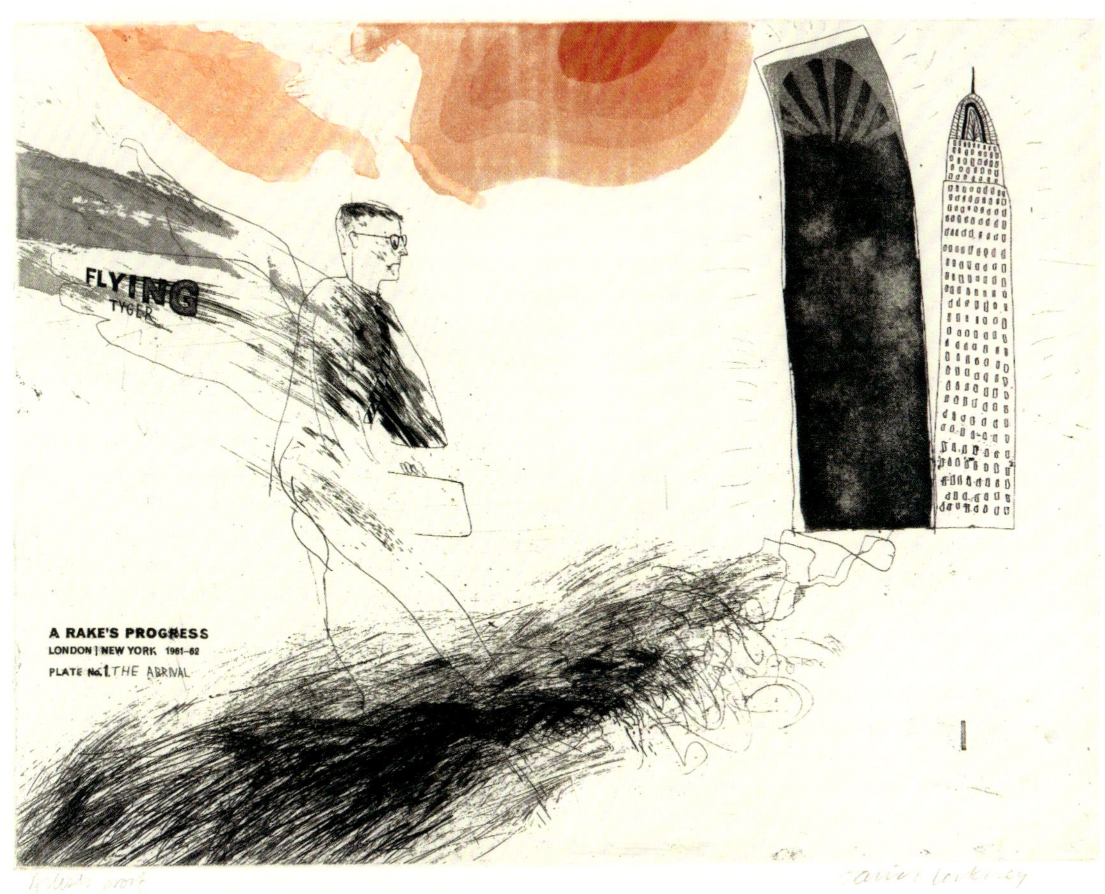

David Hockney (born 1937)
The Arrival, plate 1 from *A Rake's Progress* 1961–3
Etching with aquatint on paper 30 × 40

David Hockney began etching while studying at the Royal College of Art in London, having heard that the school's printmaking department provided free materials for students.[17] Even his first etching, *Myself and my Heroes* 1961, is an advanced work, both in terms of its complex content and Hockney's combining of different etching techniques, most notably line etching and aquatint, on a single plate.

A Rake's Progress was Hockney's first series of prints, and it remains one of his most celebrated. It dates from Hockney's time in New York between 1961 and 1963 and was inspired by the series of the same name by one of Britain's first great printmakers, William Hogarth (see p.98). In Hockney's version the subject matter is radically different, and the setting translated from eighteenth-century London to contemporary New York. The prints combine black etched lines with tonal areas of aquatint and are printed in black and red – the red adds unifying dashes of colour to each print in the series.

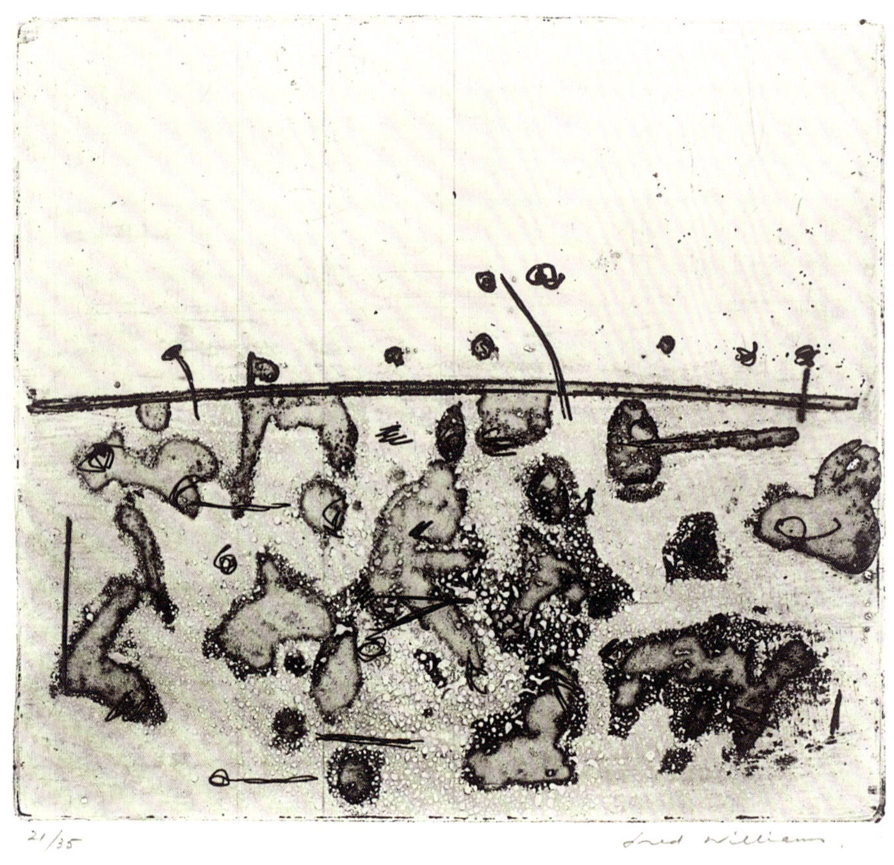

Fred Williams (1927–1982)
Chopped Trees 1965–6
Etching, aquatint, sugar lift and engraving on paper 19.8 × 22.3

Fred Williams spent five years in London, where, in 1953, he studied at the Central School of Arts and Crafts. There, he mastered several printmaking techniques. He became a prolific printmaker, creating over a hundred prints in two years. On his return to Australia in 1956, Williams saw the Australian landscape, particularly the untamed environment of the bush, in a new way; its depiction became central to his work.

Chopped Trees combines the techniques of line etching, aquatint and sugar lift with metal engraving, reflecting Williams's ability to combine different methods on his plates. Williams exploited the unpredictable aspects of etching with acid in his efforts to capture the random aspects of nature and landscape.

Cy Twombly (1928–2011)

Untitled I 1967

Etching with open-bite and aquatint on paper 59.6 × 71.7

In this print, one of a pair of etchings made in 1967 and published in 1973, the American artist Cy Twombly explored the possibilities of abstract mark-making using etching. The surface of the print echoes the appearance of handwriting, a purely visual effect which cannot be 'read'. The etchings relate to Twombly's 'blackboard' paintings and drawings, which he made on grey grounds between 1967 and 1971.

Here, Twombly achieved the blackboard-like effect by layering black ink over white before printing the plate. He worked on the plate itself using 'open bite', which involves exposing either all or part of the plate to the acid directly, without the protection of an acid-resistant ground. Although difficult to control, allowing the acid to eat away at the metal in this way can create interesting, unexpected effects, and many twentieth-century printmakers embraced open bite's unpredictability.

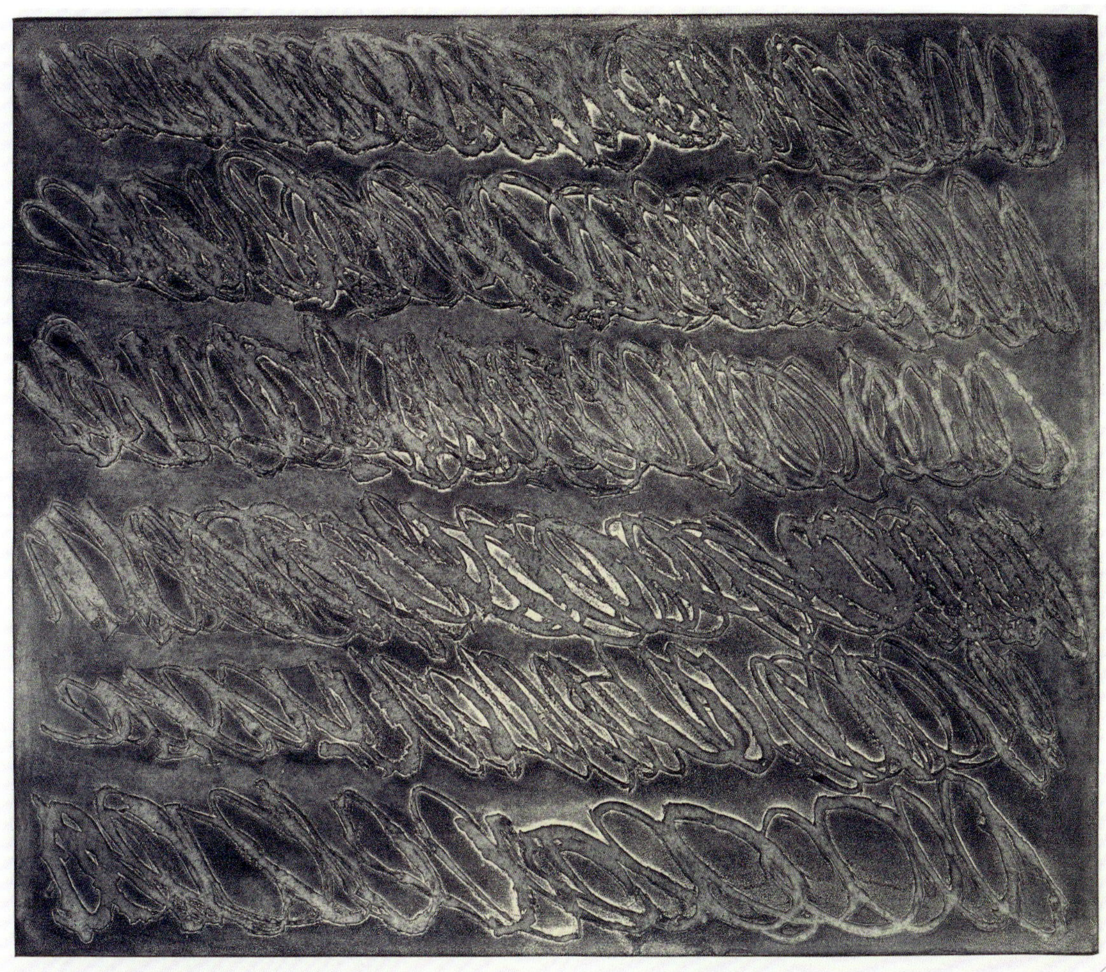

Kim Lim (1936–1997)
Red Aquatint 1972
Etching and aquatint on paper 44.5 × 44.5

Kim Lim was born in Singapore and spent much of her childhood in Malaysia before moving to London to pursue her artistic career. She began experimenting with printmaking at the Slade School of Fine Art.

Her prints display a simplicity of form and a balance also seen in her sculptures. They tend to be small and intricate, with self-descriptive titles such as *Blue Disc*, or, in the case of this print, *Red Aquatint.* This work is not quite as simple and restrained as it first appears: the cut-away area at the upper right corresponds with a series of linear patterns covering the image, which produce an effect similar to looking at the sideways-spread pages of a book, each with the corner missing. There are numerous other examples of Lim's etchings in the Tate collection; they demonstrate her interest in the etched line in relation to the simple geometric forms of squares, circles and rectangles. Her use of colour ranges from very subtle to bold and vibrant, as seen in *Red Aquatint*.

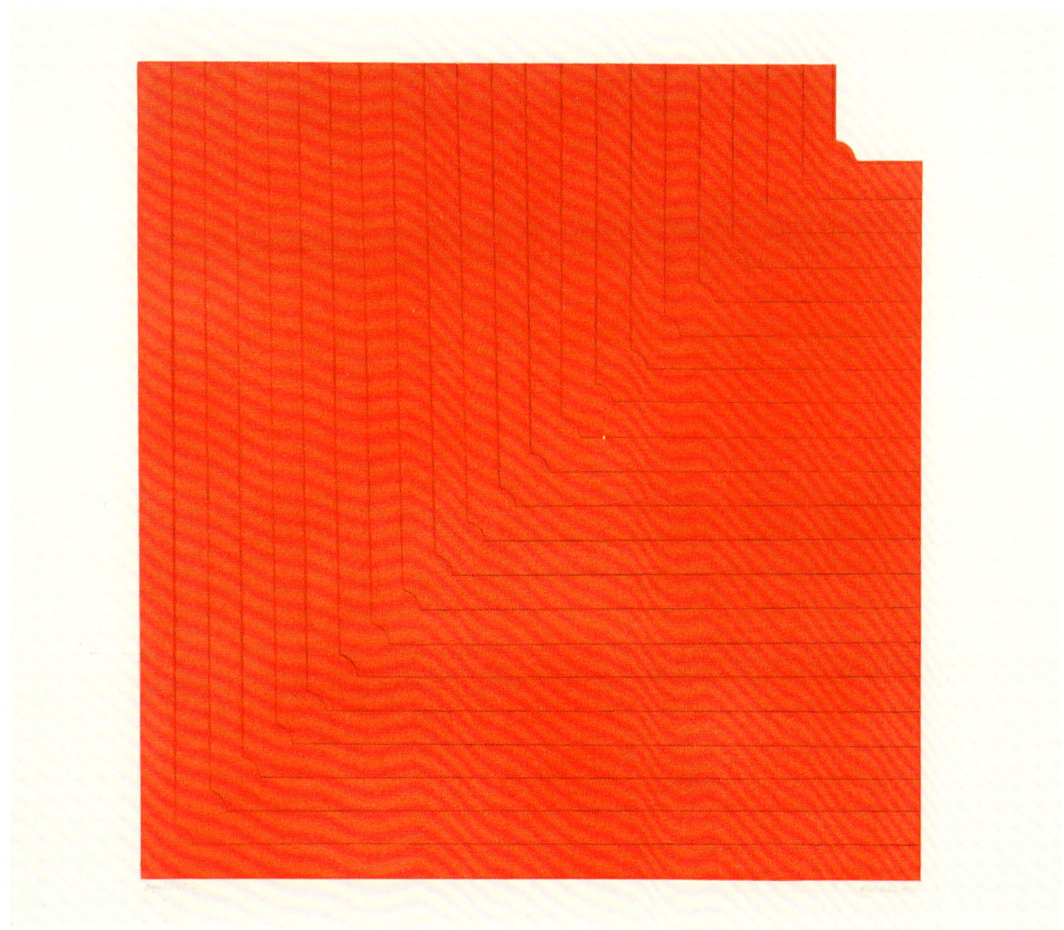

Stanley William Hayter (1901–1988)
Loop 1978
Etching and soft-ground etching on paper, state iii/iii 64.1 × 49.2

Stanley William Hayter, an astonishingly experimental printmaker, spent much of his adult life in Paris, punctuated by a spell in New York after the outbreak of the Second World War; in both cities his print studio Atelier 17 attracted important artists.

Loop was one of Hayter's favourite prints.[18] It demonstrates his achievements in the field of colour printing, utilising the method he developed to combine different colours on a single plate: the stiffest, most viscous inks were applied in a different stage to the thinner inks, with the lower and upper parts of the metal plate holding different colours. By the time he made *Loop*, Hayter's technique was well honed and he completed the plate in two days. His later prints tend to be large and colourful, and Hayter spoke of 'feeling' the colour of his plates as he worked on them, believing they assumed their own colour field.[19] His imagery became increasingly geometric, and the undulating forms of *Loop* seem suggestive of both movement and space.

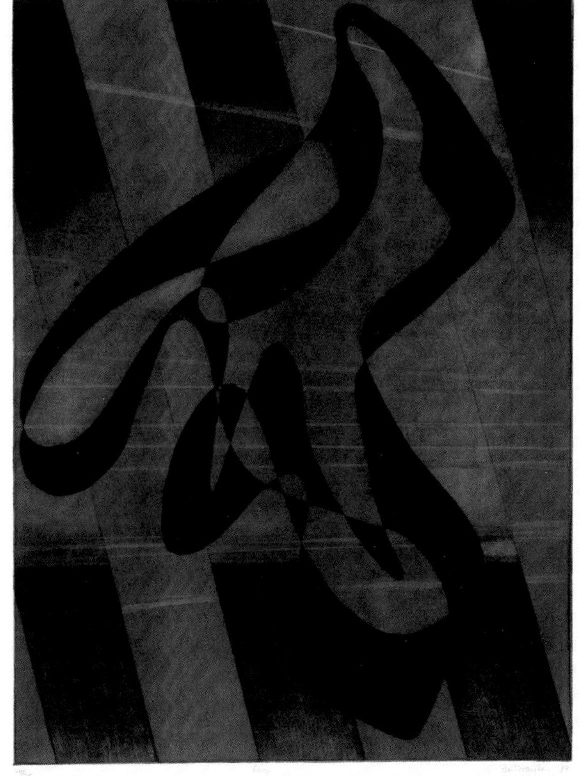

Pat Steir (born 1940)
Long Vertical Falls #2 1991
Etching and aquatint on paper 114 x 57.9

Waterfalls feature in many works by the North American artist Pat Steir. When making her 'Waterfall Paintings', she saw pouring the paint as allowing nature 'to paint a picture of itself', taking inspiration from sources including Chinese literati painting as well as the idea of 'non-intention'.[20] She achieved similar effects in the print medium, exploiting etching's potential for creating accidental-seeming marks to create a print surface alive with drips and tonal contrast, as seen in *Long Vertical Falls #2*.

Steir considers all of her work unfinished, 'a search and an experiment ... only a step along the way.'[21] She made many of her prints at the Crown Point Press in San Francisco.

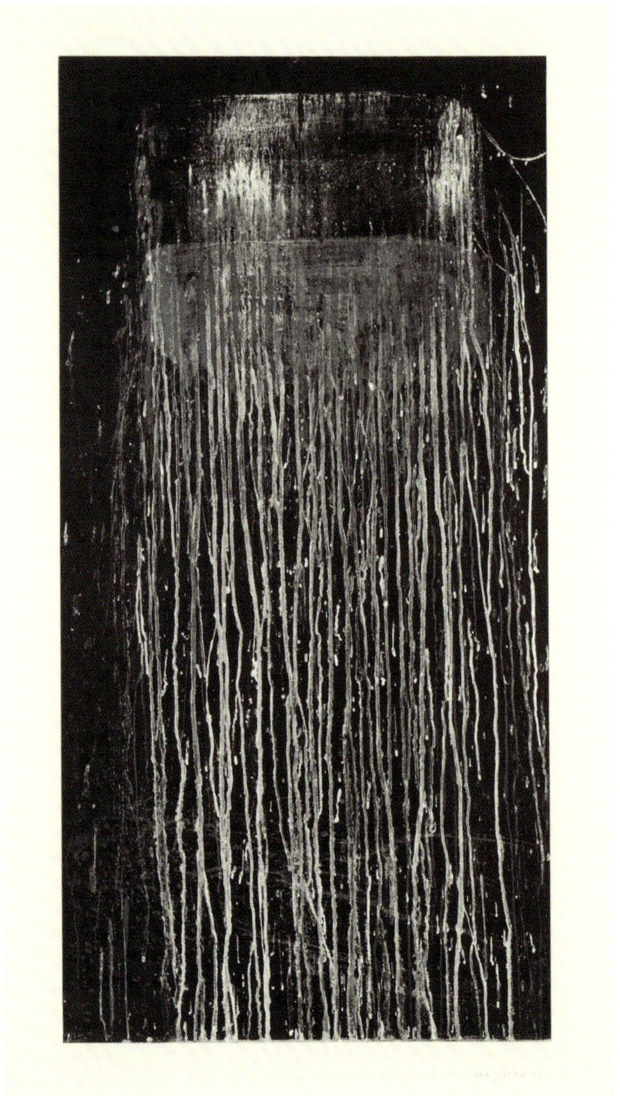

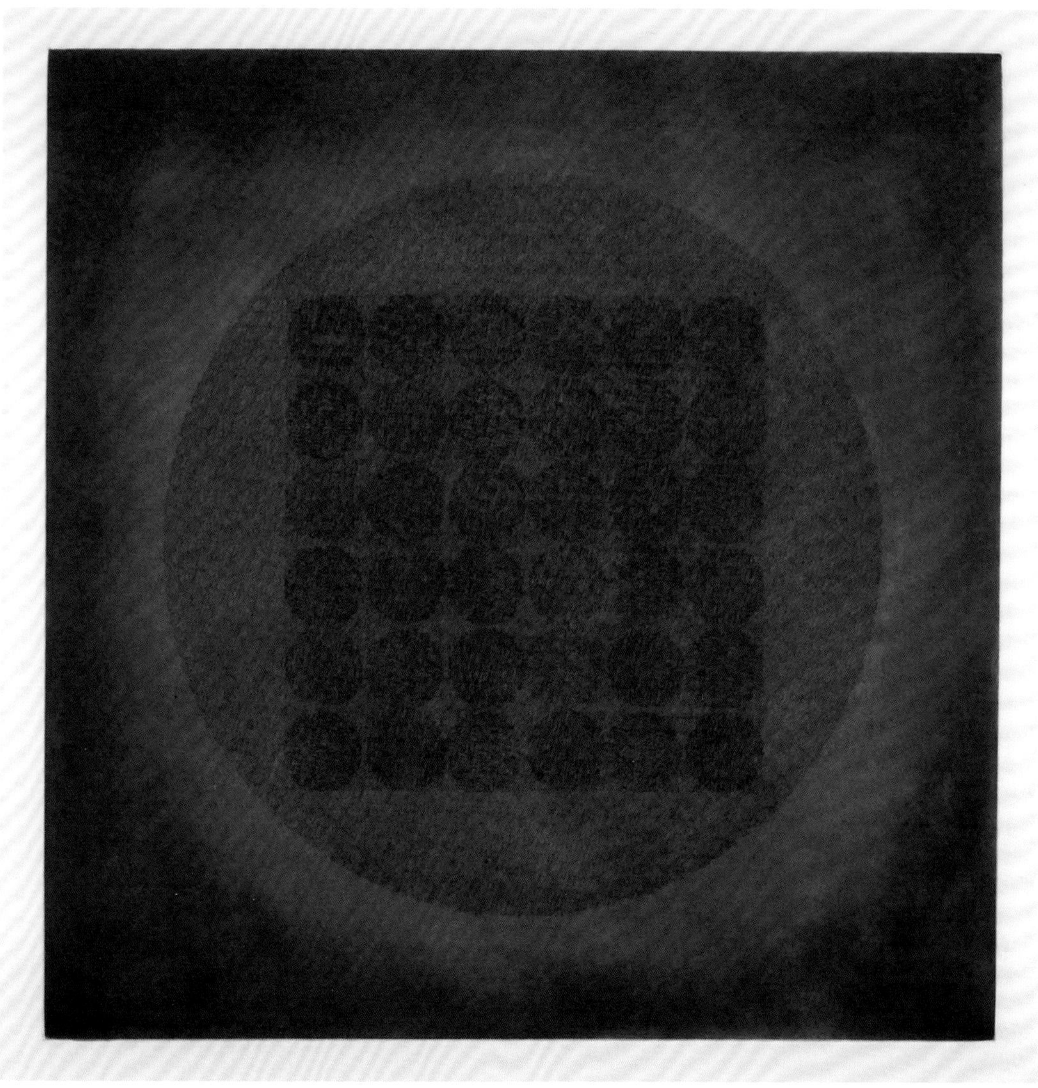

Shirazeh Houshiary (born 1955)
Untitled print from *Round Dance* 1992
Etching on paper 60.5 × 60.5

This print is from a series of five colour etchings, each of which was printed in turquoise and black. The prints were published in a portfolio entitled *Round Dance*, along with five poems that inspired them by the thirteenth-century Persian poet Jalāl al-Dīn Rūmī. The images reference the rotation of the earth and the planets. Jalāl al-Dīn Rūmī was a Sufi mystic and Islamic mysticism is an important influence on Houshiary's practice.

Houshiary was born in Shiraz, Iran, and moved to London in 1974, where she studied and established herself as an artist. She was initially known for her sculptures, but turned to painting and drawing in 1992, also the year she made this etching.

Paula Rego (born 1935)
Flood, from *Pendle Witches* 1996
Etching and aquatint on paper 39.5 × 33.5

This slightly surreal image of a woman in a little bath, afloat on a stormy sea full of unlikely objects and creatures, is one of Paula Rego's finest prints. The lines were etched, and Rego used aquatint to create the different grey tones. From a technical point of view, the graphic depiction of the water and rain is particularly remarkable. The nineteenth-century Spanish artist Francisco de Goya inspired Rego, and the way she has combined etching and aquatint to create an unsettling narrative image echoes Goya's approach to the etching medium in his *Los Caprichos* of 1799, which also combine tragic themes with touches of humour. At the same time, Rego's images have their own unmistakable visual language.

Rego grew up in Portugal during the military dictatorship of António Salazar. Her work in both paint and print explores themes from her childhood, from folk and fairy tales, and reflects feminist concerns.

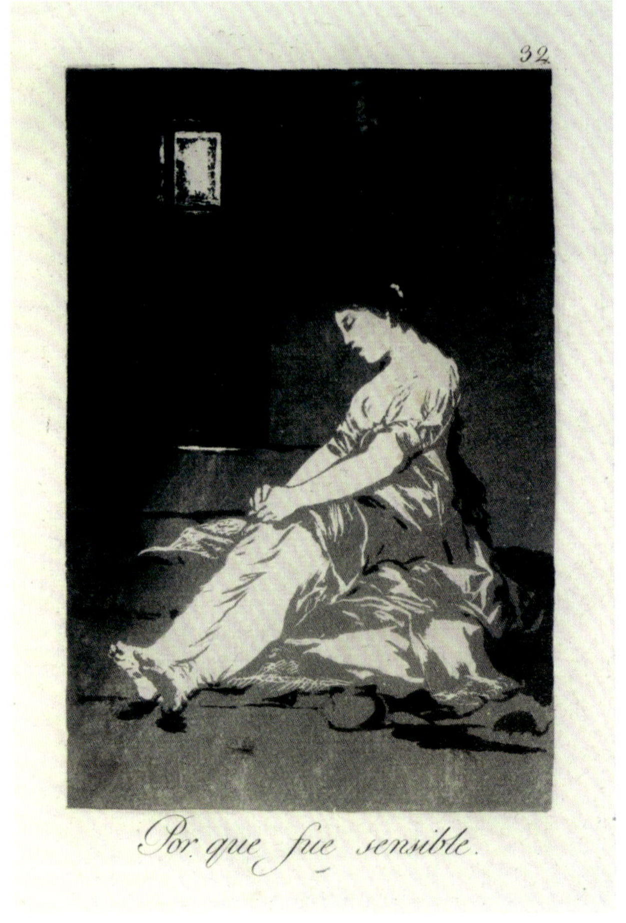

Francisco de Goya, *Por que fue sensible* (Because she was susceptible), from *Los Caprichos*, 1799, aquatint on paper. British Museum, London

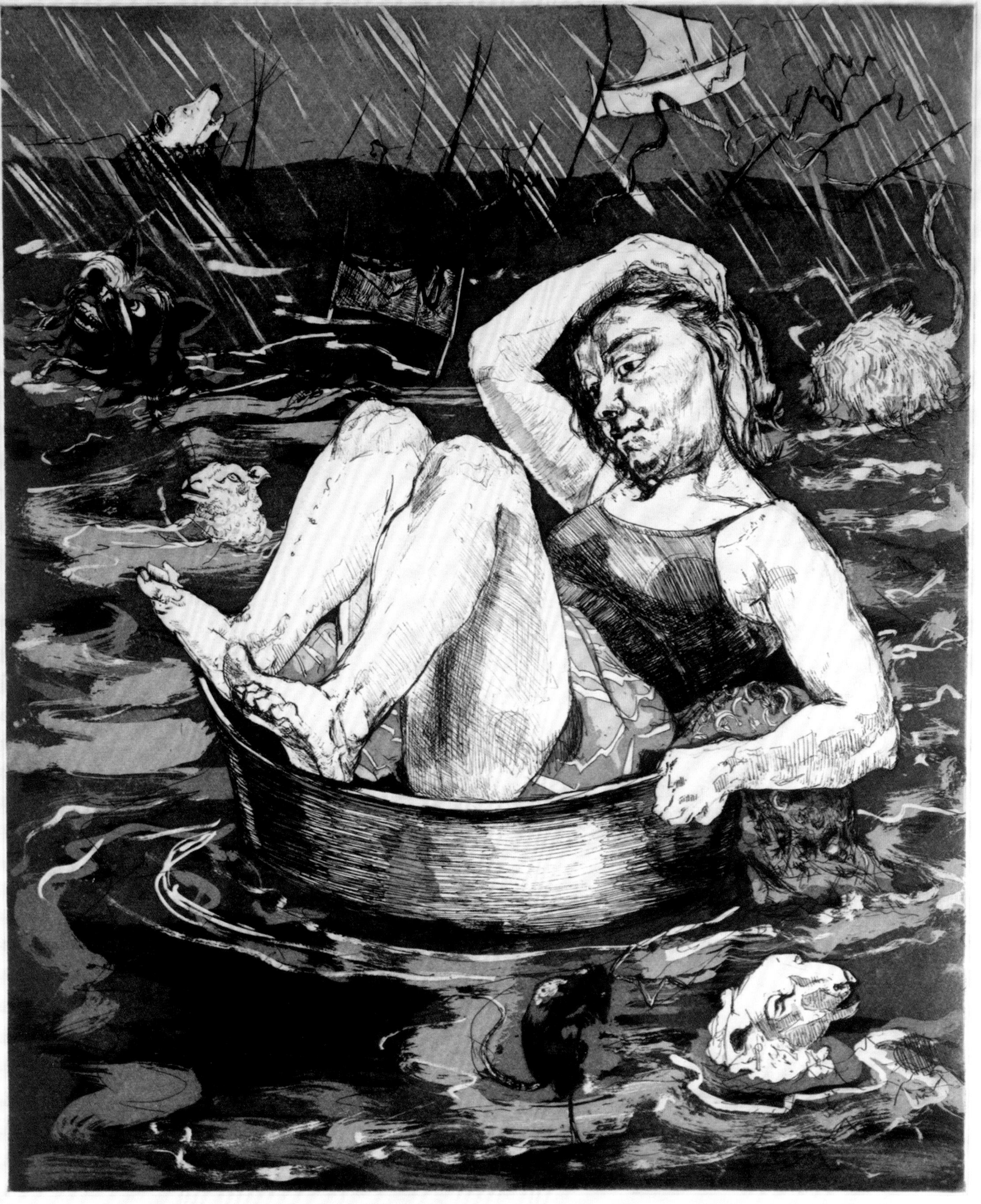
6/30
Paula Rego

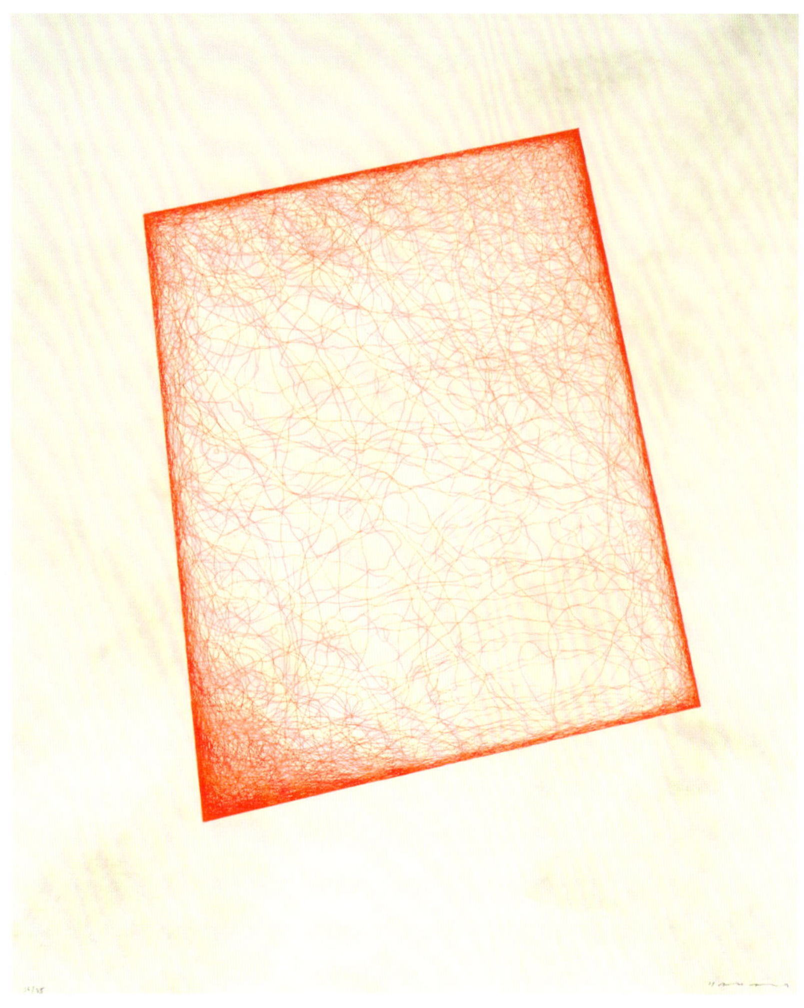

Yukinori Yanagi (born 1959)
Untitled print from *Wandering Position* 1997
Etching on paper 61 × 50.9

While this large etching might seem at first glance to be an attractive and purposefully abstract image designed for visual effect, Yukinori Yanagi's approach to image-making is more conceptual than it first appears. To make this work, an exploration of imprisonment, he placed an ant onto a metal plate and traced its movement with an etching needle; the marks are concentrated around the edges because the ant kept trying to escape. The artist, however, had placed barriers around the edges of the plate.[22]

Yanagi is a Japanese artist who has also spent considerable time in the United States. The attitude of humans towards other living creatures is a key theme in his work: he said in relation to the ants (or 'friends') used in his work: 'I let the ant [be] free to wander. It creates a natural line.'[23]

Chris Ofili (born 1968)
Untitled print from *Cubitt Print Box* 1999–2000
Aquatint and drypoint etching on paper 26 × 21

This image of a woman's head and shoulders is printed in striking orange-red ink. Like much of Chris Ofili's work, it seems to both reference and reinterpret stereotypical views of race. The afro hairstyle is an image Ofili has returned to repeatedly in his exploration of recognisable characteristics – rather than presenting a portrait of an individual, Ofili is concerned with creating a stylised 'type'.

Tate's recent print collecting has embraced the rise of editioned portfolios, including those by mixed groups of artists. This print is from the 2000 *Cubitt Print Box* portfolio, which aimed to raise funds for the move of the London artist-run gallery and studio Cubitt from King's Cross to Islington. Tate also holds a copy of Ofili's *North Wales* portfolio of etchings, one of a number of print series inspired by his trips to different areas.

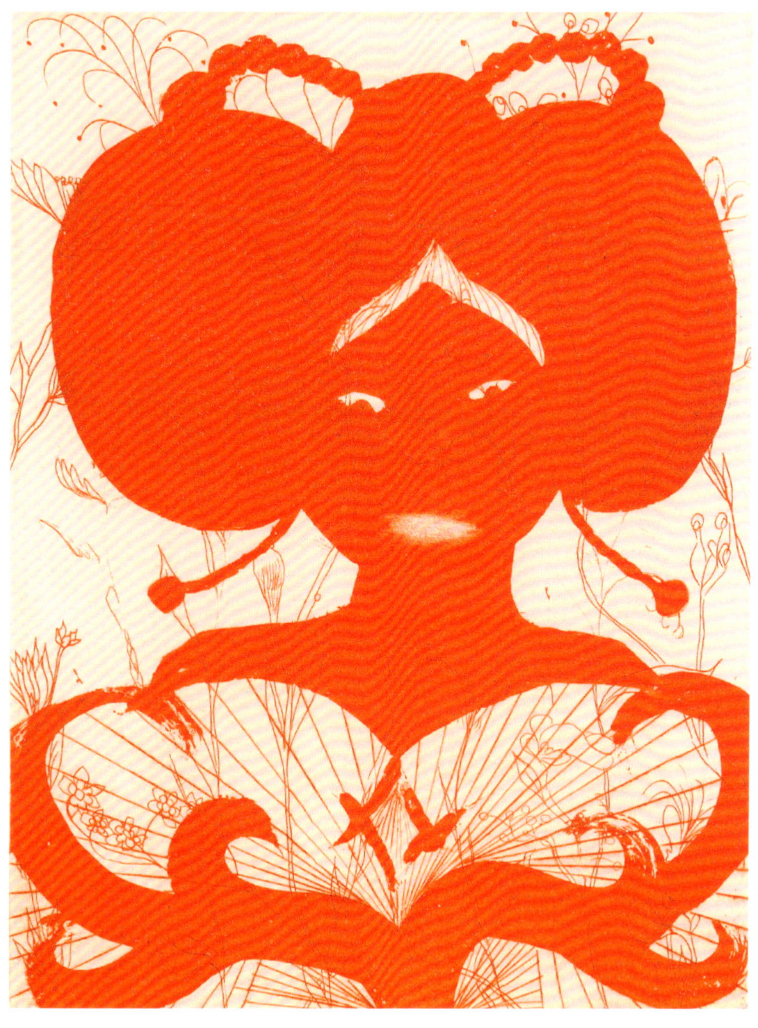

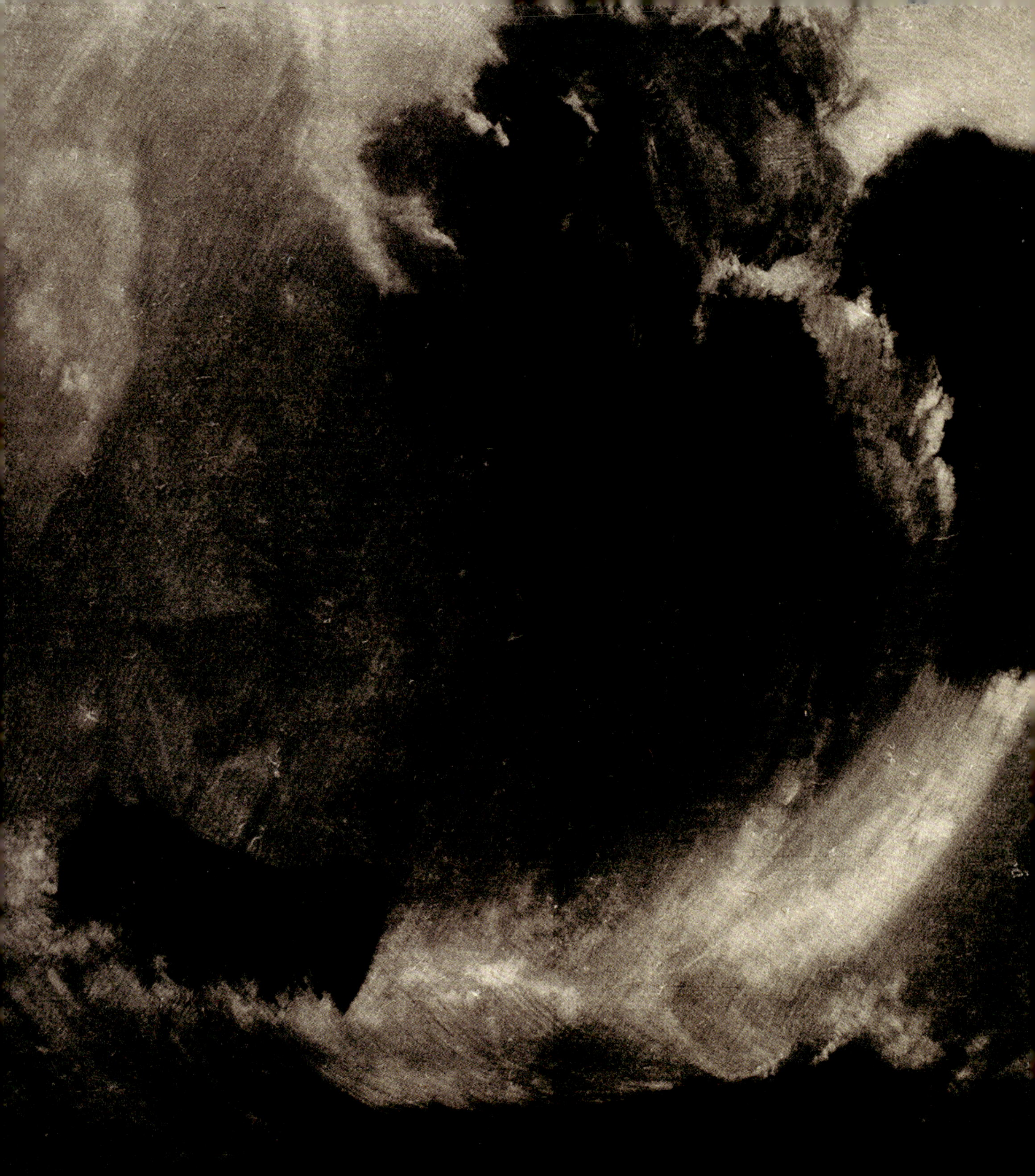

4 Metal on Metal

Joseph Mallord William Turner *Ship in a Storm* c.1826 (detail)

4 Metal on Metal

The prints in this section were made by marking metal printing plates using metal tools. A close relationship exists between these methods and etching (see pp.56–8); in both cases incised marks hold the ink when the plate is wiped and printed using a rolling press, so those marks print as black (or the colour of the ink used). But while etching employs acid to mark the metal, the following techniques rely on the direct incisions of metal tools.

Engraving involves using a sharp tool to make incisions directly into a metal plate, which can then be inked, wiped and printed. Engraving is laborious and involves a high level of technical skill.

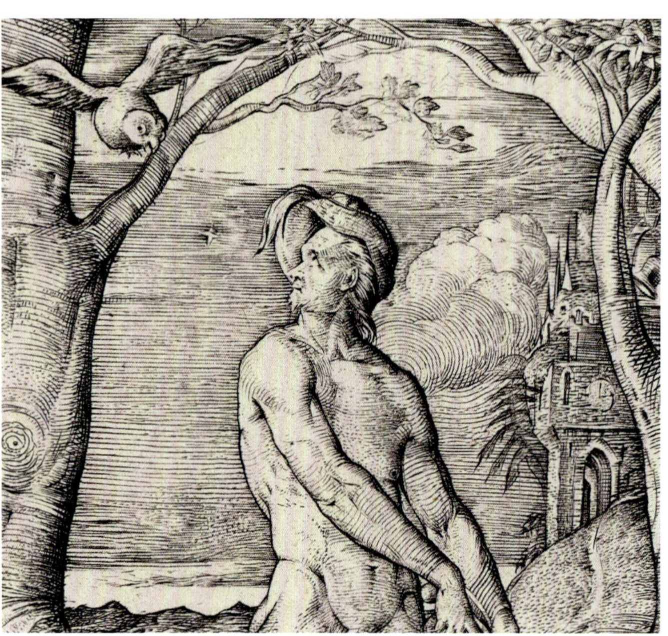

Detail from George Richmond, *The Fatal Bellman* 1827

Drypoint involves using a metal needle to scratch marks directly into a soft metal plate, which can then be inked, wiped and printed. It is a straightforward technique to learn, but only a few prints can be made before the artist's delicate marks, characterised by a fuzziness caused by each incision's roughened edges, start to wear.

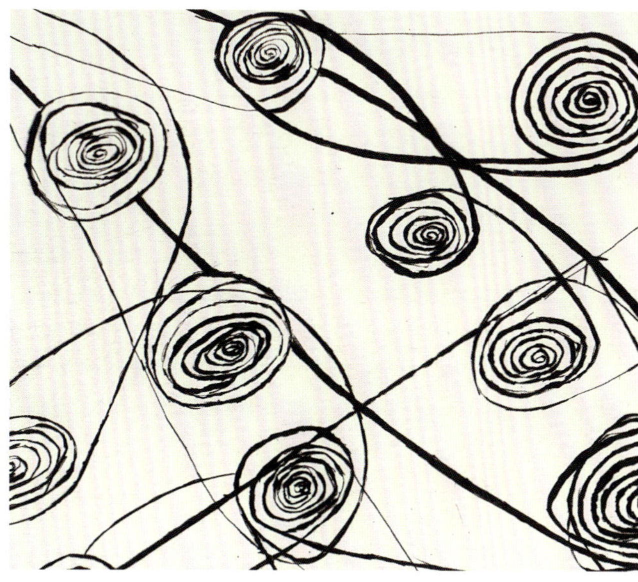

Detail from Louise Bourgeois, *Untitled (Safety Pins)* 1991

Mezzotint is a tonal technique in which the printmaker works from dark to light. A metal plate is first 'rocked' (or roughened) all over using a metal tool; the newly roughened surface would print as pure black if inked at this stage. The artist then works into the plate with another tool, smoothing areas to different degrees so that they will print in shades of grey. Areas of the plate burnished completely smooth do not hold any ink at all and appear in the final image as white highlights.

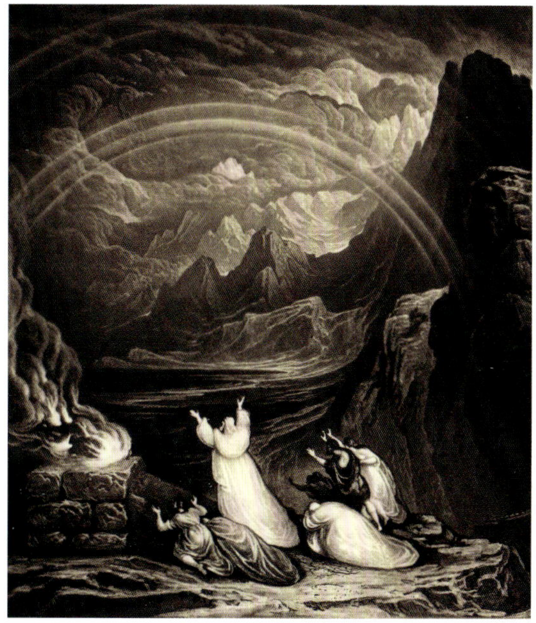

Detail from John Martin, *The Covenant*, from *'Illustrations of the Bible'* published 1832

Working With Metal

Of all the 'metal on metal' techniques, engraving has the longest and most complex history. It originated in fifteenth-century Germany and northern Italy, where the technique of engraving metal plates for printmaking evolved from metalwork. While in Italy engraving took hold as a means to reproduce painted and drawn images, in Northern Europe two key figures, Albrecht Dürer and Lucas van Leyden, concentrated on using it to create original images. By the seventeenth century, though, engraving's key role was established: it had become the primary method of reproducing images first produced in other media and was increasingly used for illustration. Artists, on the other hand, generally preferred the less laborious technique of etching when working with their own hands.

> TURNER p.99

A trade employing the skills of highly trained metal engravers flourished in centres across Europe and survived well into the nineteenth century. While much of this work was purely reproductive, artists such as Joseph Mallord William Turner actively collaborated with professional engravers to translate designs that had been made with the specific intention of creating prints in the black-and-white language of engraving. Many leading artists of the pre-photography era were aware of engraving's potential for disseminating their work. The prints made to reproduce their paintings and designs are usually termed 'engravings', but in fact often include some areas of etching as well as engraving; combining the two techniques on one plate is relatively straightforward.

> HAYTER p.105

As the need for engraved reproductions of images waned following the onset of photography, Europe's engraving workshops became obsolete. Some twentieth-century artists, notably Stanley William Hayter, attempted to revive the method for artists' prints, but it remains an unusual choice due to the high degree of specialist skill required.

If the history of engraving is dominated by the wish to reproduce images for a large audience, drypoint is, by contrast, only suited to making very small editions of artists' prints. Its delicate nature means that a plate will only produce a handful of good impressions. Although the technique dates back to the Renaissance, its most famous proponent is the seventeenth-century Dutch master, Rembrandt. His example particularly inspired British and French artists in the mid nineteenth century, who often added elements of drypoint to etching plates, sparking a revival of interest in the technique. In the twentieth century, the directness of the drypoint technique appealed to printmakers working in Europe and beyond. One, the Hungarian artist Dóra Maurer, took this directness a step further, abandoning the drypoint needle altogether and creating marks by making folds in the metal printing plate itself.

> MAURER p.108

Mezzotint was invented in the Netherlands during the seventeenth century but was most widely practised in England. During the eighteenth century it was frequently used to reproduce the tonal qualities of oil paintings, while in the nineteenth century both John Constable and Turner collaborated with professional mezzotint engravers; Turner also tried the medium with his own hands. Like engraving, mezzotint fell from favour after the 1850s, once the onset of photographic reproduction rendered its reproductive capabilities increasingly irrelevant. Artists have occasionally taken it up again, attracted by the medium's rich, tonal qualities. For example, the Latvian-American artist Vija Celmins has used it on multiple occasions to depict night skies lit by shining stars, a subject to which the technique is naturally suited.

> CONSTABLE p.103
> TURNER p.101
> CELMINS p.112

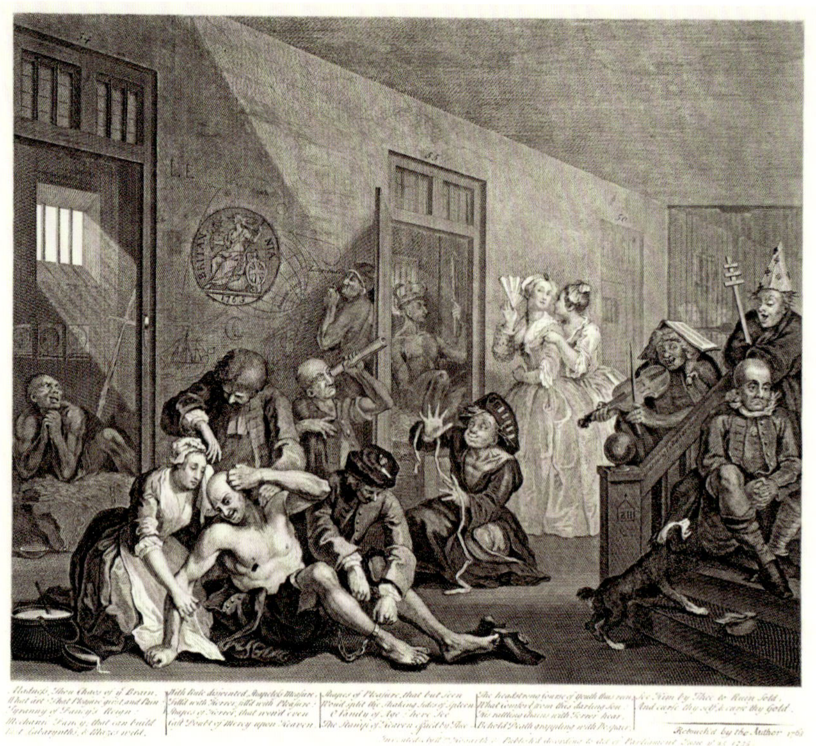

William Hogarth (1697–1764)
A Rake's Progress (plate 8) 1735–63
Etching and engraving on paper 31.8 × 38.7

This print is from *A Rake's Progress*, a series of prints by William Hogarth documenting the imagined fate of the protagonist Tom Rakewell. Having inherited wealth after his father's death, Tom is shown following a dubious path, squandering his fortune in brothels and gambling houses until his incarceration in debtors' prison. In this, the final image in the series, Hogarth reveals that Tom has ended up in Bethlem Royal Hospital, the psychiatric hospital in London from which the word 'bedlam' was termed.

Hogarth, a highly trained and skilled engraver, translated his own series of paintings (now in the Sir John Soane's Museum, London) into print. Hogarth built up this scene using meticulous grid-like engraved lines that taper at the end. He also added some etched lines, which appear thicker and more fluid. An important artist in Tate's painting collection, Hogarth's significant achievements in print were not properly reflected within the gallery until 1973, when this and a number of other prints were transferred from the reference collection and given status as art objects. As well as mastering various printmaking techniques and disseminating his own images widely, Hogarth was a leading voice in establishing a form of copyright for engravers.

Charles Turner (1773–1857) after
Joseph Mallord William Turner (1775–1851)
A Shipwreck 1806–7

Mezzotint and watercolour on paper 59 × 85.1

This large-scale print was the first to reproduce one of Joseph Mallord William Turner's paintings. The print's engraver, Charles Turner (no relation), suggested making the mezzotint after seeing J.M.W. Turner's large oil painting *The Shipwreck* exhibited in 1805. The print's success proved a turning point for both men. The widespread interest it generated encouraged the painter to pursue further print projects, which became a central feature of his career. These included the *Liber Studiorum*, an ambitious series laying out the different types of landscape composition; for this project he again chose Charles Turner as mezzotint engraver. As well as employing professionals to interpret his paintings as he did here, Turner himself experimented with the mezzotint technique in some rare unpublished plates (p.101).

For *A Shipwreck*, the artist reserved the right to publish a few prints with hand colouring in watercolour. All colour impressions are rare, but this one is particularly special as it is a unique engraver's proof (or test), part-printed in colour, with the hand-colouring in watercolour, as well as some scratching out, added by Turner himself.

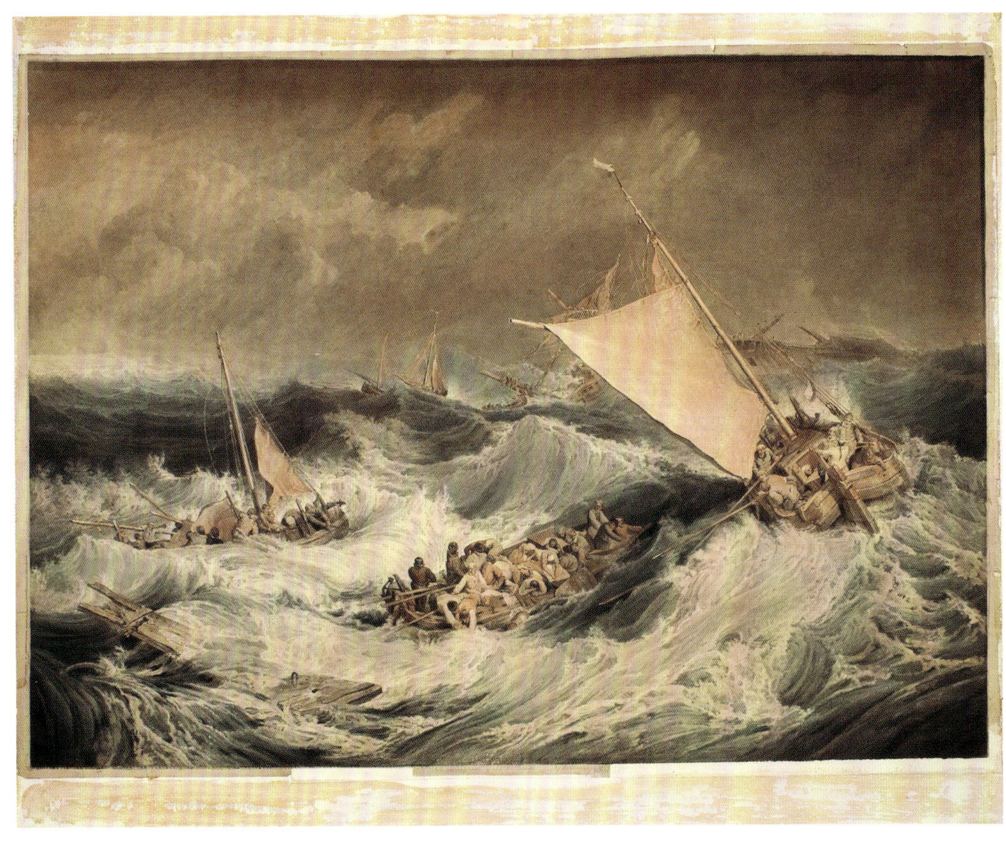

Thomas Lupton (1791–1873) after
Thomas Girtin (1775–1802)
York Minster on the River Foss published 1824
Mezzotint on paper 14.7 × 22.9

Thomas Girtin, a contemporary of J.M.W. Turner, died young, unable to make the same impact as his friend and artistic rival. It is said that for this series of prints, which reproduced works by both Turner and Girtin in mezzotint, Turner hand-corrected test prints of the plates made after both artists, providing instructions to the engraver Thomas Lupton so that the mezzotints could be improved. This was apparently out of respect for his friend's memory, although it is stated that he also claimed 'two guineas a piece' as a fee.[1] Either way, the finished print successfully uses the full range of tones possible in mezzotint to capture Girtin's vision of York Minster, shown backlit by a low sun stretching through the clouds.

This mezzotint is a proof, printed before the lettering was added. The series it is from was entitled 'The Rivers of England', published by W.B. Cooke between 1823 and 1827 and also known as 'River Scenery'.

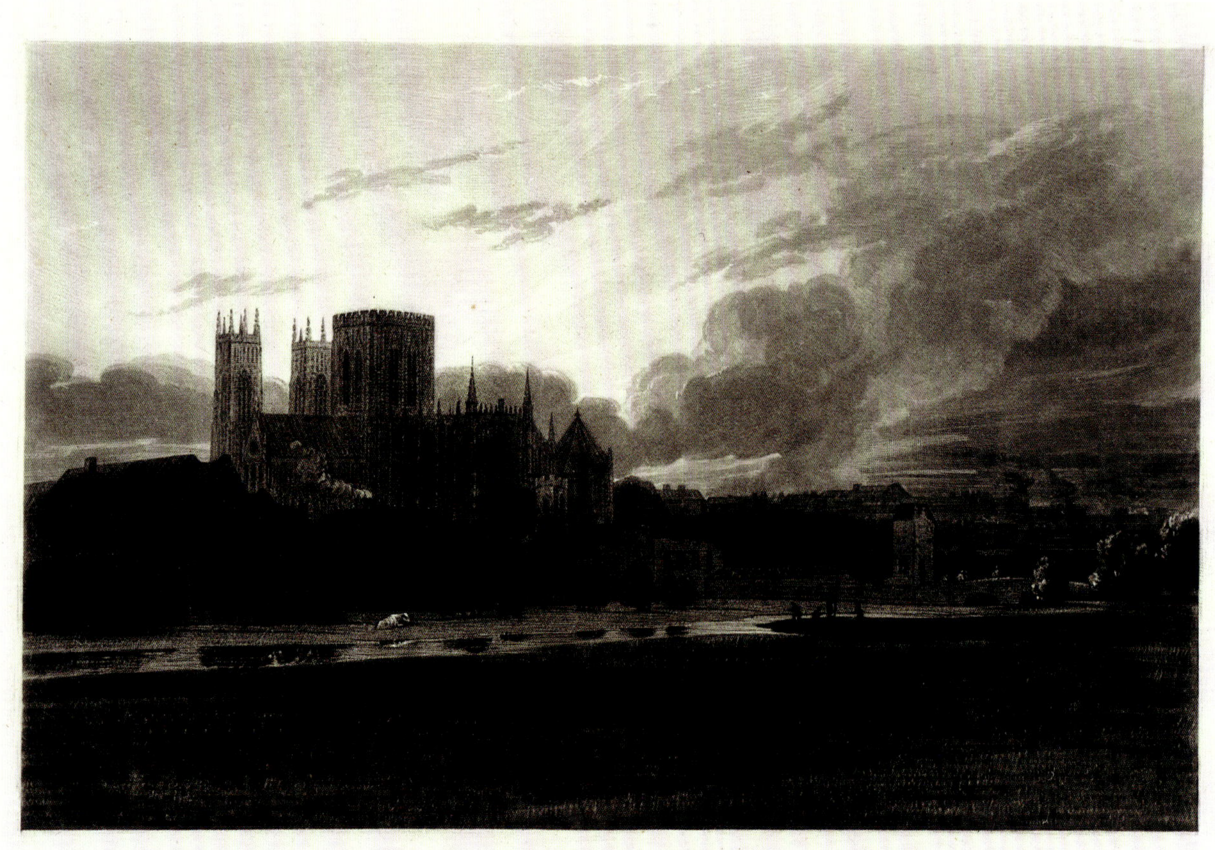

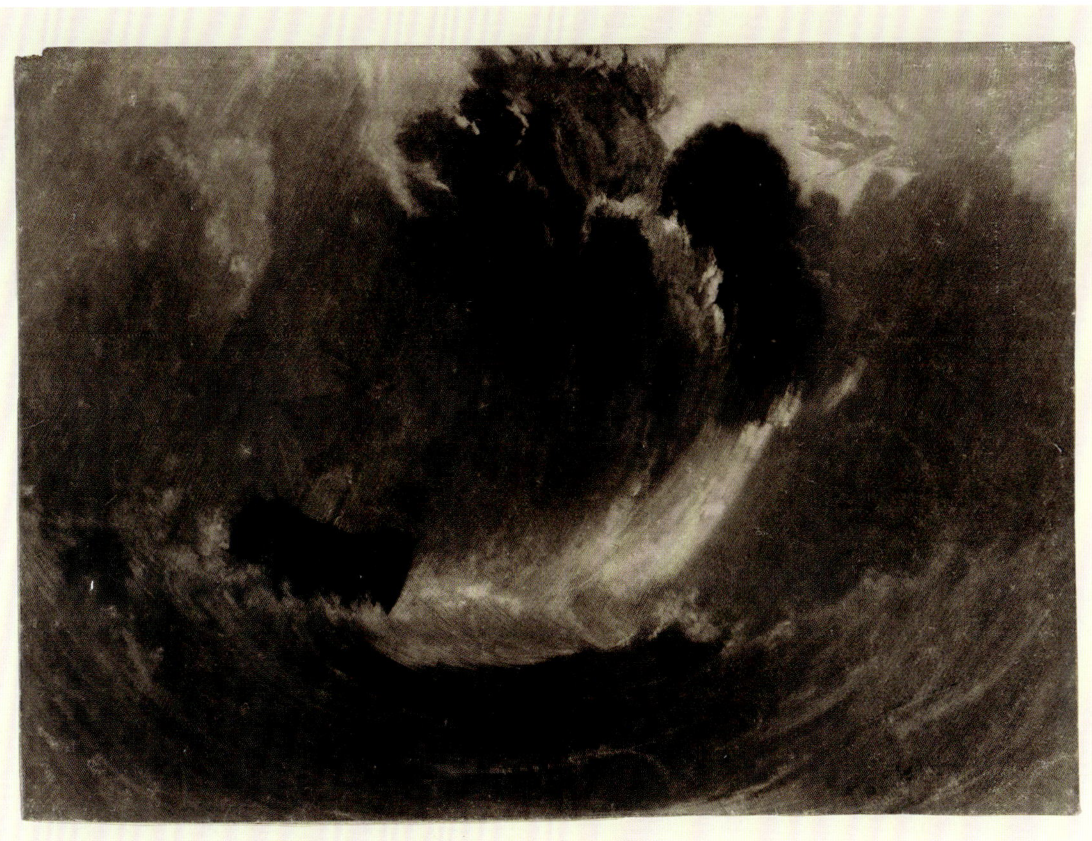

Joseph Mallord William Turner (1775–1851)
Ship in a Storm c.1826
Mezzotint on paper 15.1 × 21.3

Although much of Turner's printmaking activity involved collaborating with professional engravers, this is one of the few prints made entirely by his own hands. In the 1820s he experimented with the mezzotint technique to create a series of unpublished prints. In these remarkable and apparently private works, Turner created a mysterious group of dramatically lit night scenes and seascapes. This is an unfinished proof state, made before Turner made his final changes to the plate – in particular, by darkening the ship.

To create the print, Turner 'burnished' (or polished) the plate to varying degrees, only the stormiest clouds and the dark form of the ship left untouched to print as pure black. Meanwhile, the light coming through the clouds appears as a bright, shining white. The image has a vortex-like composition, reflecting the turbulence of the sea. Although unfinished and never published by Turner himself, this piece sees Turner use print to great expressive effect. It and Turner's related efforts take an important place in the history of the mezzotint medium.

George Richmond (1809–1896)
The Fatal Bellman 1827

Engraving on paper 7 × 4.8

A quote from William Shakespeare's play *Macbeth* runs along the top edge of this small and intricate engraving: 'It was the owl that shriek'd, the fatal bell-man'. The artist, George Richmond, took Shakespeare's line as inspiration for his own interpretation of Macbeth, here shown looking at the owl in the upper left, his tall figure framed by trees. The texture of the trees' bark is superbly rendered using the engraver's burin, a pointed metal tool used to incise metal.

Richmond made this engraving when he was eighteen. At this time he was a member of 'The Ancients', along with Edward Calvert and Samuel Palmer (pp.27, 67). The artists in this group, which was inspired by William Blake (p.26), were deeply interested in the art and literature of the past, including Shakespeare. After his marriage in 1831 Richmond turned his focus to portraiture, making this youthful engraving an all the more precious example of his early work.

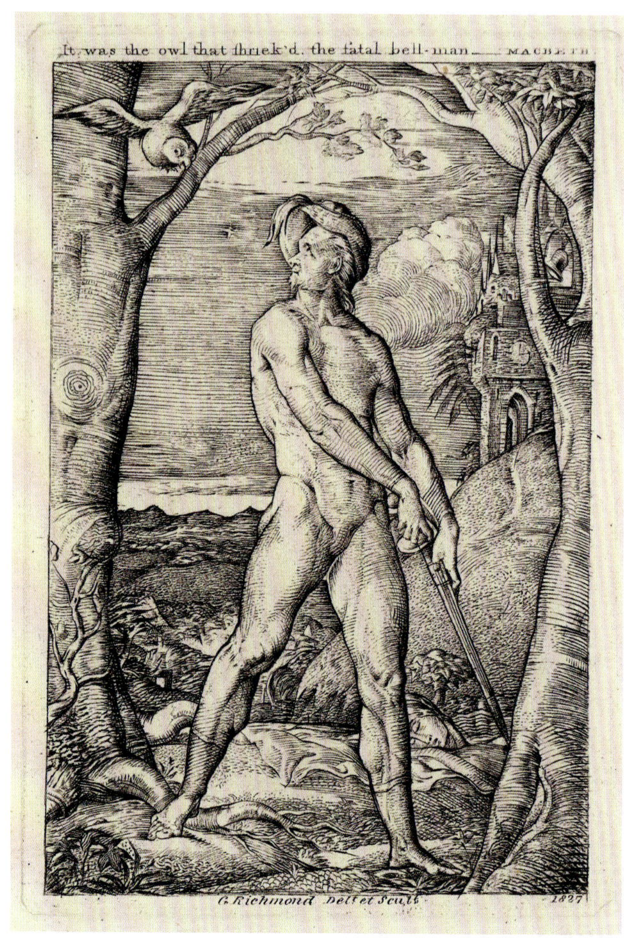

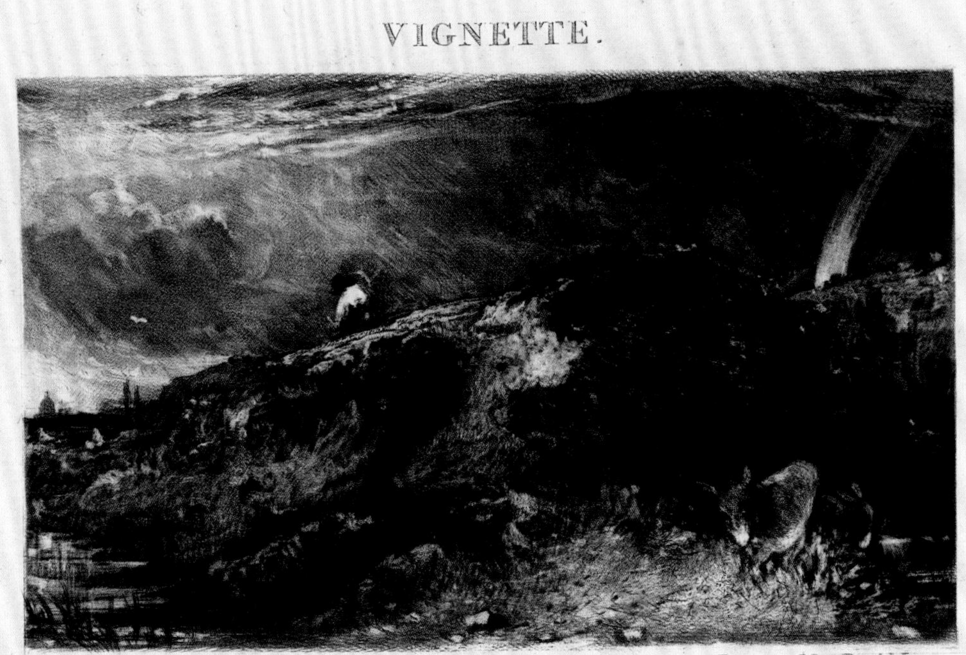

David Lucas (1802–1881) after
John Constable (1776–1837)
Vignette: Hampstead Heath, Middlesex 1831 or 1832
Mezzotint on paper 9.2 × 15.4

This is a view over Hampstead Heath in London, a favourite subject of one of Britain's best-known landscape painters, John Constable. St Paul's Cathedral can be glimpsed in the distance, on the left. The print is from Constable's only major printmaking project, *Various Subjects of Landscape, Characteristic of English Scenery, from Pictures Painted by John Constable, R.A.* (1830–2). For this publication, intended to disseminate his oeuvre, he employed David Lucas to make mezzotints based on his paintings. Finished works and oil sketches alike were translated into the black, white and grey language of mezzotint via a combination of Lucas's competent hands and Constable's resolute demands. The result was a series of images demonstrating astonishing power and tonal variation.

Although the image is nearly complete in this impression of the print, the lettering is not, and this is a late progress proof, printed as a test. Constable looked over many proof prints before the plates for the series were finally completed. The motto along the bottom edge, 'Ut Umbra sic Vita', means 'life is like a shadow'.

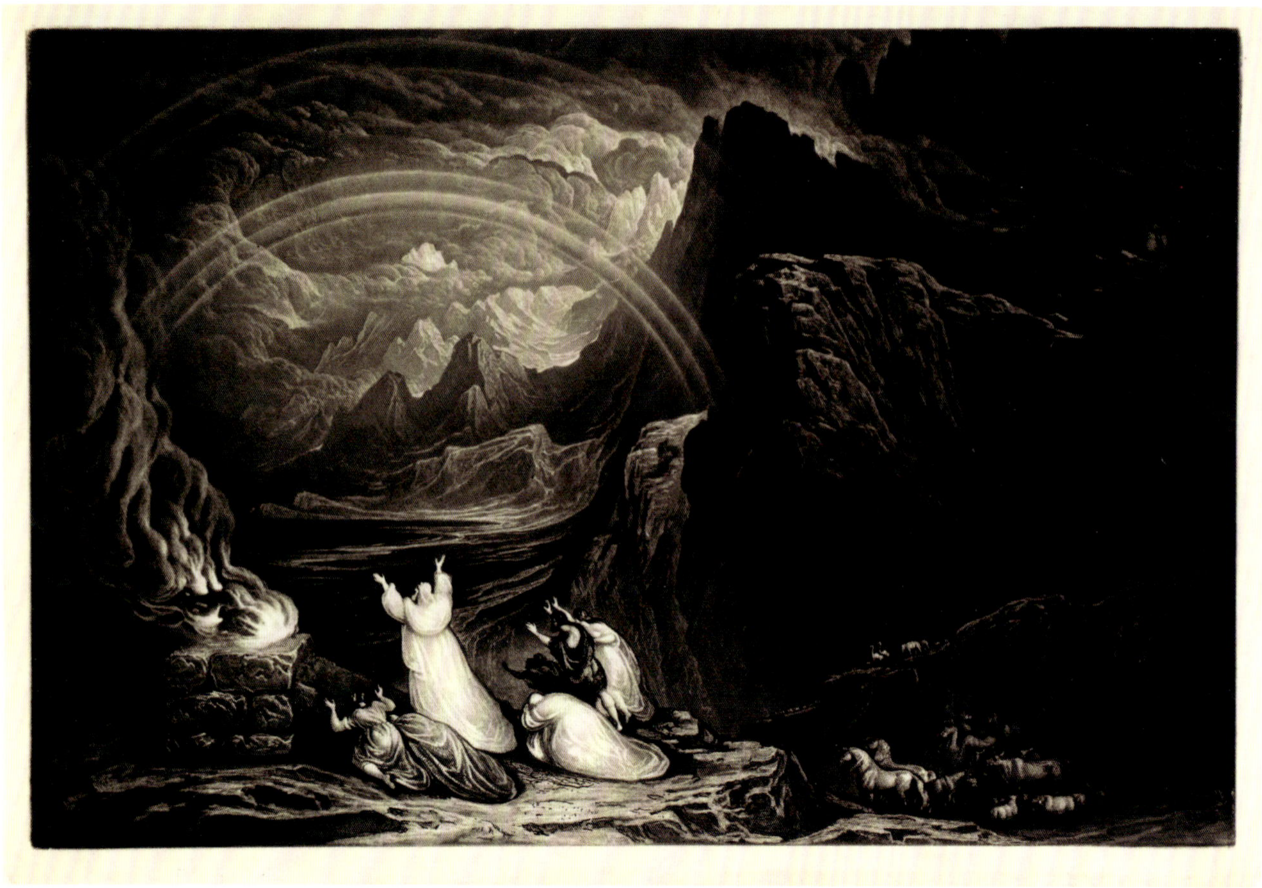

John Martin (1789–1854)
The Covenant, from *'Illustrations of the Bible'* published 1832
Mezzotint on paper 19 × 29

The British artist John Martin, known for his vast landscape paintings, was also a skilled printmaker. This mezzotint is dominated by the Old Testament figure of Noah, shown giving thanks to God following the biblical flood. Noah's ark is seen on the mountain at the right, and the animals saved from the flood can be glimpsed in the lower right of the image.

Martin published twenty plates for his 'Illustrations of the Bible', his most ambitious project, between 1821 and 1835. The prints were appreciated by critics – but rival prints, which took Martin's ideas but sold at a much lower price, soon appeared. Partly as a result of this, the project was a commercial failure and was never completed. Financial pressures left Martin with little choice but to sell his plates to a print publisher in an effort to avoid bankruptcy, and the prints became well known only after they were reissued. This particular print is a proof copy, made before the addition of lettering.

Stanley William Hayter (1901–1988)
Le Chas de l'aiguille 1946
Engraving on paper 30.2 × 18.7

The British-born printmaker Stanley William Hayter, who shared his knowledge of various printmaking techniques within his workshop (see p.60), spent much of his life in Paris. Working at a time when engraving was seen as obsolete, Hayter was a proponent for its creative potential. While engraving is usually considered a restrictive medium due to the physical difficulty of engraving marks into a metal plate, Hayter showed that engraved marks could be made to curve and spiral in an apparently free and spontaneous fashion. *Le Chas de l'aiguille*, or 'follow the needle', is an example of this surprising – and impressive – use of the engraver's burin (or needle). Hayter actively explored and challenged what can be achieved with this historic technique.

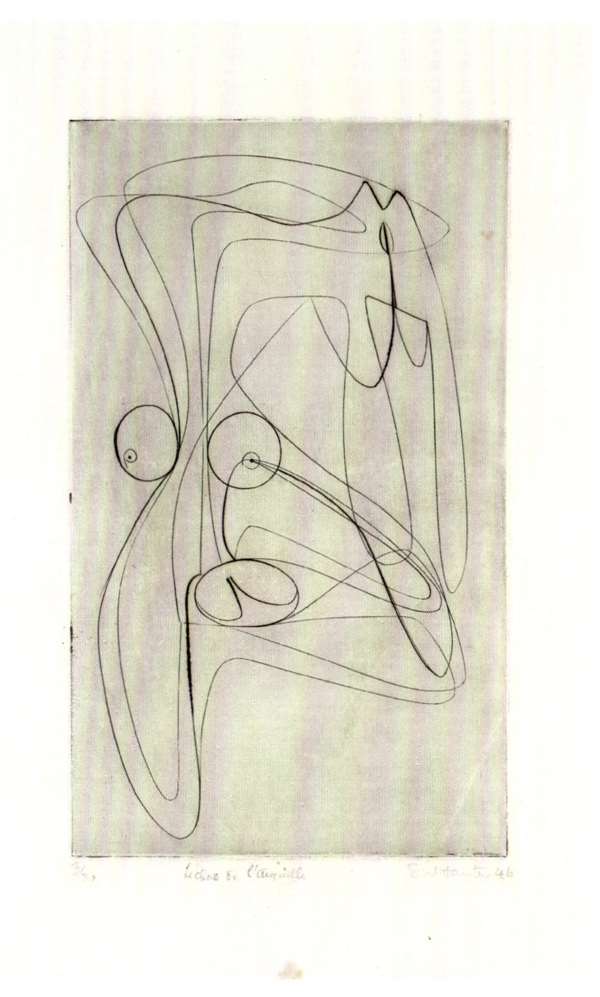

Hans Hartung (1904–1989)

24 1953

Drypoint on paper 37.8 × 51.7

By the early 1950s the French-German abstract artist Hans Hartung was a leading figure in the Paris art world. He made this print, which was published in Paris in an edition of 100, in 1953, at a time when he was also drawing prolifically using ink. The contemporaneous ink drawings feature groups of rapidly drawn straight lines, which are feathered or tapered at the ends. They relate very closely to this print in subject matter and share the same sort of line-based abstract composition. The drypoint technique is less fluid than the combination of ink and brush Hartung used for the drawings, though, making the end effect rather different.

This print, *24*, well demonstrates drypoint's capacity for creating scratchy marks of expressive power. It was this scratchiness that most appealed to Hartung.

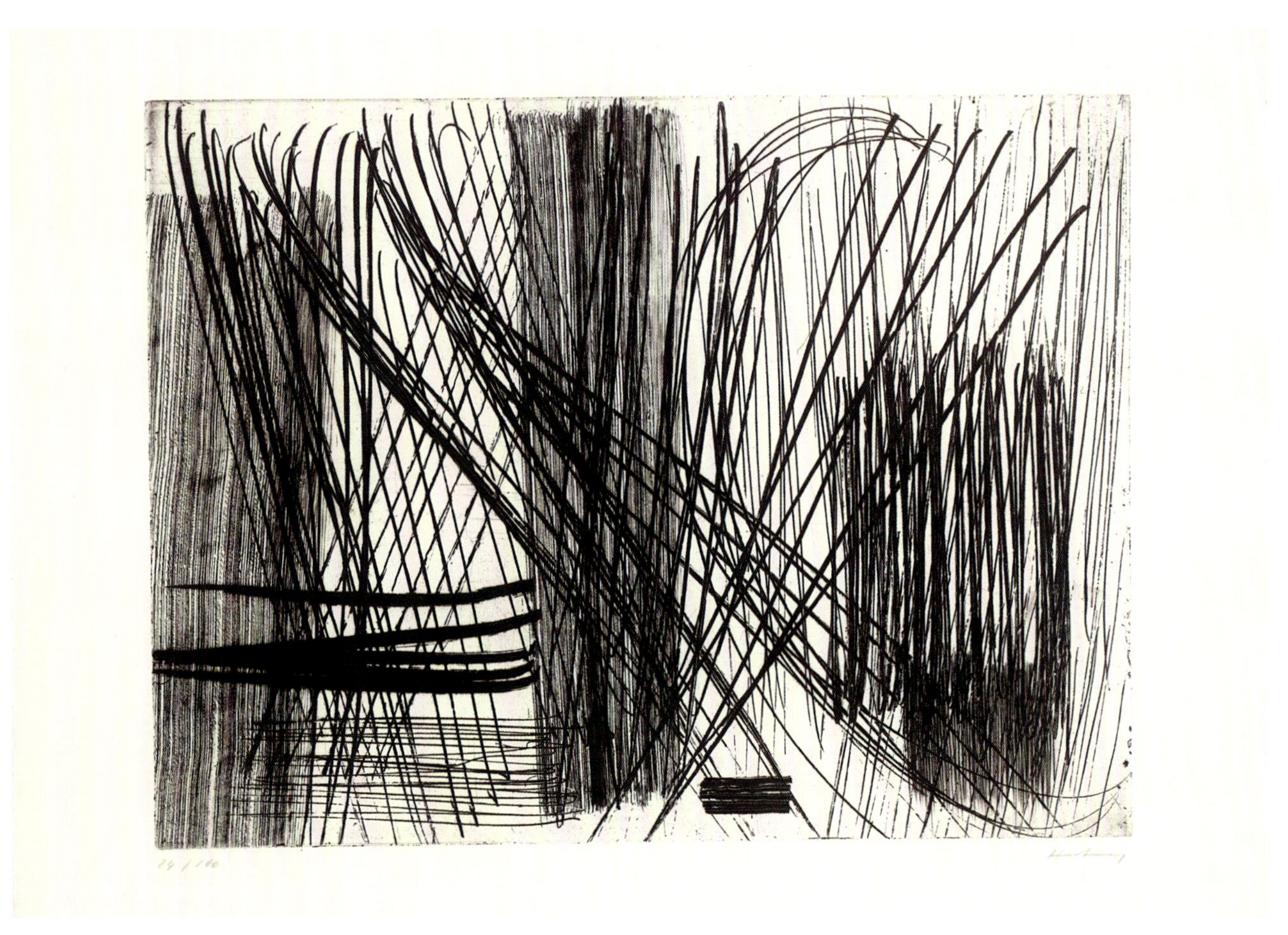

Arnulf Rainer (born 1929)
Violet Furrows 1972–9
Drypoint on paper 53 x 78.6

In this print the Austrian artist Arnulf Rainer employed the drypoint needle to create a dense network of scratchy lines. These marks seem to reverberate with the rich red colour of the ink. While the upper edges of the image reveal the scratchiness of the printed lines, surrounded by the buzz of the metal 'burr' created on either side of each line Rainer scratched into his printing plate, the majority of the image is so built up as to appear almost a solid block of colour.

Violet Furrows is from *Five Reds*, a series of drypoints printed by Karl Imhof and published by Edition Galerie Heiner Friedrich in Munich in an edition of thirty-five.

Dóra Maurer (born 1937)
Seven Foldings 1975, published 1978
Drypoint on paper 57.8 x 40

After training as a graphic artist in the 1950s, Dóra Maurer developed an experimental art practice. Her work was at odds with the 'official' art system dominating her home country, Hungary, a legacy of the Soviet-imposed system.[2] Along with other artists, Maurer participated in informal creative networks in Budapest, also collaborating with European colleagues based in other cities.

Maurer's approach to printmaking is highly unconventional. Although *Seven Foldings* is categorised as a drypoint, it is unclear how much Maurer employed the traditional drypoint needle to make it. Rather, the aluminium plate Maurer used became both printing plate and engraver's tool, as she worked by 'folding and pressing a thin plate diagonally and repeating the procedure step by step'.[3] The marks we see printed were born of the traces of this movement; the result is surprisingly beautiful. *Seven Foldings* was printed by the artist and published by Griffelkunst Editions, Hamburg.

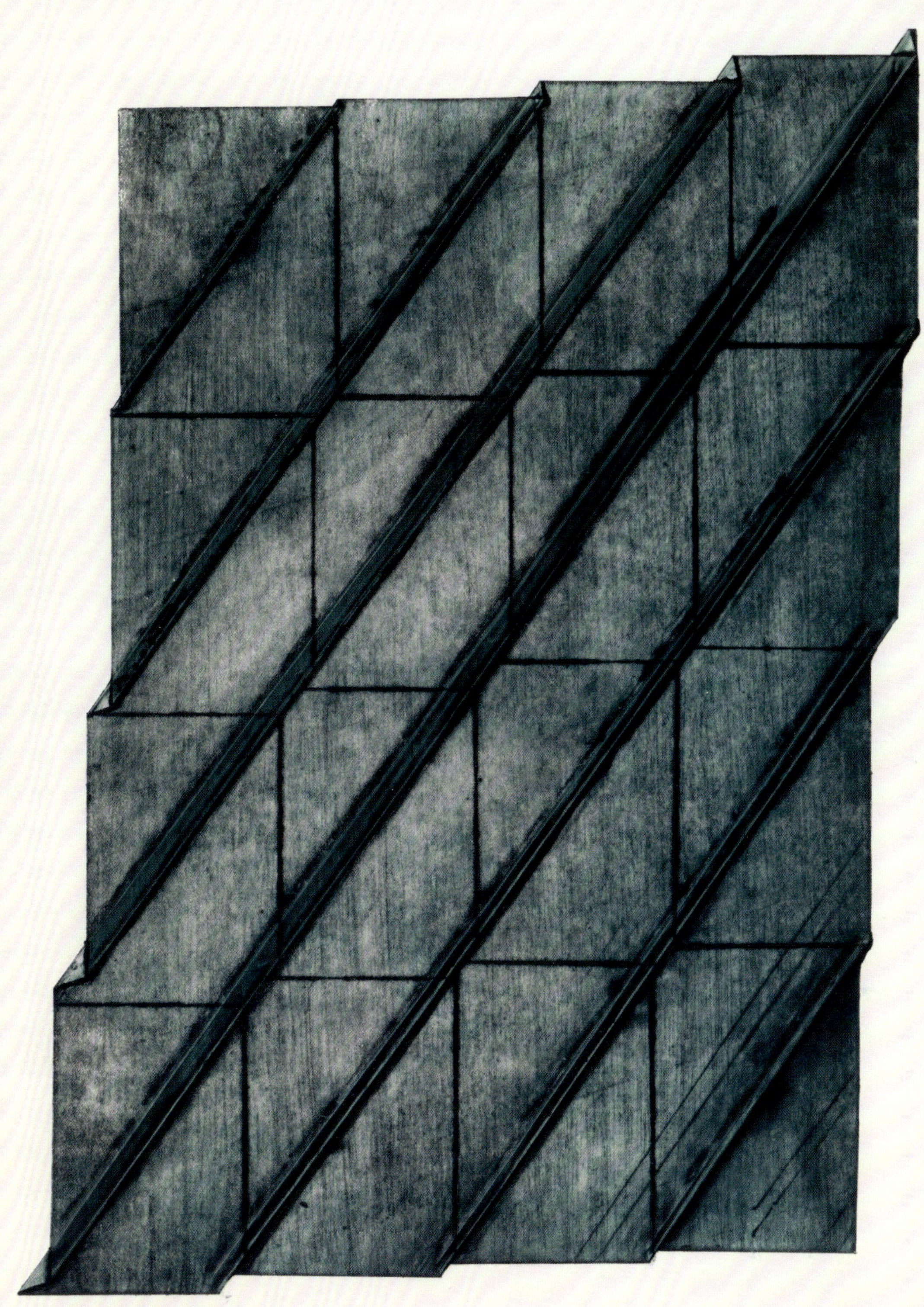

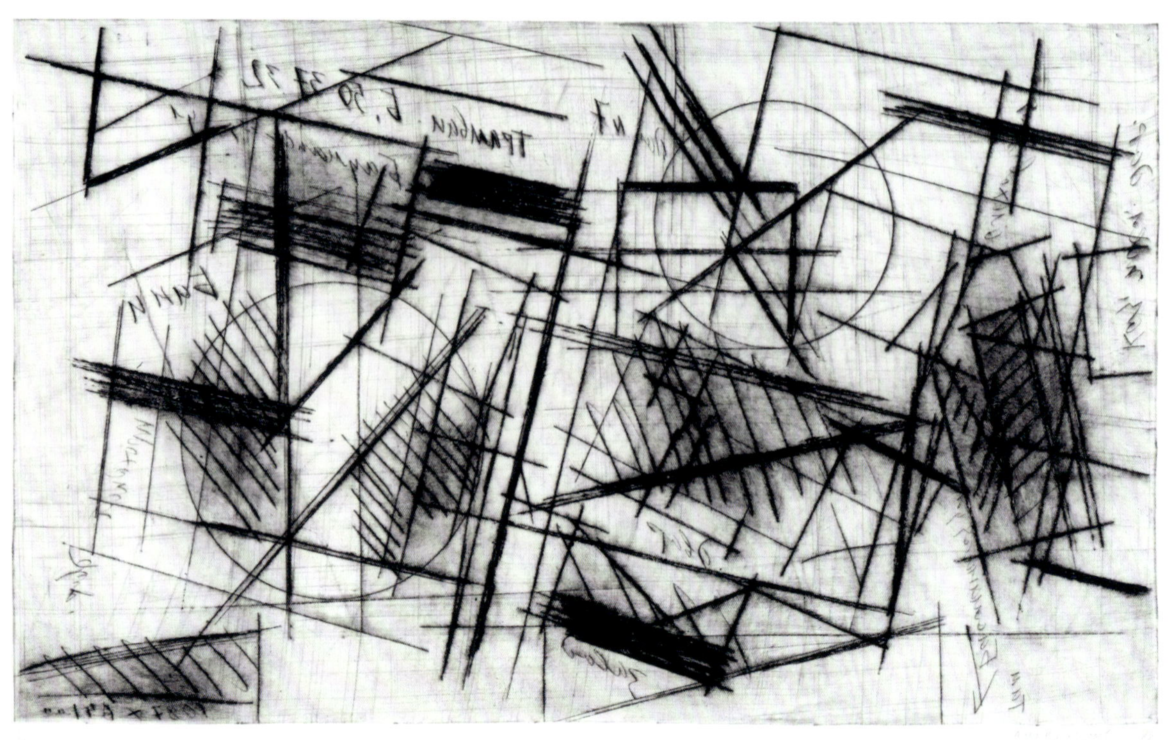

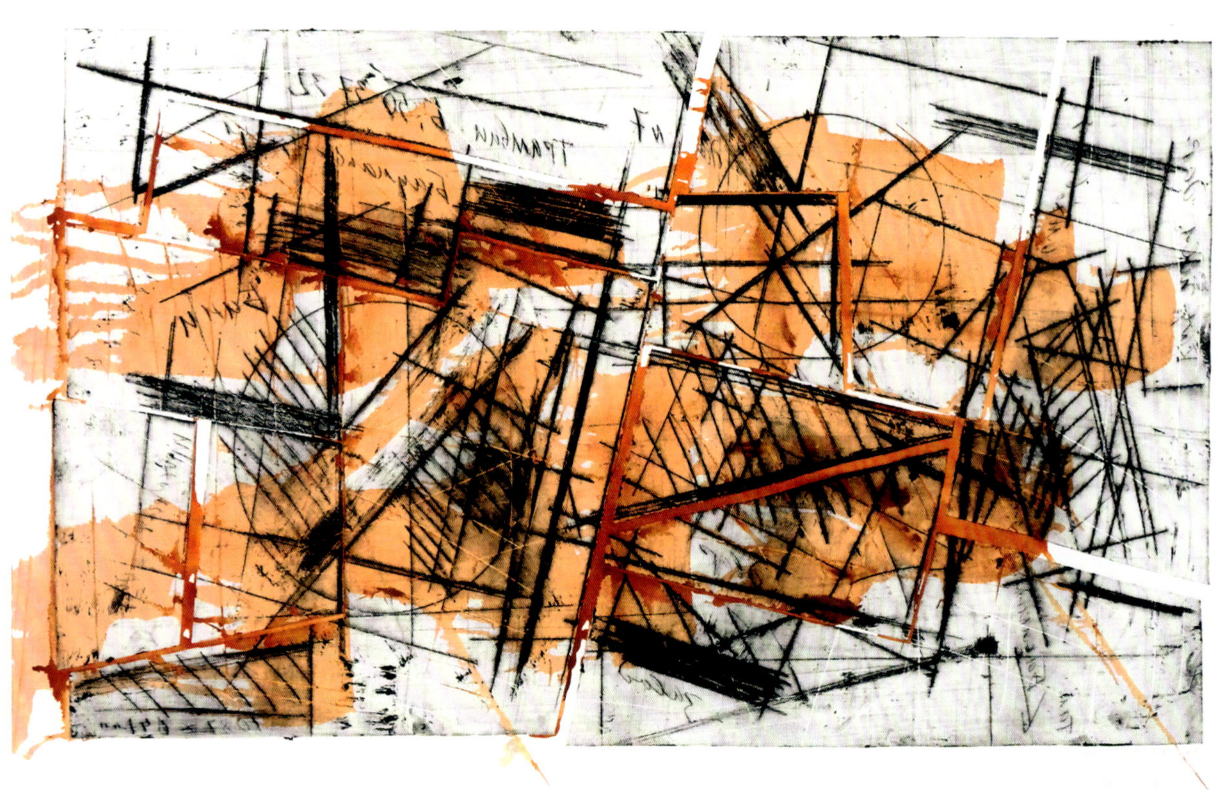

Oleg Kudryashov (born 1932)
Diptych No.21 1982
Drypoint on paper (i) and drypoint and gouache on paper (ii) Support, each: 71.9 × 121.7

The two images comprising *Diptych No.21* represent Moscow, Oleg Kudryashov's native city, and London, his adopted hometown. The artist used a separate metal plate for each image. While the plate representing Moscow was printed in black, Kydryashov added hand colouring to the 'London' plate using gouache, a medium similar to watercolour with a more opaque consistency.

Kudryashov's approach to printmaking is distinctive. For prints like *Diptych No.21* he rejected the use of chemicals or specialist printmaking tools, choosing instead to work directly on metal plates using non-specialist implements, particularly needles and brushes.[4] The drypoint technique appealed to him for its direct simplicity. Kudryashov also avoided editioning his prints.

Vija Celmins (born 1938)
December 1984 1985
Mezzotint on paper 40.7 × 38.8

Vija Celmins, who was born in Latvia and grew up in the United States, has made use of various different printmaking techniques to further her monochromatic exploration of seas, night skies and spider webs.

In this piece, part of the jointly owned Tate and National Galleries of Scotland 'Artist Rooms' collection, Celmins collaborated with the master printer Doris Simmelink to create a quietly dramatic image of a starry sky. Starting with a roughened metal plate that would print entirely black if not worked into further, Celmins created her image by burnishing (or polishing) each star until she had created the correct level of brightness. The sparkle of each star is actually the white of the paper seen in relation to the greyer tones and the black of the background.

December 1984 was published by Gemini Graphic Editions Limited in Los Angeles in an edition of twenty-five.

Susan Rothenberg (1945–2020)
Mezzo Fist #1 1990
Mezzotint on paper 49.5 × 49.5

This mezzotint demonstrates how artists using the technique work from dark to light, building up the image from a dark background. Here this has the effect of creating a shadowy, mysterious figure, characterised by the scratchy metal-on-metal lines that create a white halo around the face and – more significantly – the 'fist' of the title. The human figure was Susan Rothenberg's key subject matter at this time, and she was particularly interested in portraying the figure in motion. In this print, the artist's marks hint at the movement of the fist and arm, suggesting the figure is in the process of punching its own face.

The availability of machine-roughened mezzotint plates means artists like Rothenberg can work from dark to light without the excessive physical work required in previous centuries to prepare the plate for mezzotint. Today, an artist can purchase a plate prepared with the correct surface texture to print black and simply work the 'lights' into it as they desire.

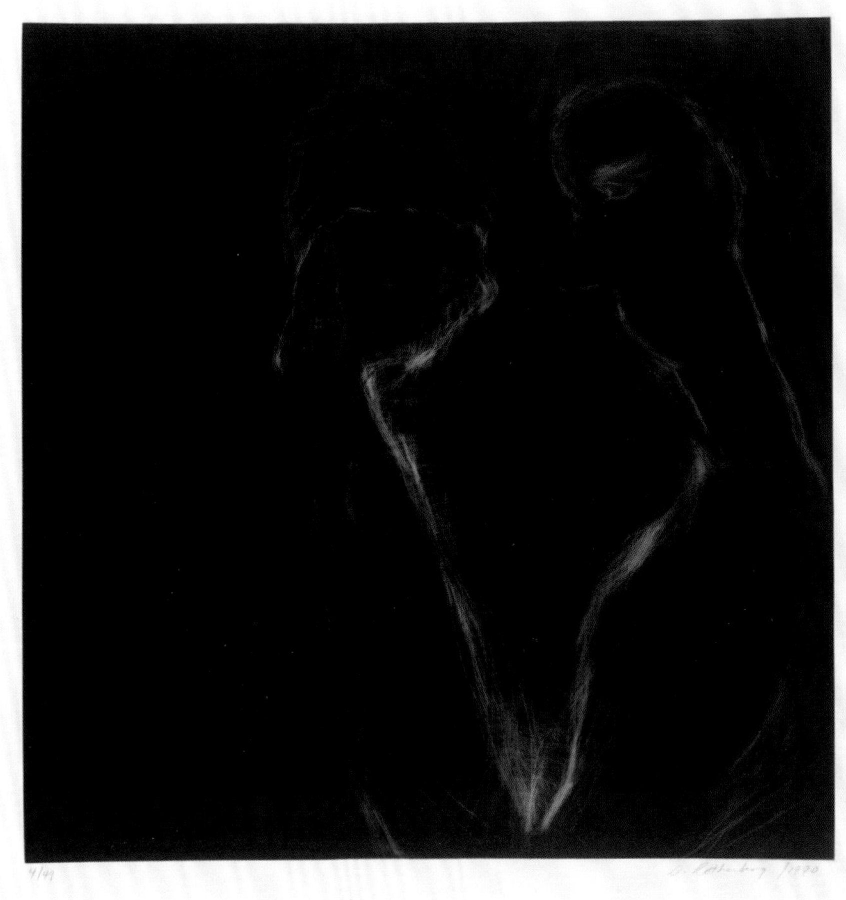

Louise Bourgeois (1911–2010)
Untitled (Safety Pins) 1991
Drypoint on paper, state iii/iii 30.3 × 37.9

The Paris-born artist Louise Bourgeois is famous for her huge sculptures of spiders. Her numerous prints, on the other hand, are probably the least-known part of her oeuvre. Although Bourgeois began making prints in 1939, studying at Atelier 17 with Stanley William Hayter (see p.60) after the Second World War, she abandoned printmaking almost completely from 1947. She returned to it with seriousness from the 1980s, becoming particularly interested in drypoint, preferring the direct method of marking metal with metal over the use of acid required for etching. She noted the potential for violence when working with a sharp metal drypoint needle, calling printmaking a positive exercise in aggression.[5]

The spiralling marks in *Untitled (Safety Pins)* display the slightly ragged edges characteristic of drypoint, which drives the 'burr' of the metal around the lines up into its edges. They are certainly suggestive of safety pins, about which the artist said: 'I like the idea of the safety pin ... it is dangerous, but it also holds up my whole attire. Safety pins can keep things together ... they can prevent catastrophe.'[6]

This print was published in an edition of sixty in 1991; Bourgeois added the title *Safety Pins* a little later, in 1993.

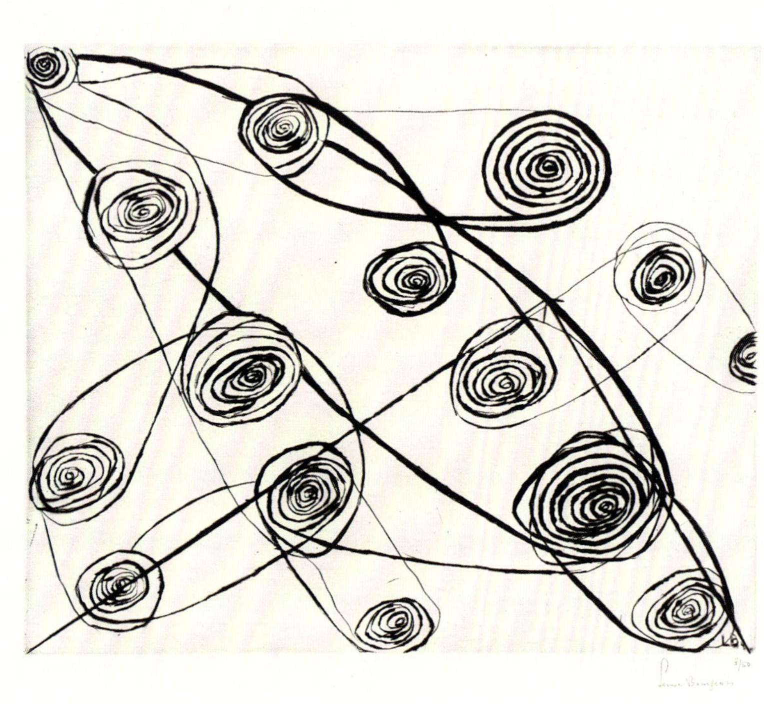

Ana Maria Pacheco (born 1943)

As Proezas de Macunaíma 10 1995

Drypoint on paper 8 × 9.3

The Brazilian-born artist Ana Maria Pacheco has embraced the techniques of etching, woodcut, lithography and screenprinting within her printmaking practice. For this print she used drypoint, a medium she has compared to the sculptural practice of wood carving in terms of its directness.[7]

This work is from a series of twelve prints responding to *Macunaíma*, a seminal Brazilian text by Mário de Andrade first published in Portuguese in 1928. The story follows the eponymous shape-shifting hero who loses an amulet given to him by his wife before her death. To retrieve it, he leaves his home in the Amazon and travels to São Paulo. Many of the characters and events he encounters along the way are drawn from Brazilian folklore, also a key inspiration for Pacheco. This particular image references an 1820–3 painting by Goya, *Saturn Devouring his Son*. Pacheco's *As Proezas de Macunaíma* was printed in an edition of twenty-five.

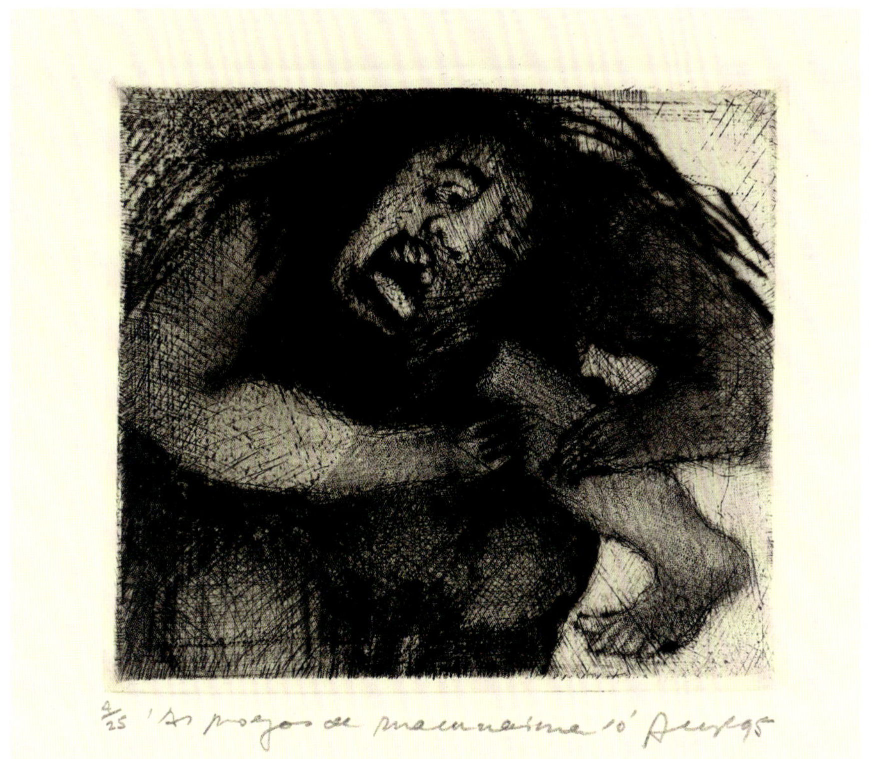

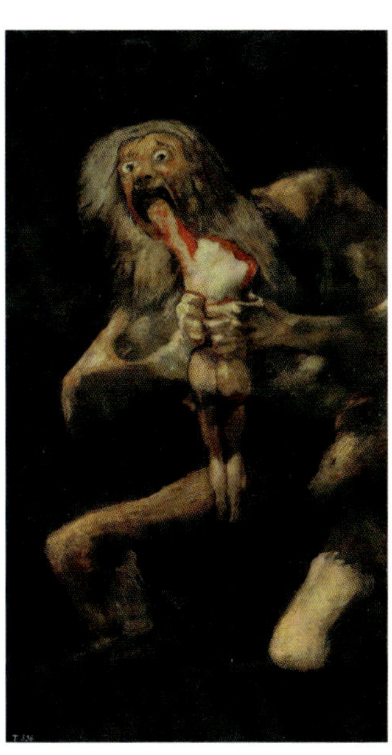

Goya, *Saturn Devouring his Son,* 1820–3, Museo del Prado, Madrid

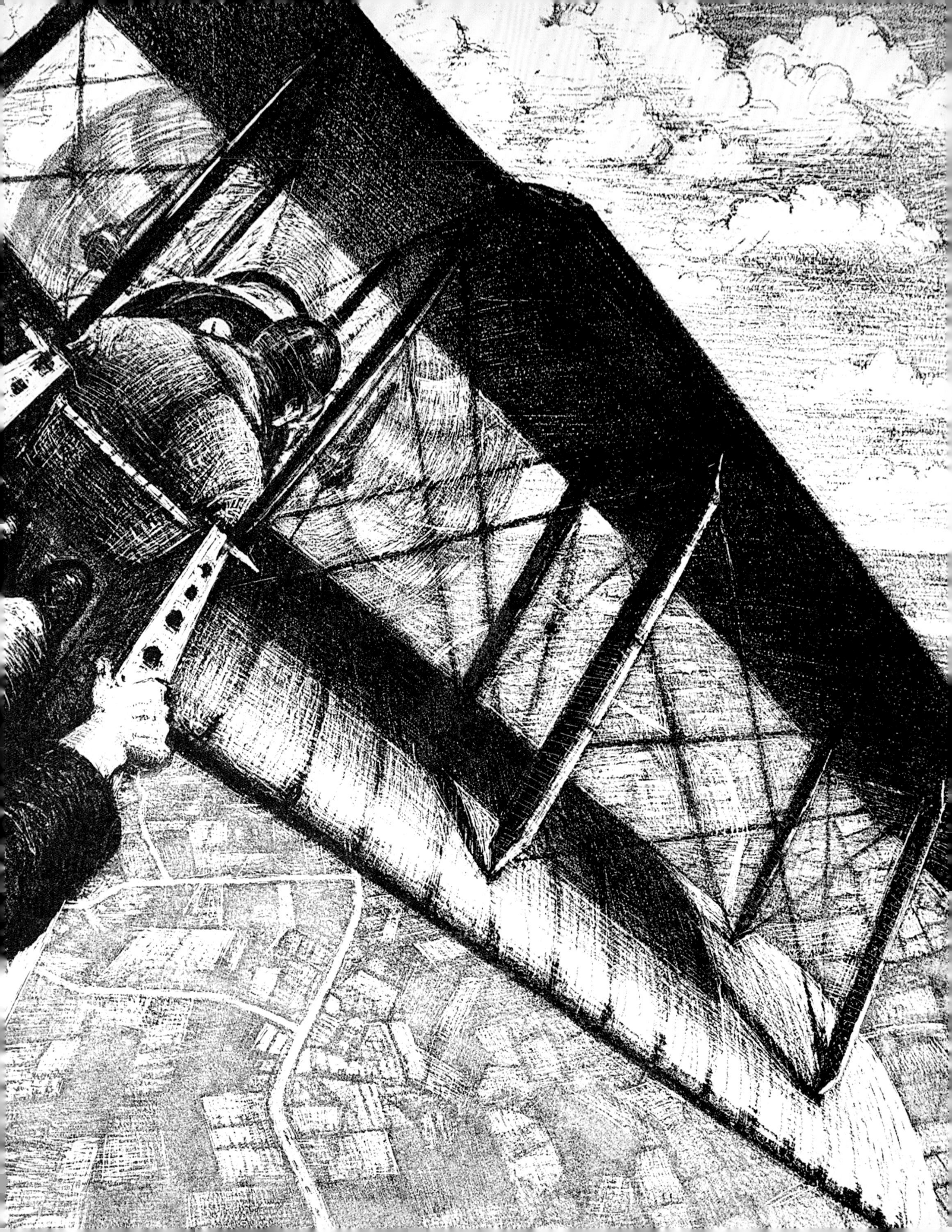

5 Drawing on Stone

Christopher Richard Wynne Nevinson *Banking at 4000 Feet* 1917 (detail)

5 Drawing on Stone

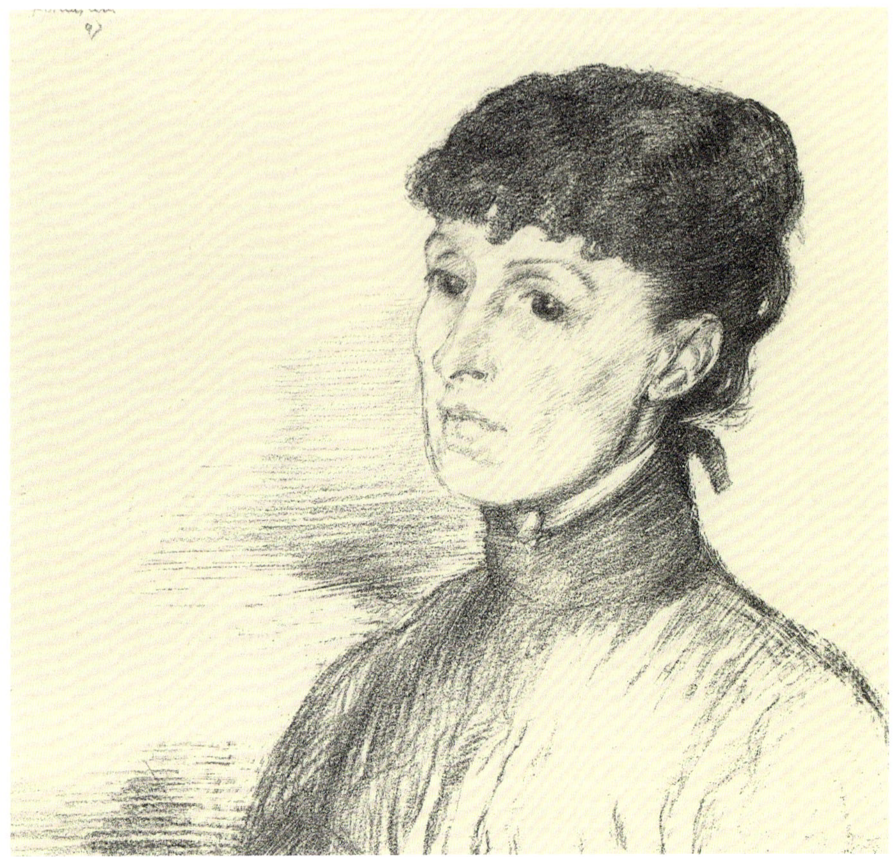

Detail from William Rothenstein, *Mrs Meynell* 1897

Lithography involves making marks on a flat stone (or sometimes a plate) using a greasy crayon or liquid. Once the image has been chemically fixed onto the stone, the surface is moistened with water. Lithography relies on the fact that oil and water repel each other: when printing ink is added, it is repelled by the stone's watery surface, but held by the artist's greasy marks. When the stone is passed through a flat-bed printing press along with paper, a print of the artist's marks is made. A key characteristic of lithography is the direct reproduction of the artist's marks, which the printing process does little to alter – 'drawn' marks generally look just the same on a lithographic print as they did when first drawn onto the stone (or, sometimes, a special transfer paper).

Colour Lithography involves preparing a separate lithographic stone for each colour used in the print.

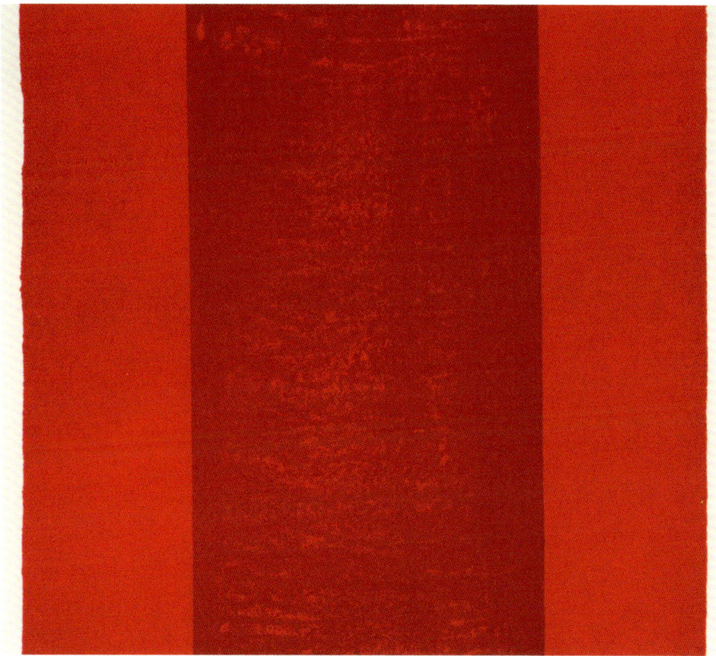

Detail from Barnett Newman, *Canto XIV*, from *Eighteen Cantos* 1963–4

Mass Reproduction and Photolithography

Artists' lithographs are usually made in limited editions to ensure their rarity. But of all the print techniques described in this book, lithography is most suited to – and most commonly used for – mass production. The print surface can be re-used an almost unlimited number of times without affecting the quality of the resulting image, making it possible to produce (or reproduce) images en masse. Artists such as Nina Vatolina exploited this potential to produce very large editions to make posters and in postwar Britain the 'School Prints' scheme brought prints by artists including Georges Braque and Picasso to the walls of British schools.

> VATOLINA p.129

> BRAQUE p.131

The potential for mass reproduction of imagery has also been utilised within the larger world of commercial printing, to print books, magazines or posters. In these cases, images tend to be transferred to the print surface using 'photolithography', which avoids the need for original, handmade images. These images can be printed first onto a rubber cylinder, which then 'offsets' (or transfers) the image onto paper or another surface, such as fabric. This method is still commonly used in commercial printing today. Some twentieth-century artists have also employed photolithography within their prints, using photo-mechanically reproduced imagery alongside more traditional direct mark-making.

Artists and Lithography

Lithography was invented at the close of the eighteenth century by Alois Senefelder, a German author and actor, as a cheap method of reproducing his theatrical works. The new medium rose to prominence during the following century, and in France it began to be used by artists, including Théodore Géricault, Eugène Delacroix and Honoré Daumier. The earliest French example illustrated here is a late nineteenth-century colour lithograph by the post-impressionist artist Paul Cézanne. Lithography also began to find favour with artists working on the other side of the English Channel. A high point for the method's use in Britain came during the First World War, when the Ministry of Information commissioned various artists to make lithographs in support of the war effort; these are represented here by a striking image by Christopher Richard Wynne Nevinson.

> CÉZANNE p.123
> NEVINSON p.124

It was during the second half of the twentieth century, though, that lithography became dominant as a technique for artists' prints in Britain. Tate's collection is particularly strong in this area, with many fine examples arriving in 1975 via the Curwen Studio Gift, one of the founding gifts of the modern print collection. This grouping includes hundreds of examples of lithographs by British artists, from Henry Moore to Barbara Hepworth. European artists based in London, such as the experimental Swedish printmaker Birgit Skiöld, are also represented. From the 1970s Tate also actively purchased lithographs to supplement its holdings, and many works by international modern artists were added to the collection in this fashion, such as a group by the Russian artist El Lissitzky.

> MOORE p.139
> HEPWORTH p.146
> SKIÖLD p.141
> EL LISSITZKY p.126

A European method by origin, lithography has, like other western print techniques, also flourished in other parts of the world. Particularly notable locations include Mexico, where early twentieth-century artists including José Clemente Orozco and Diego Rivera used the process in new ways, and the United States, which has produced some of the most experimental and inventive names within the history of the medium. While Tate's collection is not yet rich in the former area, it does reflect the significance of North American artists to the medium's development. Key examples included here are by artists ranging from Robert Rauschenberg to Kiki Smith.

> RAUSCHENBERG p.138
> SMITH p.151

William Rothenstein (1872–1945)
Mrs Meynell 1897
Lithograph on paper 13.6 x 15.2

During the nineteenth century, lithography was commonly employed to create collectable sets of prints, such as William Rothenstein's twelve-part series, *English Portraits*. This sensitively drawn portrait from the series portrays Alice Meynell, an English poet and essayist. She was one of only two women to be represented in Rothenstein's series of 'notable people'. Although little known now, Meynell's verses were popular in her day, when she was considered a possible contender for the position of poet laureate.

English Portraits was printed by T. Way and published by Grant Richards in an edition of 750. Many copies were destroyed by a fire at the binders, so only a small proportion of the 750 actually appeared.

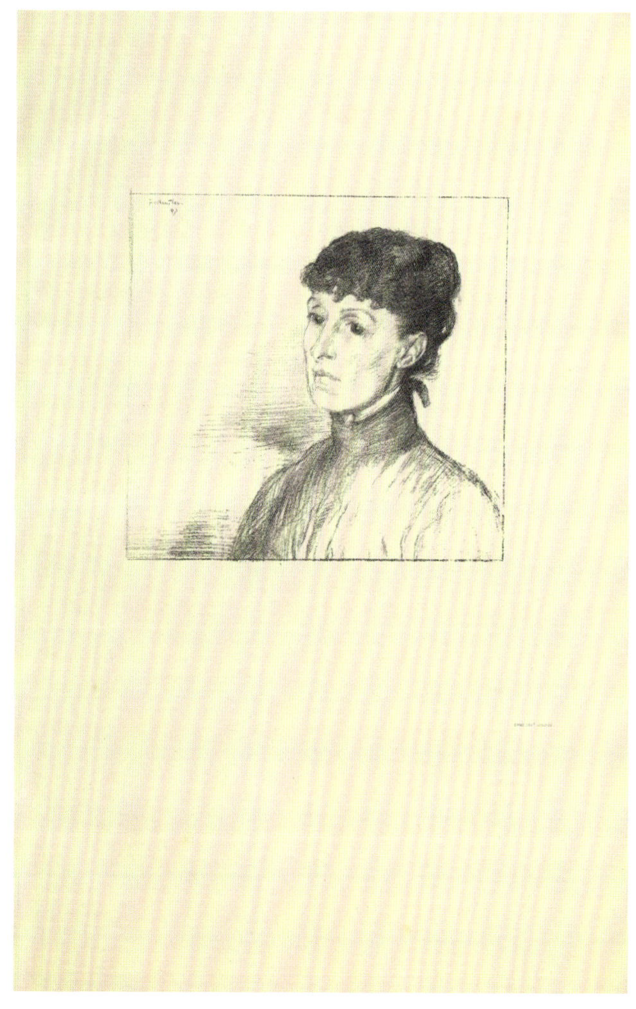

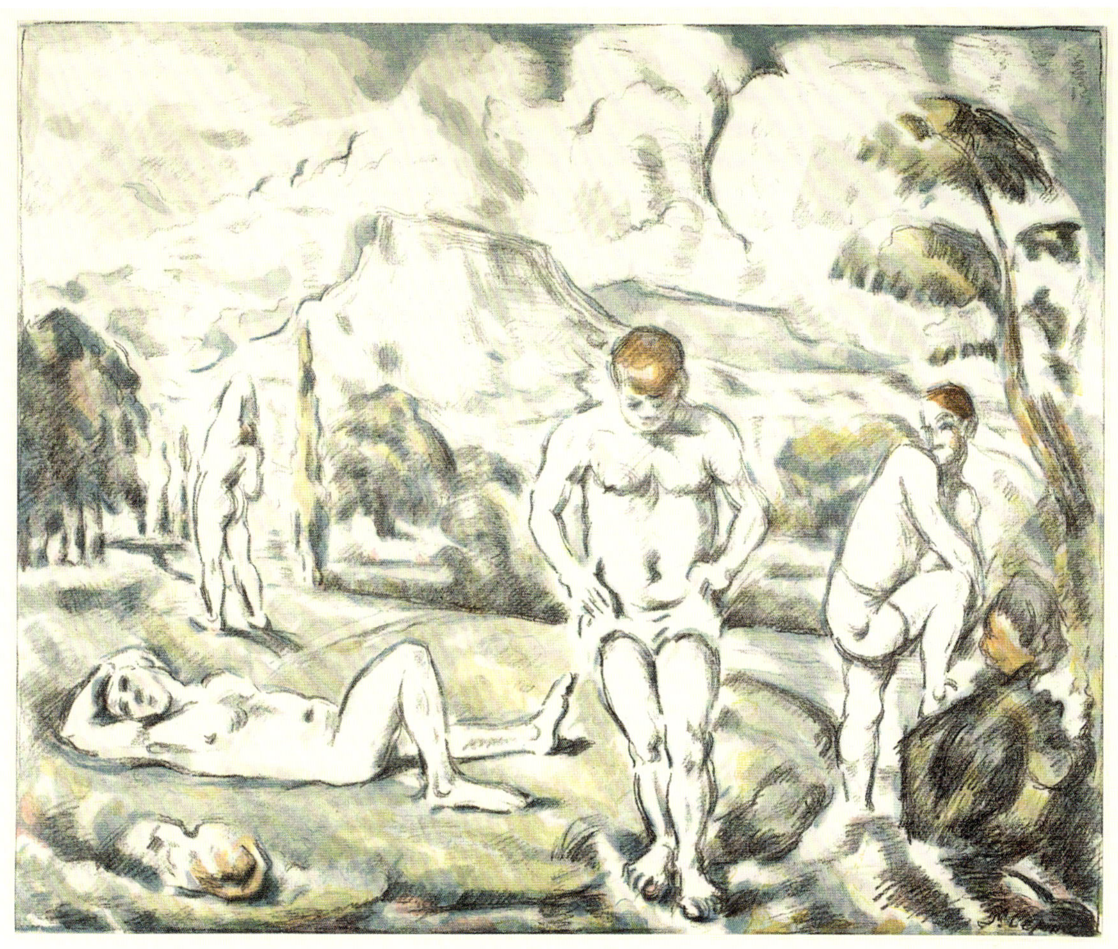

Paul Cézanne (1839–1906)
The Large Bathers c.1898
Lithograph on paper 41 × 50.7

This impressive colour print is based on an oil painting of the same name now in the Barnes Foundation, Pennsylvania: at the time the canvas was one of Paul Cézanne's best-known works. Although it echoes the painted composition, the print was designed as a discrete work, very different in visual effect to the painting. Lighter and less highly finished, the lithograph is characterised by Cézanne's fluid marks, drawn with the lithographic crayon.

Cézanne drew his design on a special transfer paper, which allowed it to be transferred onto a lithographic stone without reversing the image (reversal occurs in direct stone lithography). His design was then printed in black, and he used watercolour to work up a 'proof' of the print as he envisaged it in colour. The master printer Auguste Clot then prepared three colour stones based on the colours the artist had chosen so that the print could be produced as a colour lithograph.

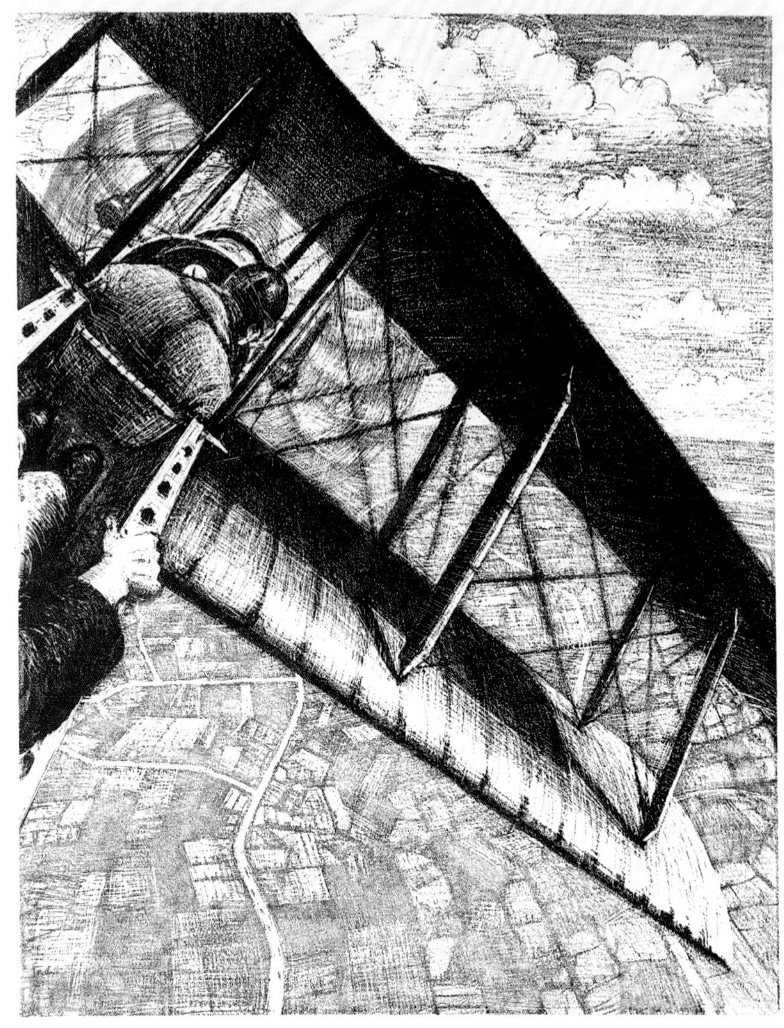

Christopher Richard Wynne Nevinson (1889–1946)
Banking at 4000 Feet 1917
Lithograph on paper 40.3 × 31.6

Christopher Richard Wynne Nevinson is best known as a war artist. This print is from *Britain's Efforts and Ideals,* a series of lithographs commissioned by the Ministry of Information in 1917. Various artists were asked to produce prints exploring different aspects of the war effort: this composition is from a group by Nevinson entitled *Making Aircraft*. In the prints, Nevinson, a skilled printmaker, documented the process of building an aircraft from manufacture through to flight. His chosen viewpoint for this scene is almost dizzying: the plane leans sideways, with the distant roads and fields appearing like a patchwork below.

The prints were published in an edition of 200 by the Fine Art Society, London, where they were also exhibited in July 1917.

Henri Matisse (1869–1954)
Little Aurore 1923
Lithograph on paper 13.6 × 20.6

In the 1920s Henri Matisse returned to lithography, a technique he had first experimented with in 1906 and 1914, with a new seriousness. He continued to focus on the human form, but his approach became more tonal and rooted in realism, something well demonstrated by *Little Aurore.* The decorative background is typical of Matisse's work of this period.

Matisse resisted the emphasis on making colour prints that preoccupied so many of his contemporaries, choosing instead to explore lithography's more traditional 'drawing-like' qualities,[1] and this print has the feel of a direct chalk drawing. Discussing his approach to working with female models, Matisse later wrote: 'My models, human figures, are never just "extras" in an interior. They are the principal theme in my work. I depend absolutely on my model, whom I observe at liberty, and then I decide in the pose which best suits *her nature*'.[2] *Little Aurore* was printed in Paris and published in an edition of fifty.

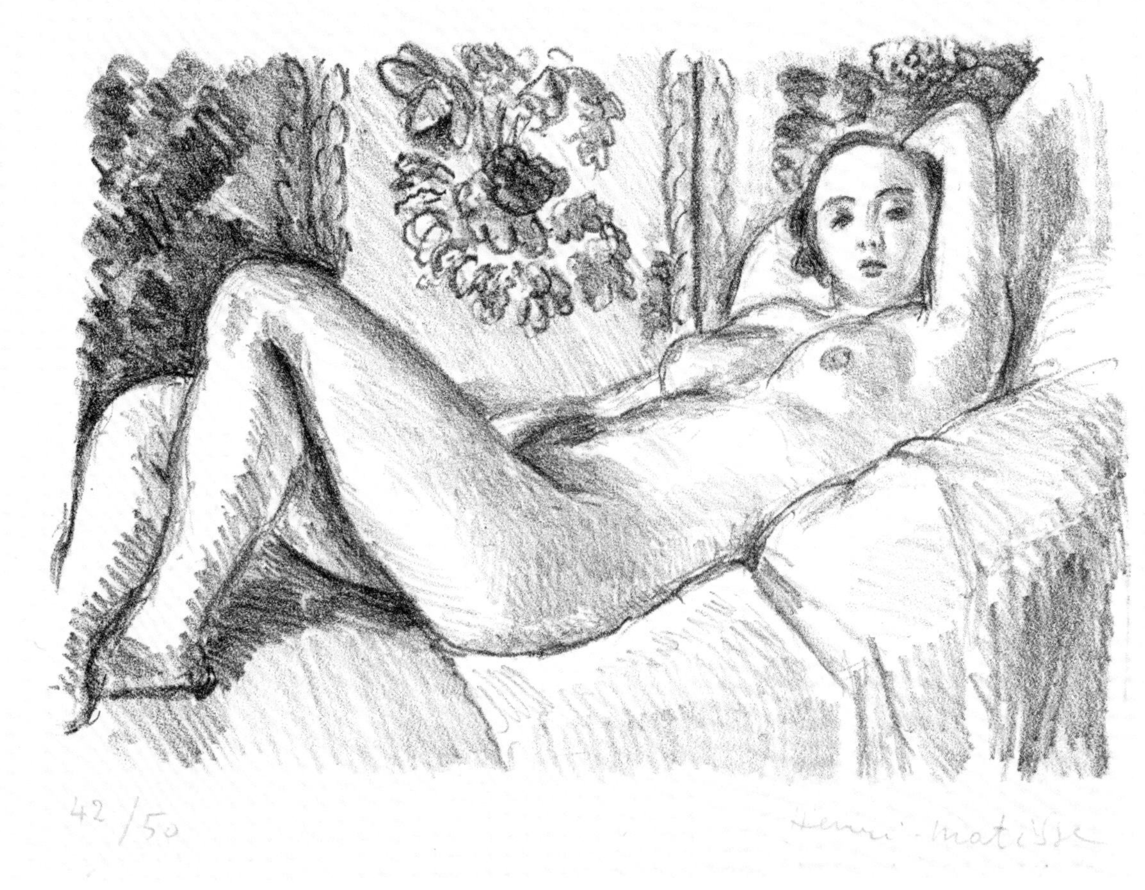

El Lissitzky (1890–1941)

1. Part of the Show Machinery, from *Victory over the Sun* 1923

Lithograph on paper 51.2 × 43

El Lissitzky was an important figure within both the Western European and the Russian art scenes. His work was diverse, encompassing painting, photography, photomontage, architecture and exhibition design, as well as lithography.

This print is from a series Lissitzky designed which imagined a mechanical theatre version of an existing opera, *Victory over the Sun*. The title page for the print series reads: 'The plastic form of the electro-mechanical peepshow Victory over the Sun from the opera written by A. Krutschonjch Moscow 1913.'[3] The artist emphasised that his aim with the prints was 'not to reform something which already exists, but to bring something else into existence.'[4] The present image, which takes stage design into the realms of abstraction and artistic invention, includes a number of reimagined characters from the opera: the 'Elocutionist', 'New Man', 'Globetrotter' and 'Gravediggers' are all reinterpreted as futuristic forms.

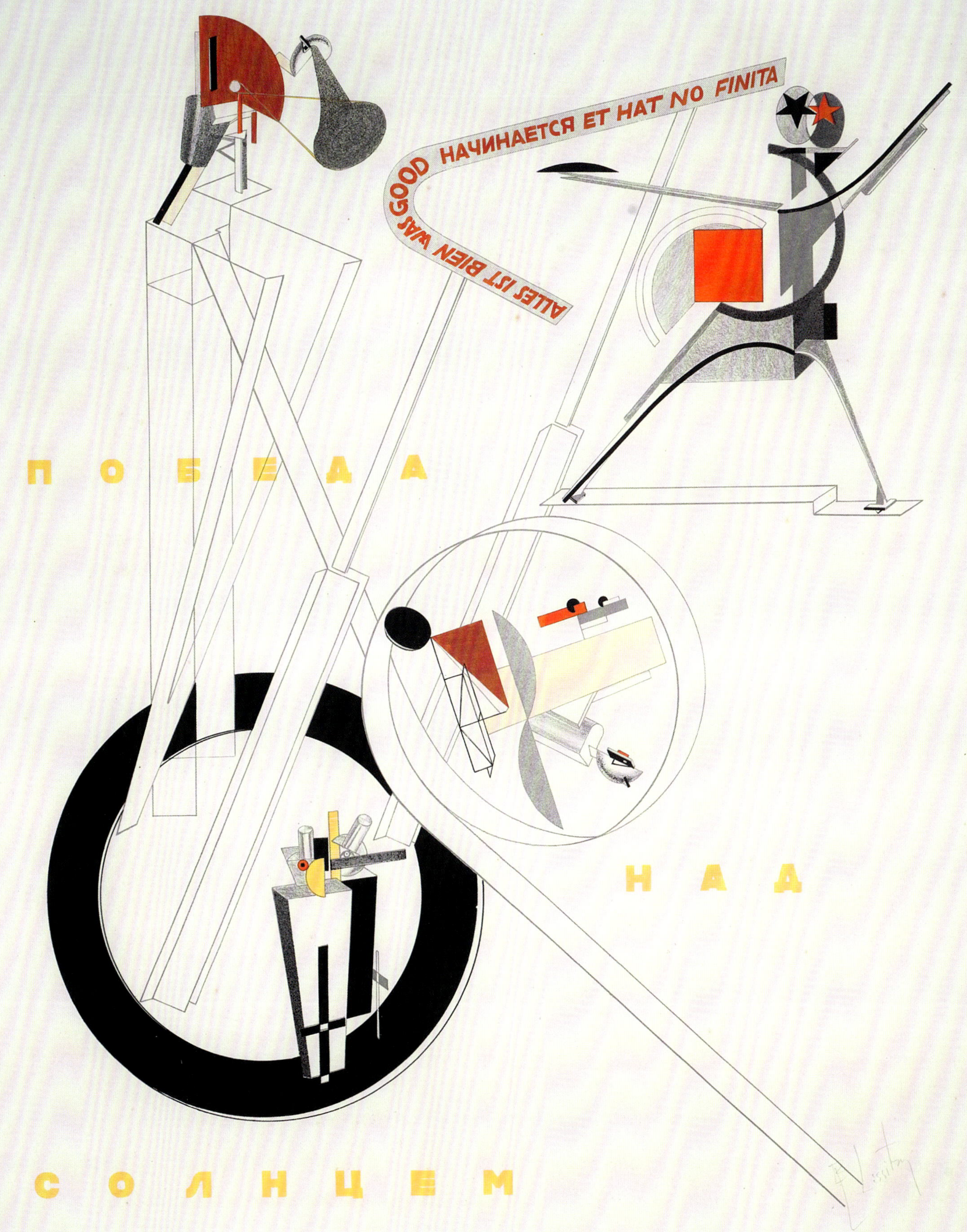
ALLES IST BIEN WAS GOOD НАЧИНАЕТСЯ ET HAT NO FINITA
ПОБЕДА
НАД
СОЛНЦЕМ

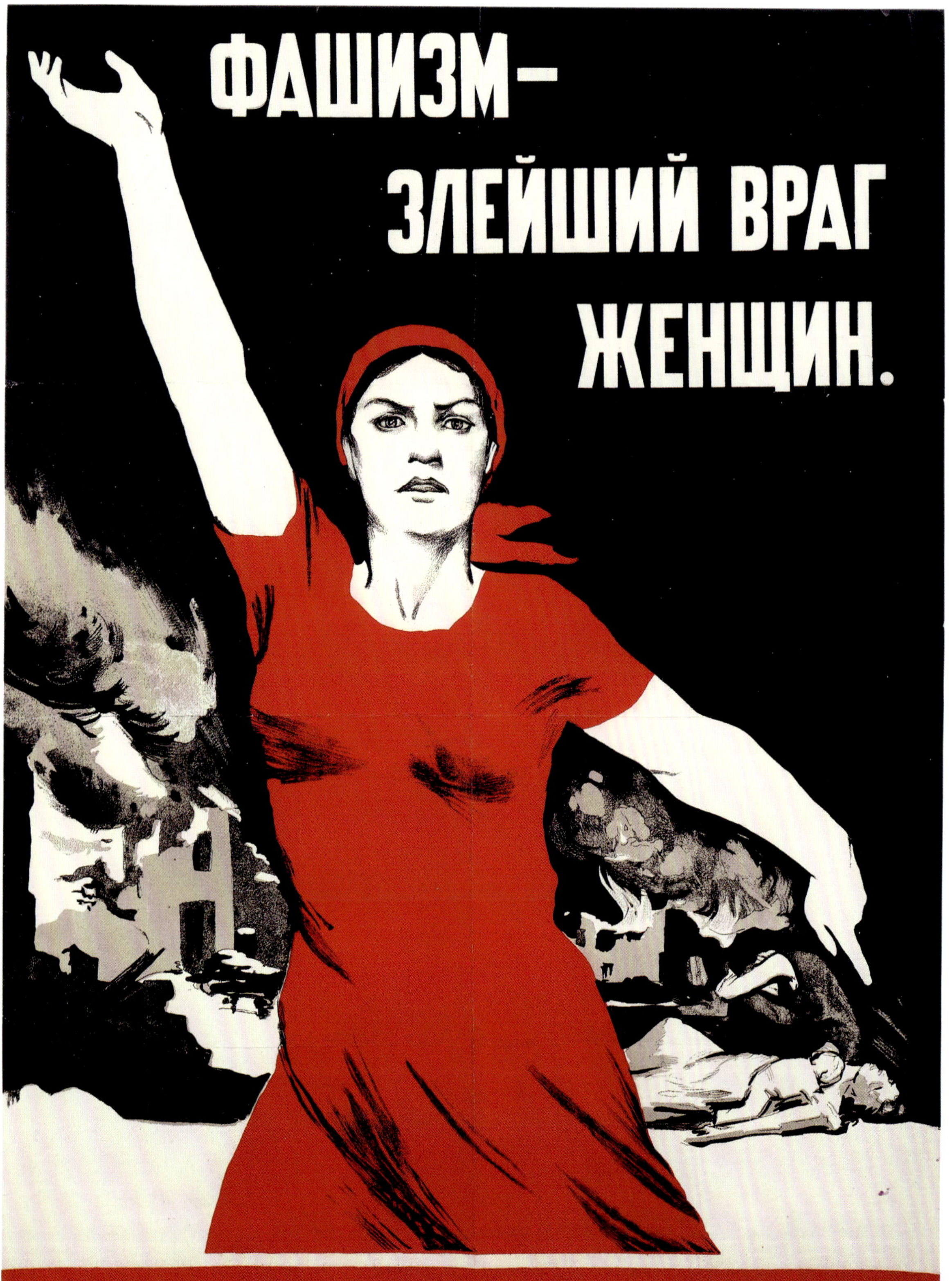
ФАШИЗМ–
ЗЛЕЙШИЙ ВРАГ
ЖЕНЩИН.
ВСЕ НА БОРЬБУ С ФАШИЗМОМ!

Nina Vatolina (1915–2002)
Fascism – The Most Evil Enemy of Women. Everyone to the Struggle against Fascism! 1941
Lithograph on paper 86 × 58.9

Although the more applied use of printmaking – in this case for poster design – is not a general focus or strength of Tate's collection, the David King Collection of Russian Revolutionary Posters forms a notable exception. This poster by Nina Vatolina, a painter who became better known for her political posters, was published in August 1941, five weeks after the Nazi invasion of the Soviet Union. Its anti-Nazi message is clear. It also demonstrates the role of artists and propaganda in Joseph Stalin's Soviet Union.

Vatolina asked her neighbour, whose two sons had already departed for the battlefield, to model for this poster with its mighty, heroic female protagonist, who symbolises the strong women of Russia.[5] While most artists' lithographs are published in limited editions, artist-designed posters could utilise the medium's potential for almost unlimited print runs. This poster had an initial run of 750,000 copies.[6]

Prunella Clough (1919–1999)
Geological Landscape 1949
Lithograph on paper 14.9 × 20.1

Prunella Clough, a British painter and printmaker, created this lithograph in her own studio. Rather than working with a print studio to produce a full edition she simply made a few impressions using her own printing press.

In her lithographs Clough explored the same concerns that characterise her drawings and paintings. She focused on creating interesting textures and used distinctive combinations of colour and shape to create semi-abstract images. While she often explored manmade and industrial forms, in *Geological Landscape* she created an image that seems to show a more natural landscape: hills, sun, water and reflections are all implied in Clough's warmly toned, but almost monochromatic, image.

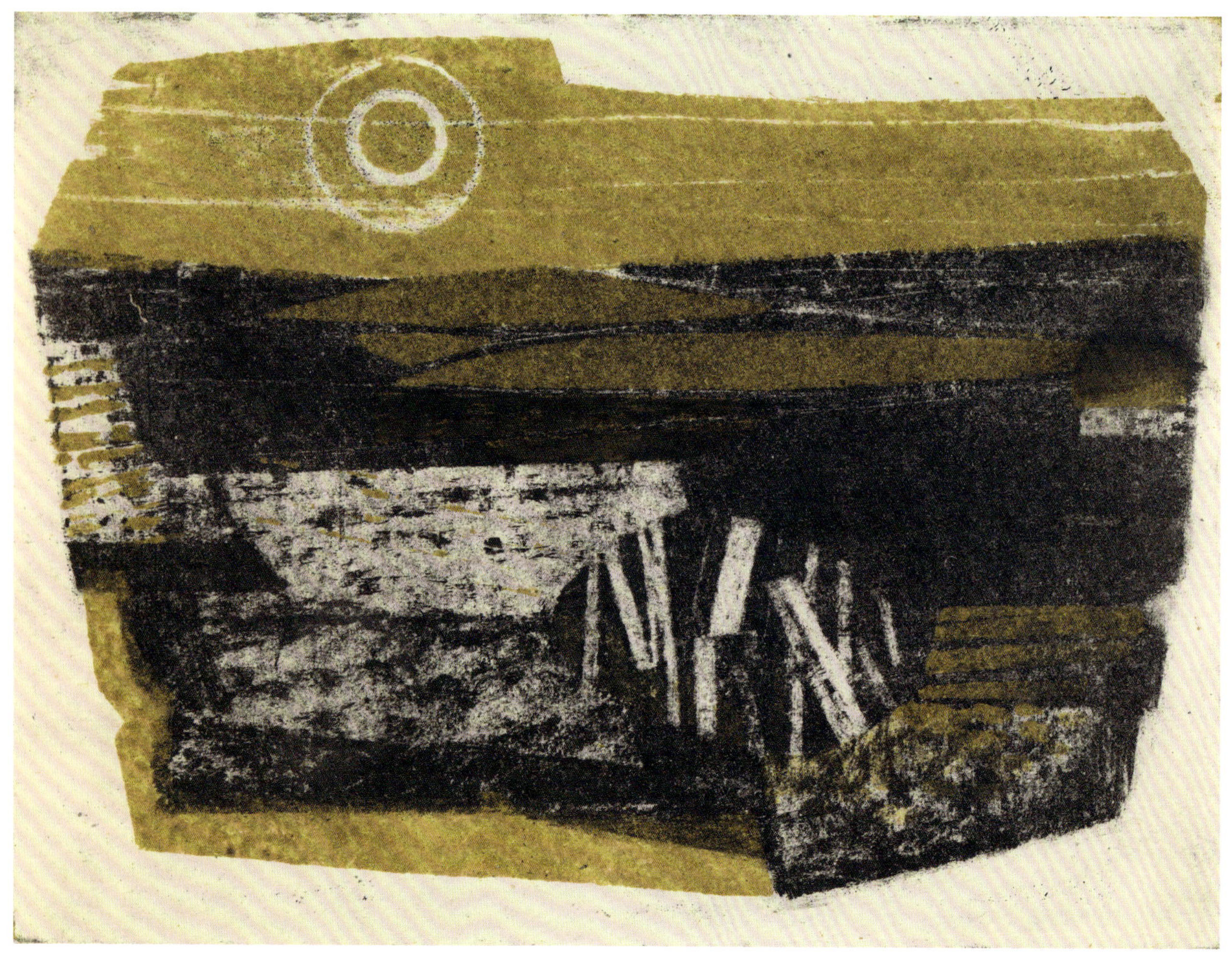

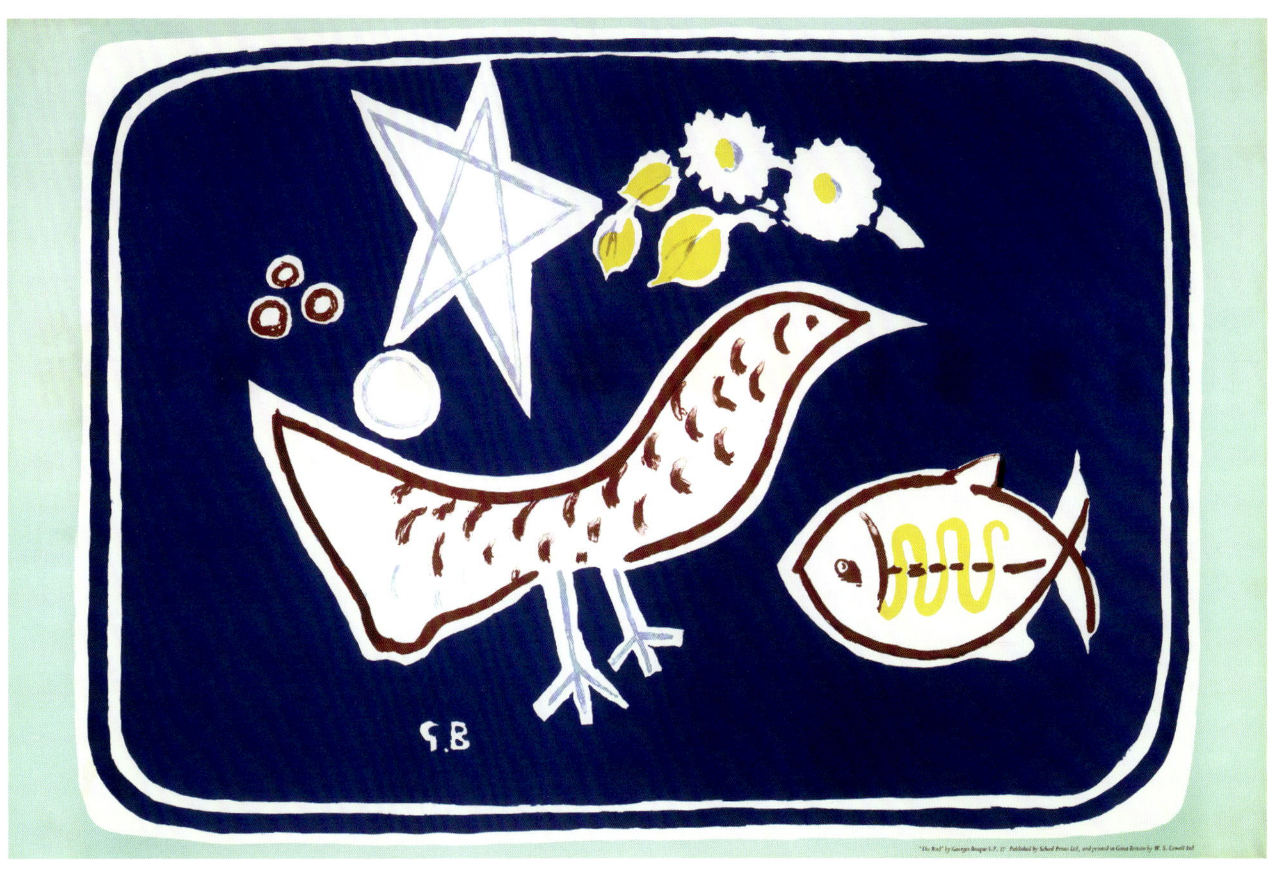

Georges Braque (1882–1963)
The Bird 1949
Lithograph on paper 49.8 × 76.2

The Bird is an example of a print made with an educational purpose in mind. 'School Prints' like this one were commissioned by the arts campaigner Brenda Rawnsley as part of a scheme to bring original lithographs by leading contemporary artists to schools across Britain. In contrast to most of the lithographs included here, the School Prints utilised lithography's potential for mass production, and were published in a large edition with the aim of reaching as many schools as possible, by being rented out on subscription to education authorities at a low cost.

The French artist Georges Braque, who enjoyed the experimental nature of printmaking, contributed to the 1949 'European' series of School Prints. Matisse, Picasso, Fernand Léger, Raoul Dufy and Henry Moore also made works for this grouping. While the venture did not turn out to be commercially successful, this does not detract from the fact that the bold playfulness of this design would almost certainly have been appreciated by many of the children who saw it each school day. For an example of an etching by Braque, see p.79.

Jean Dubuffet (1901–1985)
Peopling of the Lands 1953
Lithograph on paper 64.5 × 50

The French artist Jean Dubuffet embraced many different artistic mediums. His approach to lithography was experimental, and he used sandpaper and chemicals to alter the surface of his lithographic stones.

This print is from a series made during 'long trial sessions at the printers', when, according to Dubuffet, a 'spirit of improvisation' was required.[7] For this group of prints he used various unconventional materials, including leaves, vegetables, salt and sugar, to imbue the printing surface with different textures. In *Peopling of the Lands,* the grainy surface Dubuffet achieved is suggestive of soil, and the artist's loosely suggested forms represent figures. Tate's copy of the print is one of five proof impressions from outside the main edition of twenty, which were printed and published in Paris.

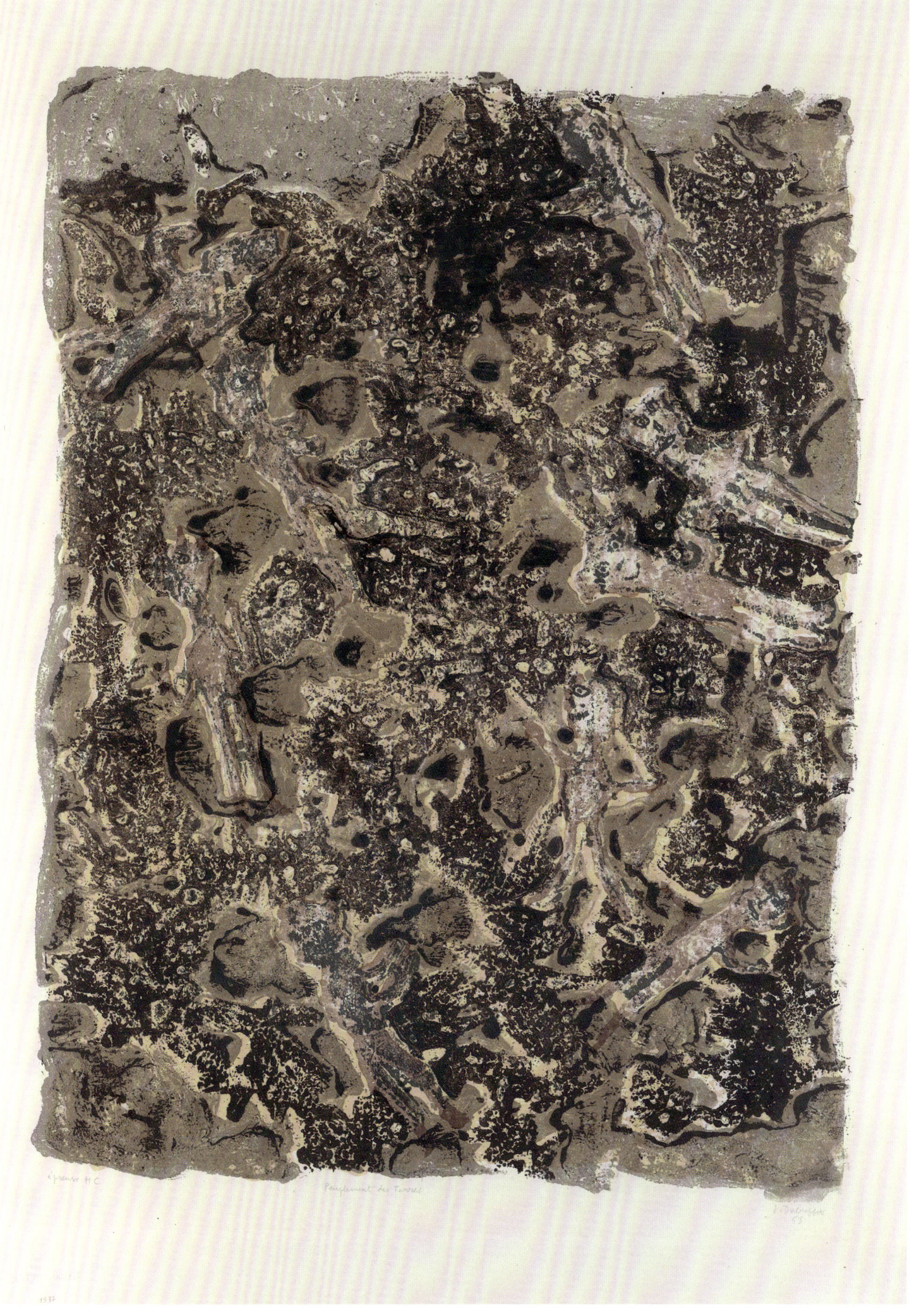
épreuve HC
Peuplement des Terres
J. Dubuffet
53
1537

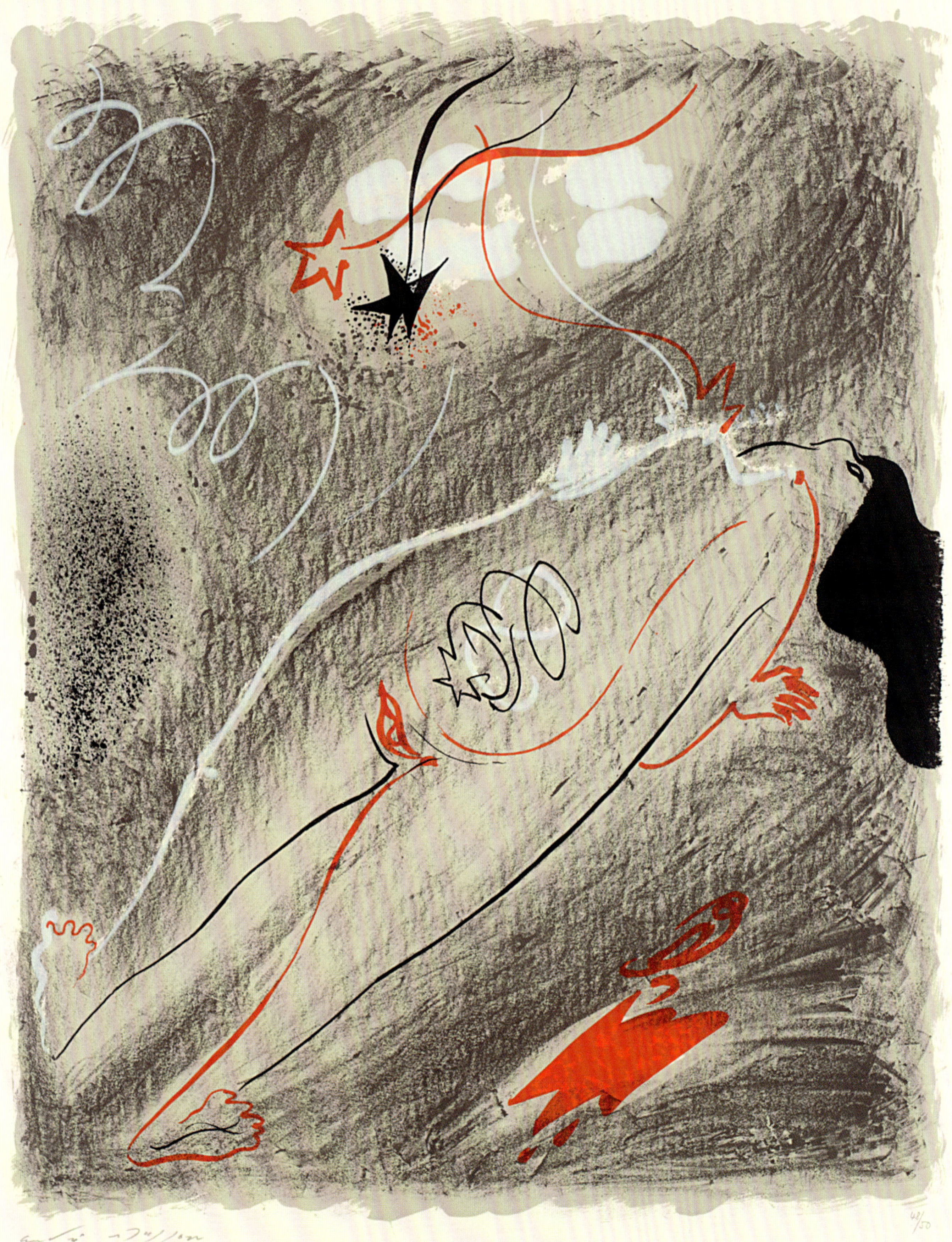

André Masson (1896–1987)
Childbirth 1955
Lithograph on paper 52.8 × 43.5

As well as being a painter, the French artist André Masson was a highly productive printmaker, completing around eight hundred prints during his career. Many were made for illustrated books.

The female form depicted at the centre of this image is accompanied by red details, which, given the subject matter of the title – childbirth – seem suggestive of blood. But the red ink denotes definite forms too, including a star in the upper part of the composition. The woman's womb is also filled with a star, an important motif in this and other works by Masson. Here it seems to connect the human act of childbirth to the cosmos, and possibly also represents the life cycle of birth, reproduction and death. *Childbirth* was printed in an edition of fifty.

Elizabeth Blackadder (1931–2021)
Dark Hill Fifeshire 1960
Lithograph on paper 47.9 × 66.7

The Scottish artist Elizabeth Blackadder, who is known as both a painter and a printmaker, studied and taught at Edinburgh College of Art. She is most famous for her depictions of flowers and plants, but has also frequently been drawn to other subjects, as in this lithograph of the Fife landscape.

This print dates to 1960, when Blackadder made some lithographs at the Curwen Studio. Her approach to the technique was free and painterly, and the print has a fluidity that suggests she made marks directly onto the lithographic stone in the same way she might work spontaneously on a brush drawing or an oil sketch. The dominant dark hill of the title is not formed of solid colour: the darker ink is broken up in places to reveal areas of ominous red.

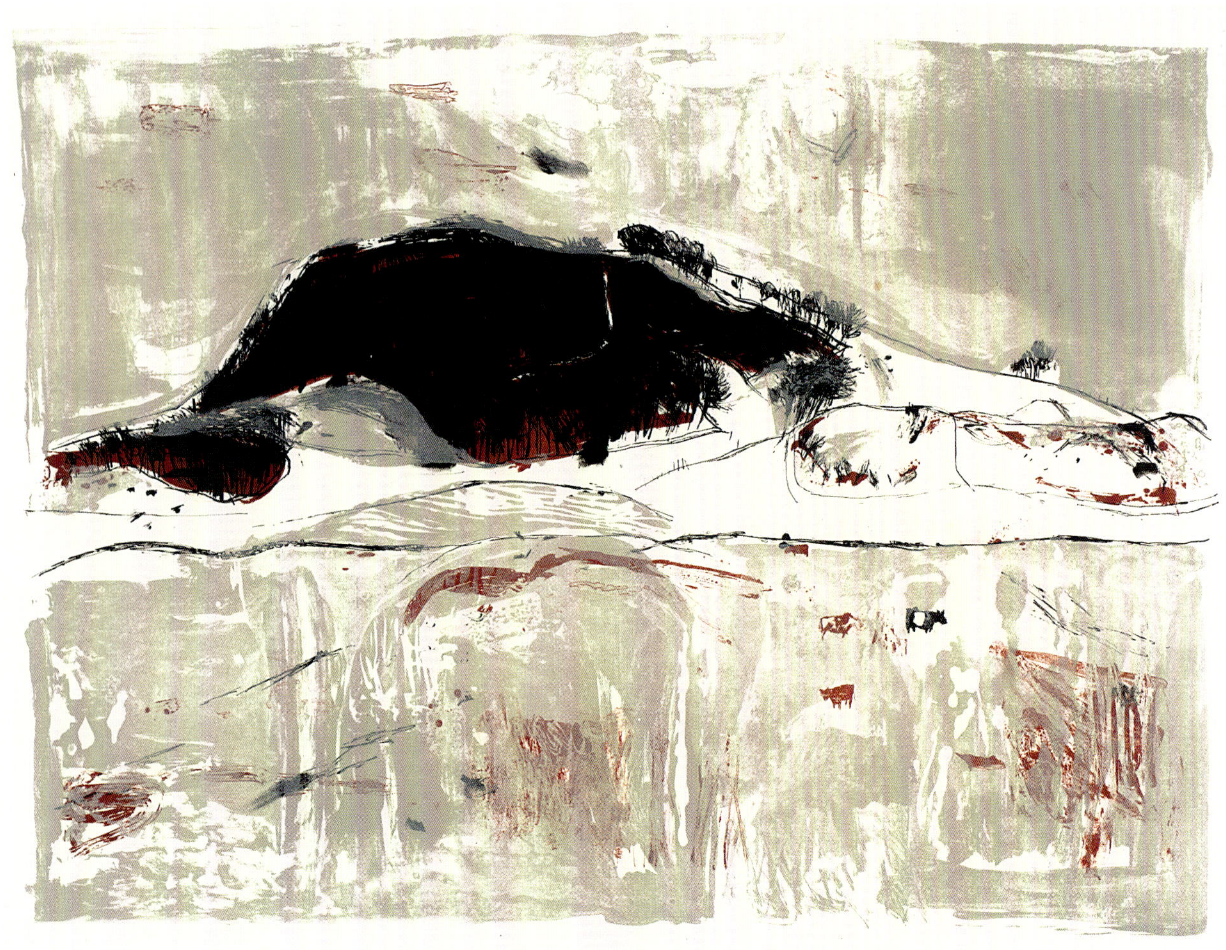

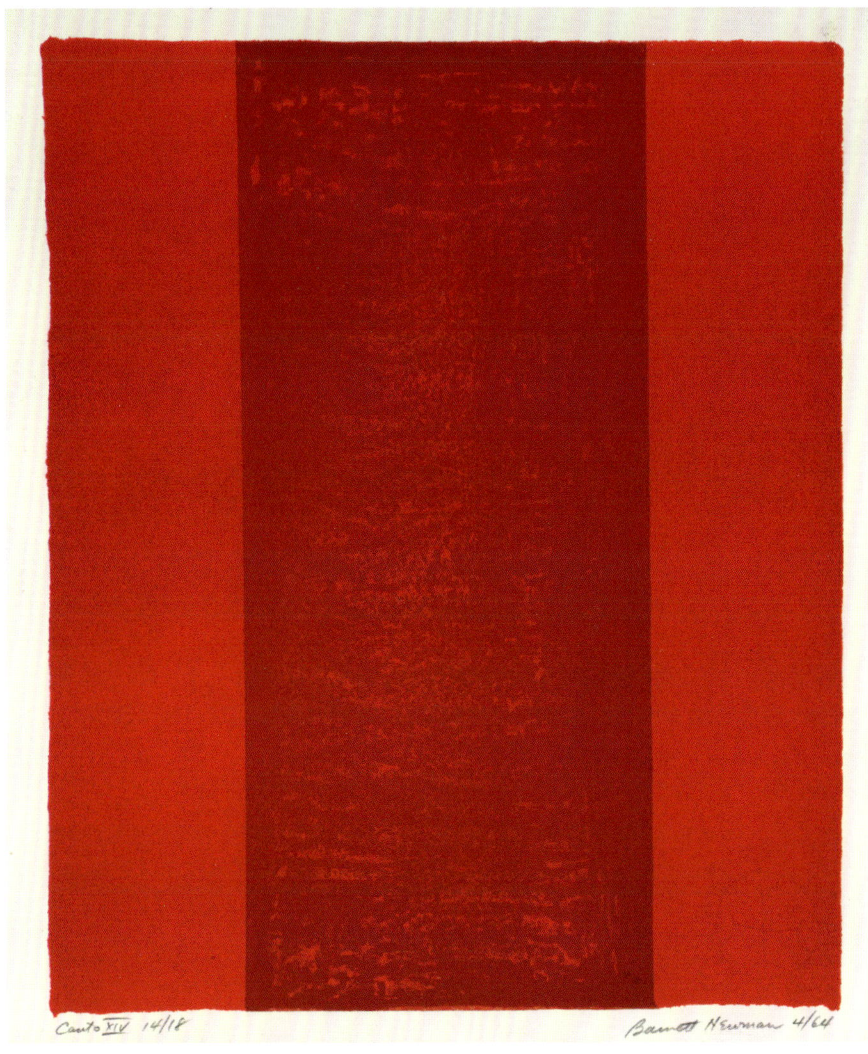

Barnett Newman (1905–1970)
Canto XIV, from *Eighteen Cantos* 1963–4
Lithograph on paper 37.5 × 31.9

The American painter Barnett Newman did not consider himself a printmaker, but he became captivated by the 'instrument' of lithography. He appreciated the medium's complexity and the need to master a different way of working when in the print studio.

Of his eighteen 'cantos', of which this is one, Newman said: 'the prints really started as three, grew to seven, then eleven, then fourteen, and finished as eighteen ... each one different in form, mood, colour, beat, scale and key.'[18] A key concern was colour, and the other cantos are printed in inks ranging from cream through to greys, blues, yellows, and greens and brown. *Canto XIV* was printed with two different lithographic stones, each using a different shade of red ink.

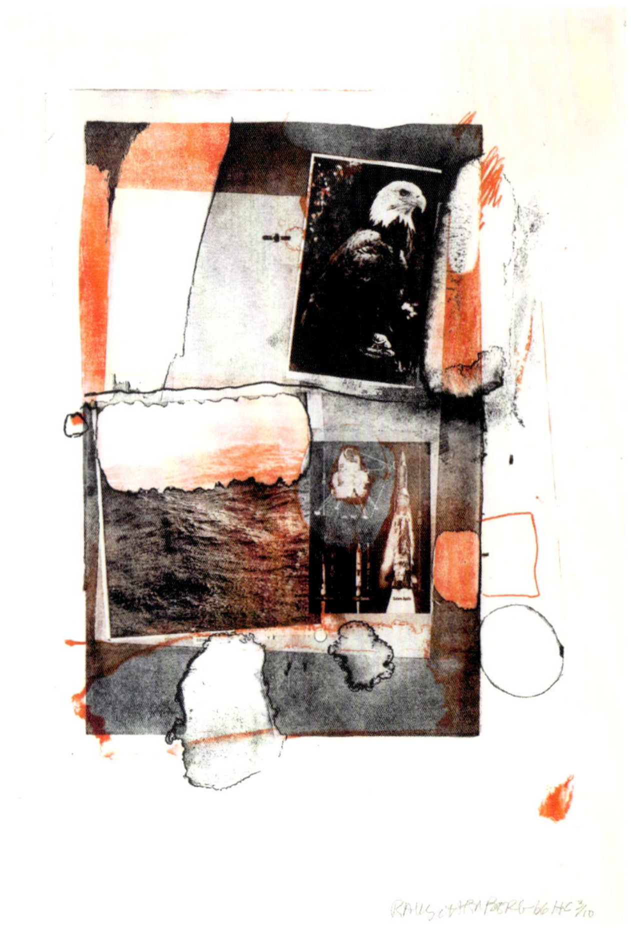

Robert Rauschenberg (1925–2008)
Night Grip 1966
Lithograph on paper 63.3 × 45.7

Robert Rauschenberg began making lithographs in New York in 1962, combining photo-derived images from newspapers and magazines with hand-drawn marks made directly onto the lithographic stone in the traditional manner. *Night Grip*, in which collaged images co-exist with direct artist's marks printed in black and reddish-brown, is an example of this innovative approach.

The photographic images collected in *Night Grip* include America's national emblem, the bald eagle; Rauschenberg also included the eagle in some of his paintings. There is also a view of the sea, and a rocket towards the lower-right. The rocket anticipates Rauschenberg's celebrated *Stoned Moon* series of lithographs (1969), which were made to commemorate the launching of Apollo 11. *Night Grip* was published in an edition of thirty-five for the New Lincoln School in New York, where Rauschenberg's son was a pupil. It was the only lithograph he made in 1966.

Henry Moore (1898–1986)
Reclining Figure 1967
Lithograph on paper 12.1 × 16.8

Although best known as a sculptor, Henry Moore began making prints in his teenage years and remained a keen printmaker throughout his life. His print practice is well represented in the Tate collection thanks to his pledge to donate an impression of every print he made to the gallery.

While some of Moore's work in the print medium feels very different to his sculptural work, semi-abstract compositions like this one share obvious common ground with his celebrated sculpted figures, with the addition of vibrant colour. This arrangement focuses on the primary colours of red and yellow, along with green. A different lithographic stone was employed for each colour. Moore's signature and the date are seen in the bottom right, drawn on the stone in red. These are seen in reverse due to the printing process: when a print is taken directly from the lithographic stone, the image is reversed.

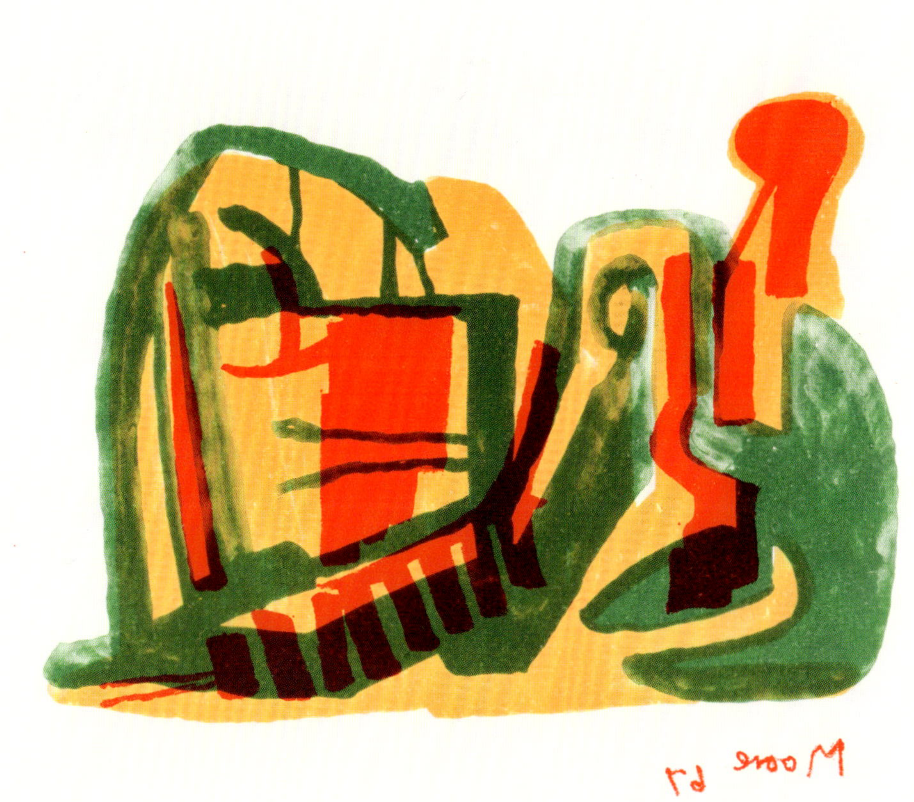

Elisabeth Frink (1930–1993)

Owl, from *Images 67* 1967

Lithograph on paper 78 × 59.4

Animals formed an important subject in the work of Elisabeth Frink, another British artist best known as a sculptor. When the Tate Gallery purchased her small bronze sculpture *Bird of Prey* in 1952, Frink became the youngest woman artist to enter the UK's national collections.[9] She was also a prolific printmaker and is well represented within Tate's print collection.

Owls were a persistent inspiration in Frink's prints; she made a series called 'Birds of Prey' in 1974, and another known as 'Six Owls' in 1977. She depicted various different species, including eagle owls, snowy owls and barn owls, often showing the birds in movement. In this print, which perhaps shows a tawny owl, the bird is shown as if about to fly away, the featheriness of its wings and the power of its talons emphasised. Its form stands out against the pale blue-green background of the print.

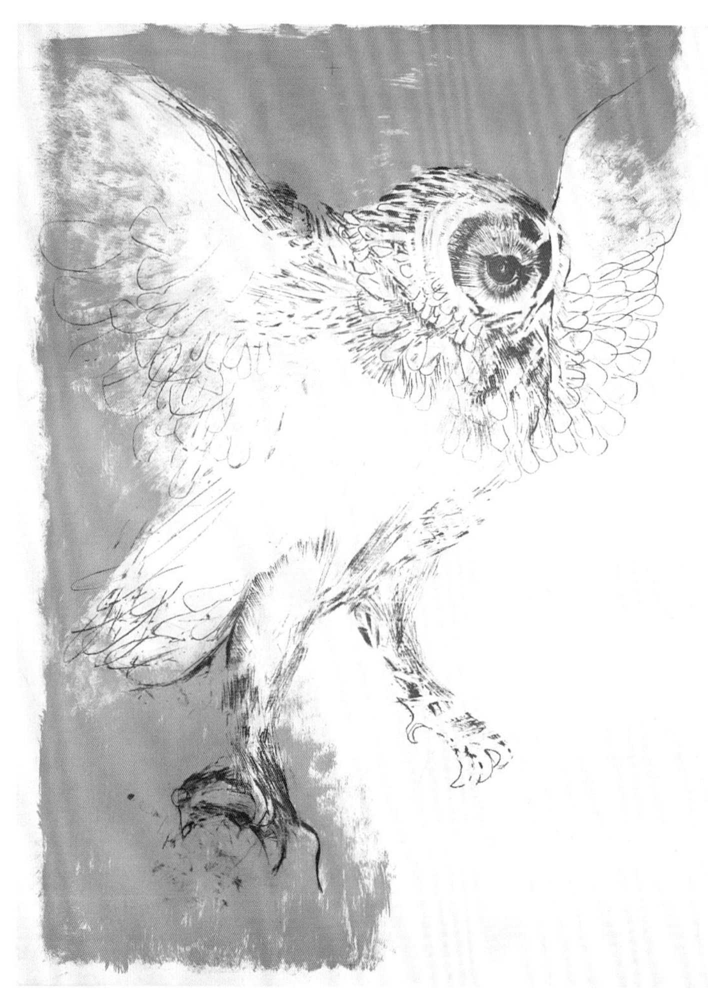

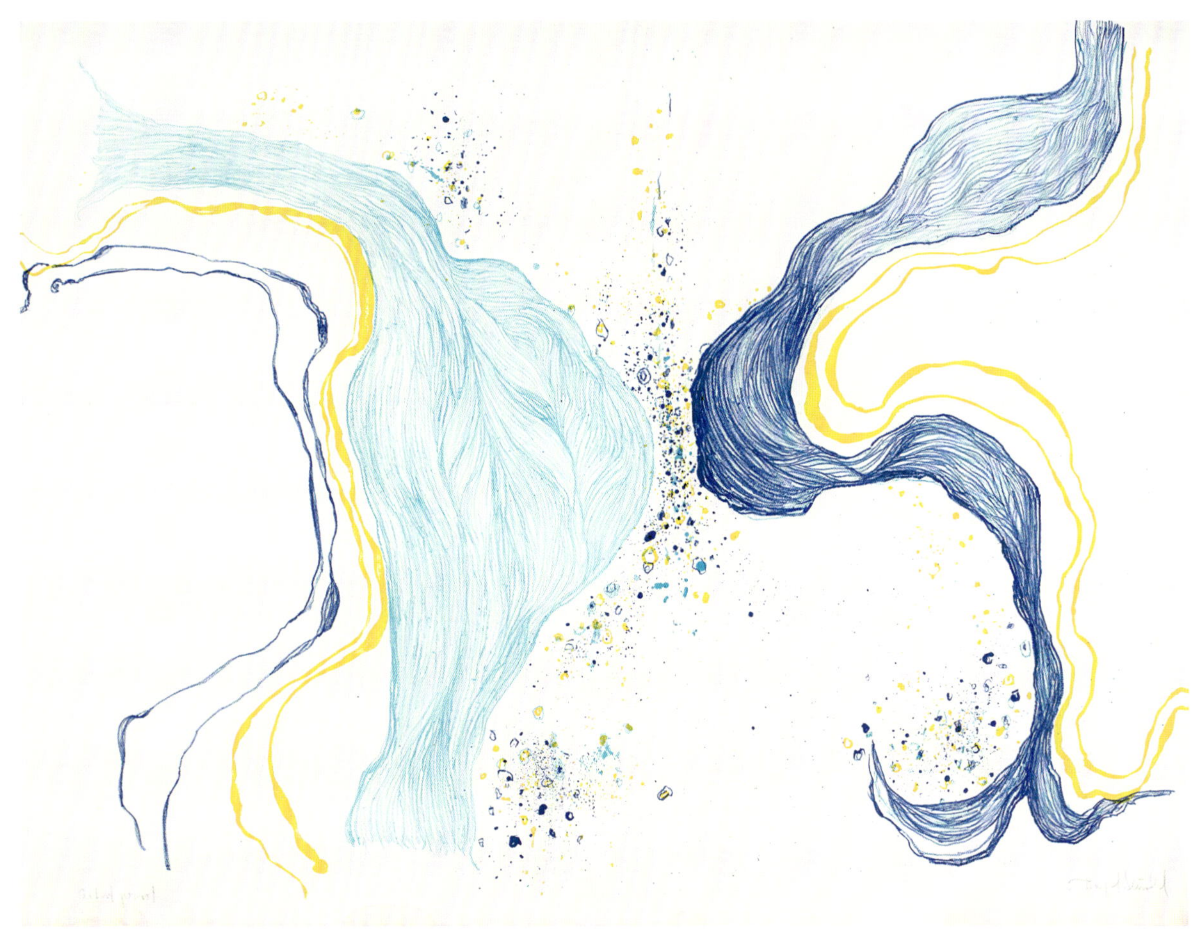

Birgit Skiöld (1923–1982)
Sea Image 1968
Lithograph on paper 59.1 × 79.1

Born in Sweden, Birgit Skiöld moved to London in 1948, where she went on to open Print Workshop, an open-access print studio for artists that filled a gap in the world of postwar London printmaking. It gained a reputation as a friendly and inspiring place to work; artists and printers visited from across Europe, as well as from Japan, Australia and North America, working alongside their British contemporaries. Skiöld also established a strong reputation as an individual printmaker, particularly in the fields of etching and lithography.

In this print, Skiöld's use of ribbons of yellow and blues creates an abstract, almost lyrical interpretation of the sea. A number of Skiöld's colour prints of the 1960s were inspired by the seascape of the Stockholm archipelago, where she grew up. It is possible the artist's memories of this home landscape also inspired *Sea Image*.[10] Tate's impression is an artist's proof. *Sea Image*, which is also known as *Seabed*, was printed by the Curwen Studio in an edition of seventy-five and published by Eugene Schuster of London Graphic Arts Associates.

Jasper Johns (born 1930)
Two Flags (black) 1970–2
Lithograph on paper 62.7 × 49.5

The US flag, an important motif in Jasper Johns's work, is here repurposed as a dual-image print. Although on first glance the image appears dark and abstract, on closer inspection the familiar stars of the Star-Spangled Banner are visible in the upper and centre left. For this print, Johns modified the two lithographic stones he had previously used for *Two Flags (gray)*, a slightly earlier print made in a landscape format.[11] He scratched into the surface of each stone to create new white lines and add further dark marks. By reworking the stones in this manner Johns achieved a dense texture, something he enhanced by printing each stone twice, top and bottom.[12] Johns's approach to lithography and printmaking in general was highly experimental. Although the twentieth century saw many printmakers break free of the medium's traditional monochromatic language by experimenting with colour, in this and similar works Johns proved that there was still plenty of room for innovation when printing in black.

Two Flags (black) was published in an edition of forty by Universal Limited Art Editions, a leading New York print publisher.

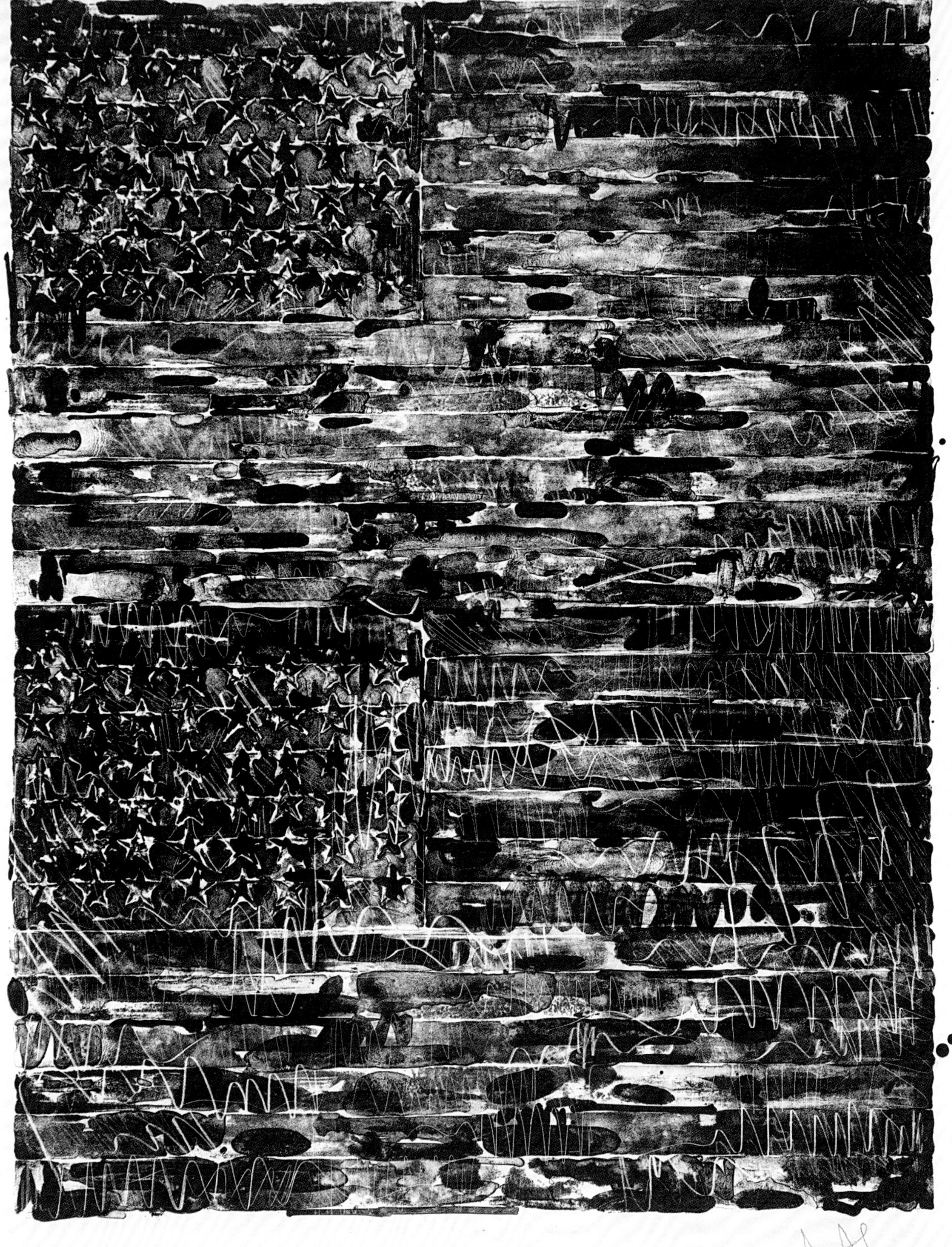

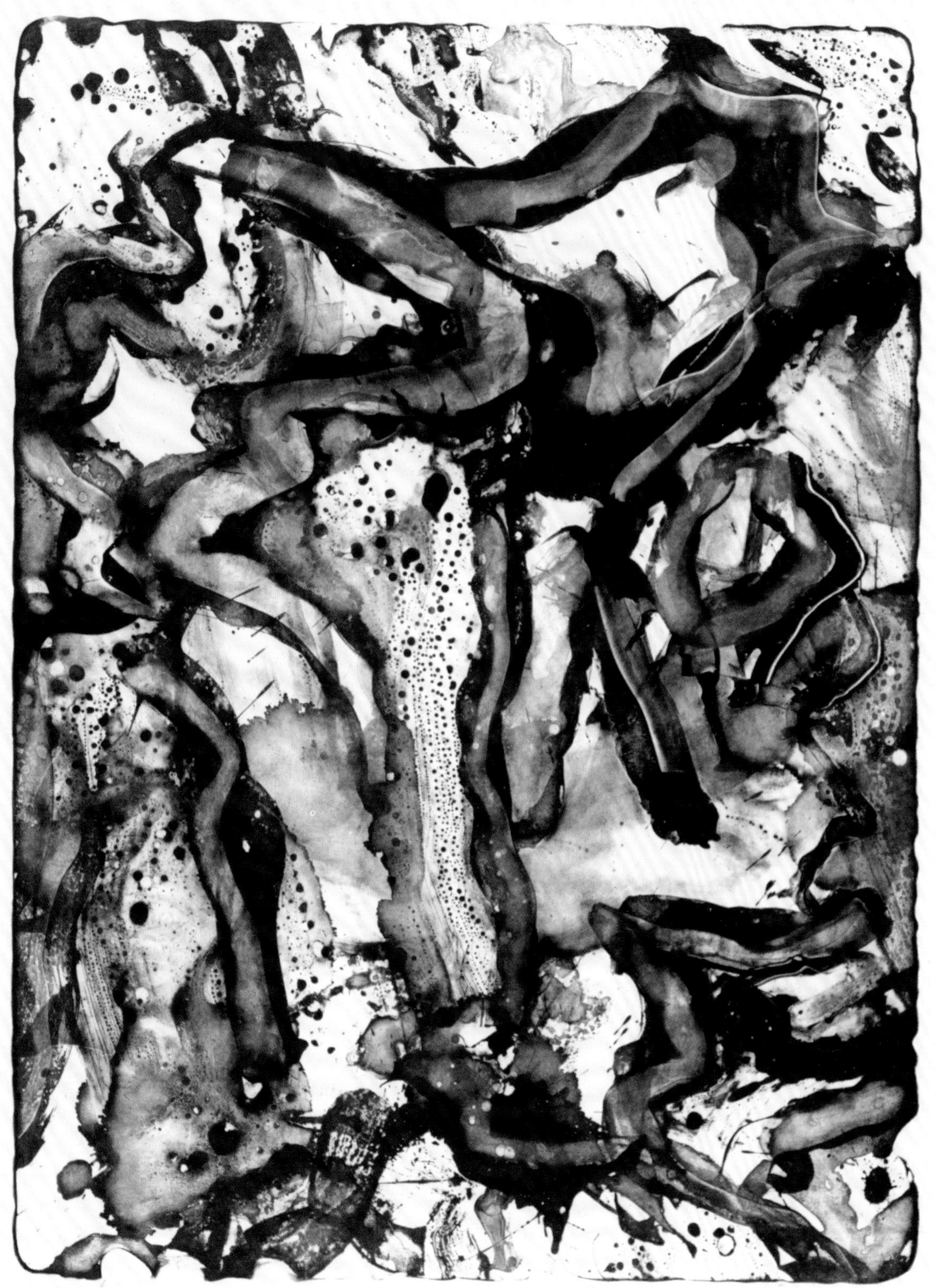

Willem de Kooning (1904–1997)
Landscape at Stanton Street 1971
Lithograph on paper 65 × 48.5

Willem de Kooning, along with artists including Jackson Pollock, was associated with the New York School of abstract painters. He is best known for his large-scale works on canvas, in which he used large brushes to make spontaneous-seeming, expressive paintings.

De Kooning made this print during a productive period of printmaking between 1970 and 1971, when he made twenty-four lithographs at the New York workshop of Irwin Hollander. These prints combine the bold, gestural marks associated with de Kooning's work on canvas with an understanding of the different characteristics of lithography. This is seen in the way the surface of this print seems to celebrate the medium's inherent dependency on the resistance of grease to water – the artist has created a textured surface, embracing incidental marks.

Although the 'Stanton Street' of the title has been connected with a street in the Lower East Side of New York, de Kooning's representation of the place is gestural and expressive rather than descriptive. While de Kooning also briefly experimented with colour lithography, the black-and-white language of monochrome lithography suited him best.

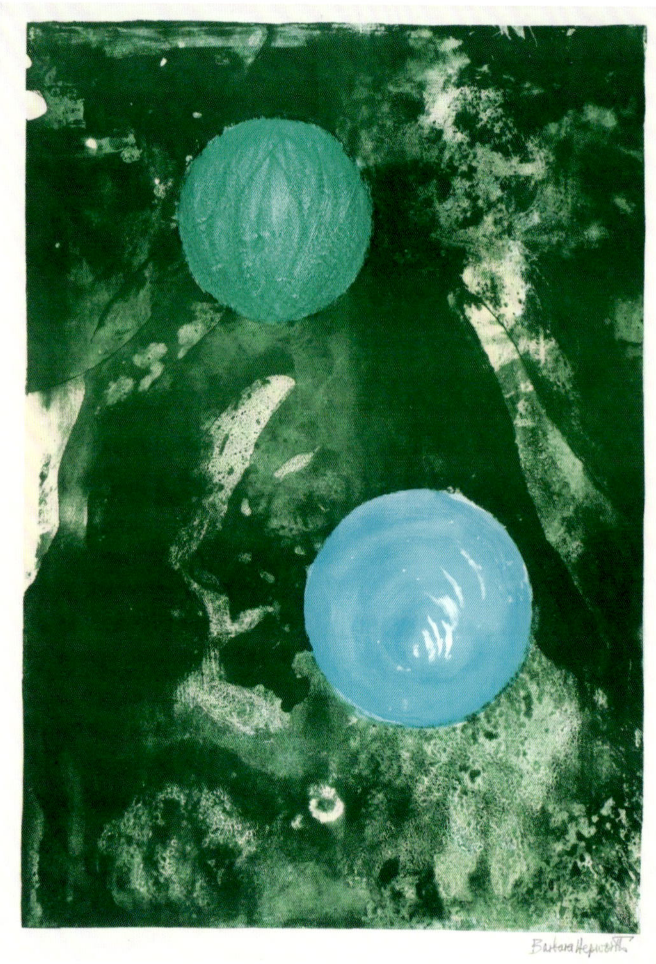

Barbara Hepworth (1903–1975)
Sun and Marble, from *The Aegean Suite* 1971
Lithograph on paper 76.8 × 54.3

The British artist Barbara Hepworth, who is best known for her sculptures, made this otherworldly print during the last decade of her life. She was at her most prolific as a printmaker during this period, making three major series, or 'suites', of prints. This example is from her *Aegean Suite* (1970–1), her second series of lithographs. She began the prints in her studio in St Ives, Cornwall, and completed them in London at the Curwen Studio, who also published the prints. *The Aegean Suite* was inspired by a trip to Greece in 1954 and Hepworth included references to ancient Greek culture and the Aegean landscape in the works.

Each print in the series of nine lithographs plays with geometric forms in relation to impressively varied surface textures. *Sun and Marble*, which is printed in green and pale blue, stands out as a particularly bold, beautiful and ethereal image.

Frances Richards (1903–1985)
Bottom 1973–5
Lithograph on paper 25 × 20.3

This lithograph is part of a series inspired by *Les Illuminations*, a set of prose poems by the nineteenth-century French poet Arthur Rimbaud. One of the poems is entitled 'Bottom'; in it the narrator describes a big blue-grey bird appearing in the home of his love interest. This is the moment depicted here by Frances Richards: in her interpretation a woman cradles the bird's head as its wings and body disappear into the ceiling or sky.

Frances Richards was a British painter, embroiderer and illustrator. She was recognised in all of these fields during her lifetime and is also remembered as the wife of the Welsh painter Ceri Richards, whom she met at the Royal College of Art in London. Her work has a visionary, surreal quality, with her influences including childhood memories as well as her love of poetry. Richards's Rimbauld illustrations came to Tate via the Curwen gift in 1975; in 1981 the gallery also purchased a set of her engravings illustrating *The Acts of the Apostles*.

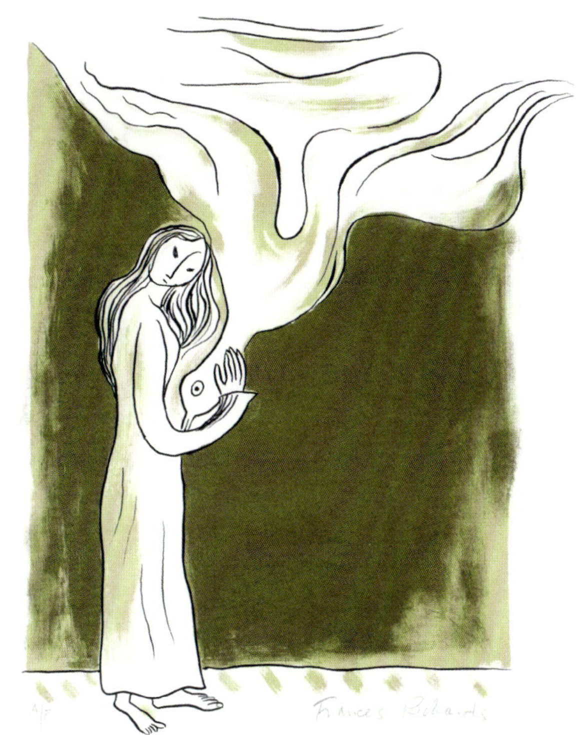

Joan Mitchell (1925–1992)
Sides of a River II 1981
Lithograph on paper 101.3 × 75

The American painter and printmaker Joan Mitchell worked in New York before settling in France in 1959. She is known for her layered, linear abstract marks.

Like much of Mitchell's work, this large-scale print is concerned with landscape. Titled *Sides of a River II*, its abstract marks, printed in yellow, purple and greens, suggest a riverbank dancing with sunlight. It was part of the *Bedford Series*, which Mitchell made in collaboration with the master printer Ken Tyler in 1981. Mitchell used lithography in a bold fashion; the need to use separate lithographic 'stones' for each colour suited her multi-layered approach to image-making.

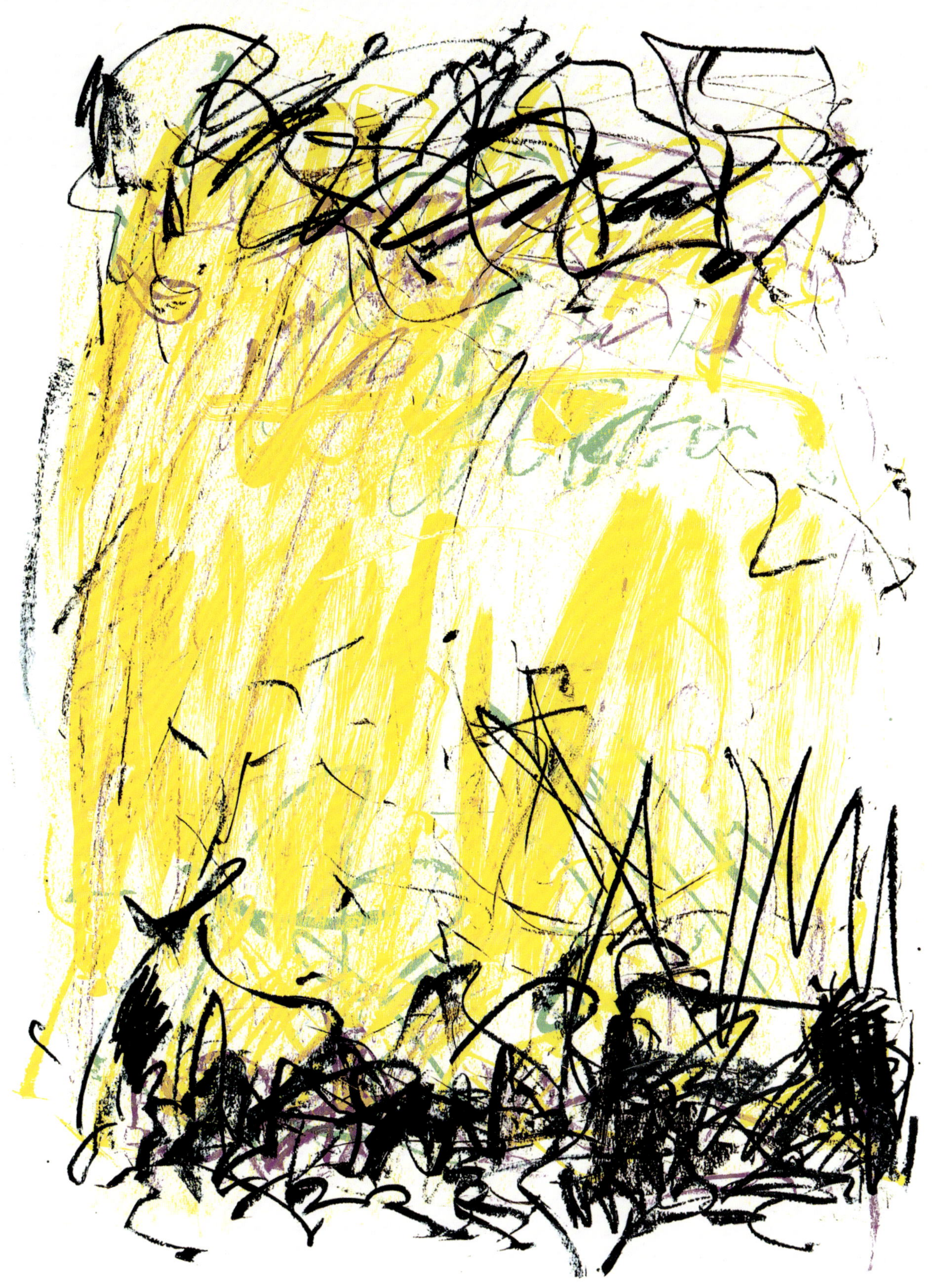

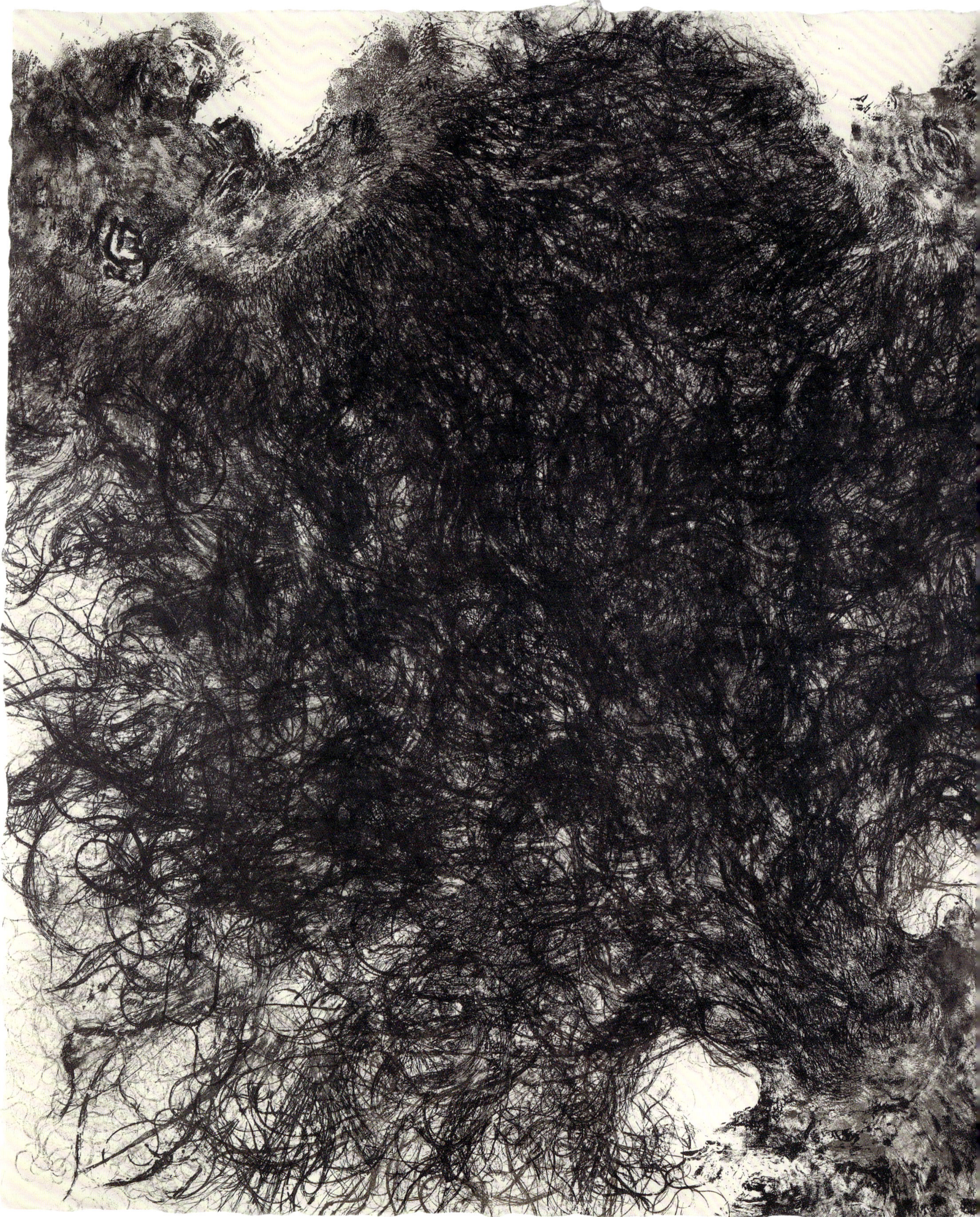

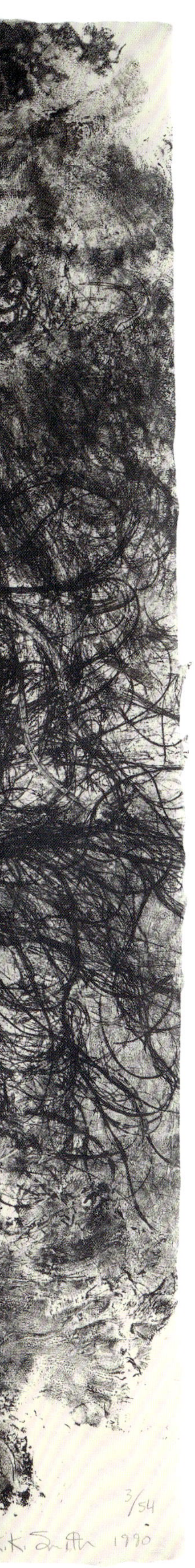

Kiki Smith (born 1954)
Untitled 1990
Lithograph on paper 90.8 × 91.2

Printmaking is central to the practice of Kiki Smith, a German-born American artist. Smith has experimented with numerous printmaking techniques, often taking an unconventional approach to the medium. The human body has been central to her work for most of her career and in this print she explored hair and its associations with feminine sexuality.

To make this multi-layered work, Smith worked with ten separate lithographic stones. Rather than taking a traditional approach to drawing on each one, Smith combined lithography with her three-dimensional work, pushing the medium to its limits. Some stones were imprinted with rubber casts of Smith's head and neck; profiles of her face can be glimpsed in three corners of the image. The dense array of lines representing hair, meanwhile, was transferred to stones from photocopies of the artist's own hair; some of the lines were also inked and printed from a wig and thread-like corn fibres.[13]

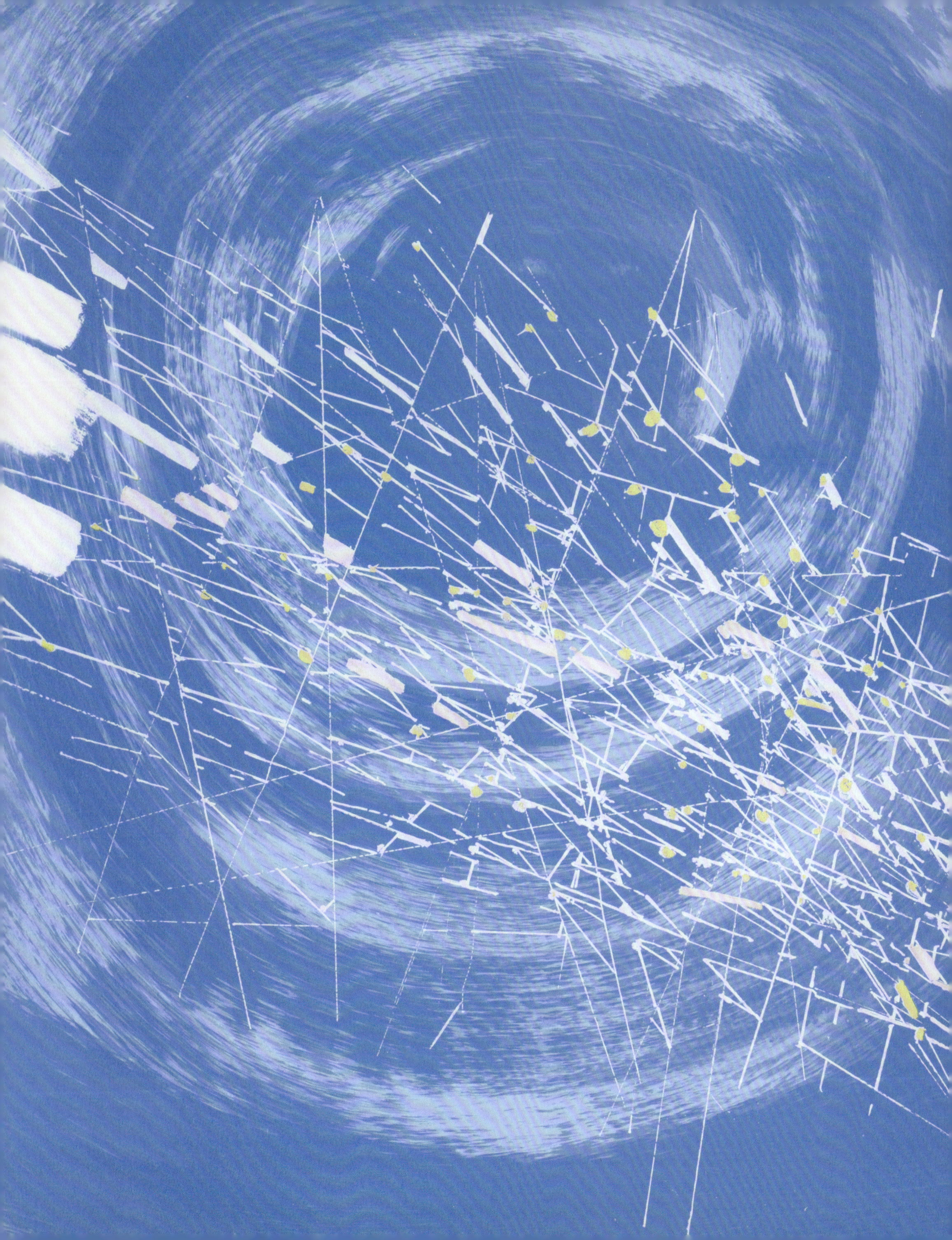

6 Through the Screen

Wilhelmina Barns-Graham *Vision in Time I* 2000 (detail)

6 Through the Screen

Detail from Berenice Sydney, *Screenprint with Balance* 1974

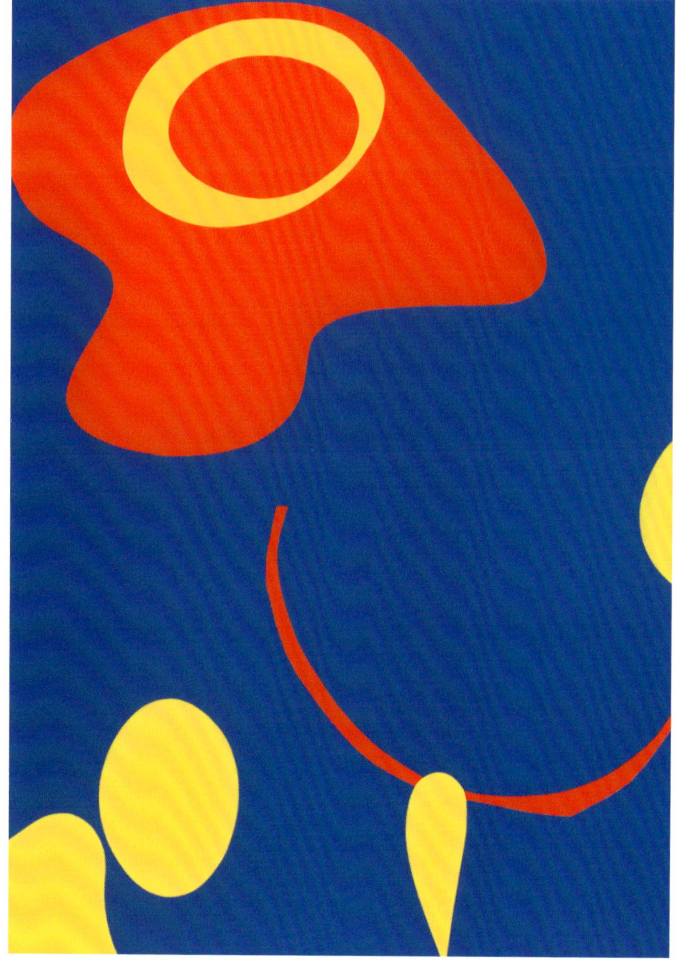

Screenprinting is a stencil-based technique. A stencil is attached to a 'screen' made from a piece of fabric mesh stretched over a frame. To take a print of the stencilled screen, the printer forces thick ink through it using a squeegee (a straight rubber blade). The ink passes through the areas not blocked by the stencil, printing onto the paper below. The method is particularly well suited to making prints with large areas of flat colour with crisp edges. Most screenprints employ colour, and a different screen and stencil is usually prepared for each colour used. An advantage of the process is that no specialist printing press is required.

Photo-stencils allow artists to include photographic images in their screenprints, or to transfer complete designs onto the screen photomechanically. The screen is coated with a photo-sensitive layer, such as bichromated gelatine; a transparency of the design is then placed over it. When light is shone through the transparency the gelatine hardens under the exposure, while the areas that are dark on the photographic transparency are protected from the light. The hardened areas of gelatine become the stencil. The process is relatively straightforward, and photographically derived images are a common feature of screenprints.

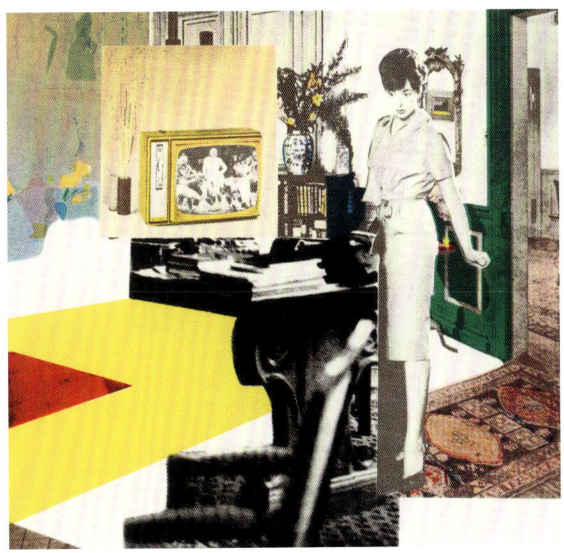

Detail from Richard Hamilton, *Interior* 1964–5

Prints Go Pop: A Brief History of Screenprinting

Screenprinting has been used for commercial textile printing in Europe and the United States since the nineteenth century. It was repurposed for artists' prints during the Depression of the 1930s, when the method's relative cheapness saw it used by American artists engaged in the Federal Art Project. These early practitioners made screenprints using a variation of the technique in which a stencil is painted directly onto the screen, avoiding the need for a paper stencil. In Europe, artists do not seem to have engaged with any iteration of screenprinting until the mid twentieth century, when printmakers in both France and Germany

> LANYON p.158

began to take it up. In Britain, Peter Lanyon tried the technique in 1948, returning to it under the guidance of an American colleague during the early 1950s. Other British artists, including Terry Frost, Alan Davie and William Turnbull, followed suit. But it was during the 1960s that screenprinting reached the forefront of print practice in Britain. This change was in no small part facilitated by the specialist screenprinter Chris Prater, who opened the Kelpra Studio in London with Rose Prater, his wife.

> PAOLOZZI p.161
> HAMILTON p.159
> RILEY p.173

At Kelpra, Prater shared his technical expertise with leading artists including the pop artists Eduardo Paolozzi and Richard Hamilton, and the op artist Bridget Riley. The Institute of Contemporary Arts print portfolio, for which several leading British practitioners made prints, was printed there. This portfolio represents an important moment in the history of screenprinting in Britain. The text accompanying it put the new popularity of the technique down to two key factors. The first was contemporary artists' increasing interest in incorporating photographic source material, which screenprinting can easily accommodate. The second was the rich, 'heavier deposit of pigment', afforded by screenprinting, said to make it 'eminently a painter's vehicle'.[1]

> LICHTENSTEIN p.164
> WARHOL p.167

The Kelpra Studio was a key centre for screenprinting from the 1960s, but exciting developments were happening concurrently in the United States. There, too, pop art became synonymous with the method, which was taken up most famously by the artistic giants Roy Lichtenstein and Andy Warhol. Like their British counterparts, these artists found that the potential to work with photographically derived images using different colour variations played well to their interest in working with mass culture imagery. The extent of the printers' role in making some of the best-known screenprints of the pop era (which could include actually creating the stencils under an artist's instruction), as well as the widespread inclusion of photomechanical imagery, created some controversy during the 1960s, as commentators on both sides of the Atlantic asked if these interpretations of photographic mass culture imagery could be called original prints.[2] In fact, many prints made using the other, more traditional, methods described elsewhere in this book saw just as much collaboration with professional printers, albeit usually without the emphasis on photographic imagery that is a key characteristic of pop art. It is also notable that for pop artists, mechanical reproduction was often an interest in itself and seen as an advantage of screenprinting.

While not all of the screenprints made during the 1960s and 1970s drew on photomechanical imagery or reflected the pop aesthetic, artists associated with pop proved to be the method's leading proponents during these years. This fruitful period for the technique is well reflected by Tate's holdings, in no small part thanks to the Rose and Chris Prater Gift, one of the founding gifts of the modern print collection. It includes prints by many leading British artists, as well as various non-British artists who worked with Prater in London. Other iconic screenprints, such as Warhol's *Soup Can Series I*, arrived in the collection via targeted purchases.

> WARHOL p.167

The holdings of screenprints from the method's heyday in the 1960s and 1970s are a key strength of Tate's collection. And screenprinting has remained a popular method for artists, something the collection increasingly reflects in terms of examples from later decades. There are interesting examples by artists including Damien Hirst, Inka Essenhigh and Sarah Morris, each of whom used the method very differently. Since 2000, Tate's increased efforts to acquire works by female and non-western artists has been reflected by some notable acquisitions. These have included important works by the feminist collective the Guerrilla Girls and the Iranian artist Parviz Tanavoli.

> HIRST p.179
> ESSENHIGH p.181
> MORRIS p.183
> GUERRILLA GIRLS p.178
> TANAVOLI p.174

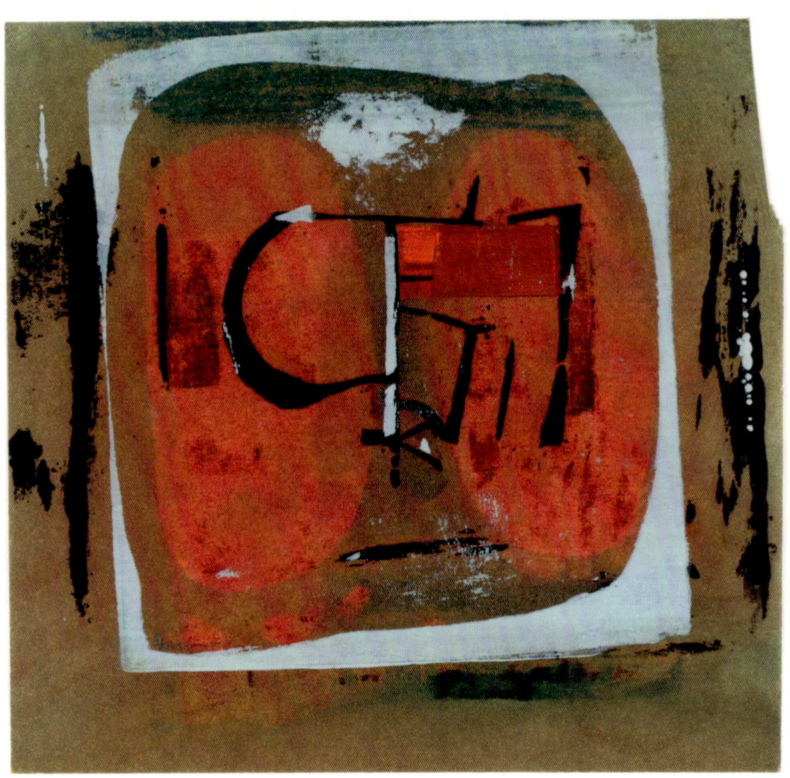

Peter Lanyon (1918–1964)
Underground 1951
Screenprint on paper 26.5 × 24.7

Peter Lanyon's *Underground* is one of the earliest screenprints by a British artist. Lanyon first attempted the method in 1948, returning to it in 1951 with the help of the American potter Warren MacKenzie. MacKenzie had learnt screenprinting in the United States, where it was more commonly used by artists. He later wrote: 'these prints were made at St. Ives as the result of Peter Lanyon asking me to teach him ... He was looking for a process that did not need the elaborate presses etc of etching and lithography'.[3] According to MacKenzie, Lanyon made a breakthrough while struggling with the process: after 'piling on colour with several stencils' he washed the ink from the surface of his paper with turpentine, resulting in the stained translucent background of this print.[4] Lanyon then screenprinted over the mysterious-looking background he had created, and repeated this adaptation of the technique in his next print.

Underground was printed by Lanyon and MacKenzie in a small edition of eight. Its abstract and painterly approach is in contrast to the refined photo-derived imagery seen in screenprints of the next decade by pop artists such as Paolozzi and Hamilton.

Richard Hamilton (1922–2011)
Interior 1964–5
Screenprint on paper 49.5 × 63.8

Richard Hamilton is closely associated with the development of pop art in Britain. The starting point for this screenprint was a collage he had made showing the same subject. When translating the idea into print, Hamilton added colour, aiming to create 'a pseudo-photographic effect'.[5] The detail of the photographic imagery is contrasted by the panes of bright colour Hamilton added to the print. The collaged imagery was drawn from various sources, with the female figure taken from an advert for a washing machine and the main interior scene from a photograph of the drawing room of Claude Monet's daughter.[6] The image was also inspired by a 1940s film still.

Interior was printed using eight stencils at the Kelpra Studio, London, and published by Editions Alecto; this impression is an artist's proof outside of the main edition of fifty prints.

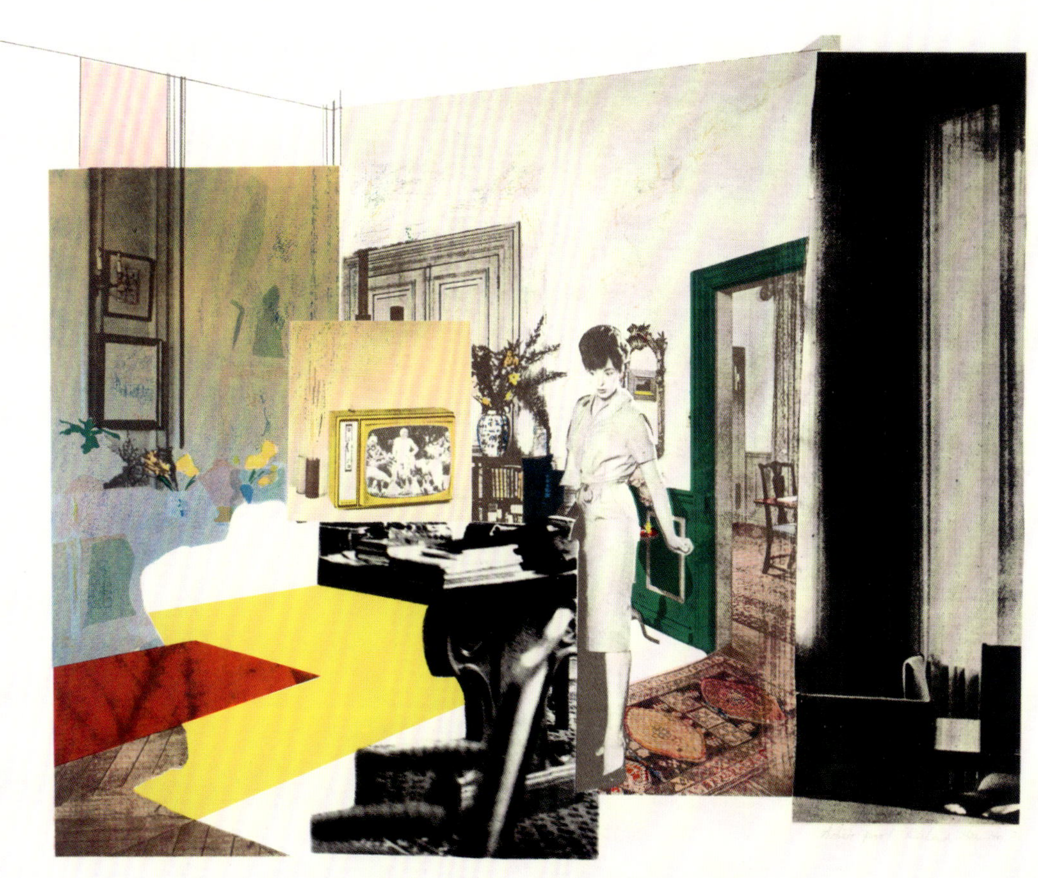

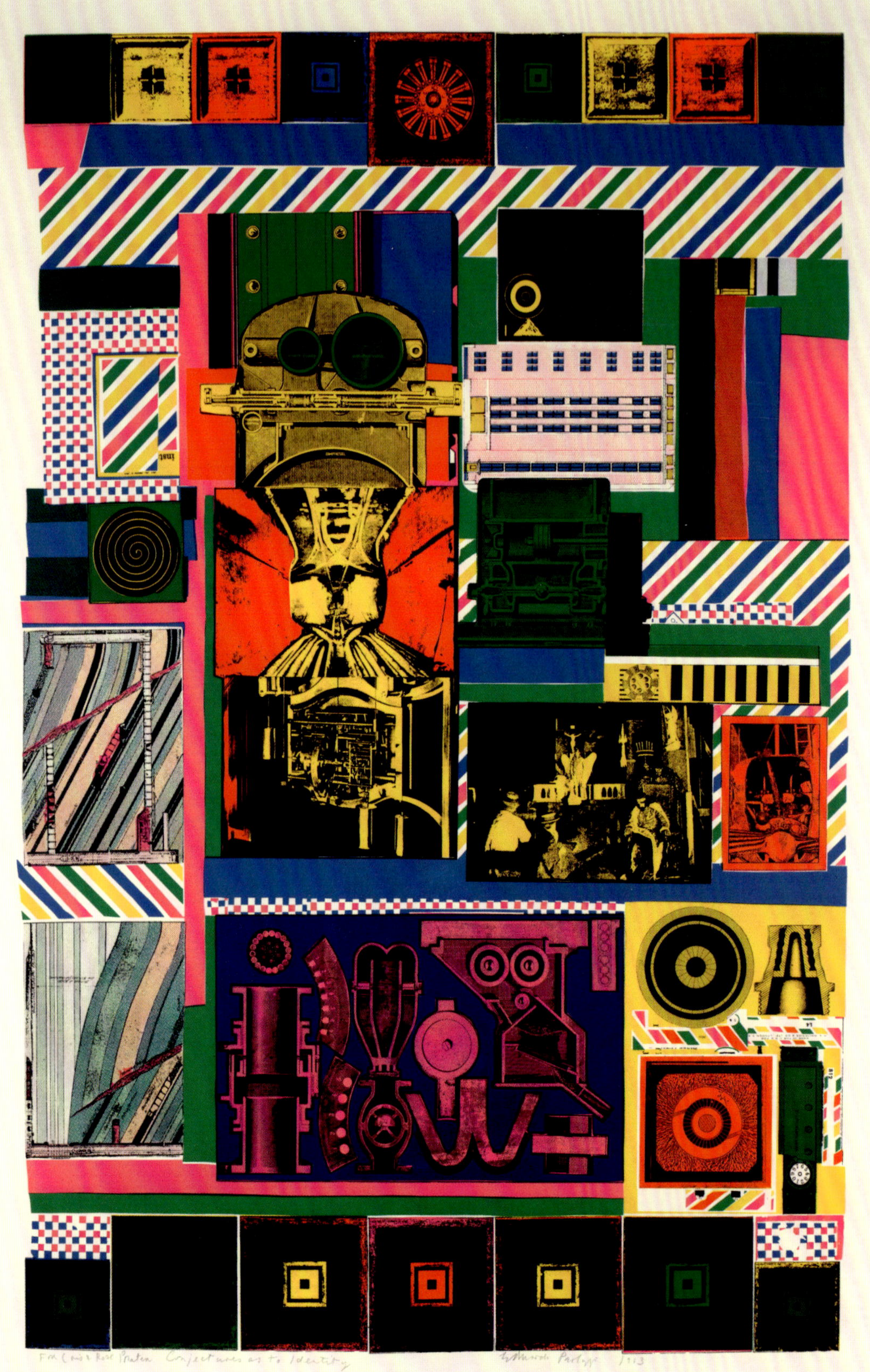
Conjectures as to Identity

Eduardo Paolozzi (1924–2005)
Conjectures to Identity 1963–4
Screenprint on paper 75.6 × 49.5

The British artist Eduardo Paolozzi was born to Italian parents in Edinburgh. He was attracted to screenprinting by its potential to reproduce his paper collages with photographic accuracy, while allowing him to alter the image with different colour combinations during the printing process. Many of Paolozzi's screenprints exist in different colour variations.

This piece was printed at the Kelpra Studio in London for the Institute of Contemporary Arts print portfolio (1964). The portfolio showcased screenprinting as the contemporary printmaking practice engaging the most important artists of the day, who were each working with print in new ways. The images in *Conjectures to Identity*, Paolozzi's first full-scale collaged screenprint, are derived from patterns, engineering drawings and photography. The piece was printed from multiple stencils, each printed using a different colour of ink.

Peter Blake (born 1932)
Beach Boys 1964
Screenprint on paper 53 × 30.8

Peter Blake was a leading figure in the British pop art movement. Like other pop artists, he embraced imagery from popular culture. His best-known work is probably the cover art of The Beatles' 1967 album *Sgt Pepper's Lonely Hearts Club Band*, which he co-designed.
The present piece, his first published screenprint, dates from a few years earlier. In making it Blake incorporated a contemporary press photograph of the American rock band The Beach Boys. Unfinished areas, like those seen around the car in this work, became a feature of Blake's screenprints.

Like some of the other prints illustrated in this section, this piece was printed in London's Kelpra Studio and published as part of the Institute of Contemporary Arts portfolio in an edition of forty, plus fifteen artist's proofs.

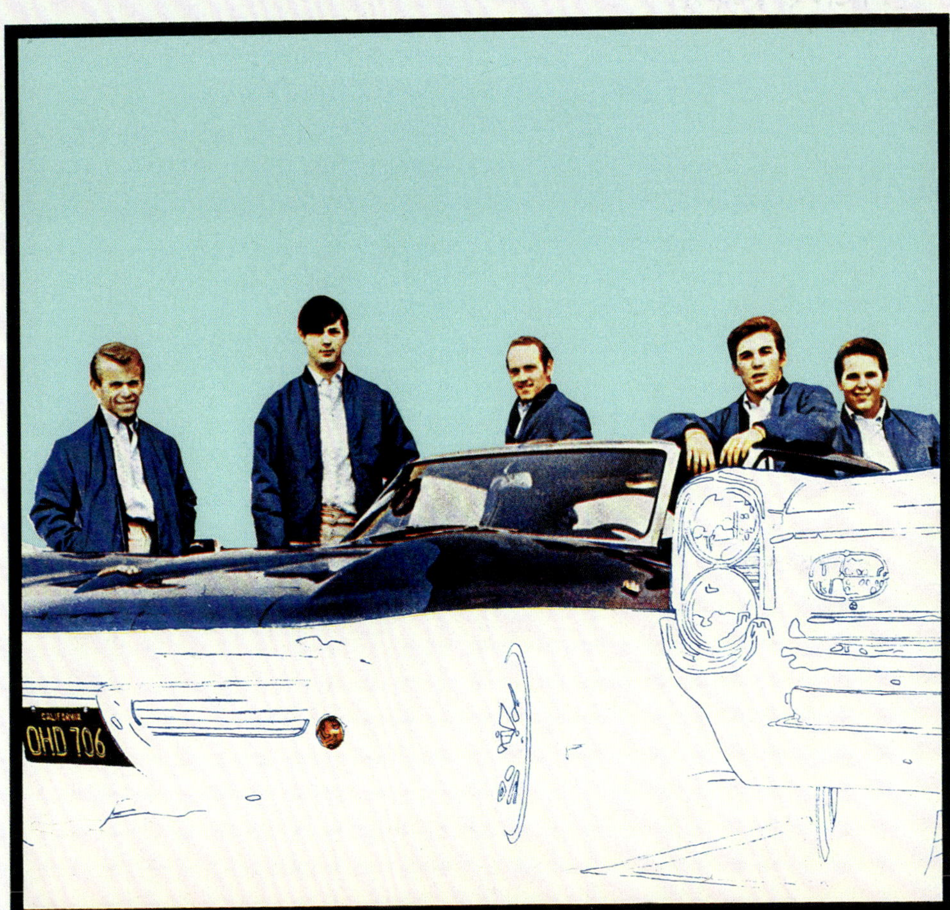

THE
BEACH
BOYS

For Chris. Pete Blake 64.

Roy Lichtenstein (1923–1997)
Brushstroke 1965
Screenprint on paper 56.5 × 72.4

The American artist Roy Lichtenstein developed a bold, graphic style as a printmaker, which encompassed popular culture and cartoon imagery. Printmaking was important to his art from the beginnings of his career in the 1940s until the end of his life.

In this screenprint Lichtenstein created an image of a brushstroke, a much-repeated motif in his work (see p.204). The result is both an arresting graphic image in its own right and a parody of the gestural, hand-drawn mark-making of abstract expressionist artists such as Jackson Pollock and Willem de Kooning (p.145). The brushstroke, like other motifs in Lichtenstein's prints, also reflects everyday imagery seen in popular culture. He later said: 'Of course, visible brushstrokes in a painting convey a sense of grand gesture; but in my hands, the gesture becomes a *depiction* of a grand gesture.'[7]

This screenprint was printed by the Chiron Press and published by the Leo Castelli Gallery, New York, in an edition of 280. Lichtenstein produced over three hundred editioned prints during his career.

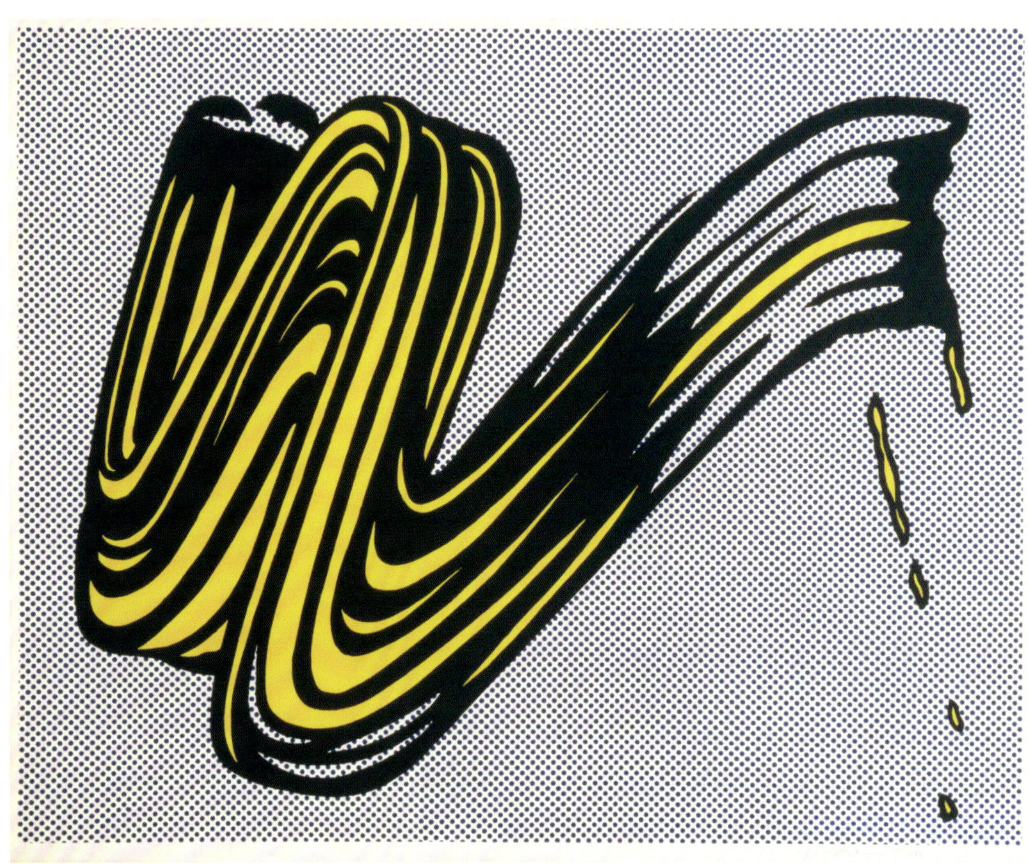

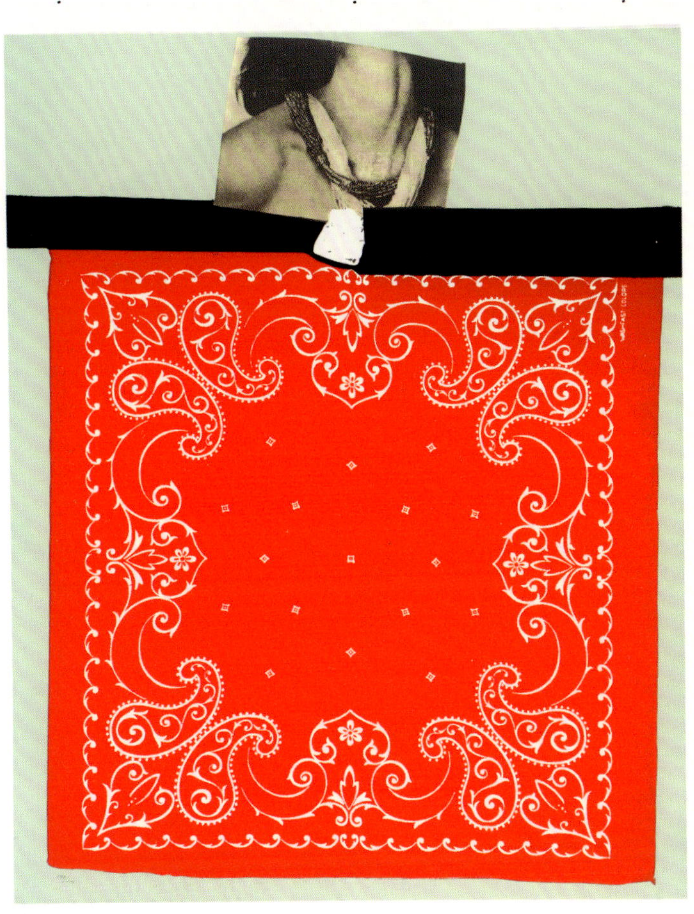

Jim Dine (born 1935)
Throat 1965
Screenprint on paper 76.2 × 61.3

The American artist Jim Dine worked as a painter, sculptor, printmaker, performance artist and poet. He became associated with the pop art movement during the 1960s and his screenprints, which often incorporate elements of collage, reflect the movement's emphasis on popular culture imagery.

The type of red patterned bandana seen here was made famous by cowboys in Western films, but was also associated with workers from farms, railroads and coal mines.[8] In the early twentieth century it came to symbolise the American labour movement, while in the 1960s the bandana was adopted as an alternative style of dress. As such, Dine's choice of imagery plays on both popular and alternative cultural associations. The print was published in an edition of 200, within the portfolio *11 Pop Artists, vol.II*, by Original Editions, New York. This portfolio, a key publication of the pop era, also included works by artists such as Allen Jones, Lichtenstein and Warhol.

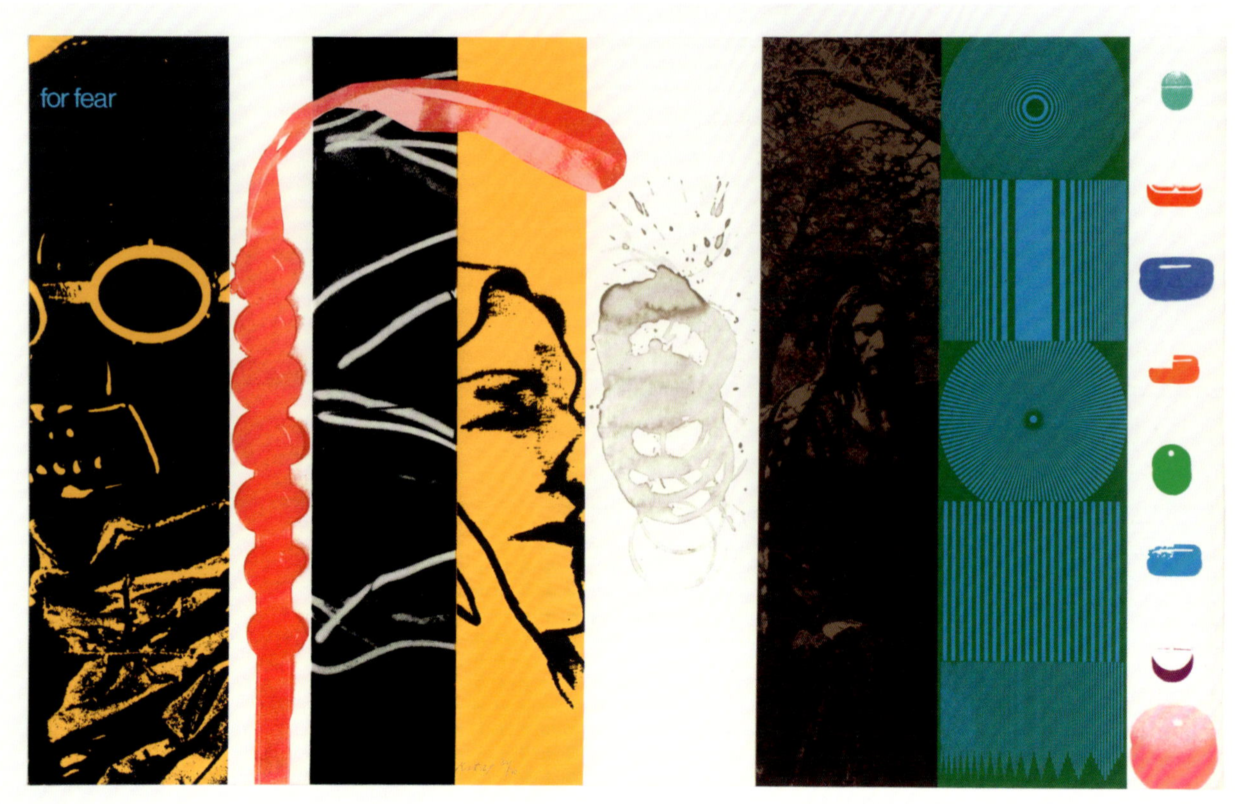

R.B. Kitaj (1932–2007)
For Fear 1967
Screenprint on paper 51 × 83.7

The American-born artist R.B. Kitaj trained in Vienna and then London, where he spent much of his career. *For Fear* is from his first print series, *Mahler Becomes Politics, Beisbol*. This series was inspired by a cycle of forty-one poems by the artist's friend Jonathan Williams, responding to the symphonies of Gustav Mahler. However, the imagery in the *Mahler* series relates to various different poets and artists, comprising fragments drawn from many places. As is the case with many of the prints in the series, the meaning of *For Fear* remains rather ambiguous, with Kitaj combining apparently eclectic pieces of imagery. These include a woman's face, a gas mask, a seal, a stain and a Christ-like figure.

Like many of Kitaj's screenprints, *For Fear* was vibrantly printed using several different colours. The series was printed at the Kelpra Studio and published by Marlborough Fine Art, London, in an edition of seventy.

Andy Warhol (1928–1987)
Black Bean from *Soup Can Series I* 1968
Screenprint on paper Sheet: 89.2 × 59.1

Familiar consumer items formed a key part of Andy Warhol's subject matter during the 1960s. Within his work everyday foods were elevated to the status of art objects to be 'consumed' in a very different way, by the viewer. *Black Bean* is from a portfolio of ten screenprints, each documenting a different flavour of soup. Warhol said he painted soup cans because he used to have soup for lunch every day.

Screenprinting suited him as it allowed photo-mechanical reproduction of his photographic source material and emphasised mechanical, rather than handmade, forms of image-making.

Soup Can Series I was published in an edition of 250 by Factory Editions, New York, having been printed by Salvatore Silkscreen Co.

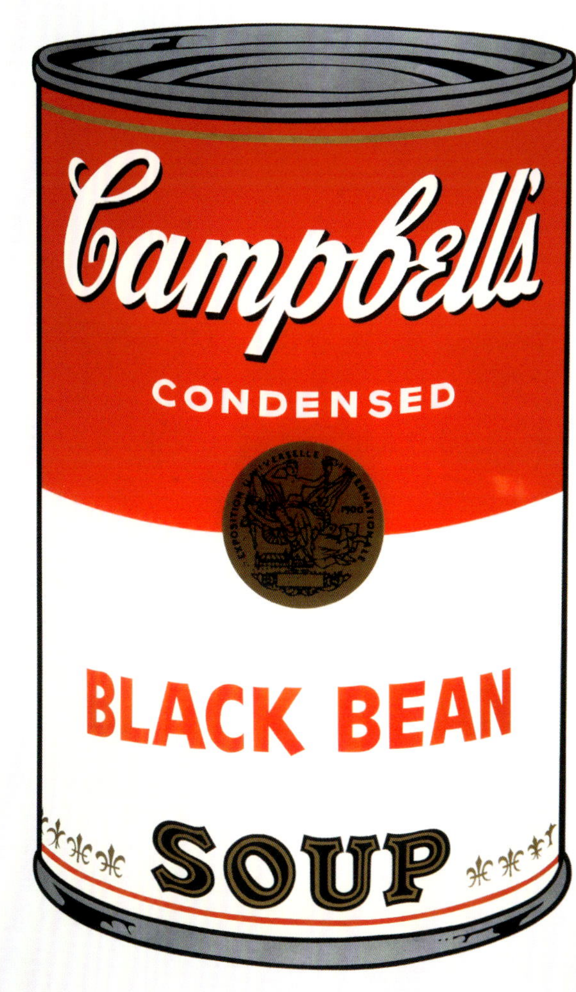

Anni Albers (1899–1994)
TR III 1969–70
Screenprint on paper 42 × 47

Anni Albers was born Annelise Else Frieda Fleischmann in Berlin. In 1922 she began studying at Germany's famous Bauhaus art school in Weimar. As a student she was steered towards textiles – at the time considered a suitably feminine discipline – and became deeply concerned with pattern. After moving to the United States with her husband, the artist Josef Albers, in 1933, she discovered the geometric patterns of pre-Columbian art, which became another strong source of inspiration.

Albers first tried printmaking in 1963, and by 1970 it was the most important part of her practice. She emphasised the importance of becoming absorbed in different print processes to make work unique to the print medium. *TR III* reflects the influence of triangular patterns seen in Mexican and Peruvian textiles. Albers made the print with the assistance of her publisher, Gemini G.E.L. in Los Angeles. The print was made by screenprinting gold ink over the entire sheet of paper. Once the ink had dried, the sheet was embossed using a matching pair of stamps.[9] The print was published in an edition of sixty along with six artist's proofs.

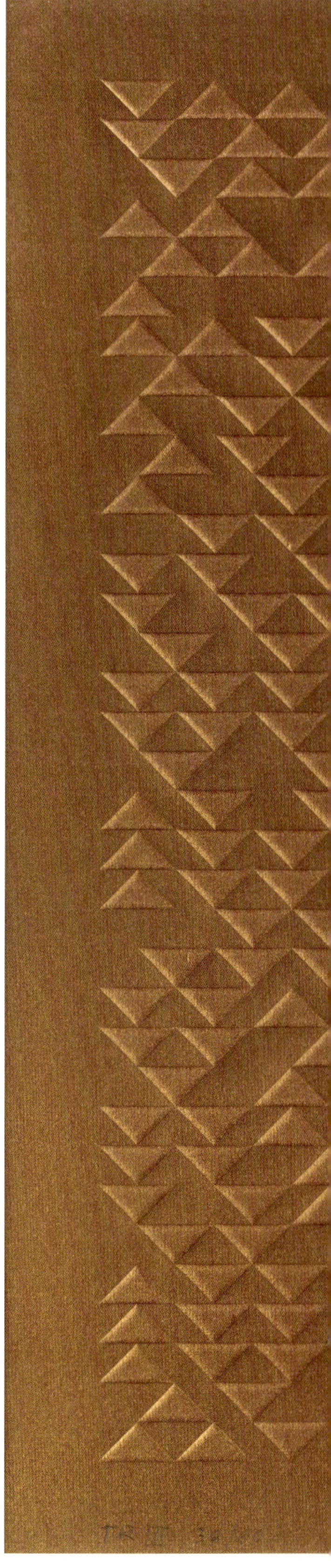

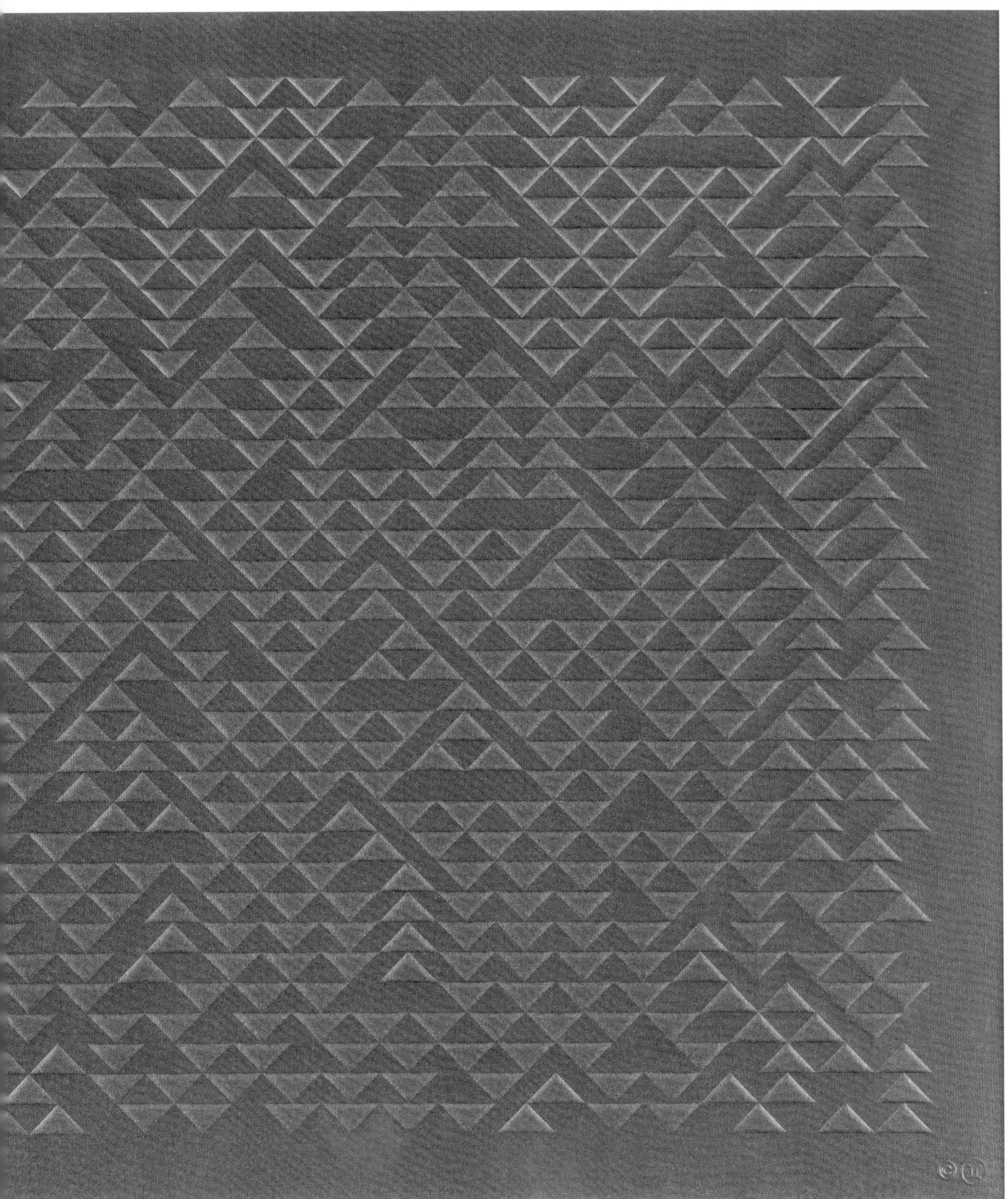

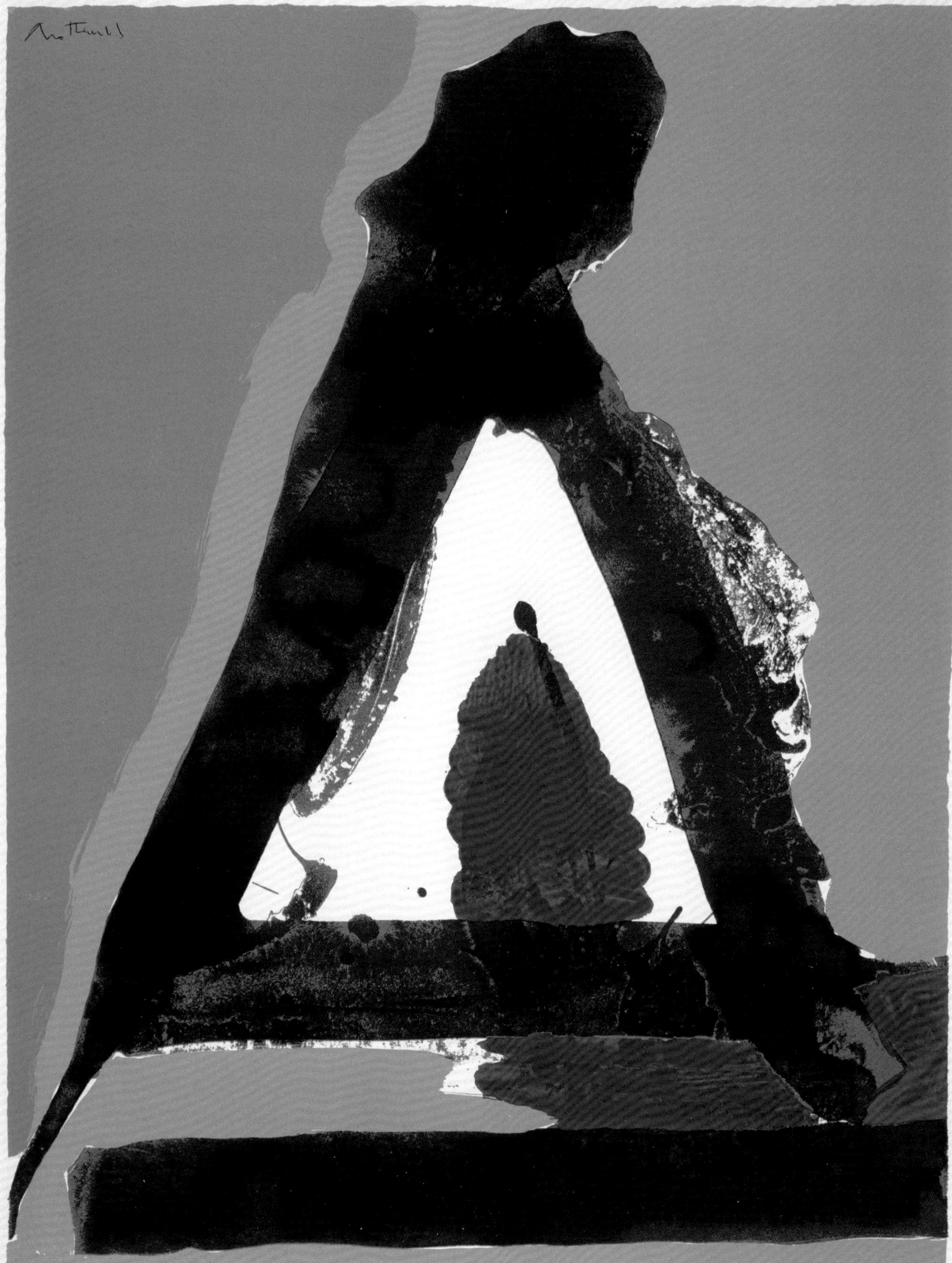

Robert Motherwell (1915–1991)
No.7, from *The Basque Suite* 1970
Screenprint on paper 71.7 × 56

The American artist Robert Motherwell is associated with the development of twentieth-century abstract expressionist painting in New York. He is known for his interest in the expressive potential of calligraphic marks: this is felt in *No.7*, which is from a series of ten screenprints comprising *The Basque Suite*. In it, Motherwell considered the singular characteristics of the Basque language spoken in north-east Spain, as well as its Roman alphabet.

Motherwell was a prolific printmaker. But although here he employed the screenprinting method, which allowed him to build up layers of rich, flat colour, he preferred other printmaking techniques, calling screenprinting 'a clumsy medium'.[10] Nonetheless, his striking experiments with the technique are demonstrations of how it can be used to make gestural, painterly marks as well as crisp graphic images.

The Basque Suite was printed in multiple colours by Chris Prater at London's Kelpra Studio and published by Marlborough Graphics, Inc., New York in an edition of 150. This sheet, the seventh in the series, was printed from three separate screens in light blue, dark blue and black.

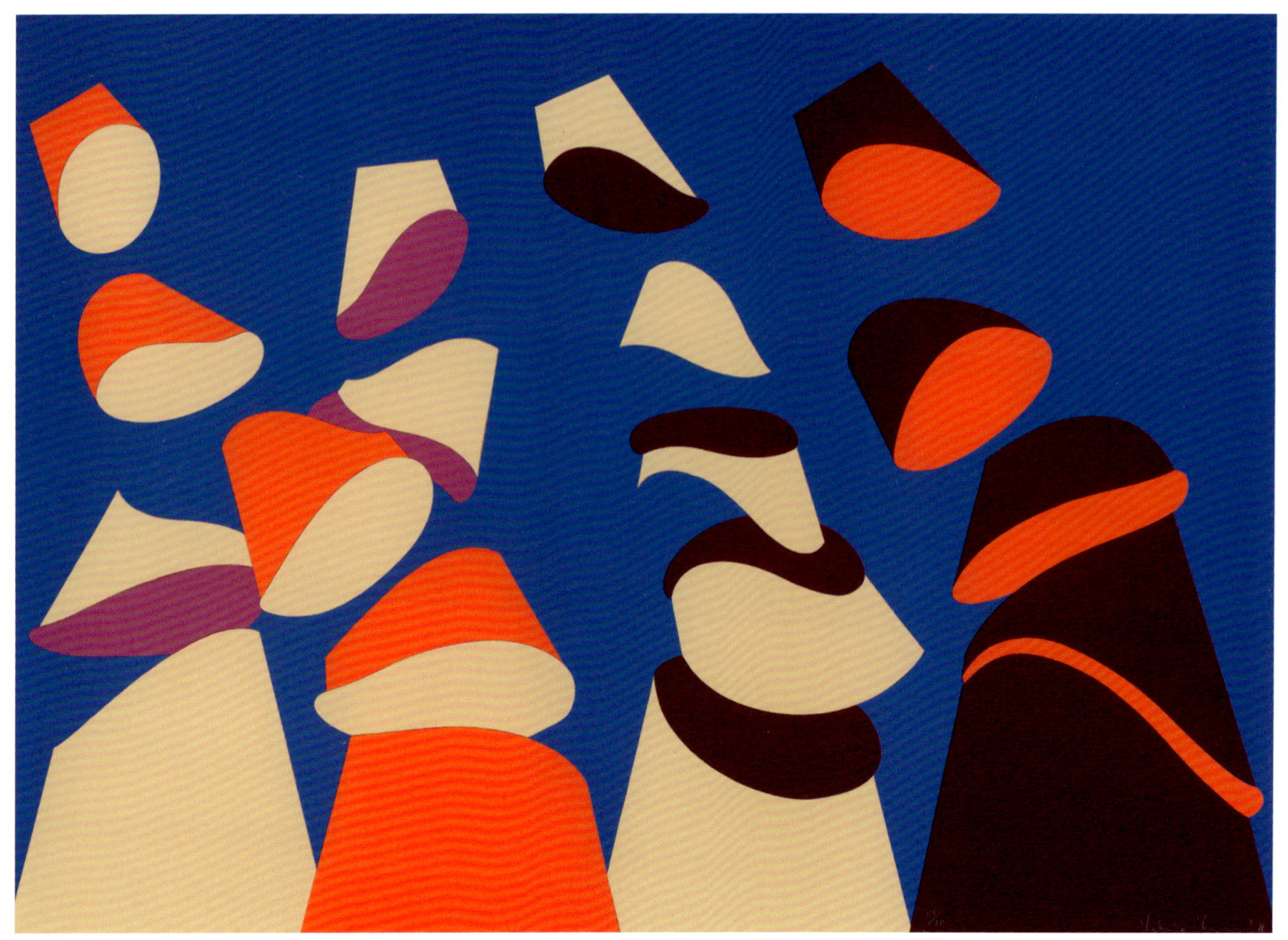

Liliane Lijn (born 1939)
Koan-Cuts V 1971
Screenprint on paper on screenprint on paper 56 × 79.6

This is one of a set of five screenprints by the American-born artist Liliane Lijn. Known as 'Koan-Cuts', these vibrant works were made during the same period as a group of conical shaped 'Koan' sculptures. A koan is a paradoxical anecdote or riddle without a solution used in Zen Buddhism to demonstrate the inadequacy of logical reasoning. Lijn refers to this idea with her titles, while also playing with language to combine the idea of a 'koan' with the tapered 'cone' shape.

In Lijn's sculpture, cones are explored in three dimensions. These flat screenprints, too, seem to suggest sculptural forms: the three-dimensionality of each cone shape is emphasised through the combination of different colours, which reveal the outside as well as the solid interior of the form.

Bridget Riley (born 1931)

Coloured Greys I 1972

57.1 x 58.4

Bridget Riley is known as an exponent of op art, a movement which saw artists use geometric forms to create patterns affecting the optic nerve. The painted surfaces of many of Riley's canvases generate sensations of movement in the eye.

While painting has been her main focus, Riley's print practice has routinely attracted attention. She first tried screenprinting in the mid 1960s, experimenting with the technique at the same time as her pop-focused British contemporaries, Hamilton, Paolozzi and Blake (pp.159, 160, 162). Like them, she found the modern method of screenprinting most suited to her needs, having previously considered prints 'what you saw in the British Museum, with that very handmade look'.[11]

Riley's early work often used black-and-white or monochrome to achieve optic effects. This piece, however, is from a suite of prints entitled *Coloured Greys*, in which she made use of subtle colour to explore the hues and movement of the sea. The prints were not individually numbered and the sequencing of the three images within the series varies from collection to collection. *Coloured Greys* was printed in an edition of 125 at the Kelpra Studio, London.

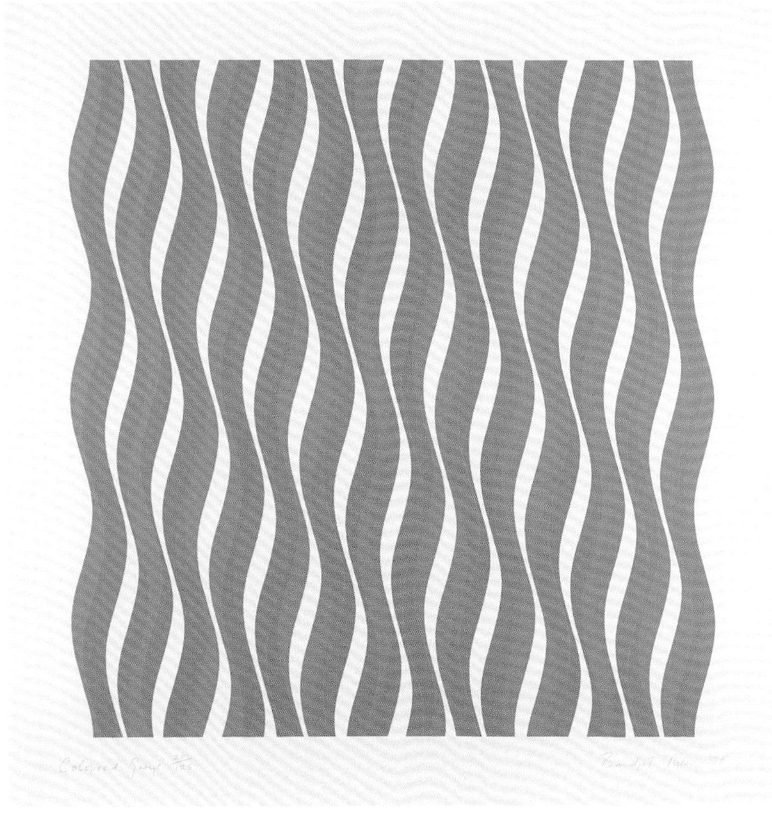

Parviz Tanavoli
(born 1937)
Poet and Bird 1974
Screenprint on paper 50 × 70

Parviz Tanavoli has been a key figure in the Iranian art world since 1960. His work, which integrates popular images from Shi'a culture, has been associated with pop art since the 1960s. Tanavoli has said he did not consider himself a pop artist until others did.[12]

This piece is from a group of prints Tanavoli made in 1974 celebrating Persian myths, poetry and symbols using a modern visual language. In them he reinterpreted icons of Shiite folk art, including the bird, using geometric forms and the modern method of screenprinting. He said of his work: 'I deliberately wanted to shake up the Iranians and get them out of their millennia-old shells. In order to do so, I picked up ordinary material and commercial paint to break down the soft lines of the Persian miniatures and those pretty faces. My lovers in new mediums with geometric lines are completely the opposite of the Persian refined taste.'[13]

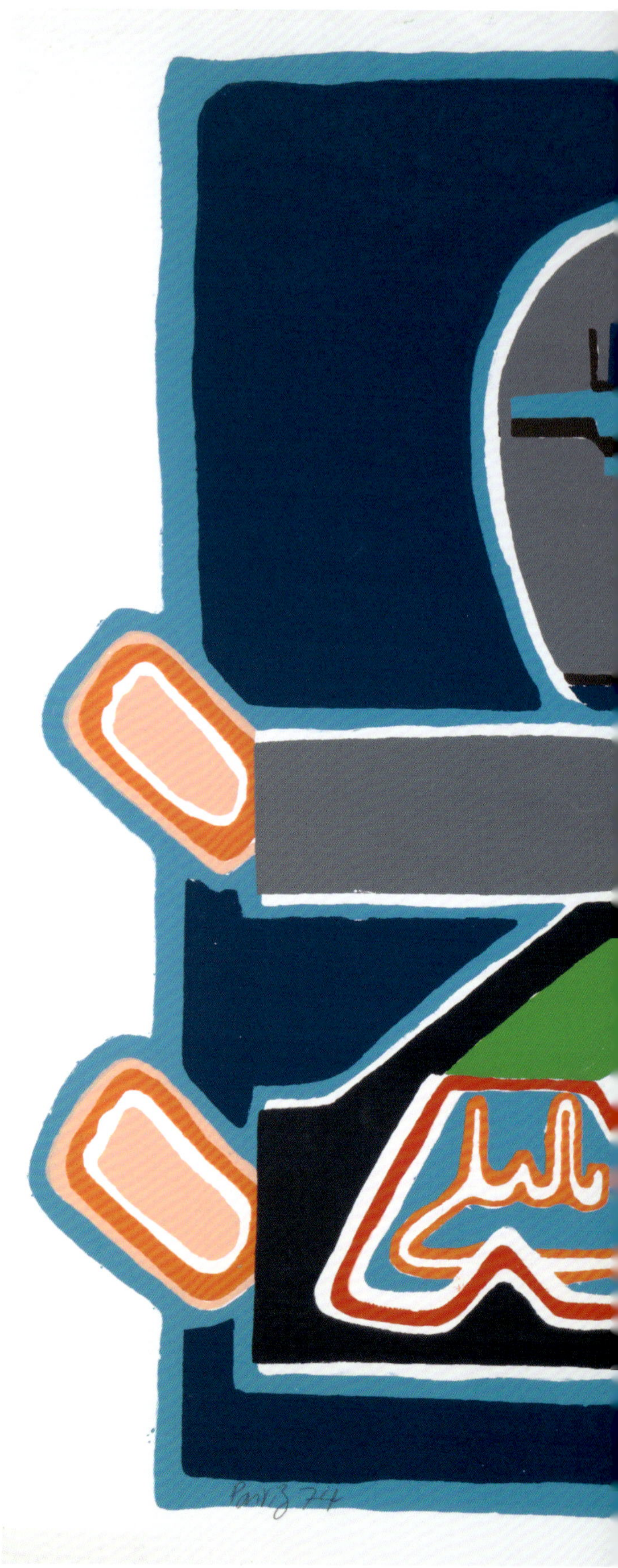

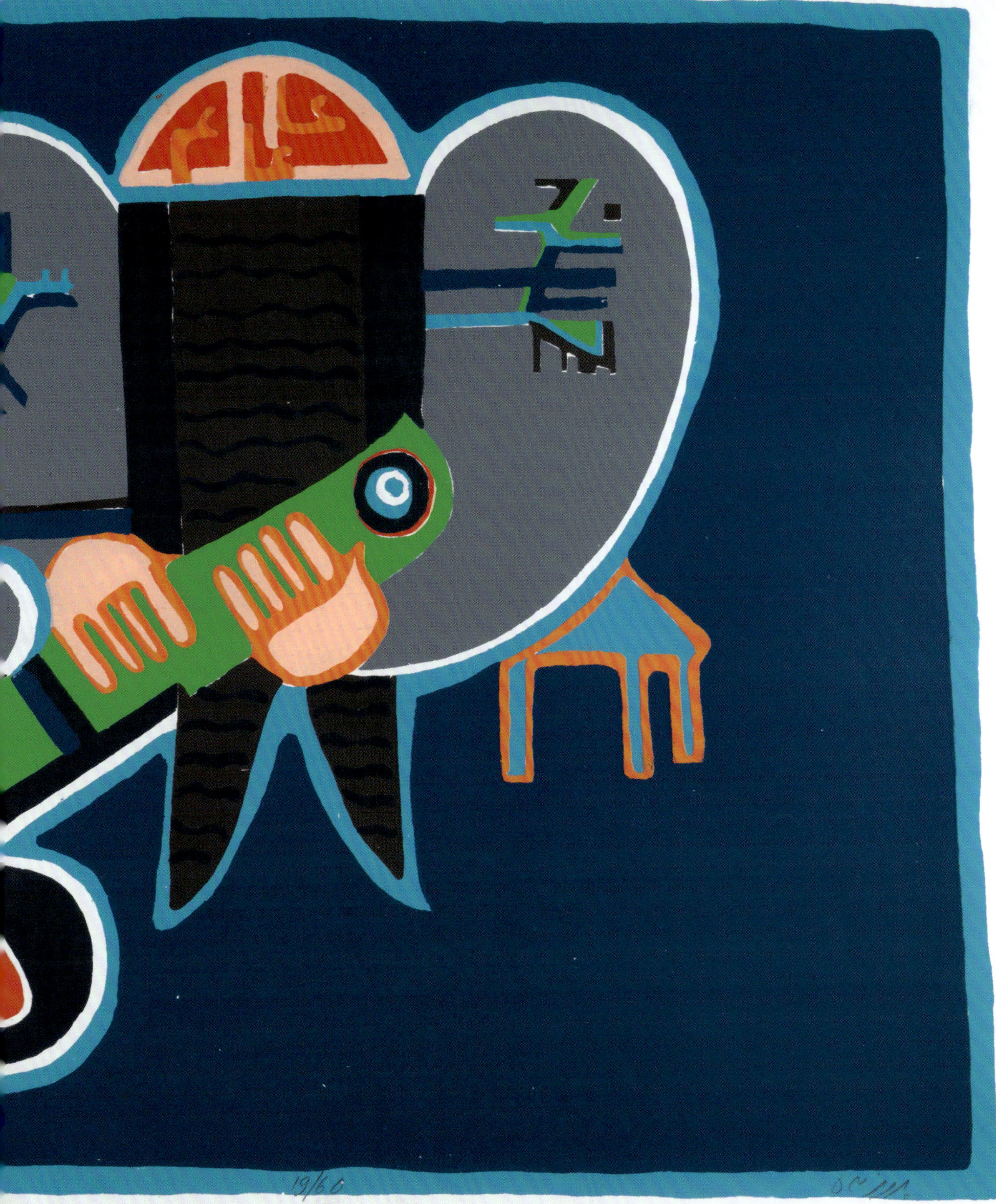

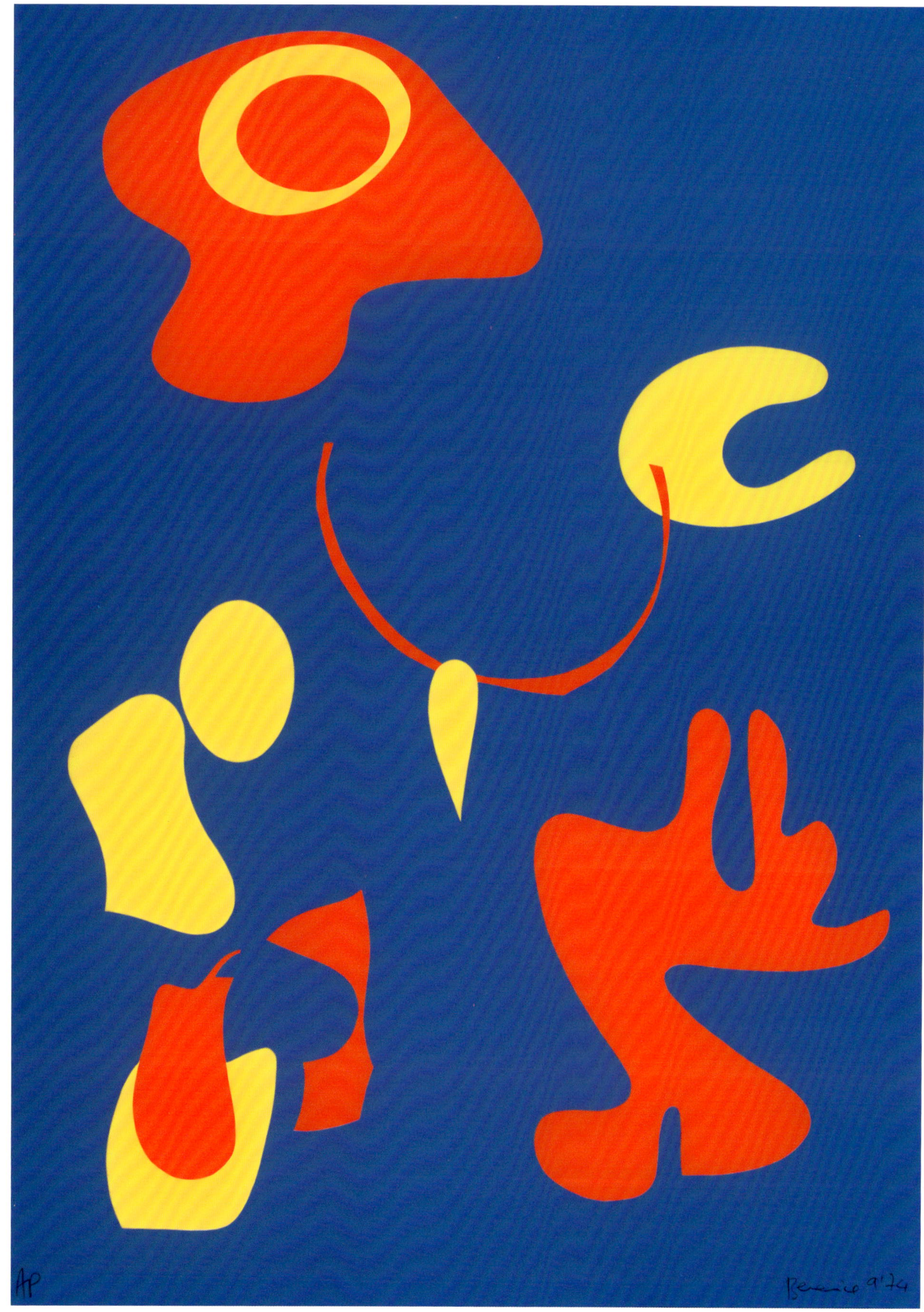

Berenice Sydney (1944–1983)
Screenprint with Balance 1974
Screenprint on paper 80 × 58.4

The British artist Berenice Sydney worked across the disciplines of painting, drawing, printmaking, children's books, costume design and performance. Her screenprints reflect her preoccupation with the aesthetic qualities of colour and form, a concern reflected by the title of this piece, *Screenprint with Balance*. The floating abstract forms have the look of paper cuts, reminding us that screenprinting is a stencil-based technique in which the stencils can be handmade if the artist chooses. Sydney selected the primary colours of blue, red and yellow for this print, creating a separate screen for each colour. In a variant of the piece, *Balance (Grey)*, the screens were printed using grey, black and red instead. Tate's impression of *Screenprint with Balance* is an artist's proof.

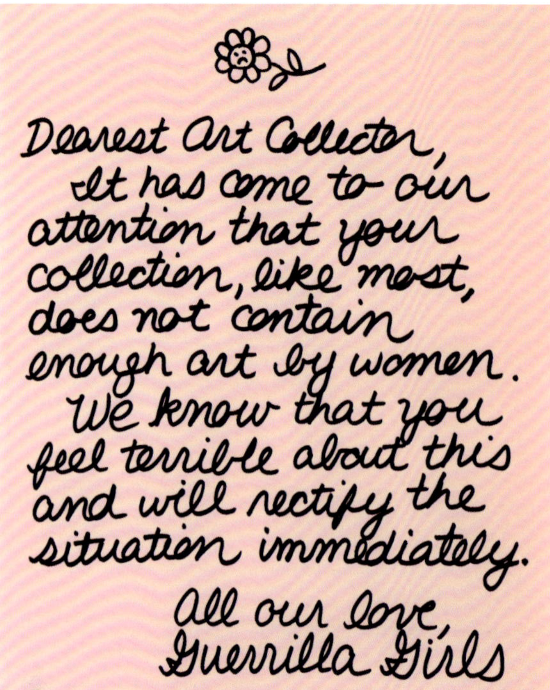

Guerrilla Girls
Dearest Art Collector, from *Guerrilla Girls Talk Back* 1986
Screenprint on paper 56 × 43

Guerrilla Girls is an artistic collective exposing sexist and racial discrimination in the art world. The group, whose members have worn gorilla masks to protect their anonymity, was formed in response to an exhibition of international painting and sculpture held at New York's Museum of Modern Art in 1984. The exhibition included work by 169 contemporary artists, only thirteen of whom were women; in addition, the comment of the show's curator that any artist not featured should rethink 'his' career angered female artists. In 1985, the Guerrilla Girls began using posters to target the museums, dealers, curators and artists they considered to be complicit in excluding women and non-white artists from mainstream exhibitions.

Dearest Art Collector emphasises the role of collectors in ensuring female artists are not discriminated against, taking the form of an enlarged handwritten letter. Pejorative notions of perceived girlishness are referenced, from the pink background to the flowing handwriting and the sad-faced flower at the top. It is from the portfolio *Guerrilla Girls Talk Back*, which includes screenprinted versions of thirty posters designed by the group. The group printed and published the prints in an edition of fifty.

Damien Hirst (born 1965)
Untitled 1992
Screenprint on paper 86 × 62.5

Damien Hirst is known as one of the Young British Artists who dominated the British art scene during the 1990s. *Untitled* was his first foray into printmaking. It shows a grid of photographic images of rocks seen against a pink background, apparently arranged in a way that reminded the artist of a 'school geography textbook'.[14] It was printed in eight colours and was partially varnished to make the background glossy and the rocks matt by comparison. Grids and organising are important themes in Hirst's work.

Untitled was published as part of the *London* portfolio, which contained prints by eleven London-based contemporary artists. The portfolio was commissioned by Charles Booth-Clibborn, who published it under his imprint, The Paragon Press, London, in an edition of forty sets, plus fifteen for artists and collaborators. The portfolio was conceived as a portable group exhibition of work by emerging artists, most of whom chose to use screenprinting.

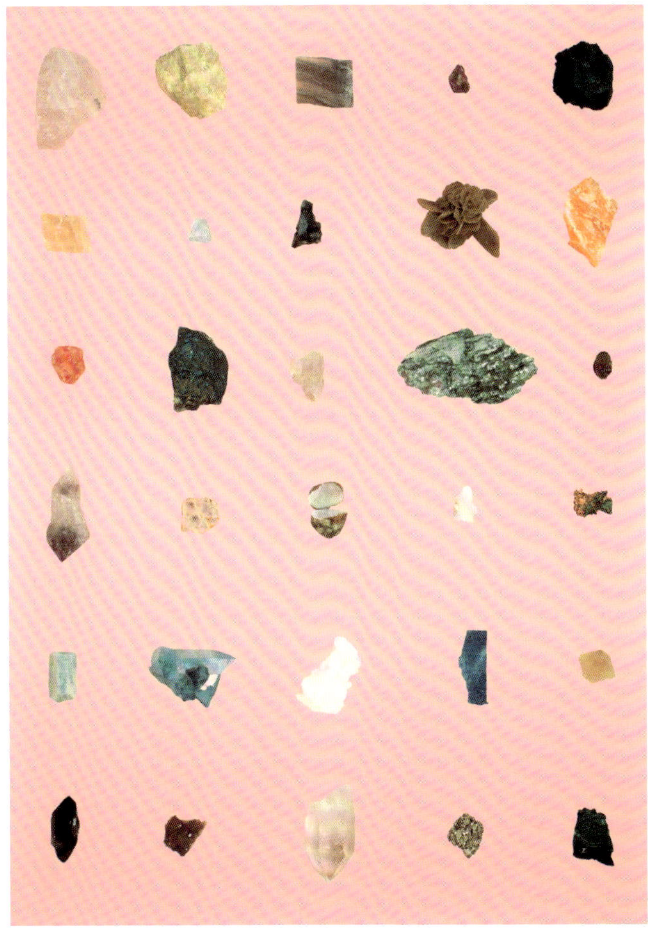

Georgina Starr (born 1968)
You Stole my Look 1997
Screenprint on paper 71.9 × 88.7

This piece by Georgina Starr explores the role of clothing in personal identity. The print presents five self-portraits of the artist wearing different outfits. It was made for *Screen*, a portfolio of prints by eleven London-based artists published by The Paragon Press, who had previously published the *London* portfolio, another effort to reflect the practice of contemporary London-based artists (p.179). The title *Screen* refers to both the screenprinting technique and the fact that most of the artists involved had also worked with photography or film.

Starr's design was originally made for a mock advertisement in the artist's self-published comic book, *Starvision*. She drew the figures by hand then edited the images on the computer using Photoshop; although screenprinting usually involves hand printing, computer-derived imagery can be used to create the stencils. Each print in *Screen* was published in an edition of seventy-five, the first forty-five of which were produced in portfolio sets.

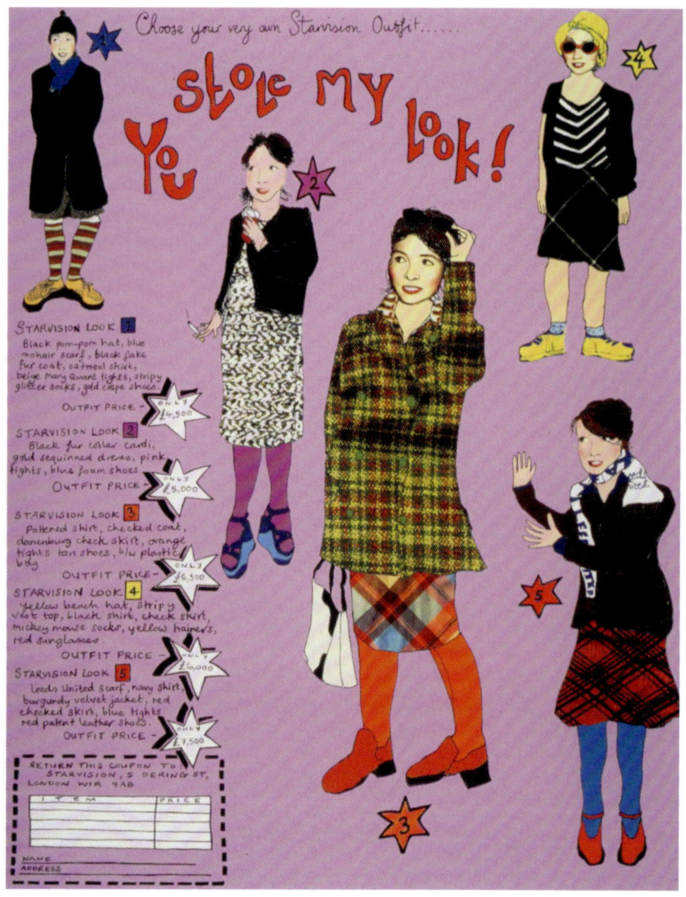

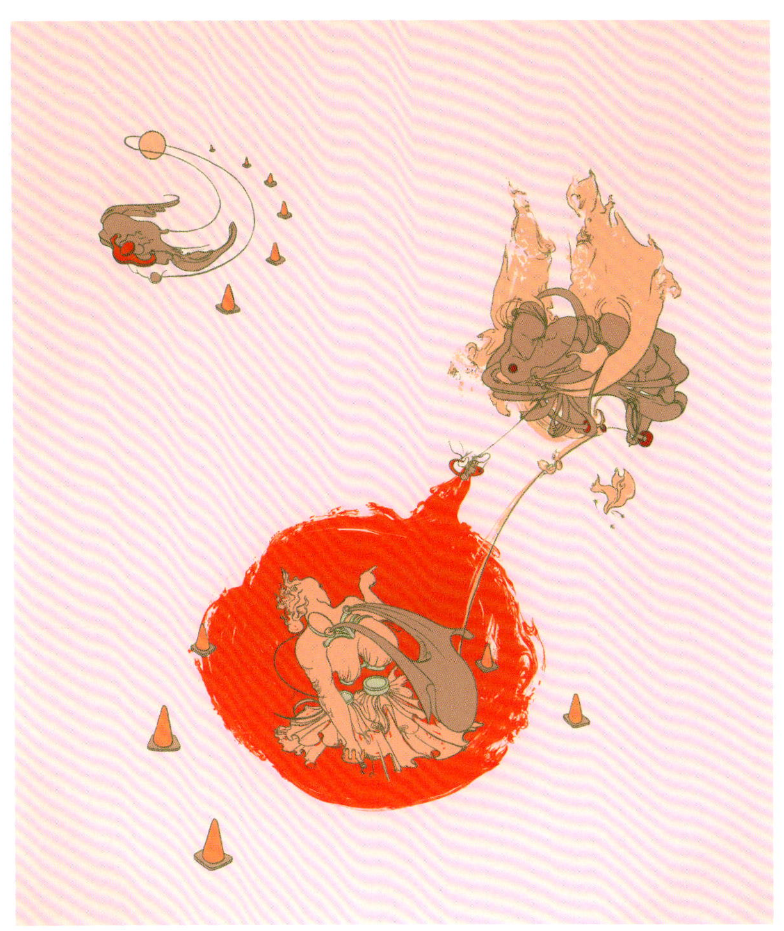

Inka Essenhigh (born 1969)
Daedalus and Icarus 2000
Screenprint with acrylic varnish on paper 76 x 66

The American artist Inka Essenhigh is known for her dreamlike paintings. *Daedalus and Icarus* reinterprets a subject from Greek mythology. In the myth, the inventor Daedalus is trapped on the island of Crete. To allow himself and his young son, Icarus, to escape by air, Daedalus makes them wings of feather and wax. Although they successfully escape, Icarus ignores his father's warning to avoid the sun's heat and flies too high: as a result, the wax in his wings melts and he falls to his death. Essenhigh's interpretation includes the key components of the story – figures, wings, the sun – but it is also strange and ambiguous; it is not a straightforward representation of the story.

Daedalus and Icarus is a ten-colour screenprint, which was coated with acrylic varnish after printing to create a high gloss finish. It was printed at Noblet Serigraphie in an edition of forty and published by Carolina Nitsch Contemporary Art, New York.

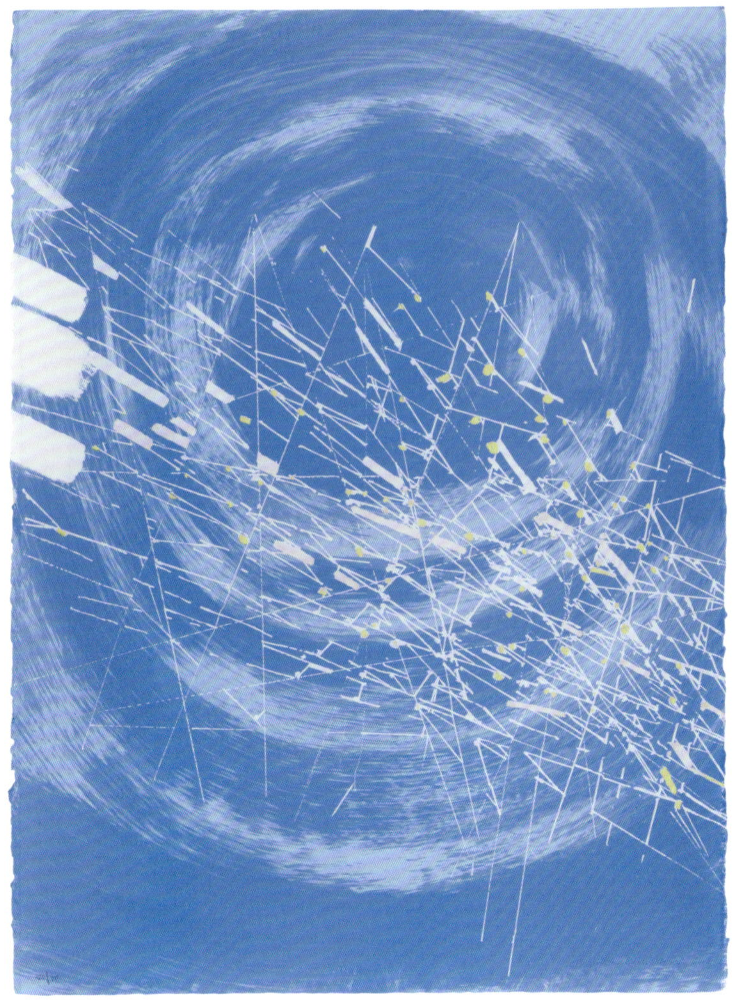

Wilhelmina Barns-Graham (1912–2004)
Vision in Time I 2000
Screenprint on paper 76.8 x 58

The British artist Wilhelmina Barns-Graham discovered her love of screenprinting during the final phase of her career, when her work became considerably more painterly and colourful. For these late screenprints, she worked closely with Graal Press, who were developing new water-based screenprinting methods. Barns-Graham was able to use her preferred paints to brush marks onto clear sheets; working with her printers, she gradually developed each screenprint as a multi-layered abstract image.[15]

Vision in Time I, from the artist's 'Time' series, reflects Barns-Graham's love of painterly effects. Screens printed in blue, pale blue, yellow and white combine to create the otherworldly image. The piece was printed in an edition of fifty (but numbered in error up to '50/70') by Carol Robertson of Graal Press, near Edinburgh.

Sarah Morris (born 1967)
Dulles [Capital] 2001
Screenprint on paper 73.7 x 73.7

This print by the American-based artist Sarah Morris demonstrates the effectiveness of screenprinting for geometric images requiring flat areas of intense colour with hard edges: in this case, white areas cleanly separate different coloured shapes. It is from her series *Dulles [Capital]*, her first major work in the print medium. The title references Dulles International Airport, which formed one of the locations in Morris's 2000 film about Washington, DC as the 'Capital' of the United States. While Morris's prints and paintings of the airport incorporate certain elements of the buildings and its colours, they do not literally represent physical characteristics of the airport's futuristic architecture.[16]

The series as a whole includes nine prints. They can be displayed either individually, as seen here, or with the complete series arranged in a grid. When the series is displayed in its entirety, 3.5cm of white wall separates each print, the white space becoming an additional part of the work. *Dulles [Capital]* was published in London by The Paragon Press in an edition of forty-five, plus ten sets of artist's proofs.

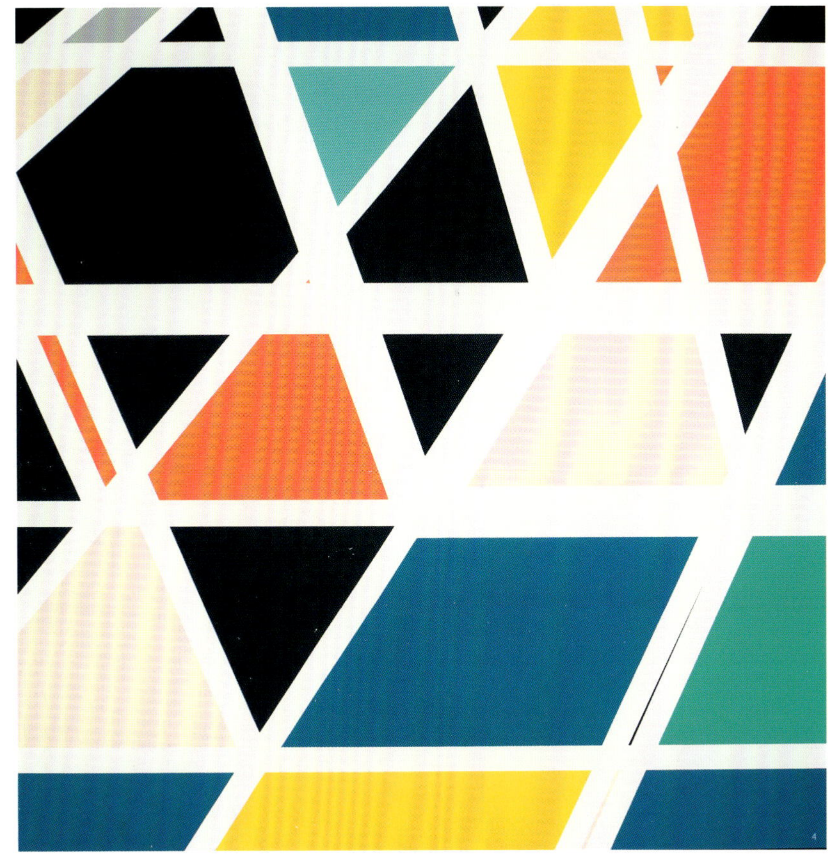

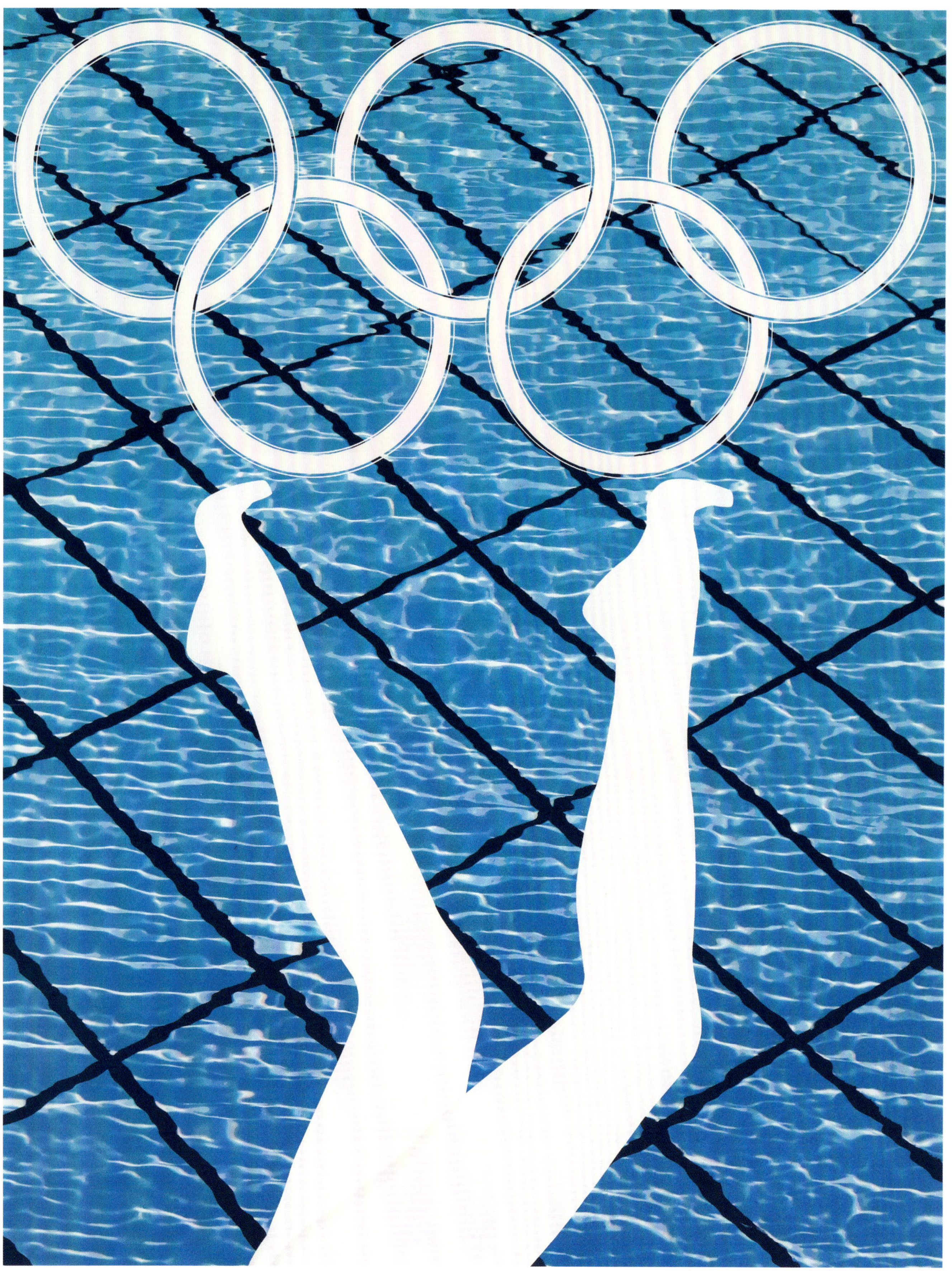

Anthea Hamilton (born 1978)
Divers 2011
Screenprint on paper 76 x 60

Anthea Hamilton was one of twelve British artists commissioned to make a print to commemorate the 2012 Olympic Games in London. The result is this thirteen-colour screenprint, which like the other prints in the *Olympic* portfolio, was printed in an edition of 150.

In the composition, the iconic motif of the Olympic rings is shown balanced on the toes of a diver or swimmer. While the print's title is certainly indicative of the Olympic sport of diving, it has been noted that the gymnastic pose seen in the image is more suggestive of the postures held in one of only two Olympic sports in which only women compete: synchronised swimming.[17] Hamilton's apparent interest in this sport in particular perhaps reflects her wider concern with the female body, a recurring theme in her practice. The combination of the white papercut-like forms making up the legs and rings and the photographic realism of the tile-like swimming pool also nods towards Hamilton's interest in collage.

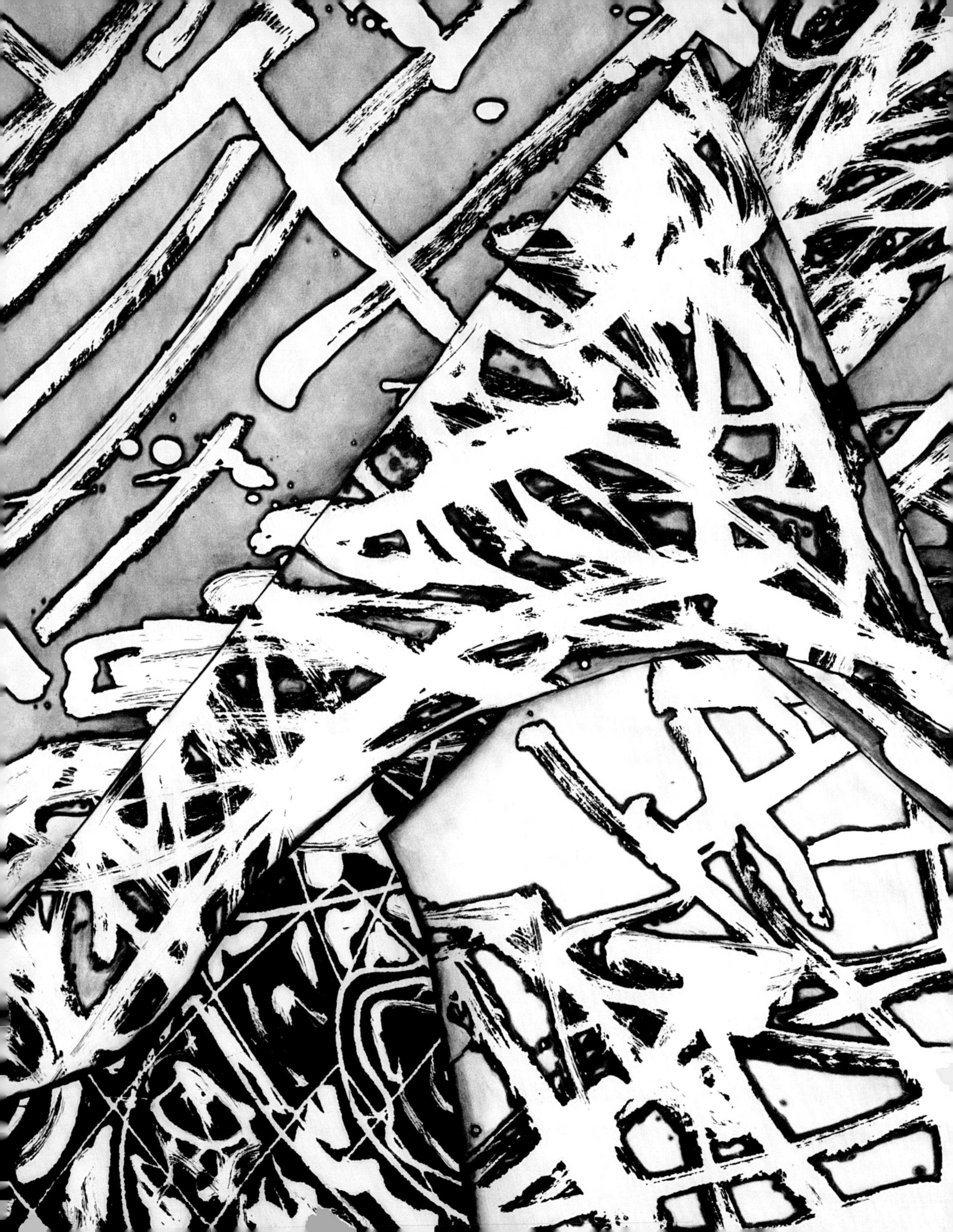

7 Print and Process

Frank Stella *Swan Engraving I* 1982 (detail)

7 Print and Process

The previous sections of this book explored the key techniques artists have used to make handmade prints. This final section is concerned with prints that present a particularly experimental approach to these and additional processes, which are often seen in unusual combinations in the examples given here. While historically print's primary purpose was to produce images in multiples, in a world awash with photographic reproductions handmade prints are no longer required to disseminate an artist's work. But even in the days when prints were still required for this purpose, a love of – and interest in – the print process itself inspired many artists to experiment with it, from William Blake to Joseph Mallord William Turner. Once the arrival of new technology had, by the twentieth century, freed artists from any need to multiply images via printmaking, the emphasis on printmaking as an experimental, technically interesting art form only increased. While this is clearly not purely a modern and contemporary phenomenon, it is probably fair to say that creating a new and different visual language with print has become increasingly important to artists over time, as the practical need to use it as a means of multiplying images has faded.

> BLAKE p.192
> TURNER p.101

Each work in this final section, then, explores the ever-evolving 'process of print' in some way, whether that involves combining different techniques in complex, multi-layered prints, engaging with digital technology or by using printmaking methods innovatively to create unique works as opposed to multiples.

The Single Copy Print

Unique elements have been added to prints throughout their history; in particular, hand colouring prints using watercolour has a long record at both the cheaper and more exclusive ends of the market. But this usually involved adding watercolour washes to prints in a standardised fashion, rather than reworking the print to the point that the line between print on the one hand, and drawing, painting or collage on the other becomes blurred. Some artists have pushed hand colouring further, into the realms of merging print with other techniques to create whole new artwork. Marc Chagall's *The Vision*, for example, exists as a single-colour etching. But the copy highlighted here, which Chagall hand coloured with gouache and pastel some years later, is so transformed by unique additions as to be barely recognisable; really this work is as much a drawing as a print. Similarly, in her 1993 work *The Colour That Was There,* Gillian Ayres used acrylic paint to work into an existing screenprint. William Kentridge, meanwhile, completed his 1999 etching *This is How the Tree Breaks* with the addition of crayon and collaged elements unique to each impression, creating a variable edition.

> CHAGALL p.194
> AYRES p.206
> KENTRIDGE p.218

While the above artists used drawing and painting media to work into prints that started life as images printed in multiples, others have purposefully used monotype, a technique which generally only produces a single print. To make a monotype, the printmaker works on a smooth surface – usually glass – using a greasy medium, such as printer's ink or oil paint. The 'drawing' they have made is then pressed directly against paper to make a print (or, if the artist has used a thin metal plate, it might be passed through a rolling press along with paper). As the artist has taken the print from an image that has not been fixed to the drawing surface in any way, it cannot usually be printed more than once, as most of the ink or paint has passed onto the paper. By its very nature monotype subverts what is often considered a principal attribute of printmaking – its ability to produce images in multiples. The fleeting and unpredictable effects created by this unstable, one-time meeting of marks and paper, forms this medium's key appeal for many artists.

Monotype has been practised since at least the 1600s, when the Italian artist Giovanni Benedetto Castiglione made monotypes from copper plates. In the nineteenth century, Edgar Degas made some of the most impressive examples of the technique. Some of his monotypes also became the starting point for print-pastel hybrids,

> DEGAS p.193

as seen in the example highlighted here. During the twentieth century, the possibilities of creating unusual visual effects using the method attracted some notable abstract painters, including the British artist Alan Davie and the German artist Karl-Otto Götz.

> DAVIE p.196
> GÖTZ p.197

Mixing Methods

A number of the prints included in this section reveal the multitude of different effects that can be created when radically different print processes are combined in a single print. Sometimes new combinations have been achieved by individual innovators, such as Blake, who developed his own relief etching and monotype techniques over two hundred years ago. At other times, making mixed method prints has been a more collaborative process, as seen in the work of Roy Lichtenstein, who created complex multi-method prints with the help of a small army of printers and technicians.

> BLAKE p.192
> LICHTENSTEIN p.204

Lichtenstein is not the only artist to require specialist help in creating particularly experimental prints, and it is notable that a high proportion of the prints included in this section came to Tate via a significant gift from Kenneth Tyler, a master printer known for his collaborations with leading American artists of his day. His print shop, Tyler Graphics, provided artists with the opportunity to work with first-rate technicians and the facilities to work on a very large scale, as well as offering Tyler's own expertise and hands-on involvement. The level of collaboration involved has sometimes been criticised, but master printers have been offering specialist, technical solutions to allow artists' ideas to fully flourish in print since the Renaissance. Sometimes this collaboration has led to visual effects unlike any otherwise achieved in the medium; Frank Stella's remarkable *Swan Engraving I*, for example, would never have been produced without the involvement of a large group of specialist printers working at the cutting edge of their field.

> STELLA p.201

Print Processes and the Future

In some ways, print has already moved beyond the handmade techniques explored in these pages. In the digital era many images exist only in digital form, and may never need to be printed in a tangible, paper-based format at all. And when they are, inkjet printing, one of the image-producers that currently surround us, is an obvious choice. It is unsurprising that artists such as Richard Hamilton soon began to take up this non-handmade method.

> HAMILTON p.215

The continued existence of handmade printmaking techniques, though, is about more than selecting the most efficient means to make images in multiples. As many of the works featured in this book demonstrate, printmaking continues to be pursued by artists actively engaged in a creative dialogue with its plethora of different methods and their potential visual effects. The continued popularity of limited edition prints as collectables is another notable factor. While some art schools have gone so far as to sell off their printmaking facilities during the past twenty years,[1] the success of independent print studios in cities across Europe and beyond suggests printmaking's continued, and perhaps even growing, popularity as an art form. It seems highly likely that all of the handmade processes described in this publication will continue to be practised alongside newer methods. Printmaking has been changing since its inception, and new generations of artists are likely to engage with it in new and surprising ways, something Tate's acquisitions of contemporary prints have continued to reflect.

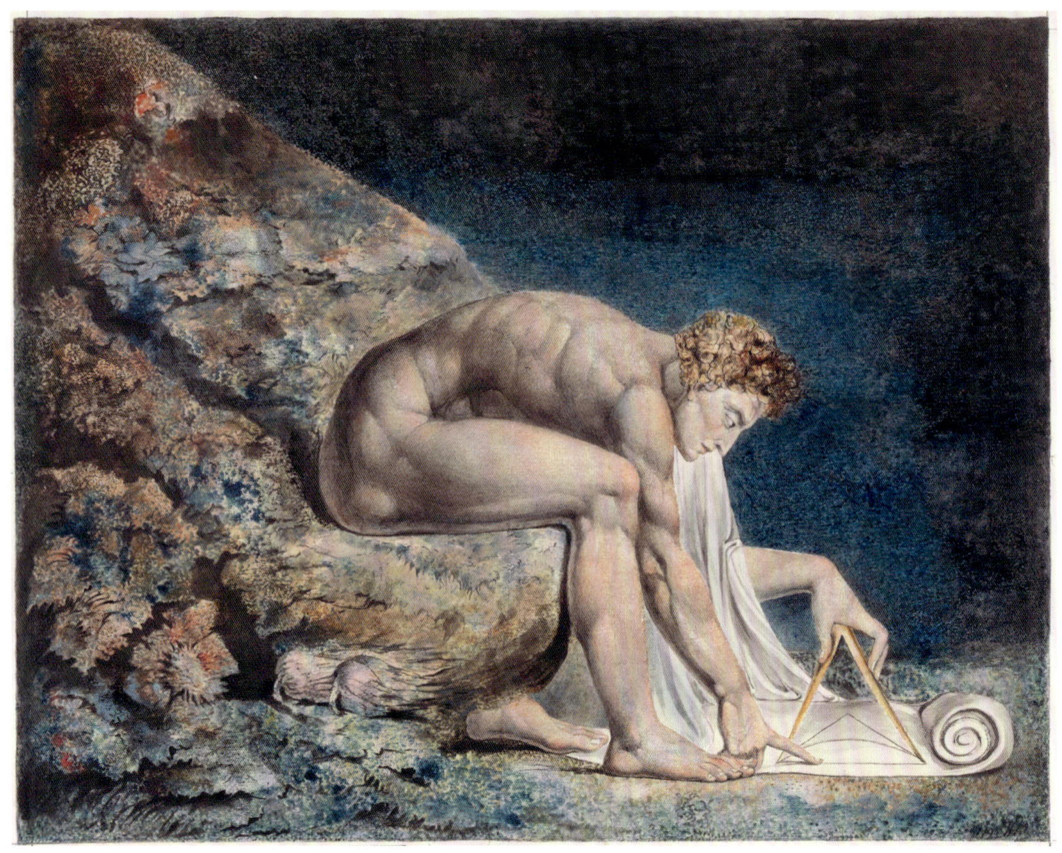

William Blake (1757–1827)
Newton 1795–c.1805
Colour print, ink and watercolour on paper 46 × 60

William Blake was proficient in various printmaking techniques, including wood engraving (see p.26) and relief etching, a method he invented himself. *Newton* is from a group of large colour monotype prints, which Blake worked up by hand to create finished works he called 'frescoes'. The subject of this 'fresco' is a young Isaac Newton; in Blake's critical vision, the influential scientist is shown following the rules of the compass, apparently blind to the beauty of the natural landscape surrounding him. It is unclear if the dreamlike landscape Blake imagines is above ground or under water.

In design the figure reflects the influence of the Renaissance painter Michelangelo. But in method the work is highly unusual, the work's surface combining printed elements with watercolour to such a degree that it is very difficult to see which areas are printed and which are hand-drawn. While the scale of this and related works is large relative to most of Blake's oeuvre, it is notably small scale by comparison to the great frescoes of Michelangelo and others that Blake seems to have been thinking of when making it.[2]

Edgar Degas (1834–1917)
Bed-Time c.1880–5
Pastel and monotype on paper 22.9 × 44.5

The French artist Edgar Degas is one of the best-known proponents of the monotype technique. In this intimate view of a woman in bed he combined the method with pastel. For this piece, the silvery marks of a monotype – which can still be glimpsed in the curtain and the pillow – formed the starting point, laying out the composition and tonal structure of the piece. Degas then worked into the print using pastel, transforming a grey, night-time scene into a lighter image, full of warm colour.

Degas used monotypes as the basis for around four hundred and fifty of his pastels, often using a second, paler impression of the monotype as a starting point for a new work. Like many of his figure pieces, this view of a woman suggests she is carrying out her daily routines while unaware of the artist's observing eye, which, like many of Degas's works, hints at voyeurism.

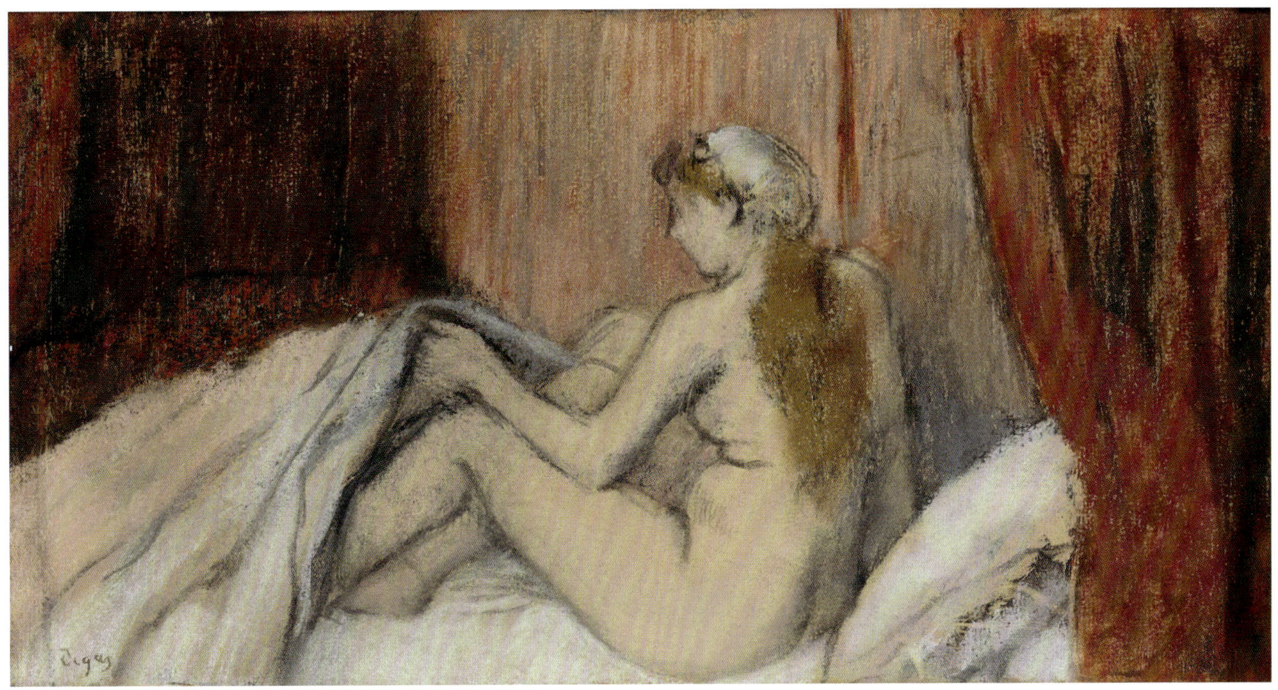

Marc Chagall (1887–1985)
The Vision 1924–5 and c. 1937
Etching, aquatint, gouache and pastel on paper 36.8 × 26.7

The Russian-French artist Marc Chagall hand-coloured some of his prints. While this is not unusual in itself, when Chagall came to work into this etching of a painter visited by an angel more than a decade after making the print, his interventions went far beyond adding washes of colour to the image. Instead, he created an entirely new work, combining printmaking with drawing and painting. To do this he worked into the etching with both gouache – an opaque form of watercolour paint – and pastel. These rich textural techniques allowed him to add a sky of brilliant blue, as well as fluffy white wings for the angel and vivid red trousers for the artist seated on the left.

Tate's impression of the etching, which dates from 1924–5, is an unnumbered copy of the print in its final state (or version), which was published in an edition of 100 and printed by Louis Fort. Chagall added the pastel and gouache elements in around 1937.

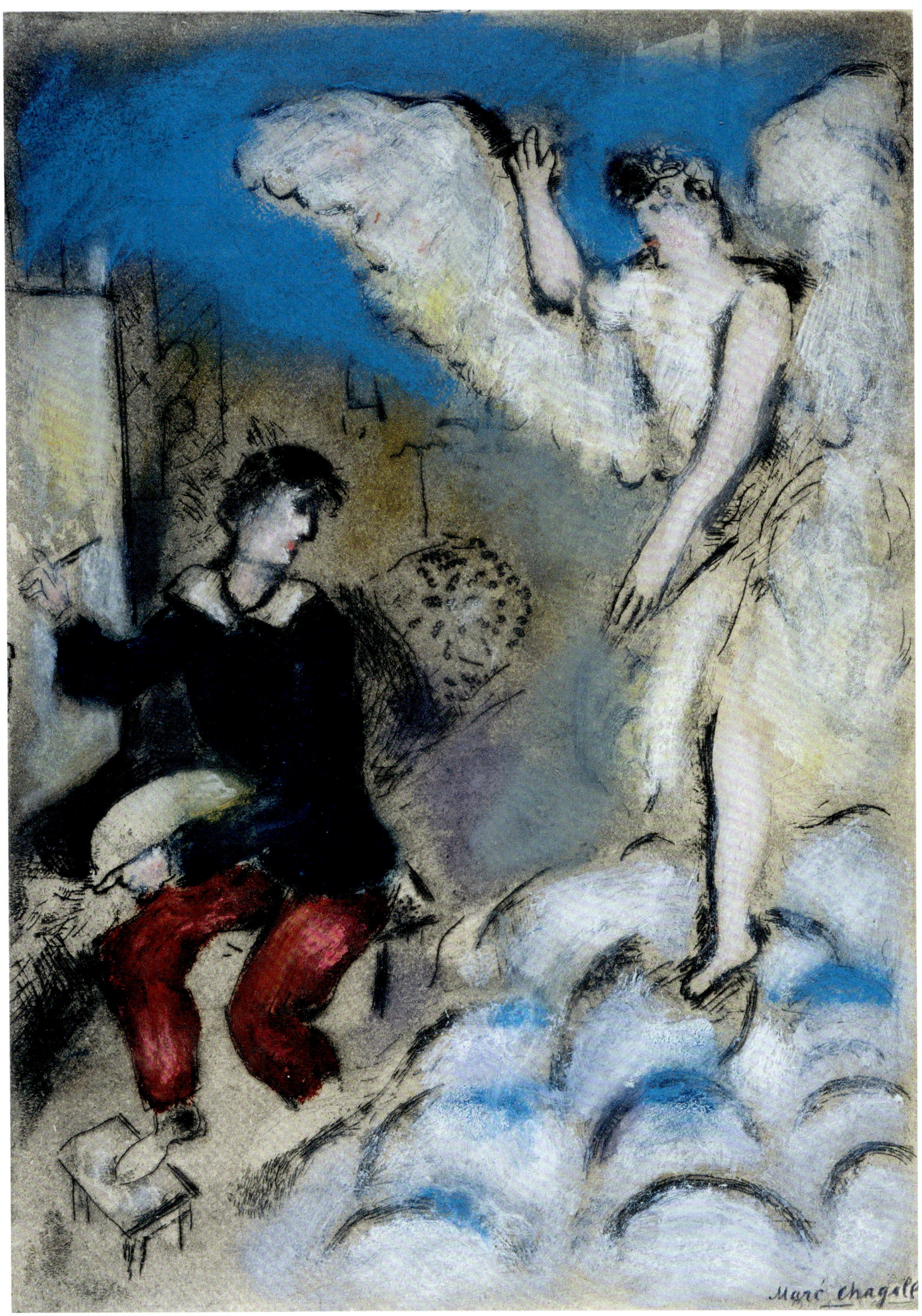
Marc Chagall

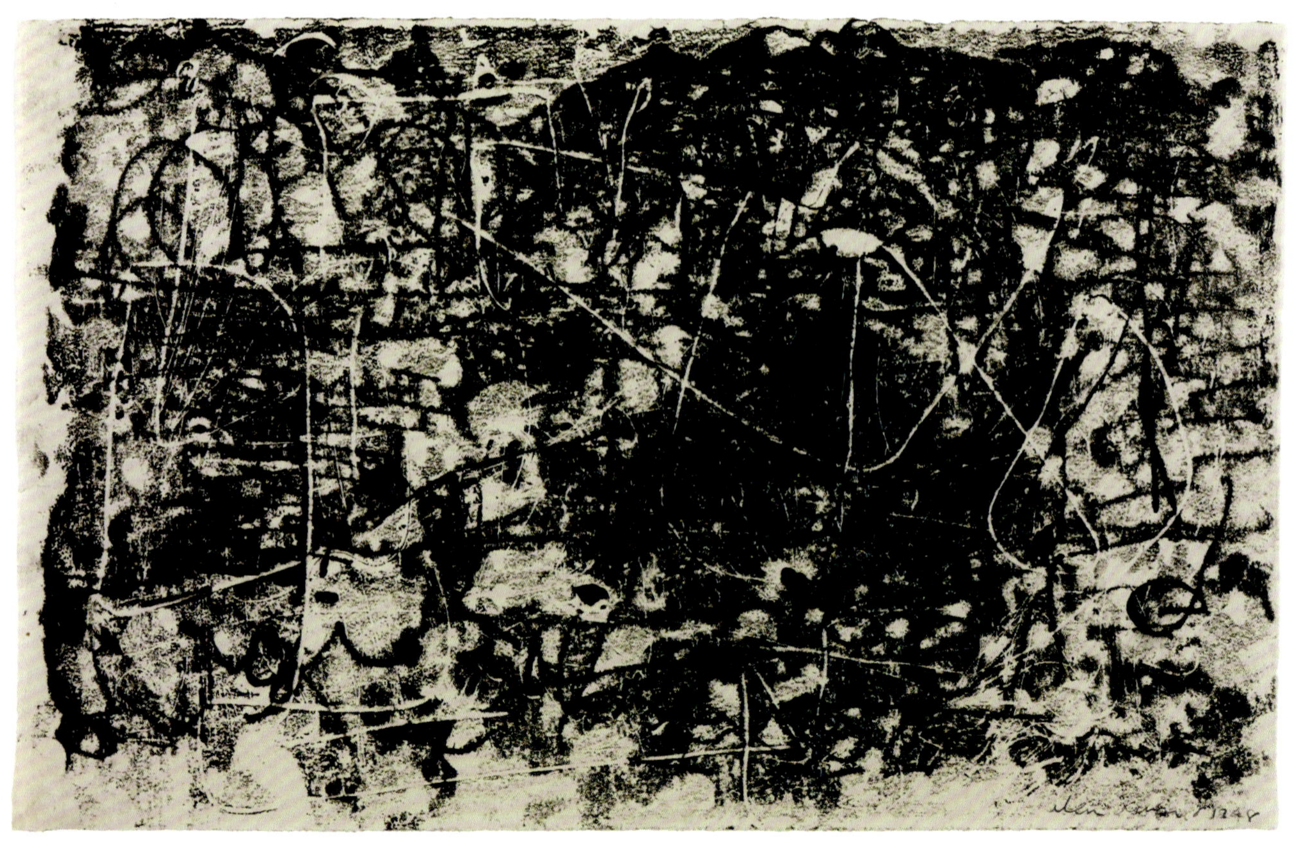

Alan Davie (1920–2014)
Spirit Over the Landscape 1948
Monotype on paper 24.9 × 40.3

The Scottish-born painter and musician Alan Davie started making abstract monotypes like this one in 1948, during a spell staying in Venice. He wrote to his father stating: 'I have perfected the technique of monotype; the secret is to use printer's ink on glass and to print on a fine Ingres paper (French). I am really finding something in the black and white mediums'.[3] Davie worked by sandwiching ink between a pane of glass and a sheet of paper. He scratched the paper with his fingers to make marks, the image only becoming visible once the sheet was lifted. This technique had the potential to make single copy prints with very rich surface textures, as seen in *Spirit Over the Landscape*.

Davie produced around a hundred monotypes between November and December 1948, only rarely using the technique again afterwards. He wrote: 'Through this wonderful medium I have discovered so much and developed so much so rapidly ... I am amazed ... my work is becoming something very strange.'[4]

Karl-Otto Götz (1914–2017)
Untitled 1954
Monotype on paper 40 × 50.2

Karl-Otto Götz was unable to exhibit work of this kind in Nazi Germany, where his interest in abstraction was deemed 'degenerate' by the government. Instead, he made a living as a landscape painter before being drafted to serve as a signal officer in the German army during the Second World War. Following the fall of the Nazi regime, Götz developed his work more freely, becoming a key figure in the postwar German art world. He was best known for his huge black-and-white paintings.

Götz became fascinated by the unpredictable chance effects possible with the monotype technique, in which he also worked in a visual language of black and white. He made this print in Paris; although he lived in Frankfurt during the 1950s he often visited the French capital. The lively forms seem to reflect his interest in surrealism, as well as the painterly, gestural abstraction that characterises his work.

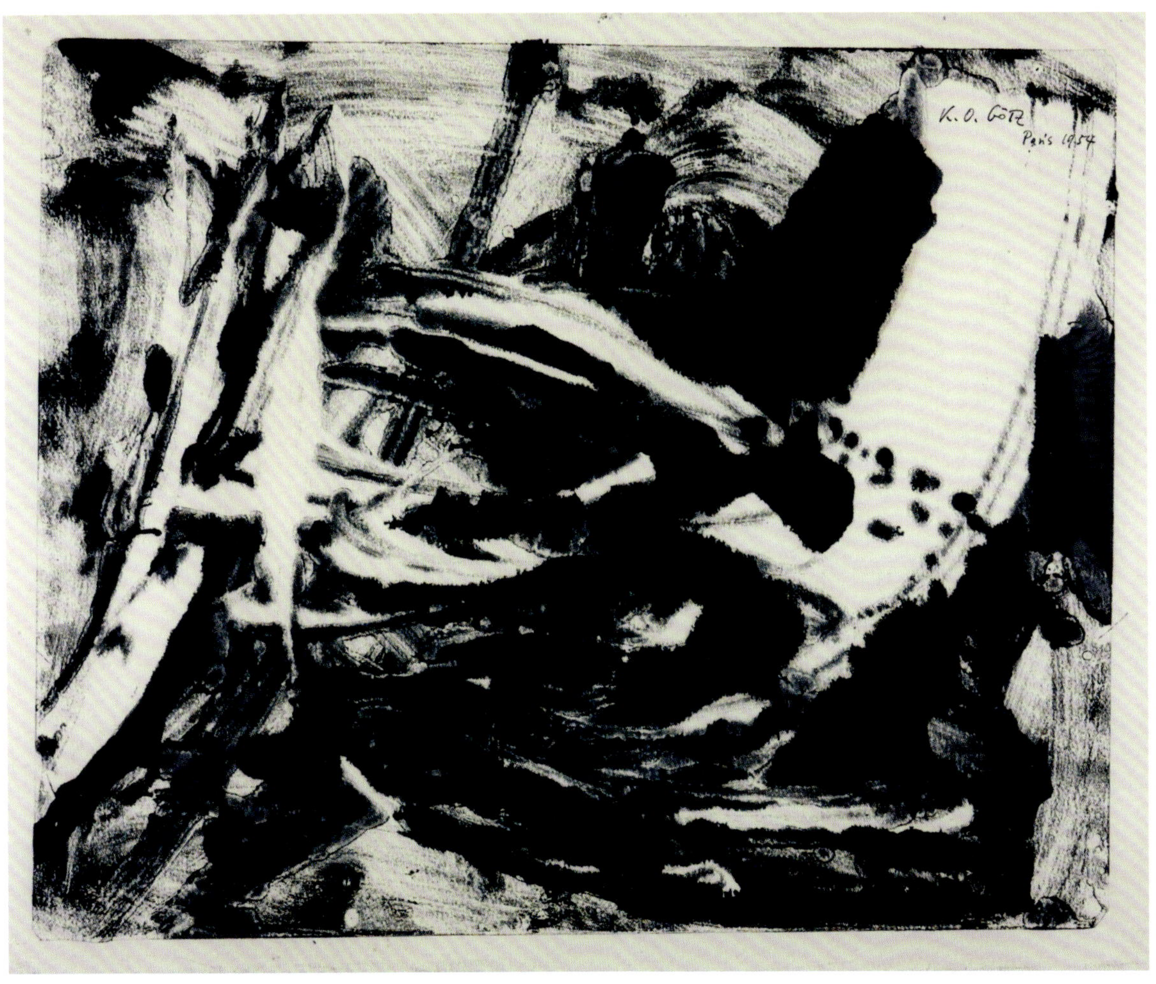

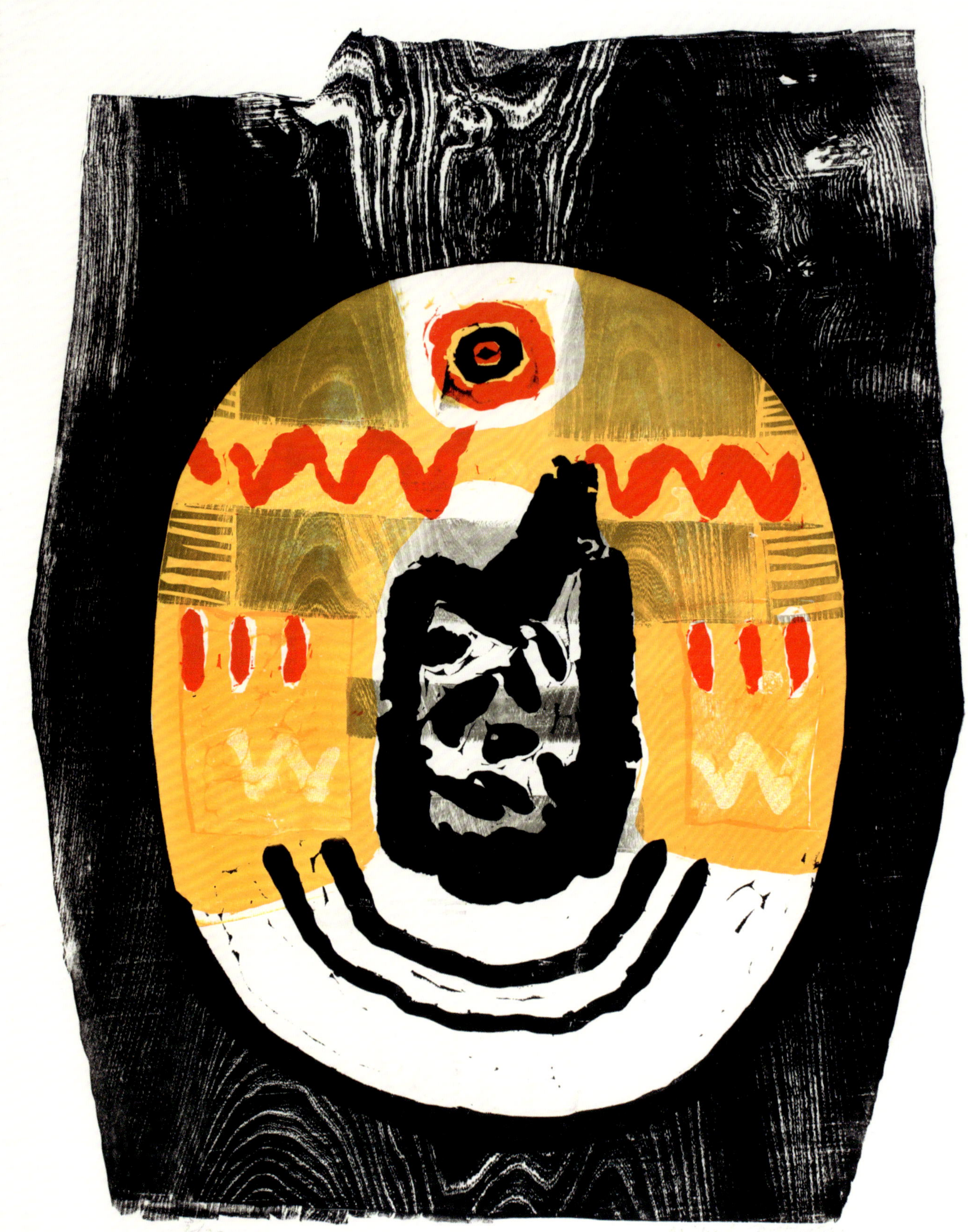

Michael Rothenstein (1908–1993)
Tournament 1963
Linocut and wood relief on paper 75.5 × 61.5

The prolific British printmaker Michael Rothenstein developed an 'open block' printing method to give him greater freedom in terms of the format and materials included in his complex relief prints. He wrote: 'the pieces of wood or other elements are assembled freely on a marked backing, thus taking on their own particular shape; the format is kept open – able to breathe – until the final arrangement is achieved.'[5]

In *Tournament*, an abstract mixed method print, Rothenstein avoided the standard rectangular shape that is the norm for prints, and combined wood and lino blocks. Preserving a sense of the wood's natural structure within the finished print was important to him, and the wood grain seen in the curving and heavy black border here is a key feature of the print. The artist said that the image was inspired by the idea of a shield from a tournament, which was itself suggested to him by the fascinating piece of elm he used for the wood block.[6]

Chila Kumari Singh Burman (born 1957)
If There is No Struggle, There is No Progress – Uprisings 1981
Etching, lithograph and paint on paper 61.2 × 81.2

The British artist Chila Kumari Singh Burman made a group of single copy prints known as the *Riot Series* while studying at the Slade School of Fine Art in London. Working with the master printmaker Stanley Jones, she combined etching and screenprint for some of the prints, and etching and lithography for others, including this work. Overlaying these very different processes – which do not lend themselves to being combined – echoes the conflict of the subject matter seen in her *Riot* series, allowing her to explore the 'democratic, versatile, colourful, creative, experimental' medium of print.[7]

This print is a response to riots seen in major English cities during the summer of 1981; the riots have been attributed to racial tension, inner city deprivation and a distrust of the police and government. Burman combined printed imagery and text, some of it reminiscent of newspaper coverage, using black and red ink as well as paint. The words and dates included relate to the riots, with the year, 1981, highlighted, and some of the cities affected, such as Liverpool, are incorporated into the image in the form of text. The multi-layered imagery includes a gasmasked riot policeman on the right, a motif also included within other prints in the *Riot* series.

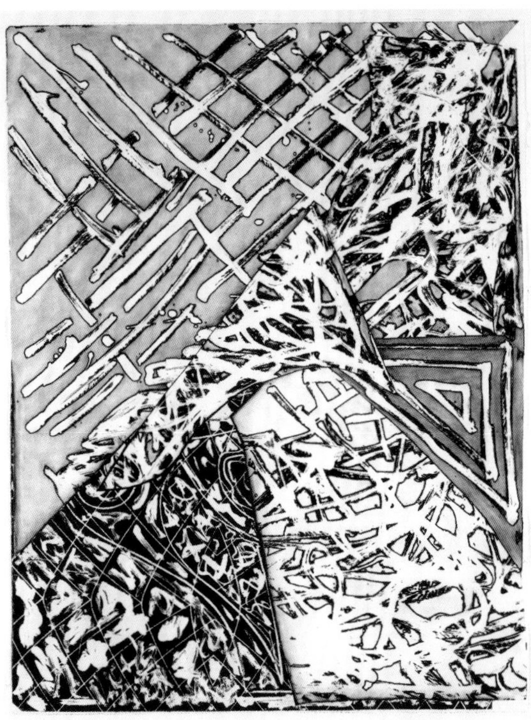

Frank Stella (born 1936)
Swan Engraving I 1982
Etching on paper 166.7 × 128.5

The American artist Frank Stella's technically inventive approach to printmaking is demonstrated by this piece from his *Swan Engravings* series. He created the print using a series of metal scraps – remnants of his *Circuits* series of paintings – which were drawn into and individually etched. The scraps were then collaged onto a large sheet of plywood alongside freshly cut pieces, creating a unique printing surface largely assembled from found objects. The resulting large-scale prints, which had to be painstakingly inked, wiped and printed in an unconventional manner by a team of specialist printers, are shimmering abstract images of black, white and grey. Some of the forms seen in them are tracings from the design tools, such as protractors, used to cut out the metal before it became scraps.[8] The true subject matter of this remarkable series is surely the printmaking process itself.

Swan Engraving I was printed in an edition of thirty by Tyler Graphics Ltd, New York, with whom Stella closely collaborated. The prints were taken from one 'collage plate'; this master plate was composed of seven irregularly cut etched magnesium plates.[9] Each plate took half a day to ink; by comparison, a traditional line etching can be inked up in minutes and is nowhere near as dependent on the methods of a particular printer to achieve a satisfactory impression.

Sue Williamson (born 1941)
Maggie Magaba 1983
Photo-etching and screenprint on papers on paper   Support: 70 × 100

The Cape Town-based artist Sue Williamson worked on the series *A Few South Africans*, of which this print is part, during the 1980s. The country was still very much in the grip of apartheid at this time, and Williamson sought to highlight the mostly anonymous women who contributed to the struggle for freedom. The subject of this particular print is Maggie Magaba, one of the many Black South African women who worked in domestic service for a white employer. One of Magaba's young charges later recounted: 'Maggie lived in the backyard of our house in a tiny room for over thirty years. During that time, she saved every penny to educate her own children.'[10] Here, Magaba's quiet, private heroism is publicly celebrated.

Williamson mixed different print techniques along with collage. The central image seen in each individual work within *A Few South Africans* was photo-etched, with elements of line etching, aquatint and drawing also added as needed, and colour screenprinting was used to create a frame. The decorative border, partly comprised of different papers, references the South African domestic practice of creating borders for photographic mementoes using coloured paper and printed ephemera. Each image was also accompanied by a description of the subject's achievements. *Maggie Magaba* was published in an edition of twenty. As Williamson wished to circulate the stories to the widest public possible, the editioned prints were also reissued as postcards.

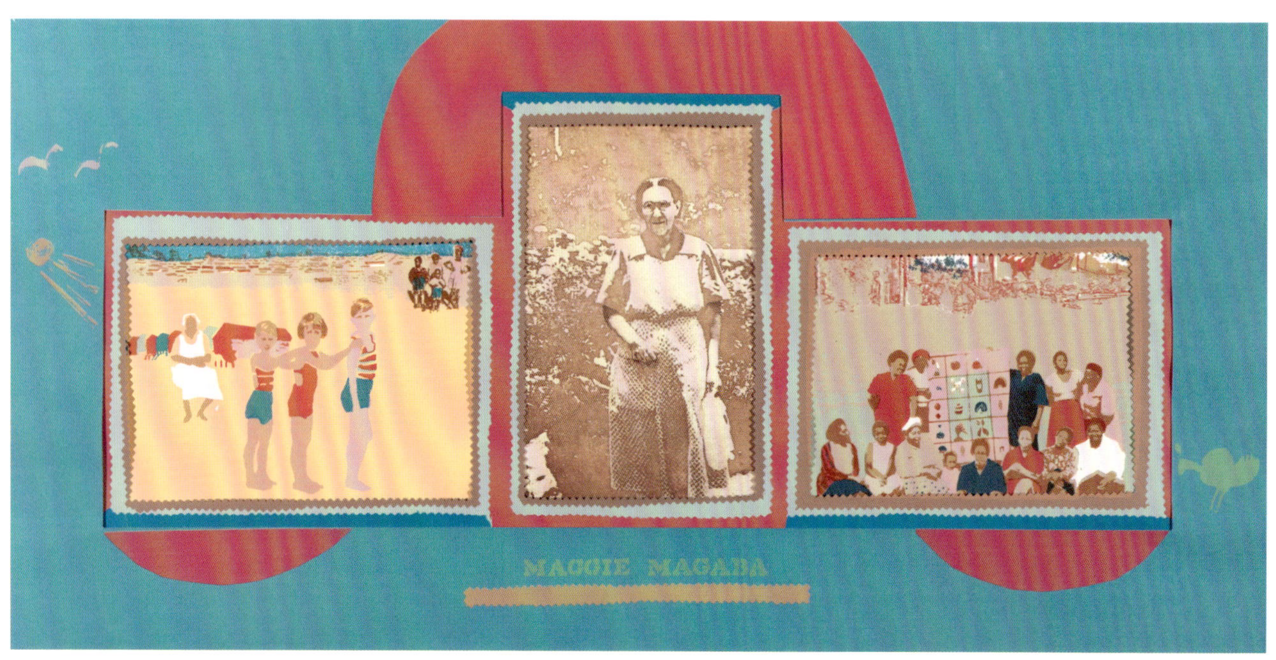

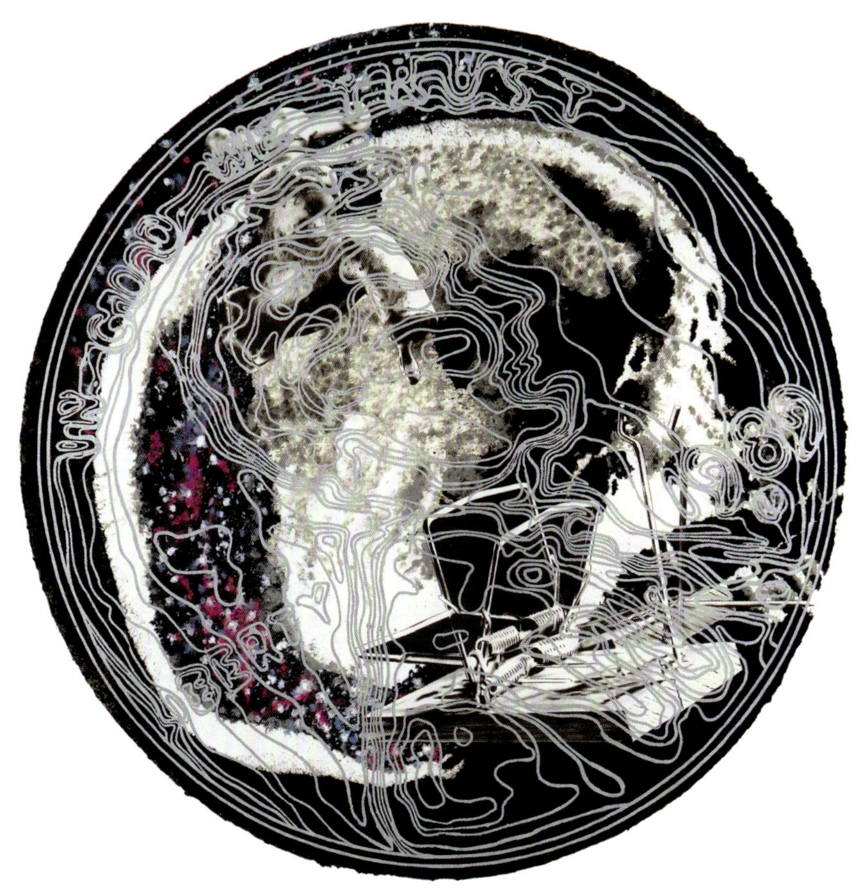

James Rosenquist (1933–2017)
Skull Snap 1989
Paper, acrylic paint, dye, lithograph and relief print on paper 151.1 × 151.1

This piece is from James Rosenquist's *Welcome to the Water Planet*, which has been described as 'a series of nine innovative paperwork multiples incorporating lithographed collage elements', each of which views the Earth in a different way.[11] Seeking a more spontaneous method of printmaking, Rosenquist worked on the series with the master printer Kenneth Tyler (see p.190).

Each work in the series is created from printed elements, but these were cut and collaged onto handmade paper to the point that the finished works are barely recognisable as prints. *Skull Snap* also includes an additional printed motif, with an image of Abraham Lincoln and the motto 'In God We Trust' from the US one-cent coin overlaid onto the final image using a relief method. The magnified, stylised version of this motif is difficult to make out and resembles a map, perhaps hinting at the global power of the US dollar. *Skull Snap* was published in an edition of thirty-eight, plus ten artist's proofs, by Tyler Graphics Ltd, New York.

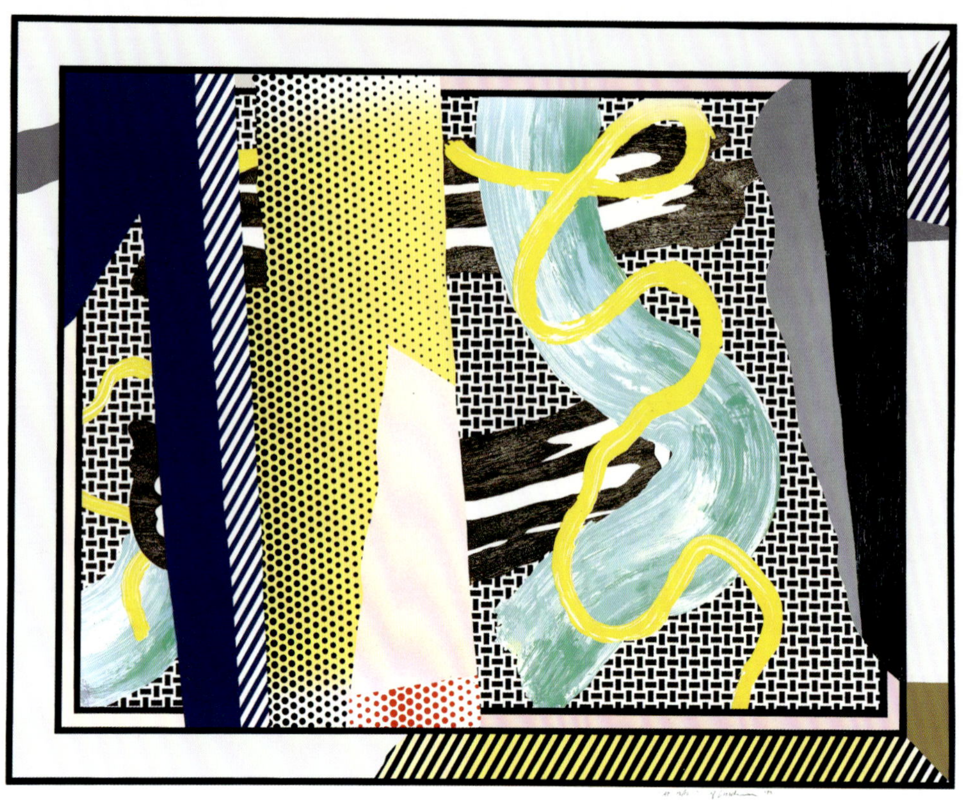

Roy Lichtenstein (1923–1997)
Reflections on Brushstrokes 1990
Lithograph, screenprint and woodcut on paper 128.7 × 165

Roy Lichtenstein's use of screenprinting is represented elsewhere in these pages (p.164). In this later work, he combined the technique with lithography and woodcut to create a complex multi-method image, the production of which was supported by several specialist printers. *Reflections on Brushstrokes* is from a series of seven *Reflections* prints, which recall the artist's comic book subject matter of the 1960s. In each of the works, the central image is partly obscured, either by reflections on glass or a mirror. In the case of this image, the reflections reference those sometimes seen when looking at a glazed painting: Lichtenstein said: 'It shows all of the paint and it has the glass in front, and the canvas and brushstrokes, so it encompasses all that is art – more or less.'[12]

The printing of *Reflections on Brushstrokes* was technically very complex; it combined numerous ink colours, metal plates, screenprint screens and woodblocks. It was printed and published by Tyler Graphics Ltd, New York, in an edition of sixty-eight with sixteen artist's proofs.

Masami Teraoka (born 1936)
Hawaii Snorkel Series: Catfish Envy 1993
Woodcut, etching, aquatint and ink on paper 65.8 × 97.9

In *Catfish Envy* the Japanese-born artist Masami Teraoka referenced techniques and imagery associated with ukiyo-e, a type of colourful Japanese woodblock print which developed in 1765 and remained popular until the early twentieth century. Teraoka drew parallels between the mass production of 'floating world' ukiyo-e prints and the later, primarily Western, style, pop art, with its celebration of mass culture imagery. Of the imagery in this scene, which reimagines typical ukiyo-e subject matter, he said: 'The middle-aged Samurai of *Catfish Envy* could represent traditional Japanese male chauvinistic thinking. He is astounded by the Western woman who is cuddling a catfish in front of him. The way she caresses the big head of the catfish could imply how much American people love animals but could also show how openly they can express their affections in public, something not culturally acceptable in Japan.'[13]

Teraoka used the woodcut technique in *Catfish Envy*, but he combined it with etching and aquatint to extend the range of tone possible. As a result, the image looks similar to ukiyo-e prints, but boasts a slightly different visual effect. Along with three other large prints, it is part of Teraoka's *Hawaii Snorkel Series*. The series was made with the input of the printer Kenneth Tyler and published in an edition of thirty, along with eight artist's proofs.

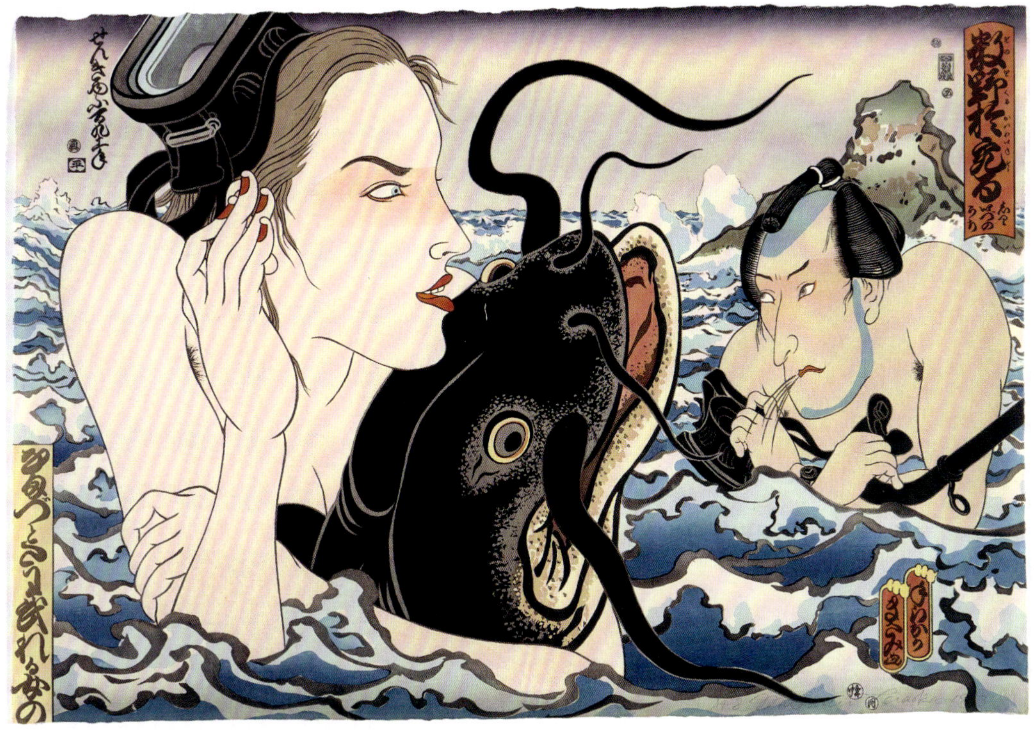

Gillian Ayres (1930–2018)
The Colour That Was There 1993
Acrylic paint and screenprint on paper 92.2 × 92

This vibrant work by the British artist Gillian Ayres is a screenprint overlaid with acrylic paint. The piece is one of five artist's proofs of a screenprint which Ayres ultimately decided not to publish. Instead, she worked into the print using acrylic paint, merging the mediums of print and painting to create a unique artwork. The image itself employs a bright colour palette to conjure a bold arrangement of abstract forms. Ayres contrasted the textured brushstrokes of the acrylic paint against the flat areas of colour provided by the screenprint below, drawing attention to the layers of artistic process inherent in the work.

Ayres made *The Colour That Was There* as an independent work, but later repurposed it as a design for a scarf at the invitation of Tate Gallery Publishing; subsequently, she offered the painted print to the museum as a gift.

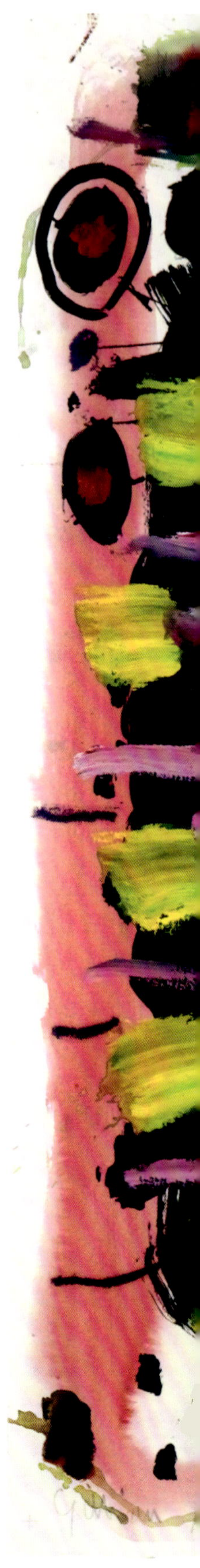

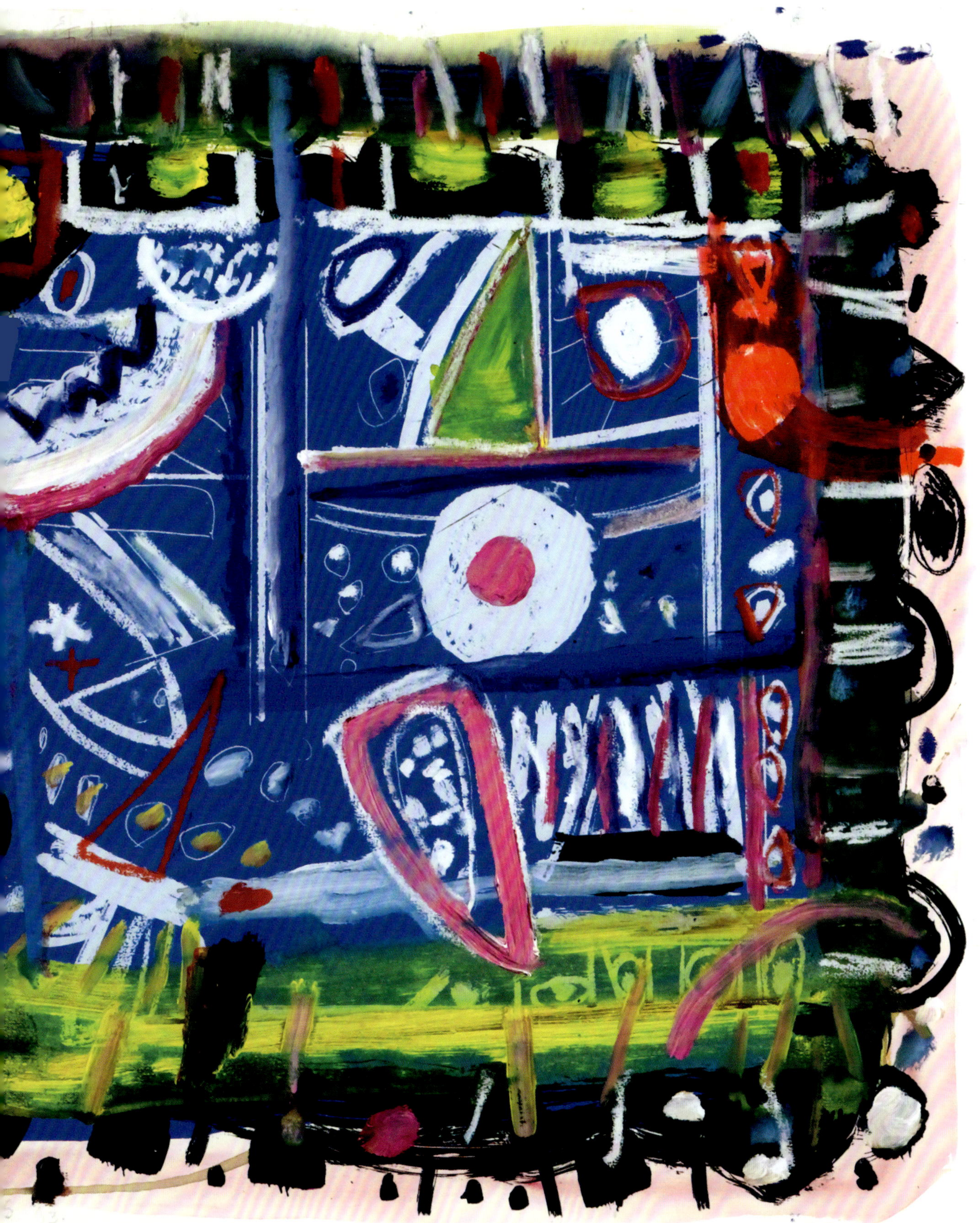

Helen Frankenthaler (1928–2011)

All About Blue 1994

Lithograph and woodcut on paper 123.2 × 73.4

Helen Frankenthaler lived and worked in New York City. Although best remembered as a painter, she also made ballet designs, ceramics, sculptures and prints, with colour the primary focus in all of her work. When she first began printmaking, she found the many stages involved in different print processes frustrating. Later, though, she embraced printmaking's potential for allowing her to rework and reuse her ideas in different formats.

All About Blue reflects Frankenthaler's increasing interest in the possibilities of printmaking and reveals the remarkable heights she reached in translating the intensity of colour seen in her paintings to the print medium. To make this multi-layered colour image she combined woodcut with lithography, which resulted in unique visual effects. *All About Blue* was printed in collaboration with Tyler Graphics Ltd, New York, who published it in an edition of thirty-eight plus twelve artist's proofs.

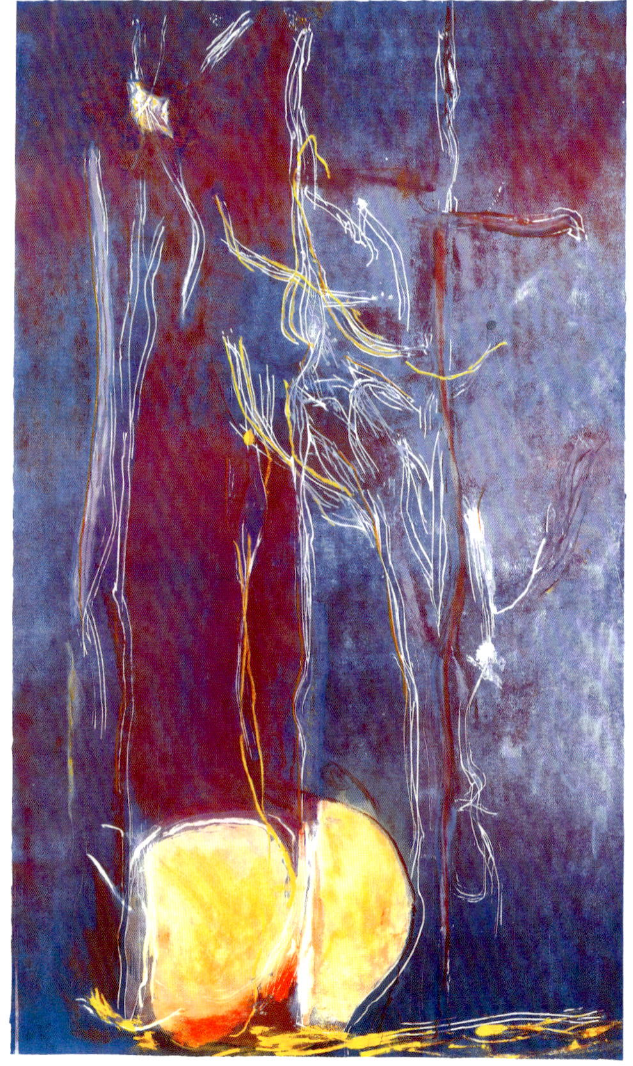

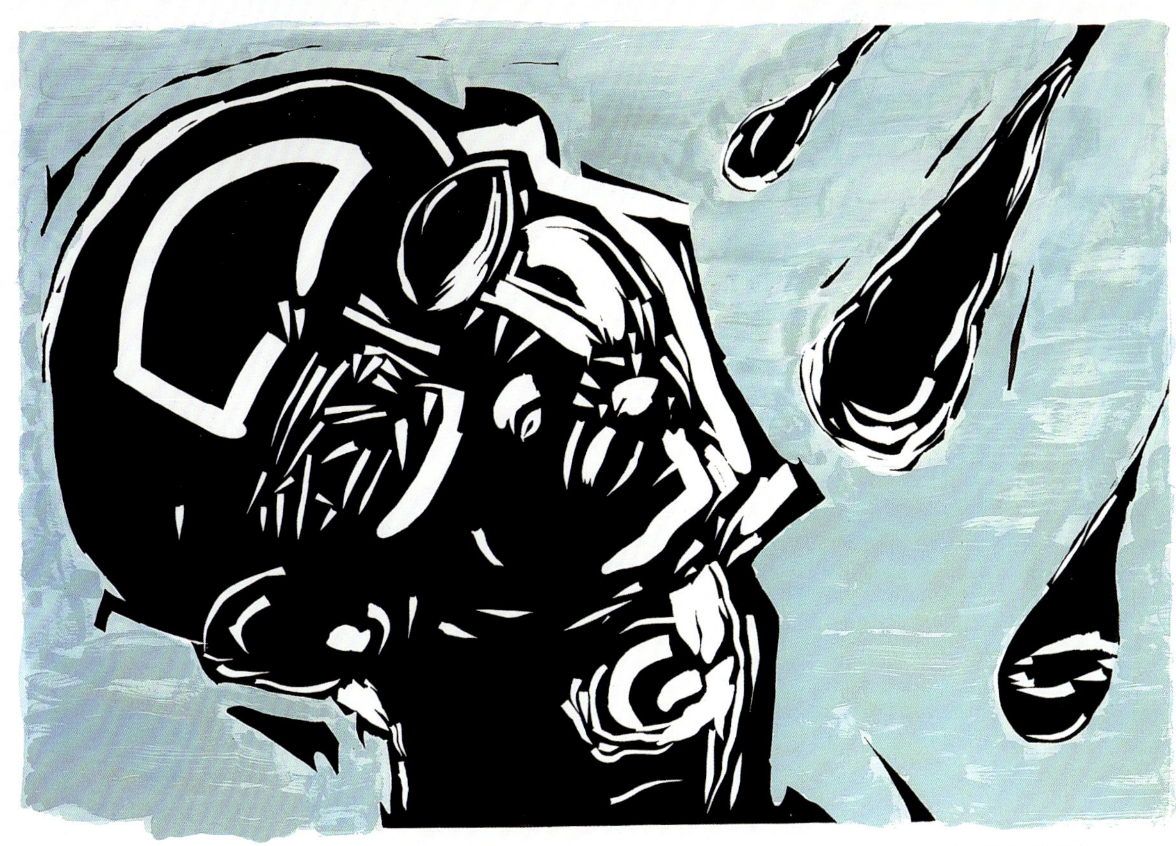

Per Inge Bjørlo (born 1952)
Drift 1996
Linocut and lithograph on paper 69.5 × 102

The Norwegian artist Per Inge Bjørlo is primarily known as a sculptor. He made this mixed method print as part of a series focused on the human head, *Heads from Balance*, which references his childhood difficulties and his search for 'balance' and 'something to believe in'.[14] In *Drift* the face, upturned towards huge droplets of water, is printed from a linoleum block, defined by its crisp edges and raw expressive power. The coloured background, meanwhile, was completed using lithography; the two processes are very different, and the contrast between the softly textured background – suggestive of water – and the stark monochrome of the main image is highly effective.

Drift was printed from three aluminium lithographic plates and one linoleum block. It was published by Tyler Graphics Ltd, New York, with whom the artist collaborated, in an edition of twenty-four plus fourteen artist's proofs.

David Salle (1952)
High and Low 1994
Lithograph, woodcut and screenprint on paper 144.5 × 113.5

David Salle is an American painter, printmaker and photographer known for his collage-like works, which juxtapose original imagery with images borrowed from sources including art history and popular culture. His multi-layered approach to image-making is suited to the kind of mixed method printmaking seen in *High and Low*, which combines lithography, woodcut and screenprinting to create a work full of textural and colour contrasts. The piece brings together seemingly disconnected imagery, from the silhouette of the South American continent on the left to gloves, cars and a couple in a diner. Photographic imagery is collaged with ink splatters and painterly marks that remind us of the artist's hand.

High and Low is one from a series of six mixed media prints. It was printed in colour from sixteen aluminium lithography plates, one woodblock and one screen. The print was published in an edition of thirty plus ten artist's proofs by Tyler Graphics Ltd, New York.

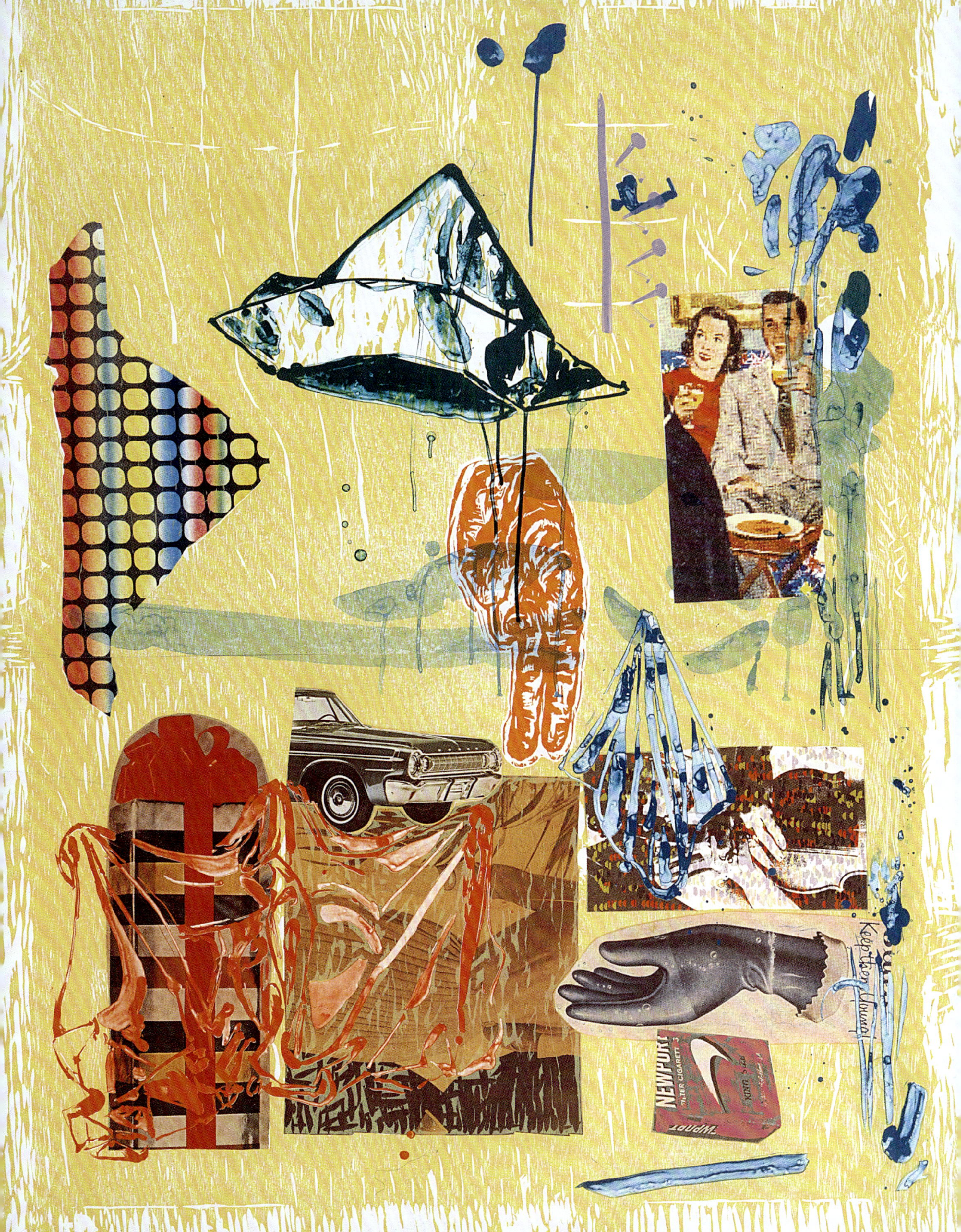
Keep them Young
NEWPORT
KING

Tracey Emin (born 1963)
Sad Shower in New York 1995
Monoprint on paper   Sheet: 42 x 59.3

The British artist Tracey Emin studied printmaking at Maidstone College of Art in Kent and learnt how to make monoprints at the Sir John Cass School of Art in Whitechapel, London. Like her drawings, her monoprints have a striking immediacy and a scratchiness; they are unique works that appear both spontaneous and deeply personal. *Sad Shower in New York* expresses the artist's loneliness when travelling abroad for exhibitions: Emin has said she felt 'pathetic and despondent' when she made it.[15] Emin's drawings and monoprints are somewhat reminiscent of early twentieth-century drawings by German expressionist artists and, particularly, the Austrian artist Egon Schiele, who Emin became interested in during the 1980s.

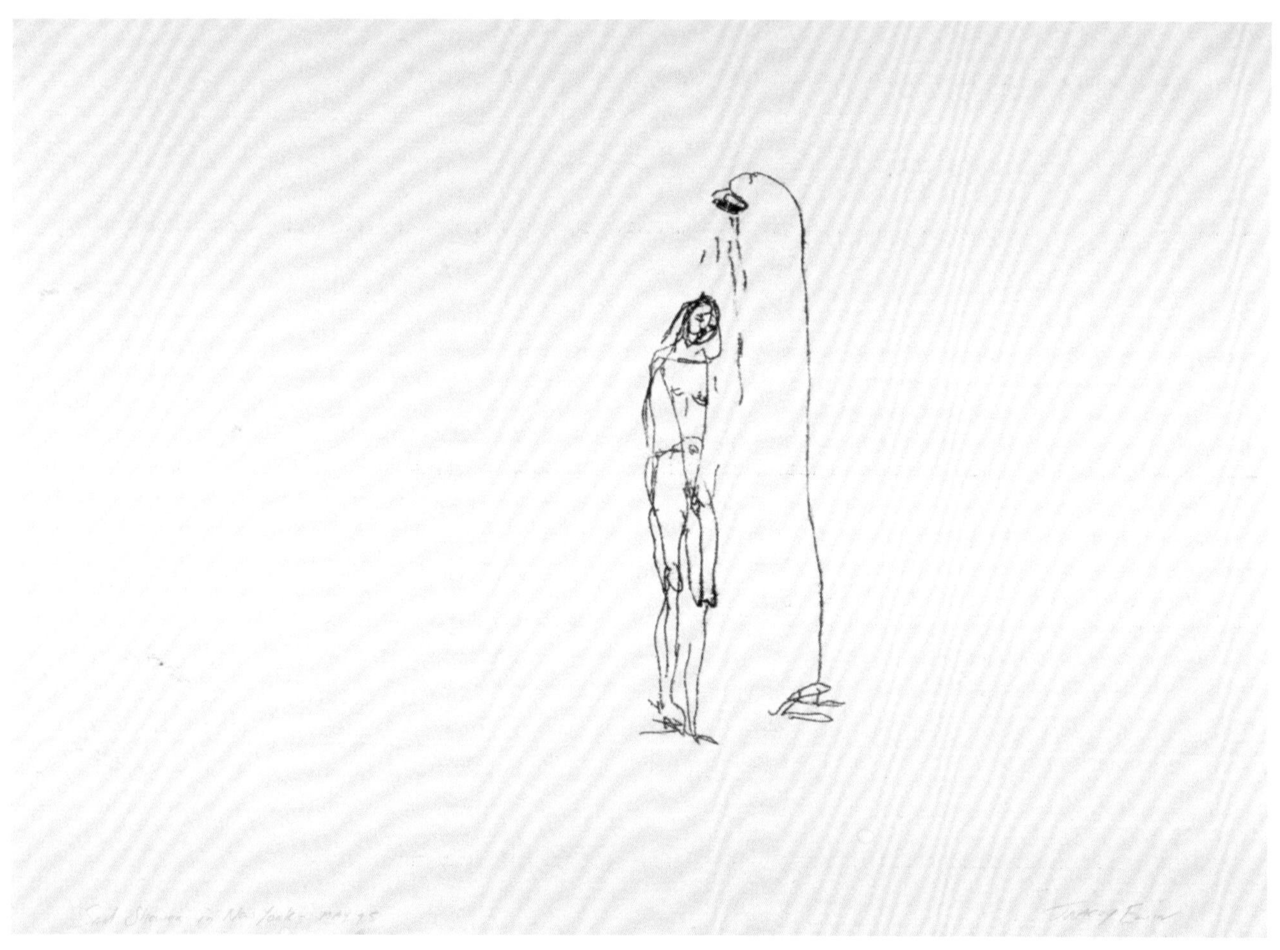

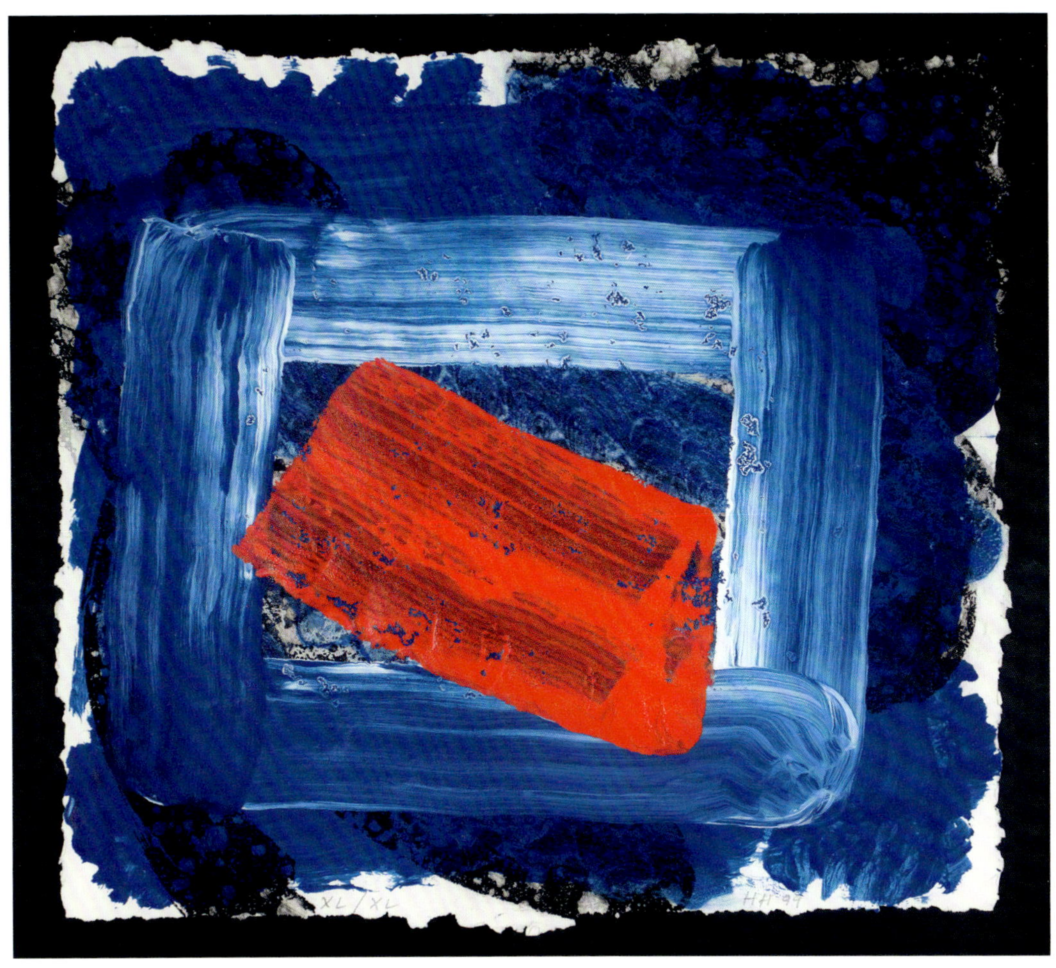

Howard Hodgkin (1932–2017)
Norwich 1999
Etching, aquatint and carborundum on paper 43.4 × 48.2

Howard Hodgkin began making prints in the early 1960s. This gem-like print of 1999 demonstrates the multi-layered approach to printmaking he had developed by the latter part of his career. Hodgkin used sugar lift aquatint (see p.58) to create bold marks, adding a substance called carborundum to the plate to create a rich texture on the surface. The hand painting then added to the piece took the layering process further, giving the print a painterly quality. The title, *Norwich*, probably refers to an event in the artist's life, using texture along with singing colours to evoke a memory.

Norwich was printed in black, grey and blue from three separate plates by the printer Jack Shirreff, who, working under Hodgkin's direction, also hand coloured the prints in red, blue and white. Shirreff printed and hand-coloured an edition of forty, working at the 107 Workshop near Bath.

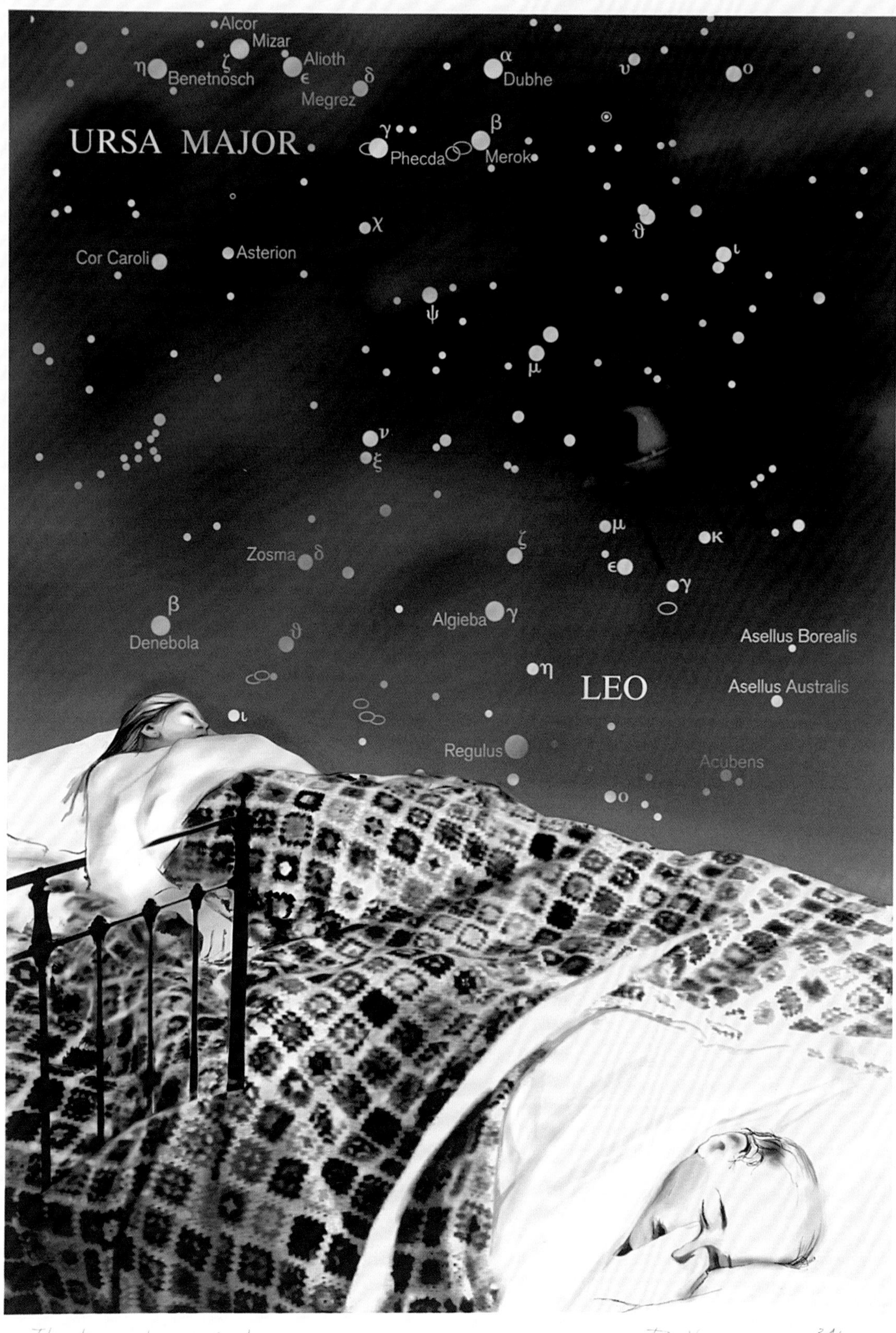

Alcor
Mizar
Alioth
Benetnosch
Dubhe
Megrez
URSA MAJOR
Phecda
Merok
Cor Caroli
Asterion
Zosma
Algieba
Denebola
Asellus Borealis
LEO
Asellus Australis
Regulus
Acubens

34/40

Richard Hamilton (1922–2011)
The heaventree of stars 1998
Digital print on paper 53 × 37.5

Richard Hamilton began making prints in the 1960s (see p.159), embracing new technologies and the mixing of different media and materials from the outset. This piece is from the latter part of his career. It followed many years of experimentation with digital collage and inkjet printing, and is an example of the impact an increasingly computerised world was having on creative printmakers by the end of the twentieth century.

The image is one of a long-running series of illustrations Hamilton made to James Joyce's novel *Ulysses* (1922) and refers to the novel's penultimate chapter and to the characters falling asleep. It is the first print in the grouping to draw on digital collage and inkjet printing. To make it, Hamilton worked on a computer to collage photographs he had taken with a scan of a map of the constellations and digital drawings. He used Quantel graphics tools.

The heaventree of stars was printed at Circa, London, and published in an edition of forty by Alan Cristea Gallery, London.

Ellen Gallagher (born 1965)
DeLuxe 2004–5
60 works on paper, etching, photo-etching, aquatint, drypoint, screenprint and lithography with additions including plasticine, velvet, glitter, toy eyeballs and coconut oil
Frame, each: 38.9 × 32.5 × 4.6

This portfolio by the American artist Ellen Gallagher combines print processes such as etching and lithography with the use of digital technology and collage elements. Sixty individual framed pieces are designed to be hung as a single work in grid formation.

Most of the imagery used is drawn from magazines of the 1930–70 period aimed at African American consumers, such as *Ebony* and *Our World*; Gallagher has repurposed adverts for products including hair and skin treatment.[16] These images are reproduced in print and further subverted through Gallagher's drawing, collage and cutting out; for example, many of the models' eyes are missing. She also added materials like coconut oil, which has associations with Afro hair care, and pieces of plasticine moulded to form shapes including new wigs for some of the figures seen in the images. Gallagher's interventions in printed imagery challenge the promise of physical transformation associated with many of the products being advertised. The piece also reflects and queries the beauty ideals seen in popular culture, especially for women, and particularly addresses the importance and politics of hair within African American culture.

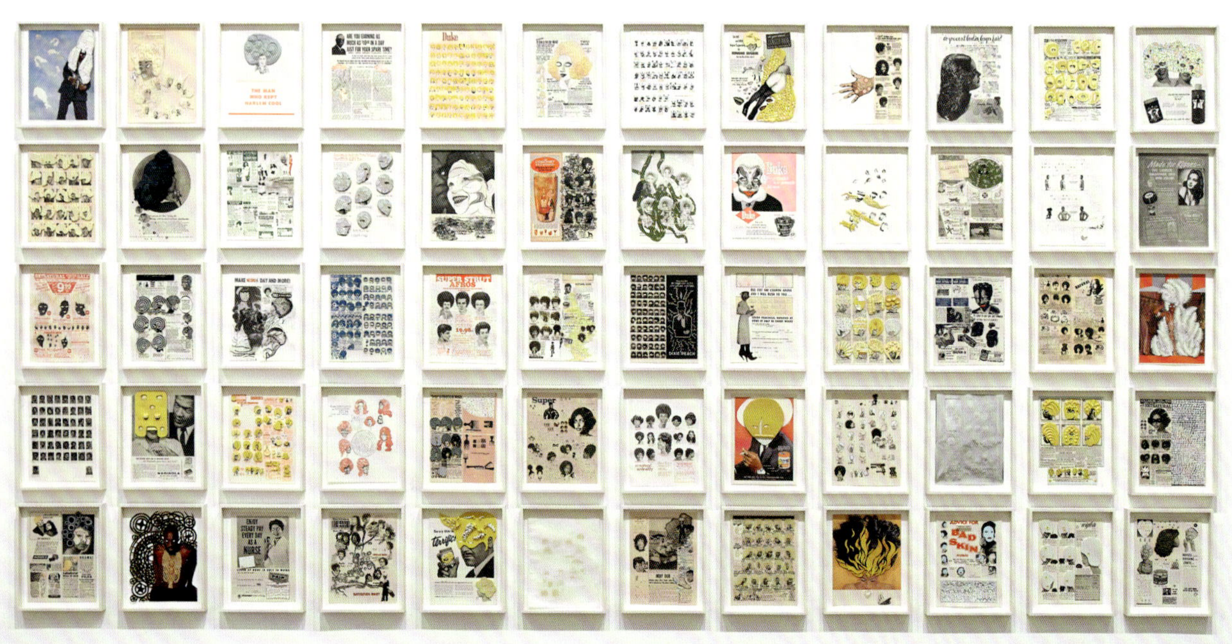

Made for Kisses–

THE LIGHTER, SMOOTHER SKIN MEN ADORE

So Let This Wonderful Bleaching Cream Give You Amazing Beauty Help!

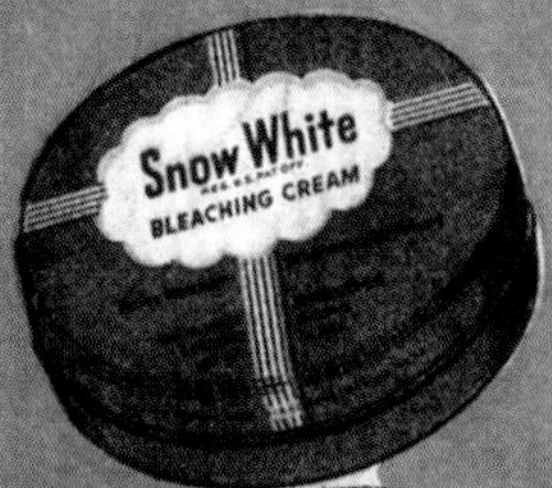

In just 3 days see the amazing difference in your complexion after you begin using Snow White* Bleaching Cream. It's so quick and easy to apply, according to the directions, at bedtime. Snow White *works while you sleep.*

Each morning see your skin appear lovelier. And on the third day, see if your skin doesn't look fairer, smoother, more alluring.

So let this wonderful bleaching cream help you have the lighter-looking skin women envy and men adore. Today, get Snow White Bleaching Cream . . . only 35¢, plus tax.

Amazing new all-purpose cream! Here's the new, satin-soft cream to use every day, every night. Snow White Lemon Creme is extra rich, extra gentle! Thus it cleanses exquisitely . . . smooths and softens . . . helps nature refine the pores. So have the fairer, fresher, smoother skin that invites cheek-to-cheek moments. Today get Snow White Lemon Creme. Generous sizes—25¢ and 50¢, plus tax.

*Registered Trade-Mark

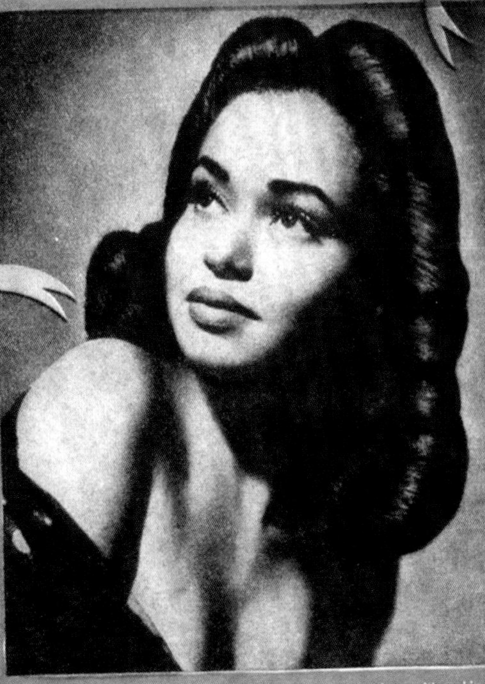

★ Famous Isabelle Cooley says: "Theatrical stars with sensitive skin must be careful of their choice of creams; so I use Snow White Lemon Creme and Bleaching Cream since they are kind to my complexion."

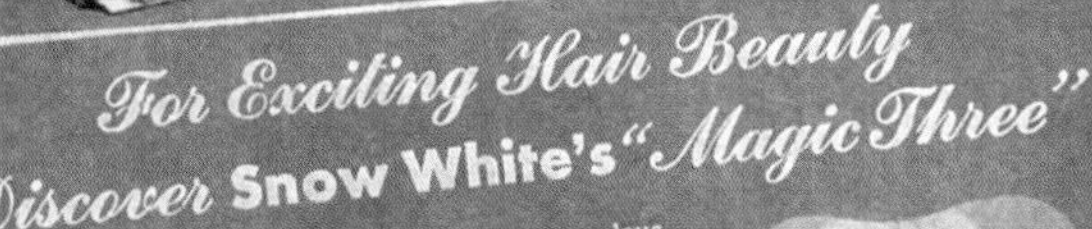

1. Snow White Hair Beautifier gives you 3 marvelous advantages! Compare to any other hair dressing you ever tried. See how Snow White gives your hair . . . *richer gloss* . . . *smoother "natural" look*—makes hair easier to manage without giving that artificial, oily look . . . *ends ugly staining*. Get this exquisite, snowy white hair dressing today. 25¢ and $1.00 sizes, plus tax.

2. Snow White Creme Shampoo. It's an exciting new beauty discovery! Not an old-fashioned cake or liquid shampoo. Snow White is a rich, fast-acting formula that's *extra-potent* so it dissolves grease, oil, and hair dressing. Instantly your cleaner hair looks smoother, softer, more lustrous. And it's easier to dress in a sleek new hairdo! Large jar, only 50¢.

3. Snow White Pressing Oil. This fine, luxurious pressing oil is truly wonderful to help you have straighter, brighter hair and a smoother, neater hairline. It dries bright—actually *protects* the hair from becoming dry and brittle. 35¢ and $1.50 sizes, plus tax.

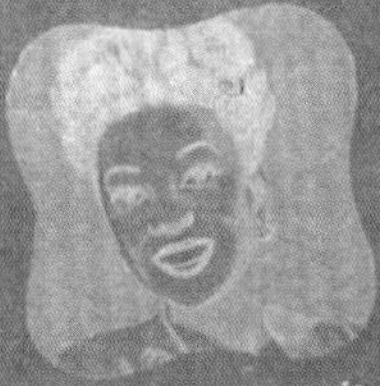

Sandra Powell, celebrated beauty consultant, says: "Famous stars of stage, screen, and radio use Snow White's 'Magic Three' for their beautiful hair. I advise you to use the same care they do."

USE
Snow White
Custom-Styled
COSMETICS

NEW LOVELINESS FOR YOUR COMPLEXION!

You'll say it's a beauty miracle! For you can instantly glorify your skin when you discover these two amazing beauty aids—Snow White Make-Up Cream and Snow White Face Powder. This glamorous make-up cream spreads quickly and evenly over your skin. Helps to cover blemishes and enlarged pores. Used with Snow White Face Powder, the effect is completely ravishing. Both come in beautiful, smart, flattering shades, custom-styled for ladies with rich-toned skin. Your skin looks smoother, more inviting all evening. So, today, get Snow White Make-Up Cream—only 50¢, plus tax . . . and Snow White Face Powder—only 25¢, plus tax.

FREE! Sandra Powell's "Guide to Correct Make-Up" at your cosmetic counter, or write Snow White Products Co., Box 3032, Rivermont Station, Va.

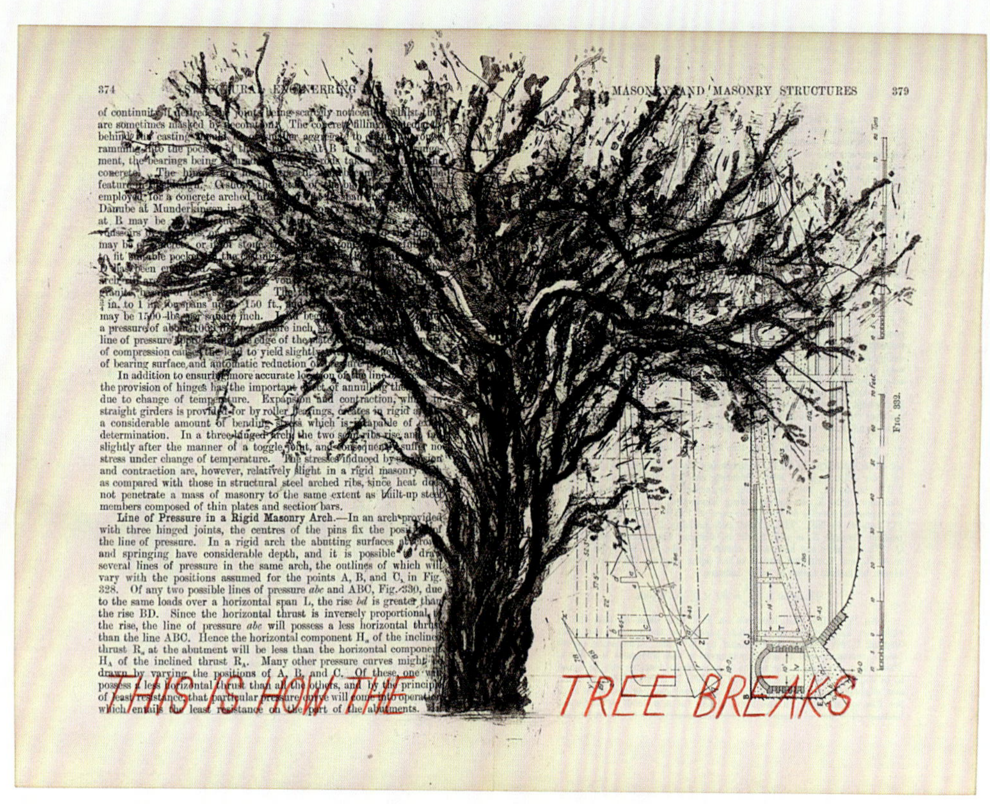

William Kentridge (born 1955)
This is How the Tree Breaks 1999
Etching, aquatint and crayon on printed paper 21.9 × 28.6

Although this work by the South African artist William Kentridge was primarily completed in etching and aquatint, each print in the edition is unique. This is due to each impression of the print having been made onto different pages of text from old, found books, and to the red crayon elements added by hand: each print is a unique collage of found, handwritten and etched elements. The tree is the central motif, its branches expanding from the spine of a double-page spread concerned with structural engineering, perhaps suggesting the fragility of the tree's structure. In a related print from the wider series of six, *Sleeping on Glass*, the tree is broken. The series title, *Sleeping on Glass*, suggests pain as well as the need to 'wake up'; it refers to the white South African psyche during the apartheid era (1948–94), when human rights abuses were deliberately ignored.[17]

Printmaking, which he has both studied and taught, has been central to Kentridge's practice throughout his career. The *Sleeping on Glass* series was printed and published by Caversham Press, KwaZulu-Natal, South Africa, in an edition of sixty.

Gerhard Richter (born 1932)
Strip (921-6) 2011
Digital print on paper face-mounted on Perspex Displayed: 201 × 441.6 × 12.2

The German artist Gerhard Richter began a new series of works, known as his *Strip Paintings*, in 2010. Despite this title, these works – which include *Strip (921-6)* – are actually digital prints laminated onto aluminium behind a thin layer of Perspex. The imagery used in their creation is drawn from paintings, however, and *Strip (921-6)* is based on photographs of Richter's *Abstract Painting 724-4* of 1990. Photographs of the painting's surface were manipulated using computer software to form the wide horizontal strips of colour seen here, a process that resulted in a different visual effect to that seen in the original painting. While the original painting is highly textured, this and other works in the *Strip Paintings* series do not share any sense of this physical texture; instead, the imagery is repurposed to create a flat and digitally altered printed surface.

The idea that *Strip (921-6)* might itself be considered a painting is interesting – and for some commentators, Richter has expanded the definition of what a painting is in an age when we consume so much imagery through digital channels, much of it manipulated. By combining digital manipulation with printed and other material elements, he also explores the role of print, and the ever-evolving relationship between painting, printmaking and reproduction.

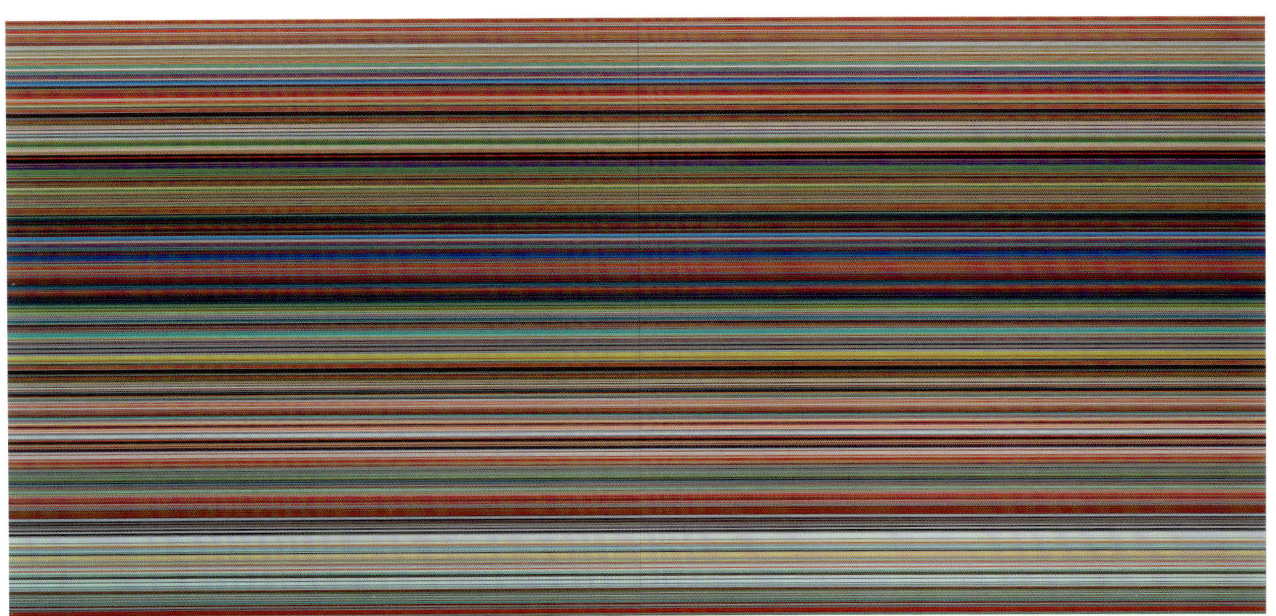

Notes

Introduction

1 Frances Spalding, *The Tate: A History*, London 1998, p.124.
2 Ibid., p.176.
3 Pat Gilmour, 'Setting Up Departments: 1. Prints at the Tate Gallery', *Print Quarterly*, vol.22, no.2, June 2005, p.161.
4 Spalding 1998, p.227.

In Relief

1 A.H. Palmer, *The Life and Letters of Samuel Palmer, Painter and Etcher*, London 1972, p.15.
2 Quoted in Carolyn Hares-Stryker, *An Anthology of Pre-Raphaelite Writings*, Sheffield 1997, p.38.
3 Paul Goldman, *Victorian Illustration*, London 2004, p.2.
4 Richard Cork, 'Introduction', in Jeremy Greenwood, *The Graphic Work of Edward Wadsworth*, Woodbridge 2002, p.7.
5 Greenwood 2002, pp.22–3.
6 Simon Brett, 'Gertrude Hermes: The Wood-Engravings', in Judith Russell (ed.), *The Wood-Engravings of Gertrude Hermes*, Aldershot 1993, p.17.
7 Chris Stephens, 'Summary: Ben Nicholson, *1933 (Profile)* 1933' (2004), https://www.tate.org.uk/art/artworks/nicholson-1933-profile-p14287, accessed 11 January 2021.
8 Ibid.
9 *The Tate Gallery 1984–86: Illustrated Catalogue of Acquisitions*, London 1988, pp.309–10.
10 Tanya Barson, 'Summary: Lygia Pape, *Weaving* 1957' (2010), https://www.tate.org.uk/art/artworks/pape-weaving-p80082, accessed 12 January 2021.
11 Ibid.
12 Ibid.
13 Christian Weikop, 'Georg Baselitz: Artist and Collector' (28 March 2014), https://www.royalacademy.org.uk/article/georg-baselitz-artist-and-collector, accessed 12 January 2021.
14 Richard Martin, 'Summary: Kara Walker, The Keys to the Coop' (2015), https://www.tate.org.uk/art/artworks/walker-the-keys-to-the-coop-p78211, accessed 8 April 2021.
15 Zarina Hashmi, 'A Conversation with Zarina in New York with Geeti Sen', in *Zarina: Paper Houses*, exh. cat., Gallery Espace, New Delhi 2007, p.13.

The Art of Etching

1 Richard Lloyd, 'Hockney: Printmaker', in *Hockney: Printmaker*, exh. cat., Dulwich Picture Gallery, London 2014, p.9.
2 Ad Stijnman, *Engraving and Etching 1400–2000: A History of the Development of Manual Intaglio Printmaking Processes*, London 2012, pp.58–64.
3 Ibid., p.64.
4 Hugh Belsey, *Gainsborough the Printmaker*, Aldeburgh 1988, p.3.
5 Alexander Cozens, *A New Method of Assisting the Invention in Drawing Original Compositions (1785)*, ed. Paola Lavezzari, Rome 1981, p.32.
6 Alan Shestack, 'Lift Ground Prints by Alexander Cozens', *Artist's Proof*, no.8, 1968, pp.82–6.
7 Kim Sloan, *Alexander and John Robert Cozens: The Poetry of Landscape*, New Haven and London 1986, p.83.
8 Elizabeth Barker in William Vaughan, Elizabeth Barker and Colin Harrison (eds.), *Samuel Palmer 1801–1885: Vision and Landscape*, exh. cat., British Museum, London 2005, p.218.
9 Katharine A. Lochnan, *The Etchings of James McNeill Whistler*, New Haven and London 1984, p.81.
10 Gordon Cooke, *Graham Sutherland: Early Etchings*, London 1993, p.3.
11 Craig Hartley, *The Etchings of Lucian Freud: A Catalogue Raisonné 1946–1995*, London and Bergamo 1995, p.11.
12 Jacques Dupin, *Miró Engraver*, vol.1: 1928–1960, Paris 1984, p.18.
13 Georges Duby et al., *Soulages: Eaux-fortes, Lithographies 1952–1973*, Paris 1974, p.19.
14 Stanley Appelbaum (trans.), *Georges Braque: Illustrated Notebooks 1917–1955*, trans. Stanley Appelbaum, New York 1971, p.65.
15 Jennifer Mundy, *Georges Braque: Printmaker*, exh. cat., Tate Gallery, London 1993, p.31.
16 Karen Kurczynski, *The Art and Politics of Asger Jorn: The Avant-Garde Won't Give Up*, Farnham and Burlington, VT 2014, p.151.
17 Lloyd 2014, p.9.
18 Peter Black and Désirée Moorhead, *The Prints of Stanley William Hayter: A Complete Catalogue*, London 1992, p.31.
19 Ibid.
20 'Pat Steir with Phong Bui' in *The Brooklyn Rail*, March 2011, https://brooklynrail.org/2011/03/art/pat-steir-with-phong-bui, accessed 8 April 2021.
21 Ibid.
22 Sarah J.S. Suzuki, *What Is a Print?: Selections from the Museum of Modern Art*, New York 2011, p.69.
23 Quoted in Ernesto Trujillo, 'Obeying Ants', in Linda Weintraub, *In the Making: Creative Options for Contemporary Art*, New York 2003, p.236.

Metal on Metal

1 T. Miller quoted in Eric Shanes, *Turner's Rivers, Harbours and Coasts*, London 1981, p.10.
2 Juliet Bingham, 'Introduction', in Bingham (ed.), *Dóra Maurer*, exh. cat., Tate, London 2019, p.9.
3 Quoted ibid., p.90.
4 *The Tate Gallery 1984–6: Illustrated Catalogue of Acquisitions including Supplement to Catalogue of Acquisitions 1982–4*, London 1988, pp.401–3.
5 *Louise Bourgeois: Selected Prints 1989–2005*, exh. cat., Marlborough Graphics, London 2005, p.[4].
6 Deborah Wye and Carol Smith, *The Prints of Louise Bourgeois*,

exh. cat., The Museum of Modern Art, New York 1994, p.164.
7 Frances Carey, 'The Prints of Ana Maria Pacheco', *Print Quarterly*, vol.5, no.3, Sept. 1988, p.273.

Drawing on Stone

1 Susan Lambert, *Matisse Lithographs*, exh. cat., Victoria and Albert Museum, London 1981, p.2.
2 Quoted in Jack D. Flam (ed.), *Matisse on Art*, Berkeley, CA 1995, p.131.
3 Ronald Alley, *Catalogue of the Tate Gallery's Collection of Modern Art other than Works by British Artists*, London 1981, pp.452–5.
4 Ibid.
5 David King, *Russian Revolutionary Posters*, London 2012, p.11.
6 Ibid.
7 Max Loreau, *Catalogue des travaux de Jean Dubuffet*, vol.IX, Paris 1968, p.103.
8 Alley 1981, pp.557–61.
9 Judith Collins, 'Frink, Dame Elisabeth Jean', in *The Oxford Dictionary of National Biography*, https://www-oxforddnb-com.nls.idm.oclc.org/view/10.1093/ref:odnb/9780198614128.0001/odnb-9780198614128-e-38274, accessed 1 March 2020.
10 'The Prints and Bookworks: A Chronological View', in Heather Maclennan (ed.), *The Prints, Bookworks and Drawings of Birgit Skiöld (1923–1982), an Interactive Catalogue Raisonné*, Gloucester 2006, http://www.birgitskiold.com, accessed 22 August 2019.
11 Richard S. Field, *Jasper Johns Prints 1970–77*, Middletown, CT 1978, no.165.
12 Ibid.
13 Wendy Weitman, 'Experiences with Printmaking: Kiki Smith Expands the Tradition' in *Kiki Smith: Prints, Books & Things*, exh. cat., The Museum of Modern Art, New York 2003, p.11.

Through the Screen

1 Institute of Contemporary Arts, *Text Accompanying an Exhibition of Screenprints*, London 1964.
2 See Wendy Weitman, *Pop Impressions Europe / USA: Prints and Multiples from The Museum of Modern Art*, exh. cat., The Museum of Modern Art, New York 1999, p.23 note 20.
3 *Tate Gallery 1984–86: Illustrated Catalogue of Acquisitions*, London 1988, p.410.
4 Letter dated 2 Dec. 1985 in the Tate Gallery Archive; also quoted in Frances Carey and Antony Griffiths, *Avant-Garde British Printmaking 1914–1990*, exh. cat., British Museum, London 1990, p.182.
5 Richard Hamilton, *Collected Works, 1953–1982*, London 1982, p.89.
6 Weitman 1999, p.43.
7 Quoted in *Lichtenstein in Process*, exh. cat., Katonah Museum of Art, Memphis 2009, p.13.
8 Annette Lynch and Mitchell D. Strauss (eds.), *Ethnic Dress in the United States: A Cultural Encyclopedia*, Lanham, MD 2015, p.18.
9 Nicholas Fox Weber and Brenda Danilowitz, *The Prints of Anni Albers: A Catalogue Raisonné, 1963–1984*, Mexico City 2009, p.76, no.27.
10 Siri Engberg and Joan Banach, *Robert Motherwell: The Complete Prints 1940–1991: A Catalogue Raisonné*, New York and Minneapolis 2003, pp.25–6.
11 Quoted in Lynn MacRitchie, 'Fragments of a Theme', in L. MacRitchie, C. Hartley and K. Schubert, *Bridget Riley: Complete Prints 1962–2010*, London 2010, p.5.
12 Parviz Tanavoli quoted in Jessica Morgan and Flavia Frigeri (eds.), *The EY Exhibition: The World Goes Pop*, exh. cat., Tate Modern, London 2015, p.124.
13 Ibid., p.145.
14 *Contemporary British Art in Print: The Publications of Charles Booth-Clibborn and his Imprint The Paragon Press 1986–95*, exh. cat., Scottish National Gallery of Modern Art, Edinburgh 1995, p.48.
15 Ann V. Gunn, *The Prints of Wilhelmina Barns-Graham: A Complete Catalogue*, London 2007, p.46.
16 Ben Borthwick, 'Summary: Sarah Morris, Dulles [Capital]' (2003), https://www.tate.org.uk/art/artworks/morris-dulles-capital-p78599, accessed 11 January 2021.
17 Leyla Fakr, *Summary*, London 2011, https://www.tate.org.uk/art/artworks/hamilton-divers-p13270, accessed 5 December 2020.

Print and Process

1 For example, Lancaster University replaced its printmaking facilities with a digital department in 2005, making the four specialisms available to Fine Art students at that time painting, drawing, sculpture and digital.
2 Martin Myrone in Martin Myrone and Amy Concannon (eds.), *William Blake*, Tate 2019, p.115.
3 Quoted in Charles Booth-Clibborn, 'Alan Davie Monotypes', *Print Quarterly*, vol.VI, 1989, p.318.
4 Ibid., p.320.
5 Michael Rothenstein, *Frontiers of Printmaking: New Aspects of Relief Printing*, London 1966, p.109.
6 'Tournament' entry in *The Tate Gallery Illustrated Catalogue of Acquisitions 1986–88*, London 1996.
7 Quoted in Hiroko Hagiwara, 'Chila Kumari Burman', *Feminist Art News*, vol.3, no.1, 1989, p.28.
8 Richard H. Axsom, *The Prints of Frank Stella: A Catalogue Raisonné 1967–1982*, New York 1983, p.25.
9 Axsom 1983, p.161.
10 Quoted on the page 'A Few South Africans' on the artist's website https://www.sue-williamson.com/a-few-south-africans, accessed 17 September 2019.
11 Judith Goldman, 'James Rosenquist's "Welcome to the Water Planet"', *MoMA*, vol.2, no.3, p.21.
12 Quoted in Mary Lee Corlett, *The Prints of Roy Lichtenstein: A Catalogue Raisonné 1948–1993*, New York 1994, p.41.
13 Masami Teraoka and Kenneth E. Tyler, *Masami Teraoka: Hawaii Snorkel Series*, Munt Kisco, NY 1993, n.p.
14 Sean Rainbird (ed.), *Print Matters: The Kenneth E. Tyler Gift*, exh. cat., Tate Modern, London 2004, p.32.
15 Tracey Emin in conversation with Tate curator Elizabeth Manchester, July 2001, quoted in Manchester, 'Tracey Emin, *Sad Shower in New York*', https://www.tate.org.uk/art/artworks/emin-sad-shower-in-new-york-p11567, accessed 1 May 2021.
16 Alice Sanger, 'Summary: Deluxe, Ellen Gallagher' (2010), https://www.tate.org.uk/art/artworks/gallagher-deluxe-t12301, accessed 21 January 2021.
17 Elizabeth Manchester, 'Summary: William Kentridge, *This is How the Tree Breaks* 1999' (2002), https://www.tate.org.uk/art/artworks/kentridge-this-is-how-the-tree-breaks-p78568, accessed 17 January 2021.

Glossary of Printmaking Terms

Aquatint See p.58.

Block The ***matrix*** often used in ***relief*** printmaking, see p.20.

Digital prints Prints made using digital technology. Digital images are either transferred by ***photomechanical reproduction*** to a traditional printing plate or screen or computer-printed using an ***inkjet*** printer.

Drypoint See p.94.

Edition Refers to the number of ***impressions*** made. Since the late nineteenth century prints have often been made in planned, limited editions and numbered as such on the print itself, e.g. '1/50'.

Engraving See pp.94–5.

Etching See pp.56–8.

Impression A particular copy of a print, e.g. 'Tate's impression is signed in pencil by the artist'.

Inkjet A commonly used type of computerised printing sometimes employed to make artists' prints.

Intaglio Prints in which ink is held by the recessed areas of the printing plate: ***drypoint***, ***engraving***, ***etching*** and ***mezzotint*** are all intaglio methods.

Linocut See p.21.

Lithography See pp.118–20.

Master Printer A leading printer/printmaker associated with a print studio who may sometimes work closely with artists to realise their vision in print.

Matrix The object upon which a design for printing has been formed, generally a block, plate or stone.

Mezzotint See p.95.

Monoprint Like ***monotypes***, monoprints are unique; they are printed from re-printable plates or blocks but with other aspects, such as hand-colouring, making the prints unique.

Monotype A single copy print taken from marks that are not fixed down or repeatable; see pp.189–91.

Photo-stencil See p.155.

Photomechanical reproduction Used within various print techniques to reproduce images photographically.

Planographic Prints made from a flat print surface, see ***lithography***.

Potato print An example of a simple form of ***relief*** print; see p.20.

Printing press Presses are often used during the printing process. There are different sorts depending on the kind of ***matrix***; intaglio prints usually require a 'rolling' press, relief prints a 'relief' press, and lithographs a 'flat bed' press.

Print Studio/ Workshop A studio equipped with the equipment needed to make prints and print ***editions***. This may either provide facilities for artists to work alone or offer professional printers to complete the printing of editions.

Proof A test print, or any print made outside of a formal ***edition***.

Publisher An individual or organisation who publishes artists' prints; sometimes the ***print studio/ workshop*** is also the publisher; sometimes artists publish prints themselves.

Relief A technique whereby prints are achieved by the surface of the plate or block being inked, while recessed areas are not: ***linocut***, ***potato printing***, ***woodcut*** and ***wood engraving*** are all relief methods, see pp.20–4.

Restrikes Prints made from a printmaker's original printing plates or blocks after the intended printing or edition, usually after the death of the creator.

Screenprint See p.154.

Silkscreen Another word for ***screenprint*** as the mesh screen was originally made using silk.

Single copy print See pp.188–90.

Soft-ground etching See p.57.

Squeegee A tool with a flexible rubber blade used to push ink through the screen in ***screenprinting***.

State Term used to describe different design stages of a print. Most prints illustrated in this book are seen in their final states, but sometimes a trial ***proof*** reveals an earlier stage in the process.

Sugar lift See p.58.

Woodcut See p.20.

Wood engraving See p.21.

Further Reading

Print history and techniques

Beaumont-Jones, Julia, *A Century of Prints in Britain*, London 2017

Black, Peter, *Copper into Gold: Whistler and 19th-Century Printmaking*, Glasgow 2003

Brocklehurst, Hannah, and Watson, Kerry, *The Printmaker's Art*, Edinburgh 2015

Carey, Frances, and Griffiths, Antony, *Avant-garde British Printmaking 1914–60*, London 1990

Coldwell, Paul, *Printmaking: A Contemporary Perspective*, London 2010

Coppel, Stephen, *The American Dream: Pop to the Present*, London 2017

Gascoigne, Bamber, *How to Identify Prints*, London 2004

Godfrey, Richard T., *Printmaking in Britain: A General History from its Beginnings to the Present Day*, London 1978

Goldman, Paul, *Victorian Illustration*, London 2004

Griffiths, Antony, *Prints and Printmaking*, London 1996
Griffiths, Antony, *The Print before Photography: An Introduction to European Printmaking 1550–1820*, London 2016

Hecker, Judith, *Impressions from South Africa, 1965 to Now: Prints from the Museum of Modern Art*, New York 2011

Lambert, Susan, *The Image Multiplied*, London 1987

Saunders, Gill and Whitley, Zoé (eds.), *In Black and White: Prints from Africa and the Diaspora*, London 2013

Stijnman, Ad, *Engraving and Etching 1400–2000: A History of the Development of Manual Intaglio Printmaking Processes*, London 2012

Weitman, Wendy, *Pop Impressions Europe/USA*, New York 1999

On Tate's print collection

Bowness, Alan, Underhill, Elizabeth and Howarth, Jill, *Catalogue of the Print Collection: Modern Collection, Tate Gallery*, London 1980

Gilmour, Pat, *Artists at Curwen: A Celebration of the Gift of Artists' Prints from the Curwen Studio*, London 1977

Gilmour, Pat, *Kelpra Studio: The Rose and Chris Prater Gift. The Artists' Prints 1961–1980*, exh. cat., Tate Gallery, London 1980

Gilmour, Pat, 'Setting Up Departments: 1. Prints at the Tate Gallery', *Print Quarterly*, vol.22, no.2, June 2005, pp.159–62

Rainbird, Sean (ed.), *Print Matters: The Kenneth E. Tyler Gift*, London 2004

Spalding, Frances, *The Tate: A History*, London 1998

Individual artists

For further information about any print in the Tate Collection visit the individual artwork page at tate.org.uk. The books listed above include further information about some of the prints, and the following list may also prove useful.

Anni Albers
Nicholas Fox Weber and Brenda Danilowitz, *The Prints of Anni Albers: A Catalogue Raisonné, 1963–1984*, Mexico City 2009

Gillian Ayres
Mel Gooding, *Gillian Ayres*, Aldershot 2001

Wilhelmina Barns-Graham
Ann V. Gunn, *The Prints of Wilhelmina Barns-Graham: A Complete Catalogue*, London 2007

Leonard Baskin
Alan Fern and Judith O'Sullivan, *The Complete Prints of Leonard Baskin: A Catalogue Raisonné 1948–1983*, Boston 1984

William Blake
Martin Myrone (ed.), *William Blake*, exh. cat., Tate Britain 2019

Louise Bourgeois
Deborah Wye and Carol Smith, *The Prints of Louise Bourgeois*, exh. cat., The Museum of Modern Art, New York 1994

Chila Kumari Singh Burman
Lynda Nead, *Chila Kumari Burman: Beyond Two Cultures*, London 1995

Vija Celmins
Samantha Rippner, *The Prints of Vija Celmins*, exh. cat., The Metropolitan Museum of Art, New York 2002

Paul Cézanne
William Rubin (ed.), *Cézanne: The Late Work*, London 1978

John Constable
Leslie Parris, *The 'English Landscape' Prints of John Constable & David Lucas*, exh. cat., Tate Gallery 1986

Tracey Emin
Carol Freedman, Rudolf Herman and Jeanette Wilson, *Tracey Emin: Works 1963–2006*, New York 2006

Lucian Freud
Craig Hartley, *The Etchings of Lucian Freud: A Catalogue Raisonné 1946–1995*, London and Bergamo 1995

Thomas Gainsborough
Hugh Belsey, *Gainsborough the Printmaker*, Aldeburgh 1988

Guerrilla Girls
Whitney Chadwick and the Guerrilla Girls, *Confessions of the Guerrilla Girls*, New York 1995

Richard Hamilton
Etienne Lullin, *Richard Hamilton: Prints and Multiples 1939–2002*, exh. cat., Kunstmuseum Winterthur, Winterthur, and Yale Center for British Art, New Haven 2003

Stanley William Hayter
Peter Black and Désirée Moorhead, *The Prints of Stanley William Hayter: A Complete Catalogue*, London 1992

Gertrude Hermes
Judith Russell (ed.), *The Wood-Engravings of Gertrude Hermes*, Aldershot 1993

David Hockney
Richard Lloyd, 'Hockney: Printmaker', in *Hockney: Printmaker*, exh. cat., Dulwich Picture Gallery, London 2014

Howard Hodgkin
Liesbeth Heenk, *Howard Hodgkin Prints: A Catalogue Raisonné*, London 2003

William Hogarth
Ronald Paulson, *Hogarth's Graphic Works*, London 1989

Jasper Johns
Richard S. Field, *The Prints of Jasper Johns 1960–1993*, New York 1994

Asger Jorn
Karen Kurczynski, *The Art and Politics of Asger Jorn: The Avant-Garde Won't Give Up*, Farnham and Burlington, VT 2014

William Kentridge
Neal Benezra, Staci Boris and Dan Cameron, *William Kentridge*, exh. cat., Museum of Contemporary Art, Chicago, and New Museum of Contemporary Art, New York 2001

R.B. Kitaj
Jennifer Ramkalawon, *Kitaj Prints: A Comprehensive Catalog of Prints*, London 2015

Käthe Kollwitz
Alexandra von dem Knesebeck, *Käthe Kollwitz: Werkverzeichnis der Graphik*, revision of August Klipstein's catalogue raisonné (1955), Bern 2002

Willem de Kooning
Lanier Graham, *The Prints of Willem de Kooning: A Catalogue Raisonné 1957–1970/1*, Paris 1991

Roy Lichtenstein
Mary Lee Corlett, *The Prints of Roy Lichtenstein: A Catalogue Raisonné 1948–1993*, New York 1994

John Martin
Michael J. Campbell, *John Martin: Visionary Printmaker*, exh. cat., York City Art Gallery 1992

Henri Matisse
Susan Lambert, *Matisse Lithographs*, exh. cat., Victoria and Albert Museum, London 1981

Dóra Maurer
Juliet Bingham (ed.), *Dóra Maurer*, exh. cat., Tate, London 2019

Joan Miró
Jacques Dupin, *Miró Engraver, vol.1: 1928–1960*, Paris 1984

Giorgio Morandi
Jennifer Munday, *Giorgio Morandi Etchings*, London 1991

Robert Motherwell
Siri Engberg, Joan Banach et al., *Robert Motherwell: The Complete Prints 1940–1991*, Minneapolis 2003

C.W.R Nevinson
Jonathan Black, *C.W.R Nevinson: The Complete Prints*, Farnham 2014

Ben Nicholson
Jeremy Lewison (ed.), *Ben Nicholson*, exh. cat., Tate Gallery, London 1993

Chris Ofili
Godfrey Worsdale, Lisa G. Corrin and Kodwo Eshun, *Chris Ofili*, exh. cat., Southampton City Art Gallery and Serpentine Gallery, London 1998

Ana Maria Pacheco
Frances Carey, 'The Prints of Ana Maria Pacheco', *Print Quarterly*, vol.5, no.3, Sept. 1988, p.273.

Samuel Palmer
Elizabeth Barker and Colin Harrison (eds.), *Samuel Palmer 1801–1885: Vision and Landscape*, exh. cat., British Museum, London 2005

Lygia Pape
Lygia Pape: Magnetised Space, exh. cat., Museo Nacional Centro de Arte Renia Sofía, Madrid 2011

Pablo PIcasso
Brigitte Baer, *Picasso Peintre-graveur: Catalogue raisonné de l'oeuvre gravé et des monotypes, 1946–1958*, vol.4, Bern 1988

Paula Rego
T.G. Rosenthal, *Paula Rego: The Complete Graphic Work*, London 2004

Bridget Riley
L. MacRitchie, C. Hartley and K. Schubert, *Bridget Riley: Complete Prints 1962–2010*, London 2010

Susan Rothenberg
Susan Rothenberg Prints 1977–1984, exh. cat., Barbara Krakow Gallery, Boston, MA 1984

Birgit Skiöld
Heather Maclennan (ed.), *The Prints, Bookworks and Drawings of Birgit Skiöld (1923–1982), an Interactive Catalogue Raisonné*, Gloucester 2006, http://www.birgitskiold.com

Kiki Smith
Wendy Weitman, *Kiki Smith: Prints, Books & Things*, exh. cat., The Museum of Modern Art, New York 2003

Georgina Starr
Georgina Starr, exh. cat., Ikon Gallery, Birmingham 1998

Pierre Soulages
Georges Duby, Christian Labaye and Pierre Soulages, *Soulages: Eaux-fortes, Lithographies 1952–1973*, Paris 1974

Graham Sutherland
Gordon Cooke, *Graham Sutherland: Early Etchings*, London 1993

Frank Stella
Richard H. Axsom, *The Prints of Frank Stella: A Catalogue Raisonné 1967–1982*, New York 1983

J.M.W. Turner
Luke Herrmann, *Turner Prints: The Engraved Works of JMW Turner*, London 1994

Cy Twombly
Heiner Bastian (ed.), *Cy Twombly: The Printed Graphic Work. Catalogue Raisonné*, Munich 2017

Edward Wadsworth
Jeremy Greenwood, *The Graphic Work of Edward Wadsworth*, Woodbridge 2002

Mark Wallinger
Mark Wallinger: Credo, exh. cat., Tate Liverpool 2000

Andy Warhol
Jorg Schellmann, Freya Feldman and Claudia Defendi, *Andy Warhol Prints: A Catalogue Raisonné 1962–1987*, New York 1997

Sue Williamson
Sue Williamson, *Resistance Art in South Africa*, Cape Town 1989

J.M.W. Whistler
Katharine A. Lochnan, *The Etchings of James McNeill Whistler*, New Haven and London 1984

Fred Williams
Laura Murray Cree (ed.), *Fred Williams: Infinite Horizons*, Canberra 2011

List of Works

All works with individual entries are in the Tate collection. Measurements given in the captions are in centimetres, height before width, and refer to image size unless otherwise stated. The page numbers in brackets below refer to the full illustration.

Anni Albers, *TR III* 1969–70. Presented by the American Fund for the Tate Gallery, courtesy of Melinda Shearer Maddock 2017. © The Josef and Anni Albers Foundation / Artists Rights Society (ARS), New York and DACS, London 2021
[p.168]

Milton Avery, *Dawn* 1952. Purchased 1985. © Milton Avery Trust / Artists Rights Society (ARS), New York and DACS, London 2021
[p.39]

Gillian Ayres, *The Colour That Was There* 1993. Presented by the artist 1996. © Gillian Ayres
[p.206]

Wilhelmina Barns-Graham, *Vision in Time I* 2000. Presented by the Barns-Graham Charitable Trust 2012. © Wilhelmina Barns-Graham Trust
[p.182]

Georg Baselitz, *Von vorne* [From the Front] 1985. Purchased 1985. © Georg Baselitz 2021
[p.46]

Leonard Baskin, *The Anatomist* 1952. Presented by the Museum of Modern Art, New York 1976. © The estate of Leonard Baskin, courtesy Galerie St. Etienne, New York
[p.38]

Per Inge Bjørlo, *Drift* 1996. Presented by Tyler Graphics Ltd in honour of Pat Gilmour, Tate Print Department 1974–7, 2004. © Per Inge Bjørlo
[p.209]

Elizabeth Blackadder, *Dark Hill Fifeshire* 1960. Presented by Curwen Studio through the Institute of Contemporary Prints 1975. © Elizabeth Blackadder
[p.136]

Peter Blake, *Beach Boys* 1964. Presented by Rose and Chris Prater through the Institute of Contemporary Prints 1975. © Peter Blake. All rights reserved, DACS 2021
[p.163]

William Blake, *The Blighted Corn* c.1821. Presented by Herbert Linnell 1924
[p.26]

William Blake, *Newton* 1795–c.1805. Presented by W. Graham Robertson 1939. © The Easton Foundation/VAGA at ARS, NY and DACS, London 2021
[p.192]

Louise Bourgeois, *Untitled (Safety Pins)* 1991. Purchased 1994. © The Easton Foundation/VAGA at ARS, NY and DACS, London 2021
[p.114]

Georges Braque, *The Bird* 1949. Presented by Patrick Seale Prints 1975. © ADAGP, Paris and DACS, London 2021
[p.131]

Georges Braque, *Black Chariot* 1958. Purchased 1988. © ADAGP, Paris and DACS, London 2021
[p.79]

Chila Kumari Singh Burman, *If There is No Struggle, There is No Progress – Uprisings* 1981. Presented by Tate Members 2014. © Chila Kumari Burman
[p.200]

Edward Calvert, *The Chamber Idyll* 1831. Presented by S. Calvert 1912
[p.27]

David Young Cameron, *The Admiralty* 1889. Presented by Ernest Marsh 1909
[p.69]

Vija Celmins, *December 1984* 1985. Acquired jointly with the National Galleries of Scotland through The d'Offay Donation with assistance from the National Heritage Memorial Fund and the Art Fund 2008. © Vija Celmins
[p.112]

Paul Cézanne, *The Large Bathers* c.1898. Presented by Lord Duveen 1927
[p.123]

Marc Chagall, *The Vision* 1924–5 and c.1937. Presented by Lady Clerk 1947. © ADAGP, Paris and DACS, London 2021
[p.195]

Prunella Clough, *Geological Landscape* 1949. Purchased from the artist (Grant-in-Aid) 1984. © Estate of Prunella Clough. All Rights Reserved, DACS 2021
[p.130]

Alexander Cozens, Plate 2, *A New Method for Assisting the Invention in the Composition of Landscape* c.1785. Purchased as part of the Oppé Collection with assistance from the National Lottery through the Heritage Lottery Fund 1996
[p.64]

The Dalziel Brothers after Dante Gabriel Rossetti, *Maids of Elfen-mere* published 1855. Purchased 1924
[p.28]

Alan Davie, *Spirit Over the Landscape* 1948. Purchased 1989. © The Estate of Alan Davie. All rights reserved. DACS 2021
[p.196]

Willem de Kooning, *Landscape at Stanton Street* 1971. Purchased 1986. © The Willem de Kooning Foundation / Artists Rights Society (ARS), New York and DACS, London 2021
[p.144]

Edgar Degas, *Bed-Time* c.1880–5. Presented by C. Frank Stoop 1933
[p.193]

Jim Dine, *Throat* 1965. Presented by the Museum of Modern Art, New York 1976. © Jim Dine / ARS, NY and DACS, London 2021
[p.165]

Jean Dubuffet, *Peopling of the Lands* 1953. Purchased 1986. © ADAGP, Paris and DACS, London 2021
[p.133]

Tracey Emin, *Sad Shower in New York* 1995. Presented by the Patrons of New Art (Special Purchase Fund) through the Tate Gallery Foundation 1999. © Tracey Emin. All rights reserved, DACS 2021
[p.212]

Inka Essenhigh, *Daedalus and Icarus* 2000. Purchased 2001. © Inka Essenhigh
[p.181]

Helen Frankenthaler, *All About Blue* 1994. Presented by Tyler Graphics Ltd in honour of Pat Gilmour, Tate Print Department 1974–7, 2004. © Helen Frankenthaler Foundation, Inc. / ARS, NY and DACS, London 2021
[p.208]

Lucian Freud, *Girl with a Fig Leaf* 1947. Purchased 1988. © The Lucian Freud Archive/ Bridgeman Images
[p.74]

Elisabeth Frink, *Owl*, from *Images 67* 1967. Presented by Curwen Studio through the Institute of Contemporary Prints 1975. © The Elisabeth Frink Estate and Archive. All Rights Reserved, DACS 2021
[p.140]

Naum Gabo, *Opus 7* 1956–73. Bequeathed by Miriam Gabo, the artist's widow 1995. © Nina & Graham Williams/ Tate, London 2020
[p.40]

Thomas Gainsborough, *Wooded Landscape with Two Country Carts and Figures* 1779–80. Presented by A.E. Anderson 1910
[p.63]

Ellen Gallagher, *DeLuxe* 2004–5. Purchased 2006. © Ellen Gallagher
[pp.216–17]

Karl-Otto Götz, *Untitled* 1954. Presented by the artist 1990. © Karl-Otto Götz
[p.197]

Guerrilla Girls, *Dearest Art Collector*, from *Guerrilla Girls Talk Back* 1986. Purchased 2003. [p.178]

Anthea Hamilton, *Divers* 2011. Presented by The London Organising Committee of the Olympic Games and Paralympic Games 2012. [p.184]

Richard Hamilton, *Interior* 1964–5. Presented by Rose and Chris Prater through the Institute of Contemporary Prints 1975. [p.159]

Richard Hamilton, *The heaventree of stars* 1998. Purchased 1999. [p.214]

Hans Hartung, *24* 1953. Purchased 1987. [p.106]

Stanley William Hayter, *Le Chas de l'aiguille* 1946. Purchased 1972. [p.105]

Stanley William Hayter, *Loop* 1978. Purchased 1981. [p.85]

Barbara Hepworth, *Sun and Marble*, from *The Aegean Suite* 1971. Presented by the Curwen Studio through the Institute of Contemporary Prints 1975. [p.146]

Gertrude Hermes, *Waterlilies* 1930. Purchased 1984. [p.35]

Damien Hirst, *Untitled* 1992. Acquired by purchase and gift from Charles Booth-Clibborn in memory of Joshua Compston 1997. [p.179]

David Hockney, *The Arrival*, plate 1 from *A Rake's Progress* 1961–3. Purchased 1971. [p.81]

Howard Hodgkin, *Norwich* 1999. Purchased 2001. [p.213]

William Hogarth, *A Rake's Progress (plate 8)* 1735–63. Transferred from the reference collection 1973 [p.98]

Shirazeh Houshiary, Untitled print from *Round Dance* 1992. Purchased 1993. [p.87]

Gary Hume, *Untitled 02* 2006. Presented by the artist 2008. [p.52]

Jasper Johns, *Two Flags (black)* 1970–2. Purchased 1980. [p.143]

Asger Jorn, *Untitled C [Ohne Titel C]* 1958–9. Purchased 1991. [p.80]

William Kentridge, *This is How the Tree Breaks* 1999. Purchased 2001. [p.218]

William Kentridge, *Untitled (Woman Turning into a Telephone)* 2000. Purchased 2001. [p.49]

R.B. Kitaj, *For Fear* 1967. Purchased 1970. [p.166]

Käthe Kollwitz, *The Widow I* from *War* 1921–2. Presented by Tate Patrons 2019 [p.32]

Oleg Kudryashov, *Diptych No.21* 1982. Purchased 1984. [p.110]

Peter Lanyon, *Underground* 1951. Presented by Warren MacKenzie 1985. © Estate of Peter Lanyon. All Rights Reserved, DACS 2021 [p.158]

Sol LeWitt, *A Square Divided Horizontally and Vertically into Four Equal Parts, Each with a Different Direction of Alternating Parallel Bands of Lines* 1982. Purchased 1984. © The estate of Sol LeWitt [p.45]

Roy Lichtenstein, *Brushstroke* 1965. Purchased 1979. © Estate of Roy Lichtenstein/DACS 2021 [p.164]

Roy Lichtenstein, *Reflections on Brushstrokes* 1990. Presented by Tyler Graphics Ltd in honour of Pat Gilmour, Tate Print Department 1974–7, 2004. © Estate of Roy Lichtenstein/ DACS 2021 [p.204]

Liliane Lijn, *Koan-Cuts V* 1971. Presented by Waddington Galleries through the Institute of Contemporary Prints 1975. © Liliane Lijn [p.172]

Kim Lim, *Red Aquatint* 1972. Presented by Waddington Galleries through the Institute of Contemporary Prints 1975. © Estate of Kim Lim. All Rights Reserved, DACS 2021 [p.84]

El Lissitzky, *1. Part of the Show Machinery*, from *Victory over the Sun* 1923. Purchased 1976 [p.127]

David Lucas after John Constable, *Vignette: Hampstead Heath, Middlesex* 1831 or 1832. Purchased 1985 [p.103]

Thomas Lupton after Thomas Girtin, *York Minster on the River Foss* published 1824. Purchased 1987 [p.100]

John Martin, *The Covenant*, from *'Illustrations of the Bible'* published 1832. Purchased 1987 [p.104]

André Masson, *Childbirth* 1955. Purchased 1985. © The estate of André Masson [p.134]

Henri Matisse, *Little Aurore* 1923. Bequeathed by Mrs E. West 1982. © Succession H. Matisse/ DACS 2021 [p.125]

Dóra Maurer, *Seven Foldings* 1975, published 1978. Purchased 1985. © Dóra Maurer [p.109]

Joan Miró, *Untitled*, from *Series II* 1952. Purchased 1983. © Successió Miró / ADAGP, Paris and DACS London 2021 [p.77]

Joan Mitchell, *Sides of a River II* 1981. Presented by Tyler Graphics Ltd in honour of Pat Gilmour, Tate Print Department 1974–7, 2004. © The estate of Joan Mitchell [p.149]

Henry Moore, *Reclining Figure* 1967. Presented by the artist 1976. © The Henry Moore Foundation. All Rights Reserved [p.139]

Giorgio Morandi, *Still Life with Very Fine Hatching [Natura morta a tratti sottilissimi]* 1933. Presented by Señor and Señora Jose Luis Plaza 1979. © DACS 2021 [p.70]

Sarah Morris, *Dulles [Capital]* 2001. Purchased 2002. © Sarah Morris [p.183]

Robert Motherwell, *No.7*, from *The Basque Suite* 1970. Presented by Rose and Chris Prater through the Institute of Contemporary Prints 1975. © Dedalus Foundation, Inc. / VAGA at ARS, NY and DACS, London 2021 [p.170]

Paul Nash, *Promenade II* 1920. Presented by the Trustees of the Paul Nash Trust 1971
[p.31]

Christopher Richard Wynne Nevinson, *Banking at 4000 Feet* 1917. Presented by the Ministry of Information 1918
[p.124]

Barnett Newman, *Canto XIV*, from *Eighteen Cantos* 1963–4. Presented by Mrs Annalee Newman, the artist's widow 1972. © The Barnett Newman Foundation, New York / DACS, London 2021
[p.137]

Ben Nicholson, *1933 (Profile)* 1933. Presented by Alan and Sarah Bowness 2015. © Angela Verren Taunt. All rights reserved, DACS 2021
[p.36]

Chris Ofili, Untitled print from *Cubitt Print Box* 1999–2000. Purchased 2000. © Chris Ofili, courtesy Victoria Miro, London
[p.91]

Ana Maria Pacheco, *As Proezas de Macunaíma 10* 1995. Purchased 1996 © Ana Maria Pacheco/ Pratt Contemporary Art Ltd
[p.115]

Samuel Palmer, *The Weary Ploughman* 1858–65. Presented by Herbert Linnell 1924
[p.67]

Eduardo Paolozzi, *Conjectures to Identity* 1963–4. Presented by Rose and Chris Prater through the Institute of Contemporary Prints 1975. © The Paolozzi Foundation, Licensed by DACS 2021
[p.160]

Lygia Pape, *Weaving* 1957. Purchased with funds provided by the Pinta Museum Acquisitions Program and Tate International Council 2011. © copyright reserved
[p.41]

Pablo Picasso, *Faun Revealing a Sleeping Woman (Jupiter and Antiope, after Rembrandt)* 1936. Presented by Gustav and Elly Kahnweiler 1974, accessioned 1994. © Succession Picasso/DACS, London 2021
[p.71]

Pablo Picasso, *Portrait of a Woman after Cranach the Younger* 1958. Bequeathed by Elly Kahnweiler 1991 to form part of the gift of Gustav and Elly Kahnweiler, accessioned 1994. © Succession Picasso/DACS, London 2021
[p.43]

Arnulf Rainer, *Violet Furrows* 1972–9. Purchased 1982. Arnulf Rainer © Arnulf Rainer
[p.107]

Robert Rauschenberg, *Night Grip* 1966. Purchased 1981. © Robert Rauschenberg Foundation/VAGA at ARS, NY and DACS, London 2021
[p.138]

Paula Rego, *Flood*, from *Pendle Witches* 1996. Purchased 1997. © Paula Rego
[p.89]

Frances Richards, *Bottom* 1973–5. Presented by Curwen Studio through the Institute of Contemporary Prints 1975. © The estate of Frances Richards
[p.147]

Germaine Richier, *Bat* 1948–51. Presented by Mme Françoise Guiter 1990. © ADAGP, Paris and DACS, London 2021
[p.76]

George Richmond, *The Fatal Bellman* 1827. Presented by Mrs John Richmond 1922
[p.102]

Gerhard Richter, *Strip (921-6)* 2011. Presented by Tate Members 2015. © Gerhard Richter
[p.219]

Bridget Riley, *Coloured Greys I* 1972. Presented by the Institute of Contemporary Prints 1975. © Bridget Riley 2020. All rights reserved
[p.173]

James Rosenquist, *Skull Snap* 1989. Presented by Tyler Graphics Ltd in honour of Pat Gilmour, Tate Print Department 1974–7, 2004. © 2021 James Rosenquist, Inc. / Licensed by Artists Rights Society (ARS), NY. Used by permission. All rights reserved
[p.203]

Susan Rothenberg, *Head and Bones* 1980. Purchased 1982
© ARS, NY and DACS, London 2021
[p.44]

Susan Rothenberg, *Mezzo Fist #1* 1990. Presented by the American Fund for the Tate Gallery, courtesy of a private collector 2000. © ARS, NY and DACS, London 2021
[p.113]

Michael Rothenstein, *Tournament* 1963. Purchased 1987. © The estate of Michael Rothenstein
[p.198]

William Rothenstein, *Mrs Meynell* 1897. Presented by Sir John Rothenstein through the Friends of the Tate 1981
[p.122]

Thomas Rowlandson, *A Two O'Clock Ordinary* 1811. Purchased as part of the Oppé Collection with assistance from the National Lottery through the Heritage Lottery Fund 1996
[p.66]

Alexander Runciman, *Fingal Encounters Carbon Carglass* c.1773. Purchased 1983
[p.62]

David Salle, *High and Low* 1994. Presented by Tyler Graphics Ltd in honour of Pat Gilmour, Tate Print Department 1974–7, 2004. © David Salle/VAGA at ARS, NY and DACS, London 2021
[p.211]

Birgit Skiöld, *Sea Image* 1968. Presented by Curwen Studio through the Institute of Contemporary Prints 1975.
© copyright reserved
[p.141]

Kiki Smith, *Untitled* 1990. Presented by the American Fund for the Tate Gallery, courtesy of a private collector 2000. © Kiki Smith and ULAE, courtesy Pace Gallery
[p.150]

Pierre Soulages, *Etching No.2* 1952. Purchased 1985.
© ADAGP, Paris and DACS, London 2021
[p.78]

Georgina Starr, *You Stole my Look* 1997. Purchased 1998. © Georgina Starr
[p.180]

Pat Steir, *Long Vertical Falls #2* 1991. Presented by the artist 1991. © Pat Steir
[p.86]

Frank Stella, *Swan Engraving I* 1982. Presented by Tyler Graphics Ltd in honour of Pat Gilmour, Tate Print Department 1974–7, 2004.
© Frank Stella. ARS, NY and DACS, London 2021
[p.201]

George Stubbs, *A Lion Devouring a Horse* published 1788. Transferred from the British Museum 1984
[p.65]

Graham Sutherland, *Clegyr Boia*, frontispiece for *Signature No.9*, July 1938. Presented by the artist 1970. © The estate of Graham Sutherland
[p.73]

Berenice Sydney, *Screenprint with Balance* 1974. Presented by the artist 1976. © The estate of Berenice Sydney
[p.176]

Parviz Tanavoli, *Poet and Bird* 1974. Purchased with funds provided by the Middle East North Africa Acquisitions Committee 2012. © Parviz Tanavoli
[p.174]

Masami Teraoka, *Hawaii Snorkel Series: Catfish Envy* 1993. Presented by Tyler Graphics Ltd in honour of Pat Gilmour, Tate Print Department 1974–7, 2004. © Masami Teraoka
[p.205]

John Thompson after William Holman Hunt, *The Lady of Shalott* published 1857. Presented by Harold Hartley 1925
[p.29]

Charles Turner after Joseph Mallord William Turner, *A Shipwreck* 1806–7. Purchased with funds provided by Tate Grant-in-Aid 2008
[p.99]

Joseph Mallord William Turner, *Ship in a Storm* c.1826. Transferred from the British Museum 1990 [p.101]

Cy Twombly, *Untitled I* 1967. Purchased 1995. © Cy Twombly Foundation [p.83]

Nina Vatolina, *Fascism – The Most Evil Enemy of Women. Everyone to the Struggle against Fascism!* 1941. Purchased 2016. The David King Collection at Tate. © copyright reserved [p.128]

Edward Wadsworth, *The Port* c.1915 Purchased 1970. [p.30]

Kara Walker, *The Keys to the Coop* 1997. Purchased 1998. © Kara Walker [p.47]

Mark Wallinger, *King Edward and the Colorado Beetle*, from *Bugs* 2000. Purchased 2001. © Mark Wallinger [p.48]

Andy Warhol, *Black Bean* from *Soup Can Series I* 1968. Purchased 1978. © 2021 The Andy Warhol Foundation for the Visual Arts, Inc. / Licensed by DACS, London. Trademarks used with permission from Campbell Soup Company [p.167]

Andy Warhol, [No title] from *Marilyn* 1967. Purchased 1971. © 2021 The Andy Warhol Foundation for the Visual Arts, Inc. / Licensed by DACS, London [p.10, figure illustration]

James Abbott McNeill Whistler, *Black Lion Wharf, Wapping* 1859. Presented by Ernest Marsh 1909 [p.68]

Fred Williams, *Chopped Trees* 1965–6. Purchased 1992. © The estate of Fred Williams [p.82]

Sue Williamson, *Maggie Magaba* 1983. Purchased with funds provided by Simon and Catriona Mordant, and the Basil and Raghida Al-Rahim Art Fund, courtesy of Goodman Gallery, 2014. © Sue Williamson [p.202]

Yukinori Yanagi, Untitled print from *Wandering Position* 1997. Purchased 1998. © Yukinori Yanagi [p.90]

Zarina, *Letters from Home* 2004. Purchased with funds provided by the South Asia Acquisitions Committee 2013. © Zarina; Courtesy of the artist and Luhring Augustine, New York [pp.50, 51]

Photo Credits

All photography © Tate, 2021 unless otherwise stated

© Tate, 2021. Photo: Seraphina Neville p.45

© Tate, 2021. Photo: Sam Day pp.46, 52, 77, 79, 122, 130, 133, 138, 150, 201

© Tate, 2021. Photo: Mark Heathcote p.49

Courtesy the artist p.91

Courtesy the artist and Hauser & Wirth / Photo: D. James Dee p.217

Courtesy the artist and Hauser & Wirth / Photo: Alex Delfanne p.216

Courtesy the artist and Luhring Augustine, New York pp.50, 51

Image: © Mathias Johansson - mat.johansson@swipnet.se p.12

© KHM-Museumsverband p.42

© Photographic Archive Museo Nacional del Prado p.115 (right)

© The Trustees of the British Museum p.71 (right)

© The Trustees of the British Museum. Courtesy National Gallery of Art, Washington, DC p.88

© Victoria and Albert Museum, London pp.8, 9

Acknowledgements

This publication is indebted to the many art historians and curators who have written about prints and printmaking; see the 'Further Reading' section for a selection of their highly recommended books.

Thank you to everyone I have worked with in museums, print rooms and printmaking studios – you all helped me to discover a love and understanding of the printed image. Many colleagues have generously shared their knowledge with me over the years, not least Peter Black, who (possibly unintentionally) made me a print person when he trained me at the Hunterian back in 2011–12. Special thanks to David Blayney Brown, Scott Richards and Charlotte Topsfield for reading draft texts of the book, and to Jane Ace, Judith Severne and the team at Tate Publishing, together with designer Mark El-khatib, for bringing it to reality.

Index

Numbers in *italic* type refer to pages on which reproductions appear.

First published 2021 by order of the Tate Trustees
by Tate Publishing, a division of Tate Enterprises Ltd,
Millbank, London SW1P 4RG
www.tate.org.uk/publishing

A catalogue record for this book is
available from the British Library
ISBN 978 1 84976 763 7

Distributed in the United States and Canada
by ABRAMS, New York

Library of Congress Control Number applied for

Project Editor: Judith Severne
Production: Bill Jones
Picture Researcher: Deborah Metherell
Designed by Mark El-khatib
Colour reproduction by DL Imaging Ltd, London
Printed and bound in Italy by Printer Trento S.r.l.

Front cover: Ben Nicholson, *1933 (Profile)* 1933
Back cover: William Hogarth, *A Rake's Progress (plate 8)* 1735–63

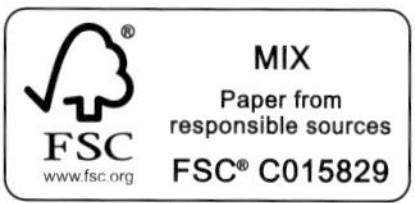